D1237356

DISOWNING SLAVERY

DISOWNING

Gradual Emancipation and
"Race" in New England,
1780–1860

C

SLAVERY

Joanne Pope Melish

CORNELL UNIVERSITY PRESS

Ithaca and London

Copyright © 1998 by Cornell University

All rights reserved. Except for brief quotations in a review, this book, or parts
thereof, must not be reproduced in any form without permission in writing
from the publisher. For information, address Cornell University Press,
Sage House, 512 East State Street, Ithaca, New York 14850.

First published 1998 by Cornell University Press.

Printed in the United States of America.

Cornell University Press strives to utilize environmentally responsible suppliers and
materials to the fullest extent possible in the publishing of its books. Such materials
include vegetable-based, low-VOC inks and acid-free papers that are also either
recycled, totally chlorine-free, or partly composed of nonwood fibers.

Library of Congress Cataloging-in-Publication Data

Melish, Joanne Pope.
Disowning slavery : gradual emancipation and "race" in New England, 1780–1860 /
    Joanne Pope Melish.
    p.   cm.
Includes bibliographical references and index.
ISBN 0-8014-3413-0 (cloth : alk. paper).
    1. Antislavery movements—New England—History—18th century.   2. Antislavery
movements—New England—History—19th century.   3. Afro-Americans—Civil rights—
New England—History—18th century.   4. Afro-Americans—Civil rights—New England—
History—19th century.   5. Slaves—Emancipation—New England—History—18th
century.   6. Slaves—Emancipation—New England—History—19th century.   7. New
England—Race relations.   I. Title.
E445.N5M44   1988
326'.8'0974—dc21   97-46669

Cloth printing   10   9   8   7   6   5   4   3   2   1

To the memory of my father,

Elton Arthur Pope, 1899–1994

ALL PROFOUND CHANGES IN CONSCIOUSNESS, BY THEIR VERY NATURE, BRING WITH THEM CHARACTERISTIC AMNESIAS. OUT OF SUCH OBLIVIONS, IN SPECIFIC HISTORICAL CIRCUMSTANCES, SPRING NARRATIVES . . . . AWARENESS OF BEING IMBEDDED IN SECULAR, SERIAL TIME, WITH ALL ITS IMPLICATIONS OF CONTINUITY, YET OF "FORGETTING" THE EXPERIENCE OF THIS CONTINUITY—PRODUCT OF THE RUPTURES OF THE LATE EIGHTEENTH CENTURY—ENGENDERS THE NEED FOR A NARRATIVE OF "IDENTITY."

—BENEDICT ANDERSON

Contents

Illustrations

Preface

In its November–December 1992 (special election issue), *Newsweek* chronicled the brief effort of Virginia's Governor Douglas Wilder, an African American, to capture the 1992 Democratic presidential nomination. In December 1991, in preparation for the early primaries, his advance team showed four New Hampshire focus groups the records of achievement of Wilder and five other leading Democratic challengers in a blind test without photographs. Wilder was the clear favorite of all four groups. But when they were shown a biographical video from Wilder's last gubernatorial campaign, staffers watching through a one-way mirror saw a dramatic change among the viewers: "'The whole room started muttering.' People turned and whispered to each other. One woman gasped out loud, 'He's black.' 'We lost every single vote,' the staffer said. 'As soon as they saw he was black, it was over.'" Wilder withdrew from the race on January 9. As *Newsweek* put it, "Wilder's dream was to rise above the old politics of race. He had succeeded in Virginia; in the North he ran into barriers."[1]

I conceived of the bare outlines of this project long before Mr. Wilder's dream was snuffed out in New Hampshire. It was in the early 1980s, in fact, when I began to be struck by messages in New England about distinctive

---

[1] "Six Men and a Donkey," *Newsweek*, Special Election Issue, November–December 1992, p. 29.

"racial" ideology on the one hand and "racial" experience on the other which resonated peculiarly with each other and suggested a contradiction that demanded exploration.

The perception that "race" is experienced or negotiated or produced in a unique way in New England is not a new insight. For well over a hundred years a succession of observers have commented on the peculiar response of white New Englanders—or sometimes, more broadly, northerners—to people of color. In *Uncle Tom's Cabin,* Harriet Beecher Stowe captured its essence in the reflections of southern planter Augustine St. Clare on the behavior of his cousin, Vermont native Ophelia St. Clare, with regard to people of color: "You loathe them as you would a snake or a toad, yet you are indignant at their wrongs. You would not have them abused; but you don't want to have anything to do with them yourselves. You would send them to Africa, out of your sight and smell."[2] This passage reflects the uneasy juxtaposition of advocacy and aversion, of desire for justice (or, at least, desire to evade complicity in injustice) and longing for erasure that characterized a broad range of antislavery thinking in its abolitionist, colonizationist, and nativist manifestations in antebellum New England.

Moreover, these qualities of response survived the nineteenth century. Some sixty years later James Weldon Johnson made a strikingly similar observation: "It may be said that the claim of the Southern whites that they love the Negro better than the Northern whites do is in a manner true. Northern white people love the Negro in a sort of abstract way, as a race; through a sense of justice, charity, and philanthropy, they will liberally assist in his elevation. . . . Yet, generally speaking, they have no particular liking for individuals of the race."[3] And later still, Zora Neale Hurston commented, "I laughed to myself watching northerners, after saying to Negro individuals how distressed they were about the awful conditions down South, trying to keep Negroes from too close a contact with themselves. The South, having been perfectly frank all along, was unembarrassed. . . . I have listened to the northern abstractions about justice, and seen the cold hardness to the black individual. . . . in some instances, the South is kinder than the North. Then the North adds the insult of insincerity to its coldness."[4]

---

[2] Harriet Beecher Stowe, *Uncle Tom's Cabin* (1852; New York: New American Library, 1966), p. 195.

[3] James Weldon Johnson, *Autobiography of an Ex-Colored Man* (1912), in *Three Negro Classics* (New York: Avon, 1965), p. 488.

[4] Zora Neale Hurston to Douglas Gilbert, clarifying remarks made to him in an interview (*New York Herald-Telegram,* February 1, 1943), quoted in Robert Hemenway's introduction to Hurston, *Dust Tracks on a Road: An Autobiography* (1942), 2d ed. (Urbana: University of Illinois Press, 1984), pp. xxix–xxx.

What these observations suggest is a level of visceral discomfort on the part of northern whites with the actual, physical presence of individual persons of color in the landscape, coupled with a willing assumption of responsibility for, and even authority over, the well-being of people of color who exist only theoretically, somewhere outside that landscape—at a safe and comfortable distance in the northern white imagination. What historical experience might have produced such a distinctive northern "racial" ideology?

The history of "racial" experience in New England is somewhat elusive, at least at the popular level. In Connecticut in the 1950s, when I was growing up, the only slavery discussed in my history textbook was southern; New Englanders had marched south to end slavery. It was in Rhode Island, where I lived after 1964, that I first stumbled across an obscure reference to local slavery, but almost no one I asked knew anything about it. Members of the historical society did, but they assured me that slavery in Rhode Island had been brief and benign, involving only the best families, who behaved with genteel kindness. They pointed me in the direction of several antiquarian histories, which said about the same thing. Some of the people of color I met knew more. One woman told me that her family had been in Rhode Island for over 250 years, the first fifty of them enslaved. And there were a few modern scholarly monographs on New England slavery, as well as one general legalistic treatment of emancipation there.[5]

I discovered that the narrative of New England slavery was not untold, exactly, but it was a kind of private narrative, told in discrete, isolated places from which it had never emerged to disrupt the public narrative of a "free, white New England." In fact, a virtual amnesia about slavery in New England had a history almost as old as the history of local slavery itself.

In 1786, for example, Robert Carter III sent his two youngest sons to Rhode Island to be educated under the supervision of James Manning, president of the Baptist College in Providence (now Brown University), for the explicit purpose of shielding them from the influence of slavery. A grandson of the legendary Robert "King" Carter, whose landholdings extended across much of northern Virginia in the mid-eighteenth century, Robert III owned sixteen plantations and some five hundred slaves when his growing doubts about the moral rectitude of slavery led him to send his

---

[5] Lorenzo J. Greene, *The Negro in Colonial New England* (New York: Columbia University Press, 1942); Edgar J. McManus, *Black Bondage in the North* (Syracuse, N.Y.: Syracuse University Press, 1973); William D. Piersen, *Black Yankees: The Development of an Afro-American Subculture in Eighteenth-Century New England* (Amherst: University of Massachusetts Press, 1988); Arthur Zilversmit, *The First Emancipation: The Abolition of Slavery in the North* (Chicago: University of Chicago Press, 1967).

sons away from "the example and custom in this neighborhood," which he took to be "very destructive both to the morals and Advancement of Youth." He wrote to Manning, "The prevailing notion now is to continue the most abject state of slavery in this Commonwealth [Virginia]. On this consideration only, I do not intend that these two sons shall return to this State till each of them arrive at the age of 21 years."[6] His choice of a New England state as a refuge from the practice of slaveholding and its contagious ideology hardly seems exceptional. Yet four years after the Carter boys arrived, according to the first federal census, there were still nearly a thousand slaves in Rhode Island.[7] On the eve of the Revolution, one person in fourteen in Rhode Island had been a slave, the largest percentage in all the New England colonies.[8] Virtually all members of the aristocracy whom Carter would have recognized as social equals, whose sons would associate with his in Rhode Island, had been well-established slaveholders (and some, slave traders); many still were. What would have led Robert Carter to imagine a Rhode Island untainted by slavery?

The construction of New England as the antithesis of an enslaved South had become commonplace by the time of the Constitutional Convention. James Madison observed in 1787 that "the real differences of interest lay, not between the large and small but between Northern and Southern states. The institution of slavery and its consequences formed the line of discrimination." Tocqueville argued that "all the differences which may be noticed between the characters of the Americans in the Southern and Northern states have originated in slavery."[9]

It was an easy leap from the erasure of the experience of slavery to the illusion of the historical absence of people of color generally. Thus, in the decade before the Civil War, Charles Eliot Norton supported the free-soil position in order to "confine the Negro within the South."[10] And as recently as 1971, Nathan Glazer explained northern racism by asserting, "Southern attitudes toward the Negro have been brought North—physically—by black and white," not only implying the absence of indigenous

[6] Robert Carter III to Robert Roger, December 7, 1778, and to James Manning, February 9, 1786, in Louis Morton, *Robert Carter of Nomini Hall: A Virginia Tobacco Planter of the Eighteenth Century* (Williamsburg, Va.: Colonial Williamsburg, 1941), p. 257; see also p. 226.

[7] Bureau of the Census, Department of Commerce, *Negro Population, 1790–1915* (Washington, D.C.: Government Printing Office, 1918), p. 57.

[8] "The 1782 Census of Rhode Island," Miscellaneous Manuscripts, Rhode Island Historical Society, Providence.

[9] *The Writings of James Madison*, vol. 3, *The Journal of the Constitutional Convention* (1787; New York: Putnam, 1902), pp. 332–33; Alexis de Tocqueville, *Democracy in America* (1835, 1840), ed. Phillips Bradley (New York: Knopf, 1945), 1:380.

[10] Charles Eliot Norton to J. R. Lowell, April 6, 1855, in *Letters of Charles Eliot Norton*, ed. Sara Norton and M. A. DeWolfe Howe (Boston: Houghton Mifflin, 1913), pp. 126–27.

people of color in the North but ingeniously suggesting that those who came brought racism with them.[11]

In summary, it seems that Mr. Wilder encountered something more complicated and nuanced than *Newsweek*'s "barriers" in his failed presidential foray into the mountains of New Hampshire. What he encountered was the power of a narrative—the narrative of a historically free, white New England—in which the emergence of a presidential candidate of color who might literally become a visible presence on billboards and TV screens and newspapers was not so much undesirable as it was literally, on some level, unthinkable.

This book represents the culmination of a fifteen-year exploration to discover how that narrative displaced a more complex reality in which economic, political, and social relations were structured by "race," itself emerging from a still earlier set of relations structured by slavery.

In my research and writing I have received the support, encouragement, and helpful criticism of many scholars and friends, for which I am deeply grateful. Rhett S. Jones guided my reading and thinking about the historiography of slavery and has steadfastly encouraged me in this project. John L. Thomas introduced me to the complexities of the intellectual history of the antebellum and Civil War periods and has remained my model of imaginative thinking and elegant writing. Robert G. Lee led me through the vicissitudes of theorizing race with relentless zeal. Wilson J. Moses introduced me to the enormous body of antebellum black literature and helped me begin to understand its variety of issues and themes. Ruth Wallis Herndon made me aware of the tremendous resource represented by New England town records and generously provided copies of documents, drafts of her work in progress, and comments on my drafts; she also offered unflagging moral support at every critical juncture. Robert K. Fitts, Matthew Jacobson, Richard McIntyre, Ann Marie Plane, John Saillant, and John Wood Sweet likewise shared their work, ideas, and sources.

David Brion Davis, Ruth Wallis Herndon, Rhett S. Jones, Robert G. Lee, John Wood Sweet, John L. Thomas, David Waldstreicher, and Shane White read and commented on at least one version of the entire manuscript, and Daniel Cavicchi, Krista DeLuzio, Kristen Petersen Farmelant, Kathleen Franz, William Hart, Richard McIntyre, Ann Marie Plane, Miriam Reumann, and Mari Yoshihara read various chapters. Their comments and advice, in some cases extensive, have improved this work immeasurably.

---

[11] Nathan Glazer, "Negroes and Ethnic Groups: The Difference, and the Political Difference It Makes," in *Key Issues in Afro-American Experience,* ed. Nathan I. Huggins, Martin Kilson, and Daniel M. Fox (New York: Harcourt Brace Jovanovich, 1971), 2:78.

Other scholars and friends, some of whom work in areas quite remote from mine, also provided great encouragement, especially Carol Frost and Sally Gabb. Peter Agree at Cornell University Press and Patricia Sterling, the freelance editor Cornell chose, facilitated publication of the book in many ways, and their advice and assistance is deeply appreciated.

I especially appreciate the assistance of the staffs of the American Antiquarian Society, the Rhode Island Historical Society, the Connecticut Historical Society, the Massachusetts Historical Society, the Providence City Archives, the Boston Public Library, the Connecticut State Library, the John Hay Library at Brown University, and the Rhode Island Court Archives. I am particularly grateful to Philip Lapsansky at the Library Company of Philadelphia, who shared with me his collection and extensive knowledge of nineteenth-century antiblack broadsides and led me to other sources.

Finally, I am grateful to Elton Pope, Rachel Johnson, Jennifer Melish, Matthew Johnson, Tara Melish, and Gabrielle Prochaska—all members of my family who believed, with varying degrees of certainty, that I would finish this work—and especially to Jeff Melish, who helped so much.

JOANNE POPE MELISH

Providence, Rhode Island

Archives Cited

American Antiquarian Society, Worcester, Mass.
Boston Public Library, Boston, Mass.
Connecticut Historical Society, Hartford
Connecticut State Library, Hartford
Hopkinton Town Council Records and Hopkinton Justice Court Records, Town Hall, Hopkinton, R.I.
John Hay Library, Brown University, Providence, R.I.
Massachusetts Historical Society, Boston
New London County Probate Records, Connecticut State Library
New London Probates, City Hall, New London, Conn.
Newport City Court Records, Newport Historical Society
Newport Historical Society, Newport, R.I.
Newport Town and City Council Records, Newport Historical Society
Providence Town Council Records; Providence Town Meeting Records; and Providence Wills, Providence Archives, City Hall, Providence, R.I.
Providence Town Papers, Rhode Island Historical Society
Providence Wills, Providence Archives, City Hall, Providence, R.I.
Rhode Island Court Archives, Pawtucket, R.I.
Rhode Island Historical Society, Providence
Rhode Island State Archives, Providence
South Kingstown Town Council and Probate Records, Town Hall, South Kingstown, R.I.
Stonington Probate Journal and Record, Town Hall, Stonington, Conn.
Sturbridge Village Research Library, Sturbridge, Mass.

DISOWNING SLAVERY

Introduction

I n the lifetime of New England slavery, whites across a spectrum of belief held a common set of assumptions about the limits and possibilities of the behavior and mental capacity of enslaved people of
color—assumptions that were conditioned, however, by the belief that
these characteristics had been heavily affected by enslavement and might
be altered radically by freedom.

The emancipation of slaves in New England, beginning around 1780,
was a gradual process, whether by *post nati* statute, as in Rhode Island and
Connecticut, or by effect, as in Massachusetts and New Hampshire, where
ambiguous judicial decisions and constitutional interpretations discouraged slaveholding without clearly outlawing it. The gradual nature of the
process encouraged whites to transfer a language and set of practices
shaped in the context of slavery to their relations with a slowly emerging
population of free people of color. The rhetoric of antislavery and revolutionary republicanism fostered this transfer, undergirding whites' assumptions that emancipated slaves, likely to be dependent and disorderly,
would constitute a problem requiring firm management in the new republic.

The emancipation process took place during a post-Revolutionary period of social and economic uncertainty that interrogated the stability of social identity and the meaning of citizenship for whites as well as people of
color. In this context, emancipation raised questions about the nature of

difference and citizenship which affected the social identity of whites as well as people of color. Previously accepted environmental explanations of difference suddenly seemed to leave whites vulnerable to radical and unwelcome alterations in their social entitlements. I argue that the sudden appearance of a large popular literature on cases of albinism and vitiglio, on the one hand, and on the enslavement of whites in Algiers (the so-called Algerine captivity), on the other, was symptomatic of a great nervousness about the stability of social identity, nervousness produced by the coincidence of post-Revolutionary social change and emancipation. Could freedom, and perhaps citizenship, turn people of color "white"? Could enslavement transform republican citizens into slaves? Turn them "black"? By 1820 whites had answered these questions with a resounding "No!" and were turning to new "scientific" explanations of difference as innate, permanent, and residing in the body to define whites as citizens and people of color as inferior by nature and thus ineligible for citizenship.

Even more problematic was the promise implicit in antislavery rhetoric that abolition, by ending "the problem"—the sin of slavery and the troublesome presence of slaves—would result in the eventual absence of people of color themselves. In other words, whites anticipated that free people of color, would, by some undefined moment (always imminent), have disappeared.

New England whites employed an array of strategies to effect the removal promised by antislavery rhetoric and to efface people of color and their history in New England. Some of these efforts were symbolic: representing people of color as ridiculous or dangerous "strangers" in anecdotes, cartoons, and broadsides; emphasizing slavery and "race" as "southern problems"; characterizing New England slavery as brief and mild, or even denying its having existed; inventing games and instructional problems in which the object was to make "the negroes" disappear; digging up the corpses of people of color. Other efforts aimed to eliminate the presence of living people of color: conducting official roundups and "warnings-out"; rioting in and vandalizing black neighborhoods. Finally, some efforts involved both symbolic and physical elements, such as the American Colonization Society's campaign to demonize free people of color and raise funds to ship them to Africa.

By the 1820s the discourse of slavery had been transformed into the discourse of "race." The process of gradual emancipation had mapped the old assumptions about slaves onto a new class of person, "free negro"; the old assumptions about the mutability of servile characteristics had been transformed into a new conviction of their innateness and immutability. The new generation of antislavery activists and reformers of the late 1820s and after similarly shared with proslavery advocates—and the merely indifferent—not some universal, underlying hostility toward "free Negroes" but a common set of assumptions about their incapacity, dependency, and need for external control. Abolitionists such as William Lloyd Garrison and Theodore Parker supported education, economic advancement, and other means of improving the "condition" of people of color in New England, as well as the cause of abolition, but the discourse of "race" shaped and fatally compromised all these efforts. Hence, while the proposals of colonizationists and "whites only" exclusionists were antithetical to those of radical abolitionists and reformers, both black and white, they often described the problem of the degraded "condition" of free people of color in similarly essentialist language.

An important aspect of the efforts to eliminate the presence of free people of color in New England was a kind of erasure by whites of the historical experience of local enslavement—the production of one of Benedict Anderson's "characteristic amnesias."[1] In its place emerged a triumphant narrative of a historically free, white New England in which a few people of color were unaccountably marooned, a class of permanently "debased" strangers.

I argue that these efforts to efface the indigenous experience of slavery or to minimize its significance further "racialized" both black and white identity in New England. Having largely disconnected people of color from their historical experience of oppressive enslavement in the New England states, whites could insist that the only way to account for the often impoverished condition of people of color there was their innate inferiority; at the same time, this conclusion enabled most whites to disclaim social responsibility for that condition. By the 1850s, then, New England had become a region whose history had been re-visioned by whites as a triumphant narrative of free, white labor, a region within which free people of color could be represented as permanent strangers whose presence was unaccountable and whose claims to citizenship were absurd. The narrative of a historically free, white New England also advanced antebellum New England nationalism by supporting the region's claims to a superior moral identity that could be contrasted effectively with the "Jacobinism" of a slaveholding, "negroized" South. Triumphant whiteness and debased blackness were complementary productions of the "racializing" process.

People of color themselves were not merely passive objects of the "racializing" discourse of Revolutionary-era antislavery struggles and the effects of gradual emancipation. A central conception of this work is that "race,"

[1] Benedict Anderson, *Imagined Communities: Reflections on the Origin and Spread of Nationalism,* rev. ed. (London: Verso, 1991), pp. 204–5.

as an embodied category of difference and a constructed aspect of identity, is not imposed by one group upon another, nor is it a construction by one group of its own identity in opposition to the "other"; rather, it is a product of an ongoing dialogue between dominated and subordinated peoples. "Racial" identifications therefore function as tools of both domination and resistance.

Conceptions of "racial" difference on the part of persons of color themselves became important sources of competing visions of citizenship and nationhood, as articulated in the pages of black newspapers after 1827, in speeches and position papers offered at national and state conventions of people of color beginning in the 1830s and continuing throughout the antebellum period, and in works of fiction after 1850. Efforts to strengthen their pride as a people by emphasizing the distinctiveness of African or "colored" identity based in blood and descent in turn reinforced perceptions of "racial" difference as innate, permanent, and located in the body.

Although free people of color in New England achieved a limited success in their efforts to advance their economic and political situation, the growing importance of southern slavery as a national issue focused political attention on their condition—often described as "degraded" and "wretched"—but away from its historical explanation. Blaming their own oppressed condition on the persistence of southern slavery became a dominant strategy among them, one that could be endorsed wholeheartedly by white New England abolitionists. The unintended consequence of this position, however, was to erode even further the dimming connection between local enslavement in the past and disadvantage in the present. Allowing the oppressed condition of northern free people of color to seem historically unaccountable ultimately bolstered the "innate inferiority" argument—especially when the eventual abolition of southern slavery in the course of the Civil War did not in fact result in a visible improvement in the condition of northern blacks.

This book engages debates in four areas of study: theoretical approaches to the development of ideologies of "race"; historical treatments of the emergence of American regional identities and nationalisms; interpretations of the economic history of early America; and historical interpretations of slavery, emancipation, and the evolution of black communities and cultures in the United States. In each of these areas, debate has been distorted by what I consider to be a blind spot: the assumption that the local institution of slavery and its slow demise were incidental to the economic, political, and social development of New England; that they therefore played no role in that region's engagement in national debates that culminated in the Civil War; and, finally, that they had little if any influence on the shaping of either regional or national "white" or "black" identity.

My work assumes that "race" is an ideological construction.[2] I follow Alexander Saxton in seeing "racism" as fundamentally a theory of history, in that it imputes historical causation to "racial" difference, and in attempting to develop an ideological explanation for nineteenth-century racial differentiation. Unlike Saxton, however, I argue that perceptions of difference, although they facilitated the subordination and enslavement of peoples of color in the fifteenth century, did not harden into notions of permanent and innate hierarchy—that is, "race"—in the United States until the late eighteenth century, when they began to emerge in the course of the first northern implementation of systematic emancipation. My focus is on locating and explaining this emergence.[3] My work engages Saxton's and other recent studies of the construction of ideologies of "race" which have focused on the elaboration of "whiteness" as a function of the debasement of, or appropriation from, black people and black culture.[4] Such studies seem to be saying that northern white workers "racialized" whiteness largely in response to a distant but potent southern black slavery, yet enacted their racism in reference to northern free people of color. In contrast, I contend that slavery and emancipation in the North (in my work, specifically New England) provided the context for the em-bodiment of "race" there, and that New England whites "racialized" themselves and people of color in response to concerns about citizenship and autonomy posed by emancipation and post-Revolutionary dislocation in their

---

[2] See, e.g., Barbara Fields, "Slavery, Race, and Ideology in the United States of America," *New Left Review* 181 (May–June 1990): 95–118.

[3] Alexander Saxton, *The Rise and Fall of the White Republic: Class Politics and Mass Culture in Nineteenth-Century America* (London: Verso, 1990), pp. 14–15. Although Saxton emphasizes the role of the subordination of Native Americans in the development of northern white "racial" attitudes, he does mention northern slavery: e.g., in the development of John Quincy Adams's "racial" attitudes (28–30). He also writes somewhat differently on the operation of white racism in partisan politics, class coalitions, and various cultural milieux.

[4] For example, scholars such as Ronald Takaki and David Roediger have argued that northern white workers whose expectations of republican independence were frustrated by the degradation of wage labor scrambled to define themselves in opposition to black slaves. Noel Ignatiev extends this analysis to Irish laborers who "earned" whiteness by joining the American-born white workers in labor unions and the Democratic Party in supporting white supremacy and opposing abolition. Eric Lott adds cultural appropriation to debasement in the context of minstrelsy as northern white strategies of self-definition. See Takaki, *Iron Cages: Race and Culture in 19th-Century America* (Seattle: University of Washington Press, 1979); Roediger, *The Wages of Whiteness: Race and the Making of the American Working Class* (New York: Verso, 1991); Roediger *Towards the Abolition of Whiteness* (New York: Verso, 1994); Ignatiev, *How the Irish Became White* (New York: Routledge, 1995); Lott, *Love and Theft: Blackface Minstrelsy and the American Working Class* (New York: Oxford University Press, 1993).

own region. I also see the presence and participation of free people of color themselves in the "racializing" discourse as influencing the articulation of "black" and "white" identity, often in unintended ways. Further, I extend the ideas of scholars of nineteenth-century scientific racism into the realm of politics and culture,[5] arguing that the whites' need to resolve post-Revolutionary uncertainty over susceptibility to enslavement and eligibility for citizenship provided a political justification for emerging scientific notions of "race." I am not so much interested here in the exchange of cultural practices and artifacts between black and white culture,[6] as I am in the participation of whites and people of color in a "racial" discourse from positions that were radically different in conception but, ironically, mutually reinforcing in effect.

In highlighting antebellum New England nationalism as the counterpart of the exhaustively discussed antebellum southern nationalism, I am responding to the statement of Lewis P. Simpson that New England nationalism "has not been so much neglected as suppressed in the study of American history."[7] He asserts that New England nationalism has routinely been assimilated to American nationalism; I believe that New England nationalism has in fact been naturalized in the same way that "whiteness" has been naturalized, and for the same reasons. In locating the sources of New England nationalism in the "racialization" effected by the process of gradual emancipation, I attempt to clarify and account for a relationship between "race" and New England nationalism that Simpson suggests but does not explicate. In proposing a New England exceptionalism based on "race," my work parallels studies that contrast antebellum southern and northern culture with an eye to explicating southern exceptionalism.[8]

The mythology of a free New England remains potent in the scholarly community as well as in American society at large. Hence, for example, Robert Steinfeld's otherwise excellent 1991 work, *The Invention of Free Labor*, states matter-of-factly, "By 1804 slavery had been abolished throughout

---

[5] See William Stanton, *The Leopard's Spots: Scientific Attitudes toward Race in America, 1815–59* (Chicago: University of Chicago Press, 1960); George Fredrickson, *The Black Image in the White Mind: The Debate on Afro-American Character and Destiny, 1817–1914* (New York: Harper & Row, 1971).

[6] See, e.g., Wiliam D. Piersen, *Black Legacy: America's Hidden Heritage* (Amherst: University of Massachusetts Press, 1993); Shelley Fisher Fishkin, "Interrogating 'Whiteness,' Complicating 'Blackness': Remapping American Culture," *American Quarterly* 47 (September 1995): 428–66.

[7] Lewis P. Simpson, *Mind and the American Civil War: A Meditation on Lost Causes* (Baton Rouge: Louisiana State University Press, 1989), p. 35.

[8] See, e.g., William R. Taylor, *Cavalier and Yankee: The Old South and American National Character* (New York: Braziller, 1961); Carl Degler, *Place over Time: The Continuity of Southern Distinctiveness* (Baton Rouge: Louisiana State University Press, 1977).

New England."[9] Well, no. *Post nati* statutes had ended birth into slavery in two states, and constitutional interpretations had made legal claims to slaves ambiguous in two others, but according to the second federal census, in 1800 there were still at least 1,488 slaves in New England.[10] The notion that the laws generally associated with emancipation actually abolished the institution of slavery and ended the enslavement of persons is taken for granted because it is part of the still-powerful conception "free New England."

This mythology lies at the heart of a second great misconception challenged by this work: that any responses of whites to free people of color in the North in the antebellum period were really "about" southern slavery. I beg readers to consider the contrary possibility: that northern whites' attitudes toward southern slavery, as well as their responses to the population of free people of color in their midst, were conditioned at least in substantial part by their own experience with slavery and emancipation.

Similarly, I ask readers to evaluate the antebellum concerns expressed by northern people of color in their own terms, rather than to subject them all to an acid test of their value in opposing southern slavery, as many commentators have done. For example, in his preface to the 1969 reprint of Frank J. Webb's *The Garies and Their Friends* (1857), Arthur P. Davis characterized the work as a "goodwill book" because "nowhere in the novel is there a frontal attack on slavery."[11] In fact, the book is a powerful indictment of northern "racial" violence; most of the principal characters are killed or maimed in a riot of whites against a black neighborhood. Only the notion that enslavement is the only significant form of "racial" oppression makes Davis's reading possible.

By emphasizing the significance of slavery in the evolving economy of New England as the foundation for my case for its social and cultural significance, I am trying to reinvigorate the historical arguments of Lorenzo Greene and Edgar McManus, who, from evidence of the involvement of slaves across occupational categories, insisted upon the importance of slavery to the northern economy but never made any actual economic arguments.[12] Virtually all economic historians of early America have dismissed

[9] Robert J. Steinfeld, *The Invention of Free Labor* (Chapel Hill: University of North Carolina Press, 1991), p. 12.

[10] Adam Seybert, *Statistical Annals of the United States of America* (1818; New York: Augustus M. Kelley, 1970, p. 21; Clayton E. Cramer, *Black Demographic Data, 1790–1860: A Sourcebook* (Westport, Conn.: Greenwood Press, 1997), p. 105.

[11] Arthur P. Davis, preface to Frank J. Webb, *The Garies and Their Friends* (New York: Arno Press and the New York Times, 1969), pp. xi–xii.

[12] See Lorenzo J. Greene, *The Negro in Colonial New England* (New York: Columbia University Press, 1942); Edgar J. McManus, *Black Bondage in the North* (Syracuse, N.Y.: Syracuse University Press, 1973).

New England slavery as unimportant; Jackson Turner Main is representative in finding "no economic justification" for the acquisition of slaves by as many as one in four families in Connecticut, since at least half of them performed household labor.[13] My argument for the importance of the domestic work of slaves rests partly on recent feminist scholarship that asserts the economic value of women's household labor;[14] however, I suggest not only that slaves' household labor had economic value per se but also that their performance of it released white males to engage in new professional, artisan, and entrepreneurial activities, thus increasing productivity and easing the transition from a household-based to a market-based economy. Pursuing this suggestion may make a useful contribution to the debate between social historians and market historians over the timing and nature of the transition of the New England economy to capitalism.[15]

Finally, this work contributes to the body of historical studies of slavery and emancipation in New England, especially in its exploration of their significance to the development of social identity and culture both of people of color and of whites. Modern studies of slavery and slaves' communities in New England do not investigate precisely this issue or see the gradual emancipation process itself as significant in the production of culture, ideology, or "racial" meaning.[16] In fact, there is almost no work focusing specifically on emancipation as a cultural process and its effects on the thinking of both whites and blacks in New England or the North. In contrast to most legalistic and social history approaches, this book places gradual emancipation at the center of the production and evolution of "racial" thinking and practices at the end of the eighteenth century.[17]

Amid the numerous primary sources consulted for this work, one par-

[13] Jackson Turner Main, *Society and Economy in Colonial Connecticut* (Princeton: Princeton University Press, 1985), pp. 177, 130.

[14] E.g., Nancy Folbre, "Counting Housework: New Estimates of Real Product in the United States, 1800–1960" (unpublished paper); Marilyn Waring, *If Women Counted: Towards a Feminist Economics* (San Francisco: Harper & Row, 1988).

[15] Cf. Allan Kulikoff, *The Agrarian Origins of American Capitalism* (Charlottesville: University Press of Virginia, 1992), and James A. Henretta, *The Origins of American Capitalism: Collected Essays* (Boston: Northeastern University Press, 1991), with Winifred Barr Rothenberg, *From Market-Places to a Market Economy: The Transformation of Rural Massachusetts, 1750–1850* (Chicago: University of Chicago Press, 1992).

[16] E.g., Greene, *The Negro in Colonial New England;* McManus, *Black Bondage in the North;* Piersen, *Black Yankees.*

[17] The only work on northern emancipation, Arthur Zilversmit, *The First Emancipation: The Abolition of Slavery in the North* (Chicago: University of Chicago Press, 1967), is an entirely legalistic account. Leon Litwack, *North of Slavery: The Negro in the Free States, 1790–1860* (Chicago: University of Chicago Press, 1961), examines northern discrimination from a legal and social perspective, and Saxton, *Rise and Fall of the White Republic,* attempts to chart "racial" thinking across the nation over the nineteenth century, but neither addresses the eighteenth-century emancipation process as a significant factor in "racial" ideology. James Oliver Horton and Lois E. Horton, *In Hope of Liberty: Culture, Community, and Protest among Northern Free*

ticular inclusion and one near-exclusion require special mention. I have made extensive use of town council and selectmen's records, and I recommend them as providing unparalleled insight into the nature and workings of government at the point of its actual interface with ordinary citizens. Although the writings of state and national leaders offer fascinating and informative insights into the ideological frameworks out of which public policy was articulated, what locally elected officials actually *did* in the course of interacting with citizens and, more interesting, with that absolute majority of residents who were either not enfranchised or not citizens at all—poor people, women, children, people of color—yields a very different understanding of the *practices* of "race," class, and gender.

I have, however, deliberately avoided where possible (though it was not always possible) the hundreds of antiquarian histories of New England towns, cities, and counties, most written in the 1880s and 1890s. Although they offer a rich variety of anecdotal information about the institution of slavery in New England and also about individual slaves and free persons of color, I am deeply suspicious of their rather uniformly "fond" reconstruction of relations between slaves and slaveowners. I see these products of the New England revival movement as building blocks of a kind of postbellum revision of New England mythology, reintroducing slavery into New England history with at least one rather ahistorical purpose: to suggest to a generation of white New Englanders facing a new immigration of southern people of color and "alien"-seeming southern and eastern Europeans that an even more "alien" population in their midst had been successfully managed once before.[18] Nonetheless, where I was unable to find detailed information on an important event or practice elsewhere, I resorted to these histories or depended on other historians' use of them.

My terminology requires a brief mention. I place the word "race" in quotes to emphasize that it has only ideological rather than material meaning. I use "people of color" rather than "black" wherever the phrase will not, by its length and rhythm, make the sentence containing it unforgiv-

---

Blacks, 1700–1860 (New York: Oxford University Press, 1997), and James Oliver Horton, *Free People of Color: Inside the African American Community* (Washington, D.C.: Smithsonian Institution Press, 1993), explore the social history of blacks' struggle to enact their freedom in northern states, again without addressing the impact of the emancipation process itself. John Wood Sweet, in "Bodies Politic: Colonialism, Race, and the Emergence of the American North: Rhode Island, 1730–1830" (Ph.D. diss., Princeton University, 1995), makes some of the arguments I make about the transformation of "racial" perceptions and invention of a white North following northern abolition, but he does not analyze the contribution to these changes made by the gradual emancipation process itself.

[18] Robert K. Fitts, "Inventing New England's Slave Paradise: Master/Slave Relations in Eighteenth-Century Narragansett, Rhode Island" (Ph.D. diss., Brown University, 1995), pp. 18–90, provides successive historical interpretations of New England slavery and their uses from 1840 to 1993.

ably clumsy. I prefer that term because slaves and their descendants throughout New England became quite quickly a people of mixed African, Native American and European descent—"of color" but not necessarily "African" or "black." I use the term "white" to characterize those persons who were "Europeans" before 1776 and "Euro-Americans" afterward, because for both whites and people of color it was the most common designation. The first use that I have noticed of the term "white" by people of color in New England to refer to persons of European descent (though there may be earlier ones) is in a 1780 petition of seven "Negroes & molattoes" of Dartmouth, Massachusetts, which refers to "our Neighbouers the white peopel."[19] The term "British" seems to have been used frequently before that, but by the outset of gradual emancipation—my focus—whites were no longer reliably "British."

This book as a whole takes a kind of call-and-response form. Chapter 1 thus introduces New England slavery from the white and then the black perspective; Chapter 2 deals likewise with the antislavery impulse. Chapters 3 through 6, constituting an extended third call, investigate gradual emancipation and the effort of whites to efface the history of New England slavery in favor of the narrative (noted above) of a free, white New England and a nationalism that came to extend throughout the North; Chapter 7 discusses the responding strategies of free people of color.

In 1852, Martin Robison Delany described his purpose in writing *The Condition, Elevation, Emigration, and Destiny of the Colored People of the United States* in this way: "One part of the American people, though living in near proximity and together, are quite unacquainted with the other; and one of the great objects of the author is, to make each acquainted."[20] I would argue that the alienation between whites and people of color observed by Delany was ideological, systematically produced and reproduced in a "racializing" discourse with roots in the historical experiences of slavery and, especially, emancipation. In New England, one of artifacts of that discourse is a public narrative in which the history of the relations between whites and people of color is rarely if ever glimpsed.

One of the great objects of *this* author is to explore the mechanics of the effacement of that other history and to reposition the one visibly within the other.

---

[19] Herbert Aptheker, "Negroes Protest against Taxation without Representation, 1780" in Aptheker, ed., *A Documentary History of the Negro People in the United States* (New York: Citadel Press, 1951), p. 15.

[20] Martin Robison Delany, *The Condition, Elevation, Emigration, and Destiny of the Colored People of the United States. Politically Considered* (Philadelphia: By the Author, 1852).

1

New England Slavery

"Short of the Truth": Slavery in the Lives of Whites

On May 2, 1745, Stepney, slave of the Reverend James MacSparran, drowned in Pettaquamscutt Pond. Stepney had been scowing a load of wood when his boat sank, and it was not until the next morning that his body was found. MacSparran, an Anglican minister prominent in the tightly knit aristocracy of southern Rhode Island, owned several slaves, but he referred to Stepney regretfully in his diary entry of May 2 as "my first, best and most principal servant." On May 4 MacSparran preached a funeral sermon for him in King's Chapel to "a great Assembly of negro's." Three weeks later he still occupied MacSparran's thoughts: "Stepney, poor boy, is dead and I have no Servant I can now so well depend upon to go and come quick and [do] his errands well." On June 1, when Harry went to cart and boat wood, MacSparran prayed, "Grant, Good Lord, I may have better Fortune in boating ye wood than the last, in the last Boatload whereof I lost my dear Servant Stepney."[1]

Throughout the months following Stepney's death, MacSparran continued to record the daily events of his life and the lives of his surviving slaves. As a circuit minister, he reported a constant round of visiting, officiating, meeting with, and administering the Eucharist to parishioners

[1] James MacSparran, *Abstract and Letterbook of Out Services*, ed. Wilkins Updike (Boston: Merrymount Press, 1899), pp. 24–27.

spread along a thirty-mile stretch of coastal Rhode Island encompassing villages in Old Warwick and Conanicut (now the island of Jamestown), North and South Kingstown, Charlestown, and Westerly.[2] For his slaves, there was the ceaseless farmwork and barter that sustained his household, in which he himself never participated (except once, "when necessity obliged me"): "Harry is gone this morning for Molasses. . . . Maroca carried a Calf Skin. . . . Harry and Emblo raking hay." Each Sunday he preached to the larger slave community: "Catechized ye Negro's."[3]

Many controversies and problems worried MacSparran that summer, and his irritability with his remaining slaves seems to have intensified in the weeks after Stepney's death. For example, having fretted in the past over the birth of two daughters to the unmarried Maroca—by Mingo, "Col. Updike's negro"—despite her repeated vows of Christian chastity, MacSparran resorted in June to giving Maroca "one or two Lashes for receiving Presents from Mingo."[4] Although anger was hardly an unusual response for MacSparran, his diary suggests that this particular expression of it was uncharacteristic.

Two and a half months after Stepney's drowning, MacSparran was troubled by two dreams of water. In the first, he confided to his diary, "a Boat overset with me and [I] was refused Help from ye Shore"; two nights later, as he dreamed of walking toward his brother-in-law, Dr. Silvester Gardiner, "a great Deal of Water stopt us."[5] More than six years later, when his slave Emblo gave birth to a son, MacSparran baptized the child "Stepney."[6] And when, remarkably, a white boy named Benjamin Baker drowned a day after the baptism in the very place and way the first Stepney had done, MacSparran was moved to note that "in the same fatal Pond was my fine Negro Stepney, the best of Servants drowned Some years ago," and to ruminate on the "great need to be in a [con]stant state of Preparation; lest we are suddenly snatched hence."[7]

How shall we evaluate the significance of slavery in New England life? It would be a mistake to suggest that a comprehensive understanding of the institution as it was practiced throughout New England during a century and a half can somehow be extrapolated from the brief record of relations between James MacSparran and his slaves. The plantations of Rhode Is-

---

[2] Ibid., pp. 27–32. For the extent of MacSparran's responsibilities beyond St. Paul's Parish in Narragansett, his home church, see p. 69 n. 1.

[3] Ibid., pp. 34, 26; 27–28; 32.

[4] Ibid., p. 29.

[5] Ibid., pp. 33–34.

[6] Ibid., p. 57.

[7] Ibid., p. 58.

land's Narragansett country in the mid-eighteenth century constituted a
form of social and economic organization that was rare among New England communities in its dependence upon slave labor for large-scale agriculture and its unusually dense population of people of color—as many as
one to every three whites.[8] Narragansett planter society peaked during
MacSparran's life and began to wane after 1760 (although it was still viable
on the eve of the American Revolution).[9]

Nevertheless, the diary of the Reverend James MacSparran reveals much
more than the minutiae of material and social relations within one family
in one particular slaveholding community. The domestic institution of slavery produced and sustained an ideology, a world view, and a psychology of
interpersonal relations that seem to have been widely shared by New England slaveholders, despite differences in the actual work performed by urban, rural, and plantation slaves as well as differences in the ratios of the
population of the enslaving to that of the enslaved. The institution also
produced distinctive counterparts to that ideology, world view, and psychology which seem to have been widely shared among New England
slaves, again despite differences in the nature of the work they performed.
I am suggesting that the relations of power and the kind of mutual de-
pendency/antagonism generated by the work relation, rather than the nature of the work itself, were determinative. From the diaries and records
of MacSparran and other slaveholders, we can cautiously draw some general conclusions about the significance of slavery and slaves in the everyday lives of white families in New England, as well as in the overall
development of the New England economy and culture.

MacSparran made well over a hundred references to his slaves and their
activities in a diary that spanned only thirty-four months and had been
originally intended as a record of letters received and sent and religious
services performed. His household depended upon slave labor. In this, it

[8] According to the Rhode Island census of 1755, South Kingstown, North Kingstown, and
Charlestown, the three principal agricultural towns in Kings (now Washington) County, had
a total of 3,929 whites and 1,223 blacks, or 26 percent of all blacks in the colony. In large
coastal cities the ratio of blacks to whites was also quite high: in Newport, slightly under one
in four (another 26 percent of Rhode Island's blacks); in Boston (1752), one in ten. Small
inland towns and rural areas, by contrast, had very small black populations, ranging down-
ward from 3 percent in Hartford (1756) to zero, although in Rhode Island only one town
had fewer than ten blacks. The large majority of blacks were slaves at midcentury. See Evarts
B. Greene and Virginia Harrington, eds., *American Population before the Federal Census of 1790*
(1932; Gloucester, Mass.: Columbia University Press, 1966), pp. 67, 22, 58.

[9] Robert K. Fitts, "Inventing New England's Slave Paradise: Master/Slave Relations in
Eighteenth-Century Narragansett, Rhode Island" (Ph.D. diss., Brown University, 1995), emphasizes modes of social organization and control of slaves. Christian McBurney, "The Rise
and Decline of the South Kingstown Planters, 1660–1783" (honors thesis, Brown University,
1981), is another detailed study of slaveholders' society in southern Rhode Island.

seems to have been fairly typical of gentlemen's households in the region, although its staff was somewhat smaller than those of plantations engaged in large-scale market production, which might comprise as many as forty slaves. MacSparran owned seven: Stepney, Harry, Emblo, Maroca, Moll, Peter, and Cujo. Between 1745 and 1751 he purchased two more male slaves, Hannibal and Bolico. At least three children were born to MacSparran's slaves but did not remain long in the household: Phillis, a child of Moll's, was baptized and then sold immediately; Maroca's two daughters by Mingo apparently did not survive long enough to be either baptized or sold.[10] MacSparran and his wife were childless; hence the entire household consisted of nine or ten persons, only two of whom were white.

Virtually all of the household labor was performed by the slaves. A partial listing of their physical tasks includes cutting, carting, threshing, and milling wheat and loading wheat straw into the barn; hilling, hoeing, gathering, and husking corn and cutting cornstalks; mowing, raking, and carting hay; digging and sledding stones and building stone walls; building fences; cutting and scowing wood; hoeing and picking peas, beans, and turnips; and mending baskets. Sometimes female slaves participated in the field labor: for example, Moll gathered beans with Harry; Emblo cut and topped haystacks; "the girls" (some combination of Moll, Maroca, and Emblo) dug potatoes with Harry.[11]

Beyond tasks involving primarily physical labor, both male and female slaves conducted a wide variety of errands that included ferrying MacSparran's friends and relatives to and from his house, carrying household goods to and from neighboring plantations, and relaying messages.[12] The slaves also kept MacSparran abreast of local gossip; for example, it was "my servants" who told him that a Mr. Arnold had left the Anglican church for the Quaker meeting.[13] Stepney appears to have enjoyed an exceptional level of trust and responsibility. He conducted many of MacSparran's commercial transactions—purchasing sugar, nails, salmon, and chocolate; making payments on earlier purchases—and apparently used his own judgment in negotiating the prices of articles on at least some occasions, since the way MacSparran noted the amounts Stepney had paid suggests that this was new information.[14]

[10] MacSparran, *Abstract*. MacSparran's slaves appear regularly throughout his diary, and some are identified further in the editor's extensive annotations.

[11] Ibid., esp. pp. 39, 37, 33–34.

[12] Ibid., e.g., p. 3: on July 21, 1743, Emblo carried quarters of mutton and lamb to MacSparran's from Mrs. Robinson's and reported that Mrs. Ailmy would be visiting in the afternoon.

[13] Ibid., p. 8.

[14] Ibid., pp. 2, 7.

No one reading MacSparran's diary could doubt that slaves were vitally important to the operation of his household, performing virtually all its services and its productive activities for subsistence and exchange. It is obvious as well that the activities of the slaves were integral to the effective participation of MacSparran's household in the network of households that constituted its larger economic and social sphere. Other New England slaveholders who left diaries and journals provide overwhelming confirmation of the central role of slaves in their households and communities. But the significance of slavery in the overall development of the New England regional culture is a different question. Since slaves never constituted more than a small percentage of the New England population, most historians have largely ignored the contribution of slave labor to the developing New England economy or have argued that it was incidental.[15] Numbers alone seem to suggest that slavery must have been a mere blip on the economic screen; if so, it is hard to argue that such a marginal phenomenon could have had a profound impact on New England culture and regional identity. Numbers, however, do not tell the whole story.

First of all, the slave population was not scattered uniformly across New England but was clustered along the seacoast, in major cities, and in a few agricultural areas such as southern Rhode Island and Connecticut. William Piersen emphasizes this clustering to support his argument that it was possible for a black subculture to develop in New England even though the absolute numbers of Africans were quite small. The phenomenon of clustering is equally important in gauging the impact of slaveholding and the presence of slaves on the politics and culture of white New England, since the concentration of slave populations coincided with the concentration of the region's merchant elite and its political and cultural leaders, among whom slaveowners were disproportionately represented. In Massachusetts in 1754, for example, near the peak of New England slaveholding, about one-third of the adult black population lived in Boston, as did the majority of the colony's merchant elite and many of its political leaders.[16]

The distribution of slaves—as individuals, couples and occasionally small groups—among white families, rather than as individuals among individuals, is also an important factor in the impact of the institution. According to the first general census of New England's population in 1715, there were 158,000 whites, or about 26,333 white families, and 4,150 "negroes,"

[15] E.g., David Hackett Fischer, *Albion's Seed: Four British Folkways in America* (New York: Oxford University Press, 1989), pp. 53, 312, points out that slaves were never more than 1 percent of the population in New England and suggests that slavery was "a labor system fundamentally hostile to the Puritan ethos of New England."

[16] William D. Piersen, *Black Yankees: The Development of an Afro-American Subculture in Eighteenth-Century New England* (Amherst: University of Massachusetts Press, 1988), pp. 14–15, 18.

or about one "negro" for every six white families. The Massachusetts governor, Sir Francis Bernard, reported that the colony's 1763 population of 200,000 "souls" included 2,221 "negroes and mulattoes"—noting, however, that "as all returns before mentioned were taken in order to make a rate of taxes . . . they are certainly short of the truth."[17] It is possible that by midcentury in Connecticut, Rhode Island, and Massachusetts (the three states with the largest populations of slaves), there were as many as one African for every four white families.[18] Obviously, slaves were not distributed evenly among families across New England in this way; however, Jackson Turner Main, surveying Connecticut estate inventories, found that in 1700 one in ten inventories included slaves, with the incidence rising to one in four by the eve of the Revolution, confirming the statistical incidence.[19] It is reasonable to suggest that the actual service of slaves within families gave them an impact on the culture and society that their statistical existence as randomly scattered individuals outside the household framework could not have had.

A small group of historians who have focused specifically on northern slavery and the development of African American culture in New England have, not surprisingly, argued that slavery and slaves were important economically as well as in other ways. As early as 1942 Lorenzo J. Greene noted, "The impression . . . has prevailed that because of adverse geographic and economic conditions slave labor was of little value to New England masters." Not so, he argued persuasively: "from the evidence showing the employment of Negroes in various fields it seems evident, despite frequent assertions to the contrary, that Negroes were a valuable and essential part of New England's labor supply and that they unquestionably played a role in the commercial and industrial development of that section."[20] Thirty years later Edgar J. McManus offered further evidence that "the slave force everywhere made a vital contribution to the Northern economy."[21]

These arguments have largely been ignored or refuted by mainstream historians of the New England economy. For example, from a detailed analysis of probate inventories and tax lists for the Connecticut colony from 1638 to the eve of the Revolution, Jackson Turner Main concluded

---

[17] Cited in Greene and Harrington, *American Population*, p. 16.

[18] Average family size is calculated here at seven; see ibid., p. xxiii, and for census figures, pp. 4, 16–17, 58–61, 66.

[19] Jackson Turner Main, *Society and Economy in Colonial Connecticut* (Princeton: Princeton University Press, 1985), p. 177.

[20] Lorenzo J. Greene, *The Negro in Colonial New England* (New York: Columbia University Press, 1942), pp. 101, 123.

[21] Edgar J. McManus, *Black Bondage in the North* (Syracuse, N.Y.: Syracuse University Press, 1973), p. 17.

that, although one in four living adult men owned slaves in Connecticut just before the Revolution, "probably half the investment lacked economic justification."[22]

Main based his conclusion on gender and occupational factors, pointing out that a majority of slaves in the 1680s "were not men who might supplement white laborers" but rather "household help who raised their owners' standard of living rather than engaging in production for the market." He reported that whereas in Connecticut half of all slaveowners were farmers, traders and merchants—a smaller part of the population—owned slaves equal in value to those owned by farmers. By 1774 half of all ministers, half of all lawyers and public officials, and a third of all doctors owned slaves; about two-thirds of persons leaving estates valued at more than £2,000 and over 40 percent leaving estates valued at £1,000 to £1,999 owned slaves.[23] From his reading of this fresh evidence, Main recapitulated the arguments of Henry Cabot Lodge, John Daniel, and others whose position Greene had tried to discredit nearly a half-century earlier: "the popular belief that New England slaves were used chiefly or almost entirely as house servants."[24] Even though slaves were represented in a wide range of occupations, as Greene and McManus had shown, the majority, Main found, were concentrated in household labor: "These servants performed the dirty, heavy, dangerous, menial jobs around the household, or they acted inferior roles as valets and maids to masters and mistresses of the upper class."[25] The clear picture emerging from Main's analysis is one of slaves purchased and performing primarily as status symbols for the wealthy—certainly a peripheral role. Other scholars have agreed. Jack Greene, for example, in *Pursuits of Happiness,* asserted that "slavery was a direct function of growing wealth" and that slaves served as "emblems of conspicuous consumption for urban elites"[26]

Yet the presence of slaves and slavery (one must carefully distinguish these from the slave *trade*) could not have had a significant impact on New England's regional culture had the institution and the relatively small number of individuals it inserted into New England life been entirely marginal to the economy, as Main and others have claimed. Their argument

[22] Main, *Society and Economy,* pp. 177, 130.

[23] Ibid., pp. 176, 269, 263, 261; table 5.1, p. 181.

[24] Henry Cabot Lodge, *History of the English Colonies in America* (New York, 1881), p. 442, and John Daniel, *In Freedom's Birthplace: A Study of Boston Negroes* (New York, 1914), both cited in Greene, *The Negro in Colonial New England,* p. 102.

[25] Main, *Society and Economy,* p. 130.

[26] Jack P. Greene, *Pursuits of Happiness: The Social Development of Early Modern British Colonies and the Formation of American Culture* (Chapel Hill: University of North Carolina Press, 1988), p. 71.

rests on two assumptions. The first is that the relatively sudden demand for slaves to perform non-market-oriented labor within a very specific time period was frankly irrational in economic terms. An alternative explanation requires a new interpretation of the value of slaves to so-called elite households. Such slaveholding households, as defined by occupation in Main's Connecticut study, shared more than a high level of relative wealth; the occupations of the males that headed them, with one apparent exception, tended to require substantial amounts of work to be performed away from home. As a minister, MacSparran is an excellent example: his visiting and circuit preaching, by his own account, left little time for productive labor on his small plantation (had he been inclined to perform any of the work himself). In addition, like many educated men of his time—ministers, doctors, lawyers—MacSparran seems to have practiced a second professional skill that occupied some of his time. He recorded in his diary at least three occasions on which he performed medical procedures on his neighbors at their homes: in one case he bled a man who had fallen from a cart; in another he opened and drained a carbuncle; and in a third he prescribed an emetic.[27] Public officials, too, were required to spend large amounts of time outside their immediate households. And like all these professional men, merchants and traders conducted much of their business away from home. Even farmers (the last major occupational group of slaveowners mentioned by Main), though seemingly the most bound to work in and for the household, in fact were often skilled in such crafts as leatherworking, which they performed for their neighbors for exchange or cash.

It seems reasonable to suggest, then, that far from being a marginal or luxury item in the households of the wealthy, slaves were crucially important in performing the work that a household head would have performed in a purely subsistence, or pre-market, economy, once that economy had begun to develop past the subsistence mode of the early settlement period. The 1778 will of Joseph Olney of Providence indicates that the well-to-do explicitly valued their slaves as producers, not luxuries. Olney left all his real estate to his sons and his personal estate to his daughters; then, reconsidering this division, he added a codicil ordering that "my oxen ploughs and other farming utensils Together with my Negroes, should pass and go with my lands unto my Sons."[28]

The timing of the evolution of slavery as an institution in New England would seem to support the thesis that slaves contributed to the expansion and diversification of the New England economy. From the first introduction of slaves into New England in 1638 (when colonists sent native peo-

[27] MacSparran, *Abstract*, pp. 5, 8, 15.
[28] Providence Wills, 6:211

ples captured during the 1637 Pequot War to the West Indies in exchange for Africans),[29] their number remained quite small for the next forty years, roughly doubled in the next thirty years, and then quadrupled in the next twenty—from about a thousand around 1708 to over five thousand around 1730. In the following two and a half decades this number more than doubled again, to about 13,300. In the last two decades before the Revolution, however, the increase leveled off sharply to 20 percent.[30] The years of greatest growth, between 1700 and 1750, coincided with an increase in agricultural productivity, the expansion of local and regional markets, widespread entrepreneurial activity, and the development of craft enterprises into manufactories. This period also witnessed the emergence of a significant class of traders, merchants, and ships' captains; the occupational specialization of wholesalers, retailers, and importers; and the proliferation of providers of personal, public, and professional services (tailors, innkeepers, lawyers, doctors, and so on).[31] It seems reasonable to conjecture that the introduction of slave labor into the household to sustain nonmarket or subsistence production—whose requirements and efficiency were, at the same time, increasing in order to support investment in other sectors—might have been a crucial factor in easing the adjustment of the New England economy to the fundamental shift that was taking place in the social division of labor and in the nature and demand for productive labor outside the household.[32] Someone was needed to take up

[29] John Gorham Palfrey, *History of New England during the Stuart Dynasty* (Boston: Little, Brown, 1858–64), 2:30 n; and John Winthrop, *History of New England, 1630–1649* (Boston: Phelps & Farnham, 1825), 1:260; Greene, *The Negro in Colonial New England*, pp. 15–18. Greene *The Negro in Colonial New England*, is still the best and most complete account of African slavery in New England. For an attempt to read the cultural history of Africans enslaved in New England from local town histories, see Piersen's *Black Yankees*.

[30] Composite derived from figures reported for growth in individual New England states, in Greene, *The Negro in Colonial New England*, pp. 77–99.

[31] See Christopher Clark, *The Roots of Rural Capitalism: Western Massachusetts, 1780–1860* (Ithaca: Cornell University Press, 1993); Allan Kulikoff, *The Agrarian Origins of American Capitalism* (Charlottesville: University Press of Virginia, 1992); James A. Henretta, *The Origins of American Capitalism: Collected Essays* (Boston: Northeastern University Press, 1991); Michael Merrill, "The Anticapitalist Origins of the United States," *Fernand Braudel Center Review* 13 (1990): 465–97; and, for a quite different interpretation, Winifred Barr Rothenberg, *From Market-Places to a Market Economy: The Transformation of Rural Massachusetts, 1750–1850* (Chicago: University of Chicago Press, 1992). These scholars agree that this period of increased household productivity and simultaneously increased investment of time and resources outside the agricultural sector was an essential stage in the takeoff of the market economy in New England—whether the stage itself should be characterized as the closing days of the moral economy, as Merrill and the others argue, or the first days of the market one, as Rothenberg contends.

[32] Main himself (*Society and Economy,* pp. 241–42) confirms that by the eve of the Revolution manufacturing had become almost as important as farming to the Connecticut economy; however, his data suggest that the individuals he identifies as "craftsmen" or "artisans,"

the slack, so to speak, as household heads sought to diversify their productive activities for both exchange and the market. Their solution seems to have been to import slaves.

This interpretation makes the labor of some slaves crucial to the chain of economic significance but still leaves the labor of others—household labor—valueless except for its status appeal. This is the second assumption on which Main's economic marginality thesis rests. Traditionally, economic historians have resisted imputing value to nonmarket production; only recently has the computation of Gross Domestic Product based on "gainful employment" as reflected in the U.S. census come under attack, largely by feminist economic historians concerned about the failure of conventional measures of "real product" to reflect women's nonmarket household services.[33] The dismissal of northern slavery as economically insignificant may be one unacknowledged element in the broader dismissal of all household work not performed either for the market (so that household manufactures "count," whether performed by males or by females, while nonmarket household services do not) or by white male household heads (so that work once performed by male householders becomes "women's work" and loses its formal value once white males no longer do it). If, however, nonmarket household labor in fact has value to the economy as a whole, by increasing the standard of living and by enhancing the market-oriented productivity of other household members, then the impact of slavery in New England has been vastly underrated.[34] A quantified assessment of exactly how important it was awaits further investigation.[35]

Anecdotal evidence supports the argument that the work of slaves undergirded entrepreneurship and increasing market participation among

---

who would establish manufactories during the second half of the eighteenth century, rarely bought slaves. This seems inconsistent with the thesis I propose. But Main also notes that the distinction is cloudy between farmers who became part-time artisans and artisans who acquired land and supported themselves at least partly by farming, making the assignment of a given slaveholder to one category or the other (on the basis of the tools listed in his inventory) somewhat arbitrary. "Artisan-farmers" certainly performed work outside the household. The absence of artisans per se in Main's data on slaveholders is not necessarily fatal to my argument.

[33] See, e.g., Nancy Folbre, "The Unproductive Housewife: Her Evolution in Nineteenth Century Economic Thought," *Signs* 16, no. 3 (1991): 463–84; Marilyn Waring, *If Women Counted: Towards a Feminist Economics* (San Francisco: Harper & Row, 1988); Nancy Folbre, "Counting Housework: New Estimates of Real Product in the United States, 1800–1860" (unpublished paper).

[34] Folbre suggests the contributions of household labor in "Counting Housework" (esp. p. 9) and explores the general problem of computing the value of household labor.

[35] There seems to have been little work on the value of nonmarket household production in New England before 1800, and none on the role of slaves in the region's transition to capitalism. My thesis is frankly speculative; I hope to investigate it systematically in a subsequent project.

New England slaveowners. It was not only clergy and other professionals such as MacSparran whose slaves enabled them to participate in a public, and profitable, life. Consider the astonishingly diversified activities of Joshua Hempstead of New London, Connecticut, as recorded faithfully in a daily journal over the forty-seven years between 1711 and 1758.[36]

Born in 1678 in New London, Hempstead was a grandson of one of the original grantees of land there and thus a relatively prosperous man. He began his journal in September 1711, when he was thirty-three years old and had six sons ranging in age from thirteen to two years. Three girls would be born over the next five years, the last birth resulting in the death of his wife, Abigail, in 1716. Thus, at the commencement of the journal, Hempstead was able to call upon three young male children aged eight and over to assist him with his daily work. The other children were under six years old, and Abigail was engaged in almost constant childbearing and child care.[37]

Hempstead's tasks, listed with apparent attention to completeness in the terse sentences of his journal, consisted largely of carpentry and farm labor on his own acres but also included public duties as a freeman and working for neighbors in exchange for goods and services. The first month reported in the journal is typical. He spent about seventeen days working on his own behalf. These tasks can be roughly divided into four types: carpentry (building a boat, hewing posts for a lean-to, building casements, making a hog sty, and laying a platform for corn husks); preparing food-stuffs for his family and his animals (mowing and stacking hay and cutting stalks, gathering and husking corn, gathering apples and pressing cider, killing a sheep); caring for animals (catching swine, sending cows to pasture, shoeing a horse); and doing personal business (paying bills, completing the purchase of a land parcel in Stonington). In the same month Hempstead spent about three days on public duties: serving as a juryman at the Supreme Court session, attending a freemen's meeting, and donating carpentry labor to the church. He spent about two days in activities associated with exchange or the market: making and installing casements and boatbuilding for one Joseph Truman in exchange for shoes for one of his sons and the use of Truman's cider press; making more casements and helping to launch a boat for a Mr. Coit, either for cash or in exchange for assistance he received at a later time from Mr. Coit's slave, Mingo. He performed no work on the four Sundays, and must have spent the equivalent of about four days in activities not reported in the diary.[38]

---

[36] Joshua Hempstead, *Diary of Joshua Hempstead, 1711–1758,* (New London, Conn.: New London County Historical Society, 1901).

[37] Hempstead, *Diary,* pp. ix–x.

[38] Ibid., pp. 1–2.

In the first sixteen years recorded in his journal, Joshua Hempstead spent some 70 percent of his working hours performing work neither for the market nor for exchange but to sustain his family. He also spent a modest amount of time working for neighbors who would in return perform work for him. On September 21, 1727, however, Hempstead bought a slave, Adam, and thereafter his work life, as recorded in his journal entries, changed dramatically. For example, on October 3, 4, 5, and 6, Hempstead stayed home cutting gravestones, while Adam performed a variety of farm chores: on October 3 he cleaned corn he had cut the previous day; he carted a load of wood for Hempstead the next morning and a second load for a neighbor, John Monrow, that afternoon; with Hempstead's son Nathaniel (then twenty-seven years old) he mowed all the following day; and on the next he carted corn for William Holt. From October 31 through November 30, Adam carted wood for six different neighbors, once assisted by Hempstead himself and twice by Nathaniel. Hempstead spent most of this time in court (he had become an attorney and would later be a justice of the peace and probate judge) or cutting stone, although once—with Adam and Nathaniel—he cut timber to ring Mr. Coit's cart wheels. One day Adam fulfilled Hempstead's obligation as a freeman to work on the public highways for the town. In the next year Hempstead began to spend more time away from his home, surveying lots and conducting legal business: for example, "at Groton with Mr. Chapman & Harris Dividing Lathams Estate" while Adam plowed, or "in town . . . Renewing ye Bounds of Jo Lesters Land in the 7 teer of Lots" while Adam remained "at home Carting dung." Hempstead also began to spend more time "at home all day writing," and he continued to cut gravestones, while Adam carted "loom" (topsoil), timber, dung, mulch, corn, or hay, often with Nathaniel assisting him.[39]

In July 1729 Hempstead's two oldest living sons died. The loss of Nathaniel, aged twenty-eight, who had shared with Adam the routine daily work of the farm, must have been especially keenly felt. Hempstead's solution, carried out sometime within the next four months, was to acquire another slave: throughout December and January one Haniball cut and carted wood with Adam and sometimes with Hempstead himself. The next month references to Haniball ended, possibly in connection with the "africans business" that kept Hempstead in court all day on February 19. But by mid-May of 1731 Hempstead had paid a Mr. Miller and a Mr. Adams £26 and 30 shillings respectively, to "buy a Negro man."[40]

[39] Ibid., pp. 189, 190–91, 196–97.
[40] Ibid., pp. 211–16, 218.

It was 1734, however, before the new slave, Ben, appeared. In the meantime, another of Hempstead's sons appears to have provided assistance to Adam. Ben seems to have been a less than ideal slave—inferior to Adam, at any rate—for on July 10, August 4, August 20, and August 21, Hempstead noted, "ben played truant." (When Adam could not work, Hempstead had always characterized him as "not well," never "truant.") After Ben's last truancy he was "unshipt" and appears no more in the journal. Other slaves, however, came and went, and Adam remained. After 1729, in fact, he seems to have been given responsibility for virtually managing Hempstead's 200-plus acres in Stonington, and his frequent work there in turn increased the need for supplementary slave labor in New London. In 1751, when Hempstead was seventy-three, "Adam helpt grind apples in ye foren[oon] & then gave out." It is the last time he appears in the diary.[41]

At his death, Joshua Hempstead left an estate valued at more than £7,668, including more than a thousand acres of land.[42] He had been a farmer, surveyor, house and ship carpenter, stonecutter, trader, attorney, justice of the peace, and probate judge. Although his inheritance at his father's death in 1687 is unknown (because probate records from the seventeenth century are unavailable for New London County), Hempstead's journal suggests that his wealth was substantially of his own making. And given the record of his journal, it is hard to dispute the value to Hempstead of slave labor, especially that of Adam, in amassing these resources. By performing labor for the support of the Hempstead family as well as labor that was exchanged for a range of goods and services, and perhaps cash as well, Adam and the other slaves enabled Hempstead to pursue an increasingly diverse set of professional and artisan occupations that ultimately left him a rich man.

The case of Joshua Hempstead clearly illustrates the importance of slavery in the developing New England economy. Obviously, the colonial New England economy was not based in or dependent upon slavery; but just as obviously, slavery played a key role in its transformation from a subsistence to a market economy.

In the world of James MacSparran and Joshua Hempstead, who or what exactly was a slave? How would these men have understood the formal relationship of their slaves to themselves and to their society?

Scholars have labored mightily to pin down a precise definition of slavery and to identify its unique characteristics. Historians have tended to fo-

---

[41] See ibid., pp. 280, 463–65, 232, 577.
[42] New London County Probate Records (microfilm).

cus on legalistic definitions, usually emphasizing the "principle of property in man," as Eugene Genovese put it, to distinguish chattel slavery from other forms of servitude.[43] John Codman Hurd, nineteenth-century legal scholar of slavery, asserted "the legal view of the slave or of his labor as private property, and the greater or less denial of his personality, making the disposal of his person and labor to depend on the will of a single private individual."[44] The law, then, theoretically extinguished the rights of slaves along with their personhood or, in a sense, transferred them to their owners.

In what social sphere did this transformation take place? Most recent theorists find the process connected in some way to the operation of kinship relations. Suzanne Miers and Igor Kopytoff, for example, identify a "slavery-kinship continuum" in which a society is able to enlarge itself by incorporating aliens—those who are not kin—as dependents into families and transferring their rights, in exchange for goods or money, to family heads, who may exercise those rights over them as slaves. In this view, reduction of personhood to property and extinction of rights are tacitly understood as constituting a form of extreme dependency, similar to that of very young children, rather than as the reduction of a person to a thing per se.[45] Claude Meillasoux, too, finds kinship a key to defining slavery but reaches the opposite conclusion: that slavery emerges "through the dislocation of the productive and reproductive cycles on which kinship is based." According to Meillasoux, the slave is defined as an absolute alien or non-kin by *exclusion* from kin reproduction; the mode of reproduction substituted—capture, conversion to a commodity, and sale on the market—achieves her or his permanent alienation.[46] Orlando Patterson sees the "kinlessness" or "natal alienation" of slaves as the distinguishing feature of slavery and terms it "social death."[47] James Oakes, following Patterson, elaborates various effects of kinlessness such as dishonor and perpetuity and concludes that kinlessness is what makes slavery a qualitatively distinct form of subordination, not simply an extreme end of a continuum of unfree statuses.[48] In other words, slaves are permanent strangers

[43] Eugene Genovese, *Roll, Jordan, Roll: The World the Slaves Made* (New York: Random House, 1974), p. 3.

[44] John Codman Hurd, *The Law of Freedom and Bondage in the United States* (Boston: Little, Brown, 1868), 1:43–44.

[45] Suzanne Miers and Igor Kopytoff, eds., *Slavery in Africa* (Madison: University of Wisconsin Press, 1977), pp. 11, 67.

[46] Claude Meillasoux, *The Anthropology of Slavery* (London: Athlone Press and University of Chicago Press, 1991), pp. 40, 95.

[47] Orlando Patterson, *Slavery and Social Death: A Comparative Study* (Cambridge: Harvard University Press, 1982), pp. 35–76.

[48] James Oakes, *Slavery and Freedom* (New York: Random House, 1990), pp. 3–17.

in a given society; the nature of that estrangement lies in depersonalization—their reduction to the status of chattels or things. (Meillasoux, however, makes a persuasive argument that it is not the individual relationship
of owned to owner that depersonalizes a slave, rendering her a chattel, but
the relation of the slave to the market, rendering him a commodity.)[49]

From these perceptions a working definition of slavery as a social category can be synthesized, one that would probably be acceptable to most
scholars. Slavery is a relationship structured by kinship (either inclusively
or, more persuasively, exclusively) in which the rights of one class of human beings to reproductive and other social relationships, personhood,
and labor have been assigned to another person or persons, as a result of
capture and transfer in the market, so that subjects are rendered kinless,
depersonalized, and transformed into *things*, with the ratification of the
law. This legal transformation ensures access to their labor in perpetuity
and also the permanence of their strangerhood.

How does New England slavery meet the requirements of this definition? With respect to the total depersonalization of the slave, it does not.
As Greene points out, slaves in New England "occupied a dual status: they
were considered to be both property and persons before the law." For example, although they were taxed as property everywhere in the region after 1675, slaves were permitted to hold property themselves and to testify
in court for and against white persons, even in cases that did not involve
other persons of color. Slaves had a legal right to life, and murdering them
was a capital crime. Such evidence leads Greene to declare cautiously that
New England slavery was "a curious blending of servitude and bondage."[50]
Such ambiguity undoubtedly has fostered the myth of mild treatment of
slaves in New England and the notion that New England slavery was not really slavery at all.

A case can be made, however, that this problem originates in the formulation of slavery as a juridical category. As Hurd noted a century ago in
his own attempt to produce a broadly applicable definition of slavery,
"where the law admits the contradiction of recognizing a natural capacity
for choice and action, and at the same time attributing that incapacity for
rights which belongs to the nature of a *thing*, this species of bondage would
require a legal name distinguishing the subject from natural things and
from legal persons. Under systems of law where this anomalous condition

---

[49] Meillasoux, *Anthropology of Slavery*, p. 95. This leads Meillasoux to see slaves as a class
constituted by the market, rather than as individuals defined by the law, and thus slavery as a
class relation. Genovese, too (*Roll, Jordan, Roll*, p. 3), sees slavery as a relationship of "class
rule," without, however, articulating how the individual property relation of slave to owner
constituted the collectivity of slaves as a class.

[50] Greene, *The Negro in Colonial New England*, pp. 167, 169–72, 177, 179, 168.

has been known, it has been included under the general terms bondage or slavery, and is sometimes more definitively known as chattel bondage or chattel slavery."[51] It follows, then, that New England slave law merely gave a degree of formal recognition to the inherent contradiction within the two terms of the phrase, "human property," which southern law refused to acknowledge. Or perhaps New Englanders exploited the contradiction more frankly. But southern laws, too, sometimes recognized the human agency of slaves; Louisiana's so-called Code Noir of 1806, for example, established regulations for the trials of slaves for various offenses.[52] Most scholars of slavery agree that legislators and slaveowners even in the South wrestled with the fiction of depersonalization, and southern slaves sometimes owned property, sometimes sustained long-term kinship relations of their own choosing, and so on. It was not the universal denial of personhood to slaves that distinguished slavery, then, but the assumption of power to deny it arbitrarily or, on the other hand, to ignore, sanction, encourage, or even demand personhood if such a position served the purpose of the slaveowner or the state.

Maintaining the contradiction of human agency in chattel—whether as a frank duality, as in New England, or more covertly, as in the South—was a kind of generative disorder, a cancer that spawned a host of other contradictions. Slavery in practice demanded agency and feared it, demanded passivity and was disgusted by it. The persistence of ascriptive and metaphorical language equating enslaved persons with beasts represented more than a naked attempt to derogate persons of color by representing them as subhuman or of diminished capacity; it was also an effort to resolve in language the very real contradiction presented by property in personhood. Domestic animals were both sentient beings and property; their limited agency could be exploited and controlled. In the "perfect" enslaved person, the agency of a domestic animal was extended by an opposable thumb and the ability to reason, yet control was maintained.

But in the actual behavior of slaves, one element or the other seemed always out of balance to dissatisfied slaveholders. The "Sambo" and "Nat" stereotypes, most fully fleshed out in the southern antebellum imagination but already present in pre-Revolutionary New England narratives, embody the fundamental chattel/agency contradiction as it disturbed slaveowners' peace of mind and frustrated their expectations from the outset of American slaveholding. In practice, that duality imposed upon slaves the obligation to be exactly like whites while remaining absolutely unlike them,

[51] Hurd, *Law of Freedom and Bondage*, 1:41.

[52] Louisiana territorial legislation, C.33, §§ 41–59, "An Act prescribing the rules and conduct to be observed with respect to negroes and other slaves of this Territory," in Hurd, *Law of Freedom and Bondage*, p. 157.

and herein lies what may have been the most terrible psychological burden of slavery as lived by slaves. Those who sought to prove their capabilities by meeting and exceeding their owners' expectations could find themselves alienating and, curiously, disappointing their owners; slaves who resisted and understood their resistance as an expression of their humanity saw their acts interpreted as damning evidence of the absence of any humanity at all. Being a perfect slave was inherently impossible, but failing to try could be fatal.

The contradictory requirement to be both like and unlike is highlighted by the social organization of American slavery within the rhetorical framework of kinship. As an analytical construct, kinship is most useful in explaining the origin of the category "slave" by exclusion, as stated above; that is, "slaves" are absolute aliens, or persons excluded from kin reproduction with members of the master class. Yet "the family" is the rhetorical framework in which slaveowners themselves represented slavery and formally incorporated slaves into their lives. Especially in small-scale New England slaveholding, slaves were incorporated into the household as so-called family members.[53] Piersen states flatly on the first page of an entire chapter on the subject that "in New England, bondage meant a form of family slavery." References by New England slaveholders to slaves as family members are too frequent and too unselfconscious to be dismissed as mere propaganda. A particularly compelling example is Ebenezer Parkman's expression of grief at the death of his slave Maro in 1729: "God is still the Strength of my Heart, and my Portion for Ever. But Dark as it has been with us it is become much Darker at or about the Sun setting. The Sun of Maro's Life Sat. The First Death in my Family!"[54]

For Parkman, the use of the term "family" clearly has more than a stylized institutional meaning. It is difficult to doubt the genuineness of his anguish. Yet Meillasoux, in framing slavery with reference to kinship but explicitly as its antithesis—that is, as a system that juridically excludes the slave from kin reproduction—argues that "the presentation of slavery as an extension of kinship implies approval of the old paternalistic idea which has always been used as moral backing for slavery," and, further, that "it means falling into the trap of an apologist ideology in which the slaveowner tries to pass off those he exploits as his beloved children."[55] How, then, does the historian treat the testimony of literally hundreds of New England slaves such as Tower Humphrey, "a Negro Man Who saith That he was born in the Town of Norton [Massachusetts] in the Family of Edwin Hodges,"

[53] See Piersen, *Black Yankees*, chap. 3, "Family Slavery," pp. 25–36.
[54] Ebenezer Parkman, *The Diary of Ebenezer Parkman: 1703–1782*, ed. Francis G. Walett (Worcester, Mass.: American Antiquarian Society, 1974), 1:37.
[55] Meillasoux, *Anthropology of Slavery*, p. 15.

or Cato Freeman, who said he was "born in Cambridge in the Commonwealth of Massachusetts in the Family of Capt. Ebenezer Stedman"?[56] How
can the permanent natal alienation of the slave be reconciled with the use
by both people of color and whites of a rhetorical kinship framework in
which to situate slaves in the social environment of New England?

The solution seems to lie in recognizing the kin/alien contradiction as
one of the myriad chattel/person contradictions at the root of the slave
condition, rather than in reducing it to an illogical effect of historians' (or
anthropologists') authenticating and legitimizing arguments. Among historians who have wrestled with this contradiction, Piersen points out the
tension between the ties of affection or "fictional kinship" and the social
distance it produced.[57] Eugene Genovese, speaking of southern slavery
nearly a century later, said that "the slaveholders' insistence on having a
'black family' must be taken with deadly seriousness," despite its "contradictory quality and dangerous consequences"; elsewhere he noted "the
self-deception inherent in the idea of a 'family, black and white.'"[58]

The contradiction at the heart of family slavery was the demand placed
upon it to incorporate and maintain difference simultaneously. Whites
needed a context within which to recognize, mark, formalize, and institutionalize the ontological status of "alien" or "stranger," which distinguished
one group of persons from another and made one of them enslaveable.
But slaveholders also needed a site in which to incorporate this marked difference into what was, especially in New England, a quite homogeneous
society. The family provided a site that was in some ways ideal for making
difference compatible while keeping it different. Thus a single set of necessarily contradictory conventions had to be established for both maintaining "difference" and assimilating it.

Although some historians have been more comfortable discussing slavery in a household rather than a family context, "family" is the structure
more appropriate to a discussion of New England slavery—for reasons that
have nothing to do with slaveholders' use of the term. In the patriarchal
social order of seventeenth- and eighteenth-century New England towns
and cities, relations between individuals and their community and polity
were mediated through family, not household, membership. For example,
"family" members—including women, children, slaves, and other household servants—were assumed to obtain a degree of representation (although certainly not an equal one) in community institutions and the

[56] Providence Town Council Records 5:291, October 11, 1784; 5:415, February n.d.,
1787.
[57] Piersen, *Black Yankees*, pp. 25–36.
[58] Genovese, *Roll, Jordan, Roll*, pp. 74–75, 133.

polity through the voting rights in town government of the white male head of a family household as a "freeman." Such representative citizenship would not extend to boarders or other sojourners in the household.[59]

In the seventeenth and eighteenth centuries, when the family was still the primary unit of production as well as reproduction, the role of the slave was infinitely more significant and integral than, for example, the role of a hired domestic laborer would be in the late nineteenth, when the work of the privatized family had become almost exclusively reproductive. In fact, one can argue that in the nineteenth century the restriction of the work of the family to reproduction and the growing importance of "racial" difference as a barrier to family membership—reflected in the increasing elaboration of a discourse of miscegenation—were reciprocal developments. But in the seventeenth and eighteenth centuries, the set of perceived differences that made persons of color infinitely available as laborers restricted their incorporation into the family solely to the realm of labor (in theory, at least). The location of the family as the site in which slave relations were enacted—in which difference was incorporated and yet stringently maintained—inevitably set up sexuality as a realm of contradiction. It may have been the demand to *maintain* "difference" in the family context—the permanence of the non-kin identity—that fostered the possibility of sexual relationships between white family members and slaves, even as the contradictory need to *incorporate* "difference" in a quasi-kinship relation invoked (again, in theory) the incest taboo against sex with slaves.

Slavery in the family context, therefore, was fraught with sexual tension. Greene cites considerable evidence of sexual relations between whites and slaves in the New England colonies; Massachusetts even placed a tax on every slave entering the state "for the Better Preventing of a Spurious and Mix't Issue." Greene points out that some of these relations occurred between slaves and indentured servants rather than members of the slaveowner's immediate family.[60] Some divorce and bastardy cases, however, clearly involved whites who were not servants; for example, John Rich, a

---

[59] For a clear exposition of the economy and polity of the British colonies as a "corporate system of agrarian household production sustained by a patriarchal political and ideological structure" in which "the family, often subordinate to the household, was an inseparable part," see Stephanie Coontz, *The Social Origins of Private Life: A History of American Families, 1600–1900* (London: Verso, 1988), esp. chap. 3, "Households and Communities in Colonial America," pp. 73–115. For the "family membership" of servants, see John Demos, *A Little Commonwealth: Family Life in Plymouth Colony* (New York: Oxford University Press, 1970), p. 108. On virtual representation in colonial political thought, see Joan R. Gundersen, "Independence, Citizenship, and the American Revolution," *Signs* 13, no. 1 (1987): 62–63.

[60] Greene, *The Negro in Colonial New England*, pp. 204–8.

freeman of Fairfield, Connecticut, was granted a divorce in 1742 because "his wife had a Negro child."[61]

Sexual relationships between owners and slaves in New England can be inferred from a number of sources, such as the distribution of property to favored slaves. Lewis Lyron of Milford, Connecticut, who died in 1738, left two male and two female slaves to his nearest relatives without comment, but he devoted the bulk of his will to providing for the future comfort of a fifth slave, Bess, whom he also manumitted. Lyron left Bess the entire use and improvement of his house and land in Milford, a stillpot and limbeck with which to carry on his distilling business, and additional land on which to pasture two cows. He also left instructions to his nephew (the actual heir of his Milford house and land, who could not use it during Bess's lifetime) to keep and care for the cows for Bess's benefit.[62] (The Lyron case also supports the contention that slaves assumed key roles in the production of items for exchange and sale; Bess must have been entirely familiar with the use of valuable distilling equipment in order to have been entrusted with it and may have been its principal user all along.)

The actual frequency of sexual relationships between slaves and the white members of the families in which they lived is impossible to determine. It is certainly the case that inequality of power, quasi-kinship status, and sheer propinquity made the coexistence of slaves and owners a potentially explosive situation in every slaveholding family. But whites also found the sexual relations of slaves with other slaves to be problematical. White heads of families in New England felt responsible for the sexual behavior of their slaves as part of their overall responsibility for the moral conduct of their families. But slaveowners' determination to control the sexual relations of their slaves was persistently thwarted by "inappropriate" relationships whose visible signs were the appearance of unwanted offspring; the children of Maroca, James MacSparran's slave, by Mingo, slave of his neighbor, are examples. The sexuality of slaves was, in practical fact, ungovernable, a site of resistance that could not be suppressed either by calls to Christian conscience or by threat of force. MacSparran's frustration with this problem is palpable in his musings on the day of Maroca's second daughter's birth: "Good God do thou direct me wht to do with her. I am perplexed about her Conduct with Col. Updike's negro. She is a Xn

---

[61] Benjamin Trumbull, "A List of the Divorces given in Connecticut from the first Settlement of the State, in 1635, to the close of the first circuit of the Honourable Superior Court in April 1788," Trumbull Papers, Connecticut Historical Society.

[62] William Lamson Warren, "Lewis Lyron of Milford, Connecticut: 1650–1738" (including will of Lewis Lyron dated October 9, 1736, and record of probate dated October 9, 1738), typescript, Connecticut Historical Society.

[Christian], but seems not concerned about her soul nor minds her promise of chastity, wch she has often made me."[63] But a year and a half later Maroca was still receiving presents from Mingo, and in beating her, MacSparran raged at his absolute powerlessness to change her sexual behavior.[64] Even when it did not threaten the social bonds between whites, the sexuality of slaves was an ever present source of potential dissension and discomfort in the family life of slaveholders and a mode of resistance over which whites were unable to exercise control. With slaves in as many as one out of four households in New England, it is hard to imagine that the problem of maintaining and yet incorporating "difference" did not occupy an important place in the sexual consciousness of the white colonists.

The realm of sexuality is only one area of white consciousness that was shaped by the presence of slaves. The diary of James MacSparran provides a rich source of insight into the psychology of New England slaveholders. MacSparran's inner life as he recorded it in 1743–51 cannot be disentangled from the lives of his slaves. A profoundly important element of that inner life was its spiritual dimension. MacSparran took very seriously his ministry to the slaves of his own and surrounding plantations; his diary leaves no doubt of his genuine agony over the state of their souls. His Sunday entries combine a commentary on black and white attendance at religious services with petitions to the Lord regarding a jumble of black and white souls:

> [*July*] 24th *Sunday.* . . . I catechized ye Negro's, ye white children, read Prayers and preached. Lord enlighten ye understanding and spiritualize the Affections of Cujo, the negro, who told me he has thought of Baptism. Prepare him, Good Lord, for such an Entrance into ye church, yy Kingdom here, as shall terminate in his free and welcome Admittance into ye church triumphant, thy glorious Kingdom above. Mrs. Patty Updike lodged here last night & walked to church. My wife was not at church. . . . Visited Abigail Sampson, a sick Mustee. She is desirous to be admitted into ch. Lord, pardon her sin, give her Faith in X Jesus and, in yy strength, enable her to resolve upon and live a new life.[65]

MacSparran believed simultaneously, with no sense of contradiction whatsoever, that all souls were equal before God and that all persons in their earthly, human state were placed by birth into a fixed social hierarchy that conferred rewards, roles, responsibilities, and rights differentially. Al-

---

[63] MacSparran, *Abstract,* p. 15.
[64] Ibid., p. 29.
[65] Ibid., pp. 4, 18.

though it is clear that the equality of souls before God contributed to the unity of MacSparran's household, it is less obvious that the differentiation of "Negroes" from whites and of slaves from masters in this world also contributed to that unity, because the hierarchical family was the earthly manifestation of the godly order.

MacSparran's understanding of the place of slaves in the spiritual and earthly social order as organized within the family was not a peculiarly Anglican conception. This ordering of slaves in family and society had been the subject of a lengthy treatise, *The Negro Christianized,* published by Cotton Mather in 1706. Mather told slaveholders: "Poor Negroes are cast under your Government and Protection. You take them into your Family; you look on them as part of your Possessions; and you Expect from their Service, a Support, and perhaps an Increase, of your other Possessions. . . . *Who can tell but that this Poor Creature may belong to the Election of God!*" Mather exhorted all converted slaveowners "to teach your *Negroes* the *Truths* of the Glorious Gospel" and promised earthly as well as spiritual results: "Be assured, Syrs; Your Servants will be the Better Servants, for being made Christian Servants. . . . Were your Servants well tinged with the Spirit of Christianity, it would render them exceeding Dutiful unto their Masters, exceeding Patient under their Masters, exceeding faithful in their Business, and afraid of speaking or doing any thing that may justly displease you."[66] Nearly all New England slaveholders, lay as well as clergy, routinely followed Mather's advice to provide religious instruction to their slaves as part of their religious obligation to their families. MacSparran "catechised ye Negro's" in the families of all the plantation owners in the surrounding Narragansett country with their full cooperation and encouragement.

Only within the context of the complexly defined "family" is it possible to explore the nature and meaning of MacSparran's grief for Stepney, the only household member to die during the eight and a half years recorded in the surviving fragment of MacSparran's diary. Stepney makes his first appearance on the second page of the diary, in an entry for July 15, 1743, where MacSparran reported the results of his slave's shopping trip: "Stepney payed 3d per Plant for ye Colliflowers. . . . Stepney brought home [this] morning ¾ of an hundred and 7 pound Sugar, which at £9 per ct. cost me £7:6." Not only had Stepney been entrusted with MacSparran's cash, but he had also been responsible for negotiating a fair price for the purchases. In early August, MacSparran sent Stepney to town on another series of purchasing errands and on August 16 he sent Stepney "to [the]

---

[66] Cotton Mather, *The Negro Christianized* (Boston: B. Green, 1706), pp. 2–3, 21.

Mill," while "Harry began to dig stones."[67] From these and several subsequent entries it becomes clear that Harry's role was usually confined to
heavy physical work, while tasks that required judgment or diplomacy were
reserved for Stepney.

Even these brief and incomplete glimpses make it is obvious that Stepney was indeed MacSparran's "first, best and most principal Servant," as he
said in reporting Stepney's accidental drowning on May 2, 1745. Thus, a
modern reader might conclude from MacSparran's lament that he had
"no Servant I can now so well depend upon to go and come quick and [do]
his errands well"[68] that his sense of loss was purely utilitarian. But in the
context of the interdependent, productive family household, the values
that were admired in slaves—dependability, judgment, efficiency, willingness—were also those admired in family members related by blood and
marriage; hence, the death of Stepney can be read as no less personal than
the death of a blood relative. For example, Joshua Hempstead recorded
the death of his son Thomas on July 4, 1729, with these words: "Thomas
my dear & dutyful Son died about 4 in the Morning being Aged Twenty
one years (Apr. ye 14) Two months & Twenty days." He recorded the death
of Nathaniel five days later similarly: "My eldest [living] son Nathll who
Lived with me Died about Ten of ye Clock at night. a Dear & Dutyful Son
Aged 28 years 6 months & 3 days."[69] Hempstead was hardly more effusive
than MacSparran, and he never mentioned either of these sons again in
his diary, whereas MacSparran referred again and again to Stepney as
"poor boy" and "dear servant." Stepney's drowning seems to have triggered
dreams in which water operated as a barrier to MacSparran's desires. Six
years later, MacSparran named a newborn slave after Stepney and, still ru-
minating on his death, found meaning in it in preparing for his own.[70]

Clearly, the childless MacSparran had made an emotional investment of
some kind in Stepney. Although nothing in the diary suggests that he or
any other slave ever escaped the role of servant in MacSparran's consciousness, Stepney seems to have been given additional roles in that consciousness as well, one of which was apparently that of surrogate son.
Obviously the roles of servant and son were contradictory—paralleling the
alien/kin structure of the slaveholding family and the chattel/person contradiction at its root—and MacSparran's representation of them was
painful and necessarily suppressed or at least muted. Although Stepney undoubtedly manipulated his privileged position and may even have enjoyed

---

[67] MacSparran, *Abstract*, pp. 2, 7, 8.
[68] Ibid., pp. 24, 26.
[69] Hempstead, *Diary*, p. 210.
[70] MacSparran, *Abstract*, pp. 26, 27, 33–34, 57–58.

MacSparran's trust and affection, there is no reason to think that he "lived" the role of surrogate son in his own consciousness. Moreover, the very nature of the chattel/person contradiction relieved him of any obligation to reciprocate.

MacSparran's diary reveals that his relations with his slaves ran the gamut from his great affection for Stepney through frustration with Maroca and disappointment with Harry to a battle of wills with the intractable Hannibal, a battle that MacSparran won, finally, only by selling Hannibal out of the family.[71] These varied and complex relations with slaves consume a sizable proportion of MacSparran's diary, as they must have absorbed a comparable proportion of his life illustrating the great degree to which the presence of slaves and the management of "difference" organized the emotional as well as the social experience of slaveholders.

"Difference" was the cornerstone of slavery, in the New England colonies as elsewhere in the Americas. Greene and others have noted that whites were sometimes offered for sale, along with Native Americans and Africans, but it was almost always their time that was sold, for a specified number of years. Until 1700 Africans too were sometimes freed after a limited term of enslavement; a Rhode Island law of 1652 actually limited the period of enslavement of "negers" to ten years, but it was never enforced. The text of the Rhode Island law makes clear that, even by the 1650s, the practice of enslavement for life was primarily directed toward Africans: "There is a common course practised amongst Englishmen to buy negers, to the end that they may have them for service or slaves forever."[72] By 1700, enslavement for life was effectively limited to persons who could be characterized as "Indian," "negro," or "molato" (mulatto).[73]

Restricting enslavement to persons of color evolved, according to Hurd, from sanction of the "law of nations" (common agreement of Christian European nations at the time of the establishment of the English colonies in America) for enslavement of prisoners of war from heathen and infidel nations but not from other Christian European nations. Thus, property in Africans as well as Native Americans was legal within international law. Once Africans and natives began to become Christians, the question arose of their continued enslavement after baptism; Hurd points out that although colonial courts appear never to have formally considered this question, they routinely sanctioned ownership of converted slaves (possibly

[71] Ibid., p. 63.

[72] Greene, *The Negro in Colonial New England*, pp. 40–41, 168–69, 290, 18; Hurd, *Law of Freedom and Bondage*, 1:275.

[73] See, e.g., Massachusetts law of 1698, Rhode Island law of 1750, Connecticut law of 1774, in Hurd, *Law of Freedom and Bondage*, 1:262, 272, 276.

now as legal persons held to bondage, but probably still as chattel). Judicial determination of cases involving these points created a common law, independent of statute, that sanctioned slavery of Africans, Indians, and other persons of color.[74] The Massachusetts Body of Liberties of 1641, the first legal sanction of slavery, limited those eligible to be enslaved to "lawfull Captives in just Warres, and such *strangers* as willingly sell themselves or are sold to us" (emphasis added). The word "strangers" was removed in 1670, apparently to eliminate suits on behalf of slaves' children claiming that native birth constituted free birth; but this change, by making slave status hereditary, only expanded the population of Africans and natives subject to legal enslavement.[75] There is no evidence to suggest that New England nativity was ever interpreted positively to erase the "strangerhood" of Africans and Native Americans.

The ground rules that had evolved by 1700 to govern slavery as a difference-based institution assured New England colonists of an inexhaustible supply of labor marked reliably by a set of characteristics, each assigned a sort of arbitrary value, whose total could be calculated and measured against a threshold of enslaveability, or availability to be a slave. Initially, these were simply physical traits: a darker skin might offset straighter hair or a more aquiline nose. By the mid-eighteenth century less tangible characteristics had entered the equation as well. The calculation could be infinitely subtle and complex, but (with the exception of a relatively few enslaved natives, discussed below) was always binary in its outcome: if determined to be even partly "African" or "negro," any individual could be and probably was a slave; if not a "negro," then not a slave. Colonial courts and legislative bodies in New England devoted considerable time to evaluating, on the basis of these kinds of criteria, claims of wrongful enslavement and claims of entitlement to persons wrongly set at liberty.

A richly illustrative case is a wrongful enslavement petition brought before the Connecticut General Assembly in 1757. One Jose Deming, also called Joseph DeMink (probably "Domingo"), claimed that he had been invited aboard the Connecticut schooner *Rebecka*, lying at anchor off the island of Buena Vista in the Cape Verdes, and had been wrongfully enslaved. Deming described himself as "a free Born Subject of the King of Portugal a Native and an Inhabitant of the Island of Bravo in the Indies one of the Cape De Verde Islands." He had been visiting at Buena Vista when the *Rebecka*'s captain, Phineas Cook of Wallingford, Connecticut, offered to drop him off at Bravo on the schooner's voyage to Barbadoes.

[74] Ibid., 1:161, 210–11.
[75] *The Colonial Laws of Massachusetts*, sec. 91, p. 125, quoted from 1660 ed. in Greene, *The Negro in Colonial New England*, pp. 63, 65

Instead, Cook had sailed directly to Barbadoes, where he "kept your Memorialist Confined & would not suffer him to goe on Shore." With Deming a prisoner, Cook had continued home to Wallingford, where he "immediately proclaimed that yr Memo:lst was a Negro very lately brot from some parts of Guinea, and presently sold your Memorialist to Mr. Noah Waddams of Goshen aforesaid for a New Negro and as a Slave for Life." Waddams, characterized by Deming as a man "from whom much kindness and pitty has been Shewn," had become convinced of the truth of Deming's story and had brought an action against Cook. In response, Cook had demanded the return of Deming, who now expected "soon to be disposed of in some parts remote."[76]

From Deming's point of view, the key to proving his free birth lay in establishing the fact that he was not a "Negro." Depositions of several witnesses, ranging from crew members of the *Rebecka* to the captain's father, also focused on this problem as a primary issue in the case. Deming described Mr. Waddam's transformation from slaveowner to advocate as stemming primarily from the fact that he had "been Long since Satisfied that your Memorialist is no Negro, nor in any Thing resembling a Native of Guinea, saving in his Tawny and dark Complexion which is [a] bit Common to the Portuguese Nation, Especially in the Southern Plantations." Deming asked the Assembly to "give me Leave to appear in yr Presence, and to Convince your Honors by Countenance, by my Education, by my proficiency in reading and writing of the Portuguese Language, and by other Evidence, that I am no Slave or Native of Guinea." Hezekiah Johnson, crewman of the *Rebecka*, noted that he had "heard Capt Cook say he was a likely Negro" and that he personally "took him for a Negro because of his Curled Hair." Captain Cook's father twice referred to Deming, who had been brought to his house upon the *Rebecka*'s return to Wallingford, as a "Negro" and noted that he "Proved so Thievish and So Bad I Could not Keep him." Titus Tuttle of New Haven, another crewman of the *Rebecka*, testified that he "took notice" of Deming "whom I judged to be about 15 years of Age as black as Negros commonly are I Understood him to be a Portuguese many [crossed out] some of the Portugues I saw there were as black as He and I never heard any of the Portuguese call him a Negro or treat him as a Negro And he was always offended if he was called a Negro." Tuttle confided, "I told him (to pester him) if he was mine I would Sell him for a Negro," and Deming had threatened to cut their throats. Street Hall, a Wallingford captain, referred to Deming repeatedly as "the Negro." Levi Comstock, who lived at David Cook's house in Wallingford, said Deming

[76] Miscellaneous Petitions [to the Connecticut General Assembly], 2:88–100, February–May, 1757, Connecticut State Library.

once claimed "he could Read and Rite" and then later denied it. Three witnesses noted that Deming was "thievish"; two recalled dark suggestions he had made about killing or stabbing people.[77] Deming remained a slave.

The testimony in the Deming case suggests how fatal the arbitrary assignment of "Negro" identity could be to the freedom of "strangers," and how a variety of antisocial behaviors (being "thievish" or violent) or "social" ones (being able to read and write Portuguese) could be invoked to strengthen or weaken a calculation of enslaveability based on physical traits. The arbitrary assignment of "white" identity was equally definitive. In 1784, in response to a petition from Amy Allen, a Rhode Island slave, the state legislature "voted and resolved, that the said Amy is a white person, and *of course* was born free; that therefore her being holden as a slave is an unjust deprivation of her natural right to freedom [emphasis added]."[78]

Besides Africans or "negroes," only native persons who had fallen into the hands of English colonists as prisoners in the course of the Pequot and Seven Years' Wars, and their offspring, could be enslaved. Early laws limiting the enslavement of natives demonstrate that the practice was common enough to require regulation. For example, Plymouth Colony in 1676 made the purchase of the "Indian children of any of those our captive salvages that were taken and became our lawfull prisoners in our late warres with the Indians" subject to the approval of the government, and the Rhode Island legislature outlawed Indian slavery in 1675. In contrast, what was then Hartford Colony explicitly recognized the legality of Indian slavery in 1650.[79] Legally held or not, slaves and former slaves identified as "Indian" appear frequently in New England colonial records before 1680. This designation becomes quite rare in documents produced after that date, probably less because the laws discouraged such enslavement than because of the assimilation of the small, fixed numbers of native slaves and their offspring into the growing population of African ones, or at least their redesignation.

From the point of view of whites, enslavement had a homogenizing effect on the ethnicity of the enslaved. Children of mixed African-Indian or African-white heritage were often simply designated "of colour" by whites. Recognition of some degree of native heritage among slaves and indentured servants was sometimes, but not always, preserved in the term "mustee," used quite commonly throughout the first half of the eighteenth

[77] Ibid., 2:88a, 89a, 93, 100, 97, 96a, 98a.
[78] John Russell Bartlett, ed., *Records of the State of Rhode Island and Providence Plantations in New England* (Providence: Providence Press, 1865), 10 (1784–92): 70–71.
[79] Hurd, *Law of Freedom and Bondage*, pp. 256, 275, 268.

century.[80] Courts, councils, and other institutions and some individuals intermittently used "Indian," Negroe," or "Molatto" to describe individual slaves, but the frequency with which more than one of these terms was applied to the same individual strongly suggests that the terms were subjective, flexible, and descriptive rather than ascriptive. By the Revolutionary period the general terms "Negro," "black," and "of colour" had come to express sufficient particularity to characterize any person who was a slave. Conversely, any person so identified was presumed to be a slave; the additional word "free" was required to distinguish the anomalous individual of color who was not a slave.

Nonetheless, during the entire course of slavery in New England, there was never a consensus among whites that the negative character traits and mental disabilities associated with enslaveability and servitude would persist indefinitely in former slaves once they had been emancipated. The conventional explanation for not only servile behavior but even physiognomic traits such as dark skin and tightly curled hair was that these were produced by environmental factors: first, the isolation of Africans on the "dark continent" without the knowledge of Christ; second, the oppressive experience of servitude itself.[81] As long as most people of color were slaves, the experiential middle step in the three-step chain of logic linking "negro" with "servile" ("negro" = "enslavable," "slave" = "servile," and therefore "negro" = "servile") could not be eliminated. Without experience as a slave, a person of color could be presumed to be inherently enslavable but not slavelike.

[80] Ruth Wallis Herndon and Ella Wilcox Sekatau, "The Right to a Name: The Narragansett People and Rhode Island Officials in the Revolutionary Era," *Ethnohistory* 44 (Summer 1997): 433–62, discuss what they call the redesignation of native peoples as "mustee" in the eighteenth century and as "black" or "of colour" by 1800. "Mustee" was commonly used to characterize children whose mother was native but whose father was not, a practice by which patrilineal Europeans laid the groundwork for the eventual claim that some tribes, notably the Narragansett, had "died out." Of non-Europeans considered "likely to become chargeable" and thus warned out of Rhode Island towns between 1750 and 1800, 69 percent were designated as "Indian" or "mustee" before 1776 but only 31 percent after that date; on the other hand, 88 percent after 1776 were characterized as "black" or "of colour." Herndon and Sekatau suggest that at least some of this increase reflects the redesignation of natives as "black" and cite examples of the redesignation of the same individual. On the "racial" complexity of non-Europeans in this time period, see also Rhett S. Jones, "Miscegenation and Acculturation in the Narragansett Country of Rhode Island, 1710–1790," *Trotter Institute Review* 3 (1989): 8–16.

[81] See, e.g., Cotton's Mather's dismissal of arguments that "complexion" justified slaveowners' failure to instruct slaves in the Gospel: "As if none but Whites might hope to be Favoured and Accepted with God! Whereas it is well known, That the Whites, are the least part of Mankind. The biggest part of Mankind, perhaps, are Copper-Coloured; a sort of Tawnies. And our English that inhabit some Climates, do seem growing apace to be not much unlike unto them. As if, because a people, from the long force of the African Sun . . . upon them . . . are come at length to have the small fibres of their Veins, and the Blood in them, a little more interspersed thro their Skin, than other People, this must render them less valuable to Heaven than the rest of Mankind" (*The Negro Christianized*, p. 24).

Free "Negroes" were uncommon enough throughout much of the eighteenth century in New England that whites' responses to them were somewhat inconsistent and varied considerably by locality. They were barred from some civic institutions by statute (sitting on juries, bearing arms) and from others by custom (apparently, voting) in most of New England, but their intermarriage with whites was legal everywhere except in Massachusetts. They were often included by class in statutes restricting the activities of slaves, but the enforcement of these provisions was extremely arbitrary.[82]

Nonetheless, as long as the majority of people of color in New England continued to be enslaved, "color" itself was not a fixed and insurmountable burden to economic independence and even social leadership. A good illustration of the permeability of "difference" in New England in the age of slavery, and its transformation as slavery gradually and painfully ended, can be drawn from a comparison of the careers of two men of color who made their mark in Vermont: a Congregational minister named Lemuel Haynes, and a schoolteacher named Alexander Twilight.

Born in 1753 in West Hartford, Connecticut, Lemuel Haynes was the child of a white mother and a father said to be of purely African descent. Contemporaries referred to him as "African."[83] He was raised as an indentured servant in a white Connecticut family after his mother abandoned him in infancy, and he fought in the American Revolution. Following formal preparation for the ministry after 1779, he became the first ordained black minister in America in 1785. In that year he married a white woman, and in 1788 he was called to become the spiritual leader of a white Congregational parish in Rutland, Vermont. He remained there for thirty years, publishing a series of essays and sermons and serving as an important spiritual and social leader of the white Rutland community. Early in his career his white contemporaries in the clergy praised him as an inspired preacher. But by 1818 he had been dismissed by a congregation that could no longer tolerate a black minister.[84] Haynes had not changed; what had changed was the meaning of his difference. Gradual emancipation had transformed "negro" and "of color" from a presumptive status ("slave") to a "natural" state of permanent and innate inferiority.

---

[82] Greene, *The Negro in Colonial New England,* pp. 299, 303, 208, 300–302.

[83] On Lemuel Haynes and his theology and political philosophy, see the following works by John D. Saillant: "Lemuel Haynes's Black Republicanism and the American Republican Tradition, 1775–1820," *Journal of the Early Republic* 14 (Fall 1994): 293–324; "Lemuel Haynes and the Revolutionary Origins of Black Theology, 1776–1801," *Religion and American Culture* 2 (Winter 1992): 79–102; "Lemuel Haynes" in *Makers of Christian Theology in America,* ed. James O. Duke and Mark G. Toulouse (Nashville, Tenn.: Abingdon Press, 1997).

[84] The only full-length treatment of Haynes's life is Timothy Mather Cooley, *Sketches of the Life and Character of Rev. Lemuel Haynes, A.M., for Many Years Pastor of a Church in Rutland, Vt.* (1837; New York: Negro Universities Press, 1969).

Even in Vermont, where slavery had never officially existed (although slaves had undoubtedly been held there), "racial" consciousness had become a virulent force.

A generation after Haynes and a decade into the period of gradual emancipation, Alexander Twilight was born in 1795 and reached adulthood in a fully "racialized" world.[85] Twilight was a Vermont native who was also a "first"—the first black citizen to earn a degree at an American college. Graduating from Middlebury College in 1823, he too married a white woman and studied theology, becoming a licensed Presbyterian minister. But Twilight's primary vocation was teaching school, and in 1829 he assumed preceptorship of the Orleans County Grammar School in Brownington, Vermont. Within seven years he had financed and completed an impressive new stone building dubbed "Athenian Hall" and gotten himself elected to the Vermont legislature. In 1847 Twilight retired from the Brownington academy but returned in 1852. In 1857 he died.

How had Alexander Twilight negotiated a "racialized" Vermont so successfully? Apparently, he passed for white; no contemporary writings about him mention his "race." Middlebury College's claim that he was a black graduate rests on a fragile chain of hearsay: the statement of a dean that he had heard a faculty member recall another dean's claim that Twilight was black. Local histories and local residents repeated the claim without substantiation. One conclusive piece of evidence indicates that Twilight was indeed a person of color, however: the federal census of 1800 lists his parents and their four children, following the listings for whites, in the column reserved for "all other free persons except Indians not taxed." But that evidence would not have been available to Twilight's contemporaries. It seems likely that the discovery of the census listing sparked "memory" and fueled what must have been only rumor during Twilight's lifetime.

In fact, by 1829 an avowedly black man probably could not have directed a school, financed a major building project, or won election to the legislature in the state of Vermont. While slavery existed in New England, an exceptional man of color could prosper; after emancipation, the barriers became almost insurmountable.

Slavery was a factor of sustained importance in many areas of New England life. It was instrumental in the transformation of a subsistence to a market economy; it was a key element in the organization of family life and its in-

---

[85] There are no substantial works on Twilight. The material here is taken from Gregor Hileman, "The Iron-willed Black Schoolmaster and His Granite Academy," *Middlebury College Newsletter* (Spring 1974); rpt., Orleans County Historical Society, Brownington, Vermont. See also Vincent Nicolosi, "Twilight Mystery," *Yankee Magazine* 50 (June 1986): 174, 146–53.

tegration into the larger community and polity throughout most of the region; it was a living, ever present source of ambiguity and contradiction in the organization of sexual, emotional, and spiritual life wherever it appeared. Finally, and most critically, slavery introduced a problem of managing and defining "difference" which preoccupied colonial society and which would be transformed into an even more destructive problem in the course of slavery's troubled demise.

Another Truth: Enslavement in the Lives of People of Color

On May 2, 1745, Stepney, an important member of the community of people of color in Rhode Island's Narragansett country, drowned in Pettaquamscutt Pond. Stepney had been scowing a load of wood for the Reverend James MacSparran, his master, when his boat sank, and it was not until the next day that his body could be recovered. Word of his death spread quickly, and most of the enslaved and free people of color from the towns of North and South Kingstown, and some from as far away as Charlestown and East Greenwich, came to his funeral two days later. Stepney, along with MacSparran's other slaves, had attended catechism every Sunday at MacSparran's church, and it was there that MacSparran preached a funeral sermon for him.[86]

The death of Stepney affected the entire community of color. On a practical level, others of MacSparran's male slaves were forced to take on additional tasks, as MacSparran did not increase his work force for several months. (On one occasion the master even performed some manual labor himself "when necessity obliged me.") As "first, best and most principal Servant," Stepney had been unusually skilled and resourceful, and no one else's work seemed to please MacSparran. He was irritable and demanding all spring, especially with Harry, to whom had fallen many of Stepney's tasks.[87]

Stepney's privileged position in MacSparran's household had empowered every person of color in it, and his loss shifted the balance of power. Now, Stepney was no longer available to intervene on behalf of the other slaves. In June, for example, MacSparran beat Maroca when he caught her merely receiving presents from Mingo, her longtime lover, who lived on an adjoining plantation.[88] Maroca had already given birth to two daughters

[86] MacSparran, *Abstract,* p. 24.
[87] Ibid., pp. 34, 24, 26.
[88] Ibid., p. 29.

by Mingo (while continuing to promise chastity to MacSparran, since it was easier than arguing with him); on those occasions MacSparran had not responded with anything more than sharp words. But then, Stepney had always been available to help Maroca manage her relationship with Mingo: keeping MacSparran occupied when Maroca had entertained Mingo; pointing out Maroca's youth and frailty and otherwise excellent qualities on the occasion of each of her pregnancies; deflecting MacSparran's anger when he had threatened to beat her before. In his absence it became much more difficult for Maroca and the others to negotiate MacSparran's unpredictable temper.

The memory of Stepney remained potent in MacSparran's household. Even as the other slaves dreaded the inevitable comparisons of their behavior with his, over time they also learned to evoke his memory judiciously to earn MacSparran's approval. Six years after Stepney's death, when Emblo, another of MacSparran's household slaves, gave birth to a son, she named him "Stepney." She intended this naming to honor the first Stepney, as part of the obligation of the living to the dead.[89] But Emblo also hoped that her choice might please MacSparran and strengthen her position and that of her son in the household. MacSparran, who conducted the baptism, indeed seemed pleased. A day after the baptism a white boy drowned in the very place and way the first Stepney had done. Emblo and her friends saw this death as a balancing of the scales, a kind of payment of a debt owed by the white community to the black, and found its timing meaningful. It was a sign that augured well for the new Stepney.[90]

How did Africans enslaved in a cold and alien place far from their ancestral home, and Native Americans enslaved in a familiar place made alien by their bondage in it, find meaning for their lives in the actions of the whites who enslaved them? How did they interpret demands that they fit

---

[89] Ibid., p. 57. Sterling Stuckey discusses reverence for ancestors among enslaved Africans in *Slave Culture: Nationalist Theory and the Foundations of Black America* (New York: Oxford University Press, 1987), esp. "Introduction: Slavery and the Circle of Culture," pp. 3–97.

[90] This attempt to read the events surrounding Stepney's death from the perspective of the community of slaves of which he was a part is not intended to suggest that the African American experience can simply be intuited without independent research. But that essential research too often yields a paucity of records of the thoughts and motives of eighteenth-century slaves. I believe that diaries, like other texts, are open to plural readings. Thus, it is easy to assume that MacSparran's documented affection for the first Stepney led *him* to name the second; after all, he had both the authority to choose the name, as the child's owner, and the opportunity to confer it, as his baptizer. But since slave names were often negotiated, it is equally likely that MacSparran would have concurred with a choice made by Emblo. None of the "imaginative" assumptions in this second reading stray very far from the text, although they approach it with a different reading strategy.

into families, households, communities, and cultural patterns that were unfamiliar? How did they decide how to negotiate the arbitrary hodge-podge of behaviors of whites toward them? There were threats of verbal and physical abuse, sometimes carried out and sometimes not; promises of rewards that sometimes materialized and sometimes did not; declarations that they could inherit an ultimate reward by submitting to the logic of this bewildering thicket of requirements—an afterlife in a Kingdom whose principal characteristic seemed to be that white people would act there in a way they seldom acted in their earthly lives.

At first, all whites and their lifeways must have seemed puzzling and dangerous. Then, slowly, it must have become possible for the slave to determine what whites' conventions meant to whites themselves, then to find some kind of correspondence between their ways and one's own ways; and finally, to make a life in the interstices of their demands and threats and promises, always conscious that one's own life was suspended in a web of meanings tangent to but not the same as one's own. Gradually it must have become apparent that adapting one's own meanings to whites' meanings gratified whites but also threatened them, that it never made a slave more "like" a white person but only a better slave. Yet there was power in being a better slave, if one could stomach it, could withstand the psychic cost of submitting. Some could not and ran away, or were sold out of the family and, often, out of New England. But most submitted well enough to avoid severe reprisals; and certain slaves exhibited considerable talent for manipulating the strengths and weaknesses of whites, satisfying their demands efficiently and winning their trust and approval—being better slaves—in a way that benefited the rest of the slave community at the least personal cost. Stepney, obviously, had been just such a talented man.

Slavery ordered the social lives of people of color in colonial New England to a considerable degree, but it did not constitute those lives. That is, enslaved people of color who abided within the limits of their enslavement nonetheless gave their own meaning to the institutions whites imposed upon them and also constructed alternative institutions that sometimes paralleled, sometimes intersected those of whites. Slaves who could not and would not abide within its limits acted as though enslavement did not exist—refusing to work, running away—and suffered the consequences. Reshaping, transforming, and inventing alternative meanings or simply refusing to acknowledge any meaning at all were simply different strategies to achieve the same fundamental end: to enact freedom within the institutional framework of slavery.

Slaves acknowledged and manipulated their membership in white families while they simultaneously created their own families, deliberately transgressing the boundaries established by whites to contain familymaking among slaves. Former slaves' statements that they had been "raised in the family of" their owners and the frequency with which emancipated slaves pressed their former owners for financial or other assistance[91] suggest that large numbers of slaves, if not the majority, found membership in white families meaningful in some sense. At the same time they formed families with other people of color, even outside the household, disregarding identity or status in relation to bondage, and some maintained those family bonds in the face of changes in that status. Venture Smith, for example, married Meg, another of his master's slaves, and sired children regularly, maintaining his marriage relation through his own sale to a succession of different masters, his purchase of his own freedom, and nine additional years of labor to earn enough to purchase his children and, finally, Meg herself. The fact that Smith tallied up the financial costs and benefits of these family relationships does not diminish the point that it was important to him to sustain them.[92]

Some slaves formed and sustained family relationships with others outside the household in direct defiance of restrictions imposed by their white families, as in the case of MacSparran's Maroca and Colonel Updike's Mingo, creating conflict that undoubtedly spilled over into other facets of daily life.[93] These relationships tested the skills of favored slaves such as Stepney in mediating between the disobedient slave and the master; they also tested his skills as a leader in mediating between slaves who supported the master's perspective (and who were undoubtedly called upon to help police the errant slave) and the slave herself and her supporters.

Finally, slaves sometimes participated in sexual relationships within their families, with their own masters. Where these were coerced, as they undoubtedly often were, defiance probably was manifested in small belligerent or subversive acts and perhaps in aggressively seeking other, forbidden alliances. Coerced liaisons would certainly have raised the level of daily tension in the household, magnifying friction between whites as well as be-

[91] See, e.g., the letter of Jeney to Moses Brown, her former owner, in correspondence of November 1800, and numerous other letters of Brown's former slaves, in Moses Brown Papers Rhode Island Historical Society.

[92] "A Narrative of the Life and Adventures of Venture, a Native of Africa" (1798), in *Five Black Lives*, ed. Arna Bontemps (Middletown, Conn.: Wesleyan University Press, 1971), pp. 4–24.

[93] Six years after the beating incident, MacSparran mentioned that some sugar had vanished from his kitchen on a day when the slaves had been left home alone, and that he suspected Maroca of the theft (*Abstract*, p. 45). Possibly he considered sexual misconduct an indicator of more general untrustworthiness; possibly Maroca actually had stolen the sugar as part of a broader pattern of subtle revenge against MacSparran for his persecution of her relationship with Mingo.

tween slaves and master. But sometimes slaves entered apparently willing, long-term relationships with their masters, as was likely the case with Lewis Lyron and Bess.[94] These relationships also constituted defiant acts on the part of the slaves involved—in this case flouting conventions established by the community–and complicated relations among the slaves, among the white family members, and between slaves and whites. One can imagine the helpless resentment of the other four household slaves at Bess's favored status and her expectation of not only emancipation but generous inheritance at Lyron's death; further, one can imagine Lyron's nephew, essentially disinherited in Bess's favor, harboring at least some resentment at his uncle and taking it out upon the easier target, Bess, or perhaps on the other slaves as safe surrogates.

Social life for slaves in New England, then, consisted of participating in two linked communities of families. That is, virtually every slave was a member of two families simultaneously, both conditioned by slavery—one structured by its formal conventions, the other constructed defiantly in opposition to those conventions or maintained quietly in the spaces permitted by them. Enslaved people of color in New England occupied similarly parallel universes with respect to larger units of social organization and political identity as well. Their membership in white families gained them a virtual representation in the polity through the household head, as discussed above; at the same time they participated in a political and legal hierarchy formally recognized in the annual festival of "Negro election."[95]

Beginning about 1750 and continuing for about a hundred years, slaves held annual elections of "governors" in various towns throughout the New England states.[96] These celebrations are generally considered to have been African in origin but heavily influenced by British colonial practices; Ann Plane has also suggested that they share certain characteristics with Native American crowning ceremonies and may have borrowed elements from

[94] Warren, "Lewis Lyron."

[95] The most comprehensive study of the institution of "Negro election" and other eighteenth- and nineteenth-century African American festivals is Shane White, "'It Was a Proud Day': African Americans, Festivals, and Parades in the North, 1741–1834," *Journal of American History* 81 (June 1994): 13–50. Earlier discussions include Orville H. Platt, "Negro Governors," *Papers of the New Haven Colony Historical Society* 6 (1900): 315; Hubert S. Aimes, "African Institutions in America," *Journal of American Folklore* 18 (January–March 1905): 5; Joseph P. Reidy, "Negro Election Day and Black Community Life in New England, 1750–1860," *Marxist Perspectives* 1 (Fall 1978): 102–17; Greene, *The Negro in Colonial New England*, pp. 249–55; Melvin Wade, "Shining in Borrowed Plumage: Affirmation of Community in the Black Coronation Festivals in New England, 1750–1850," *Western Folklore* 40 (July 1981): 211–31; Stuckey, *Slave Culture*, pp. 74–83.

[96] White, "It Was a Proud Day," pp. 16–17; Platt, "Negro Governors," p. 319; Reidy, "Negro Election Day," p. 103.

them as well.[97] Orville Platt speculated that such events did not occur before 1750 because the slave populations in New England did not achieve sufficient size to establish the custom until that time; Sterling Stuckey likewise suggests that the influx of slaves directly from Africa in the 1740s and 1750s may have been a catalyst for the practice.[98] These events were not necessarily statewide—an election district might encompass one, two, or a group of towns—and they were held on different dates in different places (in May in Connecticut, in June in Rhode Island) but on the same date annually in each place. Celebrations varied from place to place but generally involved a parade, voting (usually by means of lining up behind two opposing candidates), a banquet, dancing and drinking, and playing games. The governor would often appoint a lieutenant governor, justices of the peace, and sheriffs. Although these officials had no power under British colonial or American law, they did exercise considerable control over the behavior of slaves and free people of color (except tribalized natives).[99] The owner of the slave elected governor paid for the celebration. (After the 1780s, when free blacks began to be elected, they paid for the festivities themselves, limiting the field of candidates to men of relative means.)[100] Slaveowners almost universally allowed their slaves to participate in election day ceremonies, and every participating slave borrowed clothing and even horses from his master for use in the event. Women too dressed up in borrowed finery for the occasion and took part in the dancing and other festivities, although they did not customarily vote.

Scholars have debated whether this annual election represented an empowering institution for people of color or a method of white control over people of color. Certainly the event was approved and even financed by whites, and it cost them at least one and as many as eight days' labor on the part of their slaves.[101] Joseph Reidy suggests that it provided a safety valve for slaves' frustrations while extending whites' law enforcement apparatus, and that it falls within the rubric of rituals of "status reversal" discussed by Victor Turner, which reaffirm the principles of hierarchy. At the same time, he notes that it also developed black leadership and provided a struc-

[97] Ann Marie Plane, "'Of the Most Royal Blood': Colonial Redefinition of Narragansett Systems of Governance," paper presented at the annual meeting of the American Studies Association, Boston, November 7, 1993.

[98] Platt, "Negro Governors," p. 319; Stuckey, *Slave Culture*, p. 74.

[99] Platt, "Negro Governors," pp. 322–24; Stuckey, *Slave Culture*, p. 77; Reidy, "Negro Election Day," pp. 105–6, 110–12.

[100] Reidy, "Negro Election Day," p. 111.

[101] E.g., the owner of E. & C. Green Co. of Warwick, Rhode Island, noted in the company accounts for June 1806, "8 days lost at Negro Election." Blotter 1803–7, E. & C. Green Papers, Rhode Island Historical Society.

ture for black community life. Shane White suggests that "election" enabled slaves to control a portion of their lives. Stuckey thinks its principal purpose was to reinforce African cultural expression among slaves.[102] In fact, election day must have served all three purposes—black empowerment, white control, reinforcement of Africanity—but its role as a device to institutionalize an alternative government in the slave community, with white support, seems especially significant. Although their status as slaves distanced black males from active participation in formal political institutions, they were able to institutionalize a political identity parallel to that of white males by means of "Negro election."

Many male slaves could enact a relatively free and independent work life within the conventions of slave labor as a consequence of the seasonal rhythm and special requirements for labor in New England. Male slaves were frequently hired out as agricultural workers, seamen, or artisans and sent off with instructions to remit a specific amount of money to their masters at the end of a specified period of time. They were also employed as resident managers of farms and plantations miles from their masters' homes. These arrangements were not equivalent to freedom and did not necessarily make the fact or experience of enslavement less oppressive, yet they did enable slaves to establish self-directed patterns of work within the institution of slavery. For example, Newport Greene, slave of Dr. Amos Throop of Providence, was sent to sea as a mariner to earn money for his master.[103] Joshua Hempstead's slave Adam managed his master's Stonington property alone for months at a time while Hempstead remained at his New London farm.[104] Venture Smith bought land with money he had earned while a slave and, still a slave, cultivated this land "with the greatest diligence and economy, at times when my master did not require my labor," thereby earning enough in two years to purchase his own freedom.[105] These men and many others carved out independent work lives within the confines of slavery.

A last example of an institutional framework specifically adapted to slavery, one that structured and masked an experience of independence for slaves, was the Christian prayer meeting. Seventeenth- and eighteenth-century New England slaves may have maintained African religious practices in secret—as southern slaves are known to have done in the next centu-

---

[102] Reidy, "Negro Election Day," pp. 109–12; Victor Turner, *The Ritual Process* (Chicago: University of Chicago Press, 1969), pp. 176–77; White, "It Was a Proud Day," p. 30; Stuckey, *Slave Culture*, p. 77.

[103] Providence Town Council Records, 7:324–25, February 4, 1799.

[104] Hempstead, *Diary*.

[105] "Narrative of the Life and Adventures of Venture," p. 17.

ry[106]—but if so, there is little evidence of it, whereas meetings for prayer and Bible study in the homes of ministers and lay preachers are known to have attracted throngs of slaves. As early as 1693 a "Society of Negroes" met on Sabbath evenings in Boston to pray and learn the catechism.[107] Susanna Anthony and Sarah Osborne were attracting as many as 525 enslaved people of color to their Newport prayer meetings by January 1767.[108] Five years later Ezra Stiles noted in his diary an "evening religious meeting of Negroes at my house" at which were "present 70 or 80."[109] Although many slaveholders required their slaves to attend formal services in local churches, participation in informal prayer meetings in private homes was a self-motivated activity, or had become so by 1750, at any rate. (Mather's "Rules for the Society of Negroes," dated 1693, which purports to reflect the determination of slaves—"We the Miserable Children of Adam, and of Noah"—to meet, pray, and police their own behavior, suggests that the earliest efforts to organize separate religious activities for slaves may have been fairly coercive; nonetheless, the meetings were intended to be independent of direct control by whites, with only the agreement to "obtain some Wise and Good Man of the English in the Neighbourhood, and especially the Offcers [*sic*] of the Church, to look in upon us," suggesting that the participants had discretion over whites' attendance.) Opportunities to gather privately in numbers must have held considerable appeal for slaves isolated individually in white households.

Osborne and Anthony's meetings offer a particularly interesting example of a seemingly conventional framework masking a profoundly subversive activity. As women, they challenged the conventions of Christian religious practice by assuming the role of public preachers. By limiting their audience to enslaved people of color, however, they could enact a position of public leadership while disclaiming it, arguing that the nature of blacks as "children" placed this activity within the appropriate range of behavior for females.[110] It is not clear whether Anthony and Osborne actually thought of the slaves as children in the sense of undeveloped persons,

---

[106] The classic work on religion among southern slaves is Albert J. Raboteau, *Slave Religion: The "Invisible Institution" in the Antebellum South* (New York: Oxford University Press, 1978).

[107] [Cotton Mather], "Rules for the Society of Negroes. 1693," Boston, 1706–13, broadside collection, American Antiquarian Society.

[108] The activities of Anthony and Osborne are described in Mary Beth Norton, "My Resting Reaping Times," *Signs* 2 (Winter 1976): 515–29.

[109] Ezra Stiles, *The Literary Diary of Ezra Stiles*, ed. Bowditch Dexter (New York: Scribner, 1901), 1:204, January 13, 1772.

[110] Osborne, defending her preaching to her friend Joseph Fish, said, "The servants appear to me no otherwise now then [*sic*] children tho for Stature Men and women." (quoted in Norton, "My Resting Reaping Times," p. 521).

or whether they were consciously employing a characterization with a double meaning to mislead their accusers, asserting to themselves that slaves were after all "children of God." In any case, although many if not most of the slaves who attended their meetings undoubtedly held sincere religious convictions, the appeal must have been greatly enhanced by the challenge the meetings presented to white male authority: slaves were able to gather there in large numbers outside the gaze of white males and participate in an activity that was unobjectionable on its face but deeply subversive in its implications.

It should be noted that the opportunities within the institution of slavery to participate in formal structures of independent social and political experience which paralleled those of whites also paralleled the exclusion of women from those activities by whites. Opportunities to assume an alternative political identity, to work independently, to worship in a way that evaded church authority, all were nonetheless framed by an institution of slavery that was founded on European assumptions and was thus itself deeply gendered.[111]

Servitude ordered virtually every aspect of the social lives of people of color in colonial New England. For each institutional element whose purpose was to subordinate the slave, however, servitude also shaped an alternative element whereby enslaved people of color consolidated and institutionalized the human freedom they retained within slavery. Perversely, in other words, servitude institutionalized the enactment of freedom by enslaved people of color.

Even though the experience of enslaved people of color in New England led them to see themselves as a distinct people uniquely susceptible to enslavement, it did not lead them to see themselves as uniquely destined for it. They understood slavery to be unjust—and temporary. Their experience in managing enslavement—by meeting whites' expectations while evading them; by being "good" slaves while enacting freedom; by living two lives, one nested within the other; by ultimately achieving legal freedom in small but growing numbers and living relatively successful lives thereafter—prepared persons of color to expect one day to be free. Though they often, but not always, identified with their owners' politics, by the 1770s most were prepared to see possibilities for their own future in Revolutionary rhetoric.

[111] James Oliver Horton, "Freedom's Yoke: Gender Conventions among Antebellum Free Blacks," *Feminist Studies* 12 (Spring 1986): 51–76, esp. 52–54, describes the ways in which social and political roles in antebellum black society were highly gendered and argues that gender conventions among free blacks were influenced by African traditions as well as the gender assumptions of white Americans.

2

The Antislavery Impulse

"To Clear Our Spirits":
Whites' Expectations of Freedom from Slavery

On the eve of the American Revolution, "New England identity" and "the Negro," ideas that had coexisted in the context of family slavery from 1638 through the 1760s, were beginning to express a contradiction. By 1800, they had become mutually exclusive categories in the understanding of whites, the one negating and denying the legitimacy of the other. The engine of this great transformation was the discourse of antislavery.

Although the earliest antislavery protests preceded the movement for independence by more than half a century, it was only in the context of the Revolution that the antislavery movement gained support outside a fringe group of Quakers and other agitators. The languages of antislavery and revolutionary republicanism were mutually reinforcing; they seemed to offer precisely the same promise: liberty for all citizens. But both these languages were Janus-faced: to whites, they offered visions of a free republic in which slaves did not exist; to people of color, the visions were of a republic in which they could continue to live as free citizens. In other words, for whites, both abolitionism and republicanism functioned as ideologies of exclusion insofar as people of color were concerned; for people of color themselves, they promised inclusion.

On the eve of the Revolution, there were about 16,000 persons of African descent in the New England colonies, the great majority undoubtedly enslaved.[1] Because slaves and free persons of color were not routinely distinguished in pre-Revolutionary censuses, it is impossible to be certain of the proportions, and there is some disagreement over whether the institution had already begun to decline after 1760. There is evidence on both sides of the issue. On one hand, the average number of slaves in estate inventories did decline after 1760, although this may have represented a redistribution as a consequence of estate division and reduction in the average size of landholdings.[2] On the other hand, although wages to males for skilled craft labor fell by 30 percent between 1765 and 1774, wages for farm labor remained nearly constant, and both men's wages for general labor and women's wages (undifferentiated) continued to rise, probably reflecting the demand for workers to replace emigrating males; in such circumstances, slave labor must have remained practical.[3] Nearly 10 percent of the slaves carried by Rhode Island slavers at the peak of the trade in the 1760s, primarily from Africa but also from the West Indies, had been imported for the New England market, and most of them probably remained indefinitely in the area as slaves.[4]

Several different factors, however, may have reduced the number of New England slaves during and immediately after the Revolution. Some slaves, especially those in southern Rhode Island, fled during the British occupation of Newport; some sought freedom by means of service with the Continental Army; and there is sketchy evidence that a considerable number may have been sold south on the eve of the passage of emancipation statutes.[5] But there is no conclusive evidence that numbers declined precipitously, or that the institution as a practice was declining, before the Revolution.

It is undeniable that after 1700 slavery slowly emerged from the seamless web of unquestioned social and cultural practices that constituted the social fabric of New England to become an issue of intense public contro-

[1] Lorenzo J. Greene, *The Negro in Colonial New England* (New York: Columbia University Press, 1942), p. 74.

[2] Christian McBurney, "The South Kingstown Planters: Country Gentry in Colonial Rhode Island," *Rhode Island History* 45 (1986): 81–93.

[3] Gloria L. Main, "Gender, Work, and Wages in Colonial New England," *William and Mary Quarterly*, 3d ser., 51 (1994): 48–49, 62–65; Jack P. Greene, *Pursuits of Happiness: The Social Development of Early Modern British Colonies and the Formation of American Culture* (Chapel Hill: University of North Carolina Press, 1988), pp. 65–73.

[4] Jay Coughtry, *The Notorious Triangle* (Philadelphia: Temple University Press, 1981), pp. 165, 167.

[5] Greene, *The Negro in Colonial New England*, pp. 146, 190; Edgar G. McManus, *Black Bondage in the North* (Syracuse, N.Y.: Syracuse University Press, 1973), p. 182.

versy. The question is whether—and if so, when and in what ways—the growing public debate actually altered slaveholding and slave trading practices before the Revolution. Did the early antislavery movement set in motion a subtle but crucially important transformation in the ideologies of race and work in New England?

The Germantown, Pennsylvania, Quaker protest of 1688 initiated the American antislavery movement, and the language of that protest established in many ways the terms and landscape of the subsequent debate, as well as subsequent thinking about "Negroes" in general. Germantown Quakers offered impassioned testimony against the "traffick of mens-body"—specifically, the act of man-stealing. They gave primary emphasis to the sinfulness of acts of theft and trade in human beings and represented slaveholding as a constellation of secondary sinful practices—receiving stolen property, providing occasions that would demand violations of pacifist principles (to subdue slaves who might resist enslavement), oppressive treatment such as overwork and underfeeding—that necessarily resulted from the initial sinful act.[6] The Quakers themselves followed the logic of their protest, from warning against "the bringing in of any more negroes" in Philadelphia (1696), to admonishing members who purchased imported slaves (at the 1730 Yearly Meeting), to condemning the foreign and domestic slave trade and the institution of slavery itself (1758). In 1760 New England Quakers denounced the slave trade, and in 1773 they called upon all Friends to free their slaves. In 1783 they implemented a program to compensate former slaves.[7]

Nonetheless, attacking the slave trade, rather than slaveholding, as the nub of the issue remained the most common strategy among members of the Puritan clergy and other leaders who began to echo the Quaker opposition. Even Anthony Benezet, who insisted that slaveholding was every bit as sinful as participating in the slave trade, made the trade his primary target. That focus simultaneously confronted and evaded the issue of slavery. Investment in the slave trade, though considerable in areas such as Newport, was not as widespread as slaveholding, and the vessels that constituted the greatest investment could be turned to trade in other merchandise. But since slaves constituted an important part of the personal property of as many as one in four property owners in New England, a frontal attack on the practice itself would have amounted to proposing

[6] "The Germantown Protest," rpt. in Samuel W. Pennypacker, "The Settlement of Germantown and the Causes Which Led to It," *Pennsylvania Magazine of History and Biography* 4 (1880): 28–30.

[7] Society of Friends, *A Brief Statement of the Rise and Progress of the Testimony of the Religious Society of Friends, against Slavery and the Slave Trade* (Philadelphia: Joseph & William Kite, 1843), pp. 8, 13–14, 21–23, 43–47.

confiscation of property.[8] Even proposals for compensated emancipation threatened a radical alteration in the social order at a time when the day-to-day personal involvement of colonists with enslaved Africans as laborers and members of their households, as well as their more abstract dealings with them as commercial investments, was commonplace. Focusing on the iniquity of the slave trade and suggesting an end to importation as a source of additional slaves offered a solution whose consequences for the day-to-day practice lay safely in the hazy future. As such, this strategy foreshadowed its quite symmetrical successor: proposals for gradual emancipation by ending birth into slavery as a source of new slaves.

What is significant here is that pre-Revolutionary antislavery protest structured the problem as one of the presence or absence of enslaved Africans, of introducing closure to the process of open-ended increase in their numbers and in fact reducing their physical presence by attrition of one kind or another. Transforming the conditions of existence of enslaved persons of color already present in the colonies was not a primary consideration, precisely because ending slavery was understood to mean eliminating the presence of slaves. By proposing restrictions on the importation of Africans as a commodity, antislavery protesters tacitly accepted and naturalized their commodity status; by seeking to limit importation as a way of ending slavery, they implicitly equated ending slavery with eliminating people of African descent.

The Germantown protest introduced other ideas that became standard in subsequent antislavery writing and shaped the thinking of whites on both sides of the slavery issue. Germantown Quakers noted that the enslaved were "those oppressed wch are of a black Colour,"[9] confronting the fact of the basis of enslavement in color difference, and equated this source of oppression with their own persecution in Europe for the distinctiveness of their religious convictions. On its surface, this analogy sought simply to stimulate empathetic identification between Quaker slaveholders and their slaves. By suggesting a correlation between whiteness and orthodoxy and between blackness and unorthodoxy, however, this association strengthened the normative value of whiteness even as it challenged the appropriateness of behaving differently toward the white and the nonwhite. Fur-

---

[8] From a substantial sample of Connecticut inventories, Jackson Turner Main, *Society and Economy in Colonial Connecticut* (Princeton: Princeton University Press, 1985), p. 177, estimates slave ownership at about one in four property owners in Connecticut colony on the eve of the Revolution. Since slaves constituted approximately the same proportion of the population of Massachusetts and Connecticut and a much larger proportion in Rhode Island, the estimate is probably conservative for those three states but may overstate the case for New England as a whole.

[9] "The Germantown Protest," p. 28.

ther, by subtly associating blackness with Quakers' own historical resistance to external authority, radical self-possession, and ultimate flight from oppression, the Germantown Quakers invested enslaved Africans with attributes that had troubling implications in an American context.

Later Quaker and Puritan arguments, even as they continued to frame the slavery issue as a moral problem, warned of the practical consequences of slavery, associating the presence of laboring people of color with potential ill reports that might retard the growth of the colonies, result in long-term economic disadvantage, and bring the disfavor of God. By 1774, in the escalating Revolutionary crisis, Benjamin Colman of Newbury, Massachusetts, was describing British oppression as evidence of divine judgment on colonial slavery, a "God-provoking and wrath-procuring sin."[10] At the outbreak of war Samuel Hopkins could read clearly in the rupture with Britain a divine rebuke of slavery, that "sin of crimson die, which is most particularly pointed out by the public calamities which have come upon us." Even though capture, importation, and imprisonment of Africans were decried as the sinful acts of whites which might incur divine wrath, people of color themselves were inevitably construed as the actual embodiment of potential disaster.[11]

Further, Samuel Hopkins linked the presence of enslaved Africans with danger by reminding Americans that because slaves might at any moment seek freedom as supporters of the British enemy, they constituted an ever present enemy within.[12] Americans seem to have taken the threat of wartime black subversion quite seriously. For example, in May 1776, when Jack (John Anderson), the slave of Connecticut's British Governor John Skene (who was under arrest but paroled on his word and thus able to conduct his social affairs freely), was chosen "Negro governor," a committee of patriots was immediately formed to investigate the election as a possible loyalist plot to undermine the authority of the Revolutionary Council. The committee found no evidence of a plot, but its detailed, two-page report illustrates the contradictory views of slaves as foolish dupes, capable agents of subversion, and plausible patriots. It also suggests that slave culture still played a significant role in New England social life and was seen as having a powerful, and potentially negative, impact on it.[13] As the antislavery

[10] Ibid., p. 29; *Essex Journal*, July 20, 1774.

[11] Samuel Hopkins, *A Dialogue concerning the Slavery of the Africans* . . . (Norwich, Conn.: Judah P. Spooner, 1776), p. 31.

[12] Ibid., p. 31.

[13] The people of color interviewed by the committee insisted that Jack had not been truly elected but only appointed by Cuff, the previous governor, without their approval: "They spoke against it and declared they would not have a tory for a governor." Yet in the very next sentence the report noted that "the negroes had an entertainment and a dance . . . on Friday

movement evolved from its earliest Quaker stirrings through its Puritan and pre-Revolutionary phases, both adherents and foes of antislavery learned to think about people of color as the embodiment of sin, the sign of looming disaster, and the instrument of divine judgment and vengeance.

The argument against slaveholding on grounds of its sinfulness was compelling to many devout believers. Although the New England Quakers made manumitting their slaves a part of their discipline in 1773, widespread manumission was not achieved without persistent effort and much resistance. For example, the 1773 report to the Smithfield, Rhode Island, Monthly Meeting of Friends by a committee appointed to visit Stephen Hopkins, owner of an enslaved woman, noted that "he Appeared in an affable Disposition but continued to the Last of our Discoursing with him About it to Justify his holding her in Said State of Bondage by reason he Said She had Children that needed the immediate Care of a Mother and he Looked upon it to be his Duty to Keep her to nurse and bring them up." Likewise, a year later, when a different committee "Revisited Stephen Killton and laboured with him" over his slave, they reported that Killton "still Refuses to give him his freedom but allows in words that Negros have the Same Right to freedom as white People have but this is a Singular Case." Killton saw as justification the facts that "he hath Paid a large Sum for his Support when a Child," "he hath Paid money at Several times occasioned by the bad Conduct of Said Negro," and "he hath learned him a good trade." Killton insisted that these reasons warranted keeping the slave until he should become twenty-four or twenty-five, "but Refuses to make his freedom Certain at any age."[14] Despite this kind of stubborn resistance, however, by 1782 the Yearly Meeting reported that no Friends continued to hold slaves.

---

night after the election," suggesting both that Jack actually had been "elected" in some way and that the patriotic rejection of his selection by the slaves interviewed may have been assumed for the occasion. This account is taken from the appendix of "The Connecticut Captivity of Major Christopher French," ed. Sheldon S. Cohen, *Connecticut Historical Society Bulletin* 55 (Summer/Fall 1990): 229–30, derived from a footnote to "Major French's Journal," in *The Connecticut Historical Society Collections* (Hartford, 1860), 1:200–202. The story is told with a different interpretation in Greene, *The Negro in Colonial New England*, pp. 252–53, apparently from a different secondary source: R. R. Hinman, *A Historical Collection*, rev. ed. (Hartford, Conn.: E. Gleason, 1842). Hinman and Greene take at face value the refusal of so-called patriotic slaves to vote for a Tory governor. In either case, the story confirms the weight given to the affairs of people of color during the Revolution, and the extent to which the often imaginary "Negro plots" of the early eighteenth century had been perversely strengthened by an intervening half-century of antislavery rhetoric and politicized by the Revolution.

[14] "1773 Report of Committee to Visit Stephen Hopkins on Account of His Slave," and "1774 Report of Committee to Visit Stephen Killton," New England [Friends'] Yearly Meeting Archives, Rhode Island Historical Society.

The compelling natural rights argument against British "enslavement" of the American colonies inevitably led a growing number of voices to join the Quakers in condemning the slave trade and the enslaved labor of persons of color as hypocritical practices inconsistent with republican principles. The escalating rhetorical attack on slavery made an institution that had previously been unexceptional and commonplace a growing source of anxiety and dissension. Yet slaveholding remained widespread throughout New England until the outbreak of war. Revolutionary and Puritan antislavery rhetoric probably accelerated the rate of private manumissions, but in the absence of legislation indemnifying slaveowners against continuing financial responsibility for manumitted slaves (which did not come until 1777 in Connecticut[15] and later elsewhere in New England), sympathy alone could not have resulted in a substantial reduction in the ratio of slaves to free blacks before the war. The records of pre-Revolutionary private manumissions made by New England town clerks are spotty; they do not support a thesis of widespread manumission. Some slaveowners left instructions in their wills for the manumission of favorite slaves, but the number of such wills did not increase substantially until after the Revolution. In 1774 at least 14 percent of Rhode Island households still held slaves, and, as mentioned earlier, about 25 percent of estate inventories in Connecticut included slaves as property.[16] In the absence of convincing evidence of decline, it seems reasonable to conclude that the institution of slavery, although under attack, was still firmly entrenched in New England, as it was elsewhere in the colonies, on the eve of the Revolution.

Still, slavery had come under fire throughout the colonies, and the onset of the Revolution both intensified the attack and weakened the structures and practices that supported the institution. In New England the effect on it was fatal. New England was not ultimately dependent on slave labor, and the war disrupted patterns of production and trade in the very areas in which slave labor was most heavily engaged: the coastal trade, the provisioning trade with the West Indies, fishing, and shipping in general were all severely curtailed by the Revolution. The British occupation of Newport, Rhode Island, suspended activity in one of the principal ports of the American slave trade and also encouraged several hundred Rhode Island slaves to decamp, some to the British occupying forces and others to parts unknown. The Continental Army's desperate need for fresh troops

---

[15] *Public Records of the State of Connecticut*, 9 vols. (Hartford, Conn., 1894–1953), 1:415–16.
[16] Louis P. Masur, "Slavery in Eighteenth Century Rhode Island: Evidence from the Census of 1774," *Plantation and Society* 6 (1985): 140–50; Main, *Society and Economy*, p. 177.

drove Connecticut and Rhode Island (briefly) to offer freedom to slaves (with compensation to their owners) in return for combat services.[17]

By the end of the war New Englanders had learned to cope with many different kinds of changes in their living conditions and, more important, in their underlying assumptions about the conditions of their existence. Formerly colonial subjects, they had been transformed, many of them reluctantly, into republican citizens. And just as reluctantly, a significant number of them had become able to contemplate living in a society without slaves—at least at some distant, agreeably unspecific time.

Even so radical a patriot as Thomas Paine had not been able to imagine immediate freedom for existing slaves; he had insisted that after the Revolution laws should be passed which would "in time procure their freedom."[18] New England antislavery leaders were no more able than Paine to imagine immediate, wholesale freedom for slaves. Before the war, several of them had proposed schemes for the gradual elimination of slavery by various combinations of restrictions on slave importation, revision of manumission restrictions and bond requirements, the training of slaves from childhood for emancipation at some specified age of majority, and compensated manumission of selected categories of slaves. None of these plans could garner sufficient support to be enacted, or even to receive widespread, thoughtful appraisal and debate, until the war had altered both the economic and the intellectual environment sufficiently to erode knee-jerk hostility to emancipation.

A representative example of the prewar proposals that set the stage for the postwar debate was the thoughtful plan to "clear our spirits" of slaveholding offered by Levi Hart of Connecticut and endorsed, with some suggested modifications, by Samuel Hopkins of Rhode Island, two leading New Divinity clergy who were fervent opponents of slavery.[19] The elements and language of the plan merit extended attention because they framed the post-Revolutionary debate over the continued existence of persons of color in the new republic and their transformation from property into personhood—how this transformation might be achieved, and what it would mean for the relationships between whites and people of color once it was accomplished.

[17] Arthur Zilversmit, *The First Emancipation: The Abolition of Slavery in the North* (Chicago: University of Chicago Press, 1967), pp. 119, 122.

[18] *Pennsylvania Journal*, October 18, 1775, in Zilversmit, *First Emancipation*, p. 96.

[19] Levi Hart, "Some Thoughts on the Subject of Freeing the Negro Slaves in the Colony of Connecticut, humbly offered to the Consideration of all friends to liberty & Justice," (c. 1775), p. 7, Miscellaneous Manuscripts (typescript by Doris E. Cook, manuscript cataloguer), Connecticut Historical Society.

Some time before January 25, 1775, Hart sent Hopkins and others an essay titled, "Some Thoughts on the Subject of Freeing the Negro Slaves in the Colony of Connecticut, humbly offered to the Consideration of all friends to liberty & Justice." It seemed "to be now generally conceded," he wrote, that the slave trade had "proved to be criminal & inhumane," and that the general public was on the brink of becoming convinced that "if it is criminal to bring a fellow creature into Slavery (who hath not forfeited his liberty by any misconduct) it is also criminal to retain him in Slavery," which was "a constant acting over the same crime which was committed in enslaving him at first" (essentially, a violation of the Golden Rule). Hart concluded that only two objections stood in the way of all slaves in Connecticut being made free at once "& the accursed thing put away from among us" (here again placing the practice in a palpable presence/absence mode): "that the owners of Slaves will be injured by their being made free, unless they are in some way indemnified"; and that "the Slaves when made free will be an unsupportable burden to Society, through their imprudence, & vicious & immoral behaviour."[20]

Hart saw the first obstacle as the greater and devoted some two thousand words to laying out a graduated compensation plan with a complicated analysis of costs and benefits. He acknowledged that slaveowners had purchased their slaves and enjoyed their property in them "under the patronage of Government," so that "the public faith is, in effect, plighted to protect & support them in the possession of their Slaves, or indemnify them if they are taken away." His use of language commonly associated with marriage, a sacrament cementing a lifelong bond, suggests both the seriousness and the anticipation of permanence still implicit in the master-slave relationship in Connecticut on the eve of the Revolution. Hart used "Government" generically to mean the duly constituted authority that subjects or citizens are bound to obey; he did not suggest that the impending dissolution of British authority would by itself nullify the bonds of slaves to masters which had been authorized and preserved by colonial government, or wipe out the "public faith" supporting those bonds. In Hart's conception, under republican government citizens would still remain bound to slaves and slaves to citizens—a "plighted" troth. An act of the legislature could, however, make slaves free by indemnifying slaveowners "at the public cost." Hart saw that such an act would require those who had never owned or traded in slaves to "be punished together with the guilty persons, by being obliged to bear a part of the expence of their freedom," but he argued that "the whole of the community" was concerned in the slave trade

---

[20] Ibid., p. 1.

insofar as it was carried on under the patronage of the legislature, "a representation of the whole body of the people." He equated objections to the recovery of freedom by slaves with the absurdity of robbers' objections to the expense of restitution for theft.[21]

Next, turning to the practical problems of indemnifying owners, Hart proposed four conditions that he felt would ensure equity and minimize public expense: (1) that owners be paid "only so far as their interest suffers a diminution by the freedom of the Slaves" (that is, for the productive work years remaining to them) rather than for the full purchase price of each slave; (2) that slaves born in the colonies (therefore having required no initial purchase price) and "in a state of Minority" be required to serve their masters "till they have returned an equivalent for their education," which Hart estimated would be "24 or 25 years for males & something less for females"; (3) that owners of "unprofitable slaves—the infirm and elderly—receive no compensation for their freedom (since they would incur no loss); and (4) that owners of such elderly and infirm slaves be required to support them until their deaths, as they would ordinarily be required to do under existing manumission laws. Hart's elaborate calculations produced an age-graded table of values of all productive slaves in the colony between twenty-five and thirty-seven and a half years of age, based on the 1774 colony census of slaves. Calculating the average value of a slave at £50 and annual depreciation at £4 per year, he concluded that the colony could indemnify all slaveowners fairly for the "depreciated" value of their slaves at a modest cost of £21,984, a sum easily exceeded by a colony tax of a mere three pence per pound of valuation, or £24,650.[22]

Hart's allocation of value and equity reveals a number of assumptions about differential entitlement to labor power and personhood which were typical of antislavery theorists, slaveowners, and ordinary citizens alike. These assumptions persisted throughout the Revolutionary and post-Revolutionary periods and deeply colored the actual process of legally transforming property into persons when emancipation finally was implemented.

To begin with, Hart's proposal foreshadowed the erasure of the personal past of enslavement as an immediate consequence of emancipation. He defined freedom for slaves as "that invaluable jewel" and equated manumission with a robber's restitution to a person who has been robbed. The recompense for prospective labor lost to the slaveowner and the prospective enjoyment of their own labor by the slaves were cast as equivalent forms of full and sufficient restitution to the respective parties. But what of the

[21] Ibid., pp. 1–2.
[22] Ibid., pp. 2, 3–4.

loss of value of a slave's past labor to himself, the value already enjoyed by the slaveowner? An annual £4 depreciation based on value received by the slaveowner would, of course, also represent a £4 value owed to the slave.[23] Hart was not deliberately avoiding the can of worms that a consideration of full reparations would have opened; he seems to have been truly unable to see the lost value to slaves themselves of their own labor (their freedom expressed in productive terms) as an issue in equity, because his thinking was anchored in the very language and conventions he was seeking to overturn. Although Hart could conceptualize slaves' theoretical entitlement to freedom as a state of being, he could not conceive of deprivation of it as having a value equivalent in any sense to the loss of property-in-labor experienced by the slaveowner. That is partly because, to Hart, property could not experience a sense of loss of itself; property had value only in relation to ownership, use, and exchange by persons. Significantly, Hart seemed to imagine that slavery alienated the enslaved from their humanness along with their freedom. For him, government sanction of slaveowning, of enjoyment of slaves as property, had made them property in fact for the years of their enslavement. The law defined ontological status; therefore, people of color while enslaved remained property, their humanness suspended for that period of time, themselves excluded from the discourse of entitlement to property and labor value that was so significant a component of the natural rights argument. Their theoretical entitlement to freedom might extend backward throughout their enslavement, but their practical entitlement to the value of their labor could begin only with their emergence as persons through emancipation.

But the notion of the public purchase of slaves' freedom also had implications for the reemergence of personhood in emancipation. Such a transaction implied the transfer of ownership of slaves from individuals to "the public"; the "whole body of the people"—which Hart insisted was collectively implicated in the enslavement of Africans by "their voice in the enacting the laws"[24]—would, by the enactment of a law to purchase the prospective time of slaves from their masters, become slaveholders in fact, who would then simultaneously act as a body to free their slaves. This seemingly hairsplitting point has enormous significance: it reflects assumptions about continuing public responsibility for free people of color and, most important, about the obligations of people of color to the public. In other words, in debates over compensated emancipation, we can see an emerging theoretical approach toward transforming privately owned

[23] Ibid., pp. 2–3.
[24] Ibid., p. 2.

slaves into the collectively dependent class Frederick Douglass later characterized as "slaves of the community."[25]

Hart's assumptions about the way in which the suspension of agency imposed by enslavement would persist in people of color beyond emancipation emerge in his rationale for extending to the age of twenty-four or twenty-five the period during which slave children should "serve their masters till they have returned an equivalent for their education," even though this is "somewhat later than the period of life fixed upon by authority for white children to become free" (that is reach majority). Hart defended a later age of majority for children of color on the grounds that the period before majority for white children "was not fixed upon so much on account of the child's having returned an equivalent to the parent for his education, as that he is supposed capable at that time of life to regulate his own behaviour, & provide for himself."[26] Hart equated free and enslaved children's "education" in childhood yet assumed that children of color owed restitution for it, though white children did not. He ascribed value to the education of young slaves as a sort of property improvement that would incur obligation; it must be paid for by the service of the recipient, whereas for whites it was a free gift of love on the part of their parents. Hart further construed majority for whites in terms of their readiness to exercise self-determination and agency, whereas for enslaved children majority was an economic issue: it came with the satisfaction of a debt in the purchase of one's own value as improved property. Exercise of agency for newly freed persons of color was not part of Hart's calculation of their value and hence not a consideration in this first and more detailed part of his proposal, dealing with economic injury to slaveholders.

Such exercise of agency was the central issue, however, in the second part of Hart's argument, which addressed "the supposed imprudent & vicious conduct of the free Negros & the Injury which would probably be sustained by individuals and the public through their abuse of liberty." Hart recounted what "is said" of "Negros": that they "have not sufficient discretion to conduct their own affairs & provide for themselves, & that many of them are addicted to stealing, & other enormities *Now* & would probably be much more so if they were not under the care & government of masters who restrain them." But he refuted these assumptions, asserting that "our

[25] Frederick Douglass, "An Address to the Colored People of the United States," *North Star,* September 29, 1848, in Philip S. Foner, *The Life and Writings of Frederick Douglass: Early Years, 1817–1849* (New York: International, 1950), p. 333.

[26] Hart, "Some Thoughts," p. 2. It is clear that he is speaking here of childhood, not indenture, as a condition of unfreedom for white children. He is probably referring to the age of fourteen years, when guardianship of the property of orphans customarily ended, otherwise, he may have meant twenty-one, the age of majority.

national pride leads us to imagine them, by nature, much inferior to ourselves in intellectual ability," which he labels an "ungenerous self-applaud-
ing preference." He argued that slaves did not lack natural capacity to
govern and support themselves; rather, the "state of abject Slavery breaks
the spirits & benumbs the powers of the human mind." As to the likelihood
that they would become "more vicious & disorderly, & in particular, more
given to stealing," Hart listed what he imagined to be the motivations of
slaves and the countervailing motivations that freedom would introduce:
"Whereas *now* they have no property to be exposed & so no interest in good
order, & the preservation of it . . . they now feel a sense of Injury in the loss
of their liberty, & . . . apply the law of retalliation"; but if the slaves were to
be made free, "gratitude to the white people . . . would tend strongly to
unite them to our interest & preserve them from attempting to injure us."
He added that "any criminals among them might be punished according
to the laws of the land."[27]

Hart frankly acknowledged that this carrot-and-stick argument would
not sway those convinced that the slave communities contained "licentious
persons" who would lead others "into vicious & destructive courses when
they are at their own disposal, so that they will be very destructive members of Society." And here he broke abruptly from his pattern of rebutting
each imagined objection. Apparently feeling that he had exhausted his
store of argument in support of Negro capacity, he mused instead upon
the variety of perceptions among men and the difficulty of changing
minds, offering a final oblique thrust at the power of "temptations of private interest which in so many cases, insensibly blinds & influences men of
character and worth" before going on to outline his complete scheme.[28]

Hart proposed that all slaves in the colony of Connecticut be "freed" under the following conditions: (a) that those under twenty-five (or whatever age the general assembly thought equitable) should continue in service
until that age, to repay masters for their education, and then go free without compensation to their masters; (b) that those over fifty should remain
with their masters for the rest of their lives "to be supported at their expence," with oversight by the selectmen to ensure fair treatment; (c) that
the colony should redeem those between twenty-five and fifty, compensating their masters for the difference between the time they had already
served and the twelve and a half years of service Hart estimated would represent their full "value." "Redeemed" slaves (probably including those
raised to twenty-five) would continue to serve their present masters or another person approved by the selectmen for one, two, or three years, or

[27] Ibid., p. 4.
[28] Ibid.

"such a given time as shall be judged meet," at a rate of compensation to be set by the selectmen. The money "due for their service" would be paid, presumably by their masters as employers, into the town treasury, where it would be maintained, earning interest, by the selectmen as a sort of "trust fund" available for the support slaves who had earned it in case of sickness, old age, or other need (except on the part of those convicted of a crime, who would presumably forfeit their claims). After earning his "trust fund," the former slave would be free, with a year or more of supervision as needed. Law-abiding slaves would obtain their "trust funds" for use in returning to Africa. Any freed slave convicted of "stealing, house breaking, immodest conduct towards, or intercourse or pretended marriage with any white person of a different sex," or other atrocious crime (other than what was already a capital crime for whites) would be "punished by cropping, branding, or some visible mark of distinction & of their crime, & by transportation to Guinea" at the expense of their "trust funds." Ex-slaves continuing to reside in the colony would "in all other respects . . . enjoy the benefit of the english laws & secure the same treatment with the white subjects."[29]

Finally, Hart offered a fall-back position, should opposition to his compensation plan on the part of "the power of interest and prejudice" prove insurmountable. The backup plan would eliminate the publicly funded redemption of slave time up to twelve and a half years of service, keeping intact all other methods of oversight, and the repayment of value of education by time served.[30] He concluded with a typically mixed appeal to righteousness and self-interest: by following his plan to end slavery, the colonists could cast off guilt for the sin of breaking the Golden Rule and thereby remove the threat of God's punishment in the form of their own loss of liberty at the hands of the British king and parliament.

In such schemes for gradual emancipation, the centrality of assumptions about the abuse of liberty to be anticipated on the part of newly freed slaves underscores the extent to which New England slavery on the eve of the Revolution was performing as a crucial system of social control. Its role as a mode of productive capital investment remained important as well, but as a labor system per se and certainly as a form of conspicuous consumption, slavery was distinctly in decline. Plans such as Hart's proposed to salvage the crucial control function out of the deteriorating framework of institutionalized slave labor. By simultaneously defining freedom as an entitlement and requiring slaves to earn it by supervised good conduct over a substantial period of time, gradual emancipation plans reassured white

[29] Ibid., pp. 4–6.
[30] Ibid., pp. 6–7.

colonists that the manageability and containment offered by enslavement were transferable to the state of freedom, that a desirable degree of dependency could be maintained and an undesirable excess of it disciplined effectively; gradual emancipation thus promised a continuation of the benefits of slavery while eliminating its spiritual costs. Remove the stain of sin and the fear of just reprisal but retain the control: such was the allure of gradual emancipation.

Proponents of antislavery, poised to take advantage of the postwar disruption of economic, social, and political patterns and the republican natural rights rhetoric still echoing in the public ear, moved in the early 1780s to implement gradual emancipation programs in the two New England states most heavily engaged in slaveholding: Connecticut and Rhode Island. At the same time, litigation and constitutional interpretation brought an end to legal slavery in Massachusetts and New Hampshire in a manner so ambiguous, with results so protracted, as to merit consideration as a form of "gradual emancipation" as well. Only Vermont expressly outlawed slavery in its 1777 constitution, and even there, the language of the act was sufficiently vague that slaveholding may have persisted without sanction in a few areas for several years.[31]

In Massachusetts, three cases involving an attempt by one Nathaniel Jennison to assert his title to an enslaved man named Quok Walker led to a judicial ruling in 1783 that was widely (but by no means universally) understood to end legal slavery there. Beginning in 1766 there had been a long series of Massachusetts cases and petitions by and on behalf of slaves suing their masters for restraint of their liberty under various specific circumstances, with the results sometimes favoring the slave's liberty and sometimes the master's property rights; but these outcomes were not

---

[31] Even in the Vermont Constitution of 1777, the clause in the bill of rights that prohibited compulsory service for those who were "of age" left open the possibility of binding out children of blacks who had been enslaved prior to the adoption of the constitution; however, this clause apparently applied as well to poor white children who might otherwise become public charges. The official printed reports of the U.S. census until 1870 assigned sixteen slaves to Vermont in 1790, all in the county of Bennington. In 1870, however, George D. Harrington, chief clerk of the Census Bureau—a Vermonter—"discovered the mistake" and re-recorded the sixteen as "Free Other." In fact, the *Vermont Gazette* of September 26, 1791, had reported that the marshal's assistant for the census for Bennington County had returned twenty-one black males and fifteen black females, triumphantly declaring, "To the honor of humanity NO SLAVES." It is impossible to determine whether the census had reported freemen as slaves, or whether the antislavery enthusiasm of the *Gazette* and the free-soil pride of place of the chief clerk had transformed slaves into freemen. See *Records of the Governor and Council of the State of Vermont* (Montpelier: Steam Press of J. & J. M. Poland, 1876), p. 425. I am indebted to John Saillant for calling this item to my attention.

broadly applicable to questions concerning the legality of the practice.[32]
The concept of gradual emancipation had gained enough currency in
Massachusetts to be proposed by slaves themselves in 1771, when seven
slaves—including the well-known Prince Hall—petitioned the Massachusetts legislature to pass an act whereby adult slaves would be freed immediately and "their children (who were born in this land of liberty) may not
be held as slaves after they arrive at the age of twenty-one years." The petition resulted in a bill called "An Act for preventing the practice of holding
persons in Slavery," which would have freed all resident slaves over twenty-
one years of age, and would have limited the service of slaves under twenty-one to no longer than their twenty-sixth year; in effect, it proposed a
gradual emancipation. But this bill was tabled.[33] In the famous British case
of *Somerset* in 1772, which was widely construed as abolishing slavery in England (although this, too, was an ambiguous holding), the plaintiff had
been a Massachusetts slave; and some antislavery colonists had argued, un-
successfully, the application of that ruling to the institution of slavery in
Massachusetts as a British colony.[34]

These developments had prepared public opinion to interpret the ruling in the Quok Walker cases as broadly undermining the legality of slavery. In 1783 Chief Justice John D. Cushing of the Massachusetts Supreme
Judicial Court held, in the last of the three Quok Walker cases, *Commonwealth v. Jennison,* that "without resorting to implication in constructing the
constitution, slavery is in my judgment as effectively abolished as it can be
by the granting of rights and privileges wholly incompatible and repugnant
to its existence [in Article I of the Declaration of Rights of the 1780 Massachusetts constitution]."[35] This holding and other suits for freedom, antislavery petitions, and the bills that followed in the General Court slowly
eroded the institution of slavery in Massachusetts in two complementary
ways. They undermined whites' confidence in their property rights in
slaves, and they emboldened enslaved persons of color to demand manumission or wage compensation from their owners—or simply to walk away
from them. Even so, the institution of slavery in Massachusetts was not fully extinguished by Cushing's 1783 ruling.

[32] The best summary of these cases is in George H. Moore, *Notes on the History of Slavery
in Massachusetts* (New York: Appleton, 1866), pp. 112–22.

[33] Massachusetts Archives, "Revolutionary Resolves," 7:132, in Moore, *Notes,* p. 181.

[34] William M. Wiecek, *The Sources of Antislavery Constitutionalism in America, 1760–1848*
(Ithaca: Cornell University Press, 1977), pp. 28–31. Wiecek points out that Moore, *Notes,* p.
117, mentions the Massachusetts residence of Somerset.

[35] See John D. Cushing, "The Cushing Court and the Abolition of Slavery in Massachusetts: More Notes on the 'Quock Walker Case,'" *American Journal of Legal History* 5 (1961):
18–144; Wiecek, *Sources of Antislavery Constitutionalism,* p. 47.

The situation was even more ambiguous in New Hampshire. There, too, the new post-Revolutionary state constitution of 1783 included a "Declaration of Rights" by whose first article all men were to be free and equal. But in 1784 slaves were still taxed as property (although this clause was removed from the 1789 revenue bill). In 1788 Jeremy Belknap stated flatly that the state constitution had freed all New Hampshire slaves. In the same year, however, Justice Simeon Olcott of the Supreme Judicial Court of New Hampshire was asked his opinion of the status of slaves in New Hampshire by Justice Samuel A. John Jr., of the County Court for the County of Hartford, State of Connecticut. Olcott responded that "as Custom & Practice, in this State has ever been Similar to that in the other New England States, it has been deemed lawful to hold them in Servitude & to transfer them, as is usual in other States." He noted further that adjudications in New Hampshire courts had supported the legality of holding Negroes in servitude and cited a case in his own county before the Supreme Judicial Court in May 1786, which denied a Negro's action for false imprisonment under a claim that the New Hampshire constitution made negroes equally free with whites. Olcott concluded that "negros are not Liberated by the Constitution or Laws of the State of New Hampshire." In 1795 Jeremy Belknap, differing from his own 1788 statement, asserted that the New Hampshire constitution had freed only those Negroes born after its adoption.[36] The ambiguity of these diverse opinions had its effect: the first federal census in 1790 reported that there were still 157 slaves in New Hampshire.[37]

Emancipation thus proceeded gradually in fact in Massachusetts and New Hampshire, gradually by law in the two New England states with the largest slave populations. In 1784 Connecticut and Rhode Island both enacted *post nati* emancipation bills that reflected the legacy of proposals such as Levi Hart's and the abolition bill passed by the Pennsylvania legislature in 1780. The two New England states thus became the second and third states to enact gradual abolition laws, which produced somewhat similar effects on slaveholding patterns and practices. But differences both subtle and substantial in the language and mechanics of these bills, and in the mode and spirit of their respective adoption, reflect the distinctive ge-

[36] Belknap to Ebenezer Hazard, January 25, 1788, in *Collections of the Massachusetts Historical Society*, 5th ser., 3 (1891): 11; Simeon Olcott to The Honorable The Justices of the County Court for the County of Hartford, State of Connecticut, Charlestown, [N.H.], January 22, 1788, "Opinion of Freedom of African Americans in New Hampshire," Manuscripts of the Connecticut Historical Society; "Queries Respecting the Slavery and Emancipation of Negroes in Massachusetts, Proposed by the Hon. Judge Tucker of Virginia, and Answered by the Rev. Dr. Belknap," *Collections of the Massachusetts Historical Society*, 5th ser., 4 (1891): 204.

[37] Bureau of the Census, Department of Commerce, *Negro Population, 1790–1915* (Washington, D.C.: Government Printing Office, 1918), p. 57.

nealogies of slaveholding and abolition in the two states and subtle differences in the climate of relations between the whites and persons of color who lived there.

The exigencies of war had moved both Connecticut and Rhode Island in the direction of emancipation, and both states considered enlisting slaves in order to relieve wartime troop shortages. In Connecticut, although an actual enlistment bill presented in the spring of 1777 failed to be enacted, the legislature passed a bill that fall allowing slaveowners to free healthy slaves and indemnifying them from financial responsibility. Slaveowners used the provisions of this bill to entice their slaves to serve as substitutes for them in the Continental Army in exchange for their freedom, and several hundred took advantage of the opportunity. In 1778 Rhode Island actually implemented an enlistment act that offered state-financed compensated emancipation: slaves were offered manumission and soldiers' benefits in exchange for their enlistment, and slaveowners were compensated by the state up to £120 for each enlisted slave. There was considerable opposition to this law; in fact, with fewer than a hundred slaves actually emancipated under its provisions, the elections that followed close on the heels of its passage resulted in an assembly that repealed it immediately.[38] Other moves toward emancipation made little headway until the end of the war. In 1779 and again in 1780, bills for gradual emancipation failed to pass in the Connecticut legislature. In 1779 Rhode Island did ban the sale of Rhode Island slaves out of state, but no further efforts to engage the slavery issue were made during the war.[39]

In 1783 a fresh campaign to end slavery and the slave trade was mounted in Rhode Island by Moses Brown, Quaker convert and exasperated brother of wealthy slave traders Nicholas and John Brown. He produced countless antislavery articles and pamphlets, memorialized the legislature repeatedly, and assisted in drafting an emancipation bill that also made participation in the slave trade subject to harsh penalties. But with the American slave trade centered in Rhode Island and slavers forming the nucleus of Newport society, in February 1784 the legislature defeated this

[38] The standard work on the Rhode Island slave enlistments is Sidney S. Rider, "An Historical Inquiry concerning the Attempts to Raise a Regiment of Slaves in Rhode Island," *Rhode Island Historical Tracts*, vol. 10 (Providence: S. S. Rider, 1880). According to Rider (p. v.), only eighty-eight or eighty-nine slaves were actually enlisted. The number of persons of color who in fact served in Rhode Island regiments during the Revolution, recruited under this bill and possibly outside its provisions, may have been considerably larger; a significant number not included in Rider's list stated, when examined as transients by various town councils that they had served in the Continental Army. Of course, since it became desirable after the war for both whites and persons of color to claim military service, some such assertions may not have been true. See Zilversmit, *First Emancipation*, pp. 119–20.

[39] Zilversmit, *First Emancipation*, pp. 123, 120.

abolition bill; it passed another that stood silent on the issue of the slave trade but did provide for gradual emancipation. The Rhode Island act also enabled slaveowners to manumit healthy slaves between the ages of twenty-one and forty without financial obligation, as the 1779 Connecticut manumission bill had done. In both states, however, in order to obtain authorization to manumit them, owners were required to present their slaves to the town selectmen or councils for inspection to prove their good health and general ability to obtain their own living.[40]

Meanwhile, the Connecticut legislature approached abolition by the back door—and perhaps, on the part of some legislators, unintentionally. In a general code revision submitted by Roger Sherman and Richard Law in January 1784, a statute consolidating all earlier slave codes included two new provisions. First, one section established a penalty for importing slaves into the state (which went unremarked, since Connecticut's slave trade, unlike Rhode Island's, represented a relatively insignificant element in the state's economy). Second, a single, short paragraph instituting gradual emancipation appeared at the very end of the statute. The legislature adopted the revision with little discussion and, in so doing, inaugurated abolition.[41]

The Rhode Island and Connecticut abolition bills established the same mechanism for the gradual abolition of slavery: *post nati* emancipation. In both states, children born to slaves after March 1, 1784, would be "free": that is, not slaves for life. In Connecticut, such children would provide twenty-five years of uncompensated service to the owners of their mothers; in Rhode Island, female children of slaves would provide eighteen years of service and males, twenty-one years; Rhode Island's act provided as an alternative that the town councils would oversee the binding out of these children after a year with their mothers and compensate owners for the expense of raising them for that year. Presumably, many slaveowners were expected to retain the children of their slaves past that first year, obtaining the usual work from them; this provision would merely relieve them from mandatory responsibility for such children. This was apparently an unpopular provision, however: the Rhode Island assembly repealed it as "extremely burthensome" after a year and eight months. Yet few such claims seem to have been filed; the only one I found was submitted by Mr. John Smith of Providence, who "exhibited an account by him charged against the Town for Supporting a Female Negro Child born of his Negro-Woman Sarah."[42] It seems likely that the provision was more "burthensome" in

[40] Ibid., pp. 120–22.
[41] Ibid., pp. 125–26.
[42] *Records of the State of Rhode Island and Providence Plantations in New England*, ed. John Rus-

principle than in application, since it represented the same public compensation to slaveowners which Rhode Islanders had found objectionable in their state's short-lived slave enlistment plan. In the face of widespread resistance to public outlays of any kind in the shattered postwar economy and staunch objection to anything that smacked of transferring slaves from private to public ownership (with its disturbing implications of moral responsibility), neither Connecticut nor Rhode Island had included in their gradual abolition plans anything resembling Levi Hart's carefully structured depreciation scheme for compensating slaveowners. Nonetheless, Hart's assumptions underlay both acts.

As revised, Rhode Island's emancipation act, like Connecticut's, offered slaveowners the uncompensated service of slaves until they reached the ages of majority specified by law, in exchange for the expense of raising them. This represented an entirely new form of servitude. Unlike service under indenture and apprenticeship, such statutory servitude was noncontractual; it placed binding legal requirements only on the worker, and required no ongoing or terminal obligation whatsoever on the part of the owner. (The word "owner" is used here because such people still owned the slaves whose children were born "free," and they effectively continued to own the offspring themselves until they reached majority.)

How might the drafters of these abolition bills, the legislators who enacted them, and the communities they represented have imagined, at the time those bills passed, the class of "freeborn" persons that would come into being as a consequence? Their language provides clues to the answer. The provision for gradual emancipation in Connecticut came at the end of "An Act concerning Indian, Molatto, and Negro Servants and Slaves," the first half of which outlined a complicated system of seizures, fines, whippings, and other punishments for a legion of illegal activities: travel by slaves or free Negroes without a pass; vagrancy; unauthorized purchase or sale of any item; violating nine o'clock curfew; and unauthorized entertaining of slaves. The next section, because "the increase of Slaves in this State is injurious to the Poor, and inconvenient," made the importation of slaves into Connecticut punishable by a fine of one hundred pounds for every slave. The third section restated the rules under which healthy slaves might be manumitted, following the inspection and approval of the selectmen, without financial obligation to their owners; others manumitted

---

sell Bartlett (Providence: Providence Press, 1865), 10 (1784–92): 133. The town council delayed payment for several months, then underpaid, finally giving Smith £14.20 of the £29.2 he had requested (Providence Town Council Records, 5:323, August 1, 1785; 5:340, October 8, 1785; 5:356, December 13, 1785).

outside these rules would remain chargeable to their former owners. The final ten lines of the act read:

> And whereas sound Policy requires that the Abolition of Slavery should be effected as soon as may be, consistent with the Rights of Individuals, and the public Safety and Welfare. Therefore, Be it enacted . . . That no Negro or Molatto Child, that shall, after the first Day of March, One thousand seven hundred and eighty-four, be born within this State, shall be held in Servitude, longer than until they arrive to the Age of twenty-five Years, notwithstanding the Mother or Parent of such Child was held in Servitude at the Time of its Birth; but such Child, at the Age aforesaid, shall be free; any Law, Usage or Custom to the contrary notwithstanding.[43]

This act was utterly pragmatic; there was nothing idealistic or visionary about it. It addressed the notion of limiting lifetime slavery as a policy issue framed by a web of restrictions and regulations that encoded a permanent status of legal difference for "Indians," "Molattos" and "Negroes." It regulated both the behavior of people of color and the behavior of whites in their interactions with people of color, implying that the very act of contact constituted an occasion of sin by providing a set of temptations for both parties to embark upon wrongful actions that must be curbed. Limitations on the importation of slaves were couched in terms of restricting slaves' competition with the poor (one suspects the framers had in mind competition for both jobs and charity) and reducing their "inconvenience," a curiously open-ended term carrying connotations of intrusion and unsuitability. The abolition clause itself constructed an opposition between ending slavery and preserving individual rights, public safety, and welfare; by these terms both individuals and public were presumptively white, and rights, safety, and welfare were republican entitlements within the domain of citizenship from which slaves were and would remain excluded, regardless of their postslavery status. Further, the language of the statute defined the *post nati* status of the children of slaves as servitude; at the age of twenty-five each "Child . . . shall be free" but would until that time live in an undefined limbo of mandatory, uncompensated

---

[43] "An Act concerning Indian, Molatto, and Negro Servants and Slaves," January 8, 1784, in "Acts and Laws . . . of Connecticut," pp. 233–35. Unless otherwise noted, all "Acts and Laws . . . of Connecticut," "Acts and Laws . . . of Massachusetts," and "Acts and Resolves . . . of Rhode Island" may be found by title and date in *Early American Imprints, 1639–1800,* ed. Clifford K. Shipton (Worcester, Mass.: American Antiquarian Society, 1956–), hereafter cited as *Early American Imprints* (this is the Readex Microprint reproduction of all items listed in *The American Bibliography of Charles Evans* [Chicago: Blakely Press, 1903–59]).

service: not slave, not contractually bound, not free.

The pragmatism of this statute, reflecting the hardheaded commercial culture ascendant in post-Revolutionary Connecticut, contrasts sharply with the rhetorical idealism of the Rhode Island statute. Commercial interests were no less influential in Rhode Island than in Connecticut in the 1780s, but Quaker influence was stronger there than elsewhere in New England. The Rhode Island statute reflected the pietism of Moses Brown and his Quaker friends, who were instrumental in drafting the bill. It also reflected their understanding of the application of the Revolutionary rhetoric of natural rights to the problem of slavery.

The title of the bill was straightforward: "An Act authorizing the manumission of negroes, mulattoes, and others, and for the gradual abolition of slavery." The preamble, however, framed abolition as much more than a policy issue. Its language—"Whereas, all men are entitled to life, liberty, and the pursuit of happiness, and the holding mankind in a state of slavery, as private property, which has gradually obtained by unrestrained custom and the permission of the laws, is repugnant to this principle, and subversive of the happiness of mankind, the great end of all civil government"—made an unmistakable claim on behalf of enslaved people of color for inclusion within the "one people" whose rights were defined in the Declaration of Independence. Like the Connecticut bill, the act demanded restraint of practices subversive of the public good, but here those practices consisted of the customs of white slaveholders and lawmakers, not the activities of slaves and those tempted to abet them.[44]

The body of the act stipulated that "no person or persons, whether negroes, mulattoes, or others, who shall be born within the limits of this state, on or after the first day of March, A.D., 1784, shall be deemed or considered as servants for life, or slaves," and that "all servitude for life, or slavery of children, to be born as aforesaid, in consequence of the condition of their mothers, be, and the same is, hereby taken away, extinguished, and forever abolished." Noting that "humanity requires" that "children declared free as aforesaid" remain with their mothers "a convenient time" following their birth, the act required town councils to reimburse "those who claim the services" of their mothers for the costs of supporting the children during that time and for their instruction, according to the "earnest desire of this Assembly," in morality and religion and also reading, writing, and arithmetic, authorizing the town councils to bind out the children as apprentices between the ages of one year and twenty-one years if males and eighteen if females to achieve these ends. Finally, the act indemnified per-

---

[44] *Records of the State of Rhode Island,* 10:7.

sons freeing slaves between eighteen (female) or twenty-one (male) and forty, if determined healthy by the town councils, from further obligation.[45]

Superficially offering the same mechanism for gradual emancipation, this bill differed radically from the Connecticut abolition bill in its conception of the children to be affected by its provisions. The Connecticut bill left these children in an indeterminate state of servitude; the Rhode Island bill defined them explicitly as "children declared free." Practically speaking, they could be bound out, but this would place them within a contractual relationship of enforceable, mutual obligation.

As noted above, however, an amendment to the abolition act was quickly passed in October 1785 which undermined even the small degree of "freedom" granted under the act and made the status of children of slaves in Rhode Island similar to that of such children in Connecticut. The amendment repealed the public support provision and required "that every negro or mulatto child born after the first day of March, A.D. 1784, be supported and maintained by the owner of the mother of such child, to the age of twenty-one years, provided the owner of the mother shall during that time hold her as a slave." Only the manumission of the mother would discharge the owner from responsibility for the child's support.[46]

By transferring responsibility for support of slaves' children from the towns to the owner of the children's mother, the amendment effectively entitled slaveholders to the uncompensated services of their slaves' children without contract or oversight—in other words, it made the status of slaves' children exactly the same as it had always been, except that they were no longer slaves for life. It included no references to children born within the provisions of the statute as "freeborn," as had the original act. The assembly's "earnest desire" for moral and academic instruction, which would have been documented and made enforceable in indentures or apprenticeship contracts, had evaporated as well. Even though the great majority of slaves' children very likely would have been "apprenticed" to their mothers' owners under the original statute, that arrangement would have been contractual and at least nominally supervised by the town councils. The amendment eliminated all reciprocal features of the original statute, placing children born to slaves in Rhode Island in the same indeterminate status of servitude as those born in Connecticut—the condition of slave children in both states for the preceding 150 years, except that now it

---

[45] Ibid. A second, related act repealed a 1774 provision enabling Rhode Island slavers to market so-called "refuse slaves" (those who could not be sold in the West Indies) in Rhode Island but otherwise left slave trading unregulated. (10:8).

[46] Ibid., 10:132.

would end for each child on a date certain. By making the age of majority twenty-one for both females and males, the amendment effectively increased the period of uncompensated servitude for females by three years beyond that provided in the original statute. Thus the children of Rhode Island slaves would serve their mothers' owners for four fewer years than would slaves' children in Connecticut; otherwise, their situations were identical.

Finally, the amendment reduced the upper age limit from forty to thirty years for slaves who might be manumitted without further financial responsibility on the part of their owners.[47] Here again the ostensible motive was to reduce public responsibility for free blacks; its actual effect was to discourage the manumission of all but a handful of slaves in their prime work years—the ones most valuable to their owners and least likely to be manumitted anyway.

The Rhode Island amendment demonstrated a pragmatic approach much like that of the Connecticut abolition act. The use of the unvarnished word "owner," replacing the principled phrase "those who claim them," signaled a strategic retreat from the natural rights enthusiasm of the original bill. The change was brought about by several factors. The amendment was initiated by newly elected legislators from such towns as Newport, men who, though resigned to the inevitability of abolition, were generally hostile to antislavery principles and anxious to minimize the public expense it might entail; their election had been at least partly a direct consequence of dissatisfaction with the success of the abolition bill.[48] That there was no Quaker involvement in drafting the amendment was evident in its lack of moral rationale. In fact, the one reference to "principles" reversed the moral concern of the original act: by suggesting that "subjecting the towns to the support and education of such children [of slaves] . . . is incompatible with the principles upon which the said act was passed," the amendment in effect defended the white majority's entitlement to "life, liberty and the pursuit of happiness" against the perceived encroachment of "burthensome" demands from children of color who were not so entitled.[49] A final factor contributing to the new approach may have been a kind of public exhaustion with the issues of slaves, slavery, and public support for people of color, a backlash against the unremitting stream of impassioned antislavery appeals that had been churned out by Moses Brown and his supporters over the previous several years.

[47] Ibid., 10:132, 7.
[48] Samuel Hopkins to Moses Brown, April 29, 1784, Moses Brown Papers, Rhode Island Historical Society.
[49] Zilversmit, *First Emancipation*, pp. 121–22.

By 1785, abolition measures had cut off the natural increase of indigenous slaves for life in the New England states. The importation of slaves into Connecticut and Rhode Island with the intention of selling them there or otherwise making them permanent residents had also been restricted. The slave trade conducted by vessels berthed in these states, however, was enjoying something of a resurgence following its virtual suspension during the war. Across the New England states, Quakers and other foes of slavery marshaled a final local campaign, this time against the slave trade. In 1787 Rhode Island outlawed participation in the slave trade, and in 1788 Connecticut and Massachusetts did likewise. The Massachusetts act also addressed the problem of "divers peaceable inhabitants . . . carried off by force, or decoyed away under various pretences . . . with a probable intention of being sold as slaves," and made possible the prosecution of such persons and award of damages to the aggrieved parties.[50] Connecticut sought to curb the same practice with a 1792 amendment to the 1788 Slave Trade Prohibition Act, prohibiting sale of slaves out of state. Finally, in May 1797 the Connecticut assembly reduced the age at which slaves' children would be free from twenty-five to twenty-one years; in October it also amended the original "Act concerning Indian, Mulatto and Negro Servants and Slaves" to repeal the first eight paragraphs—the slave code—leaving in force only the provision for gradual abolition.[51]

From the developing pattern and language of legal restrictions on slavery in New England between the introduction of pre-Revolutionary proposals for compensated emancipation, through the passage of provisions for gradual abolition and curtailment of the slave trade, to the repeal of slave codes in the 1790s, we can make some general observations about the changing climate of opinion among the white majority in New England regarding slaves and slavery. Appeals to conscience and patriotic republicanism by Quakers and other religious and civic leaders called into question assumptions about the "naturalness" of slaveholding but did little to undermine assumptions about the "naturalness" of the condition of servitude for people of color. Antislavery presumed to demonstrate the godliness and humanity of whites and the triumphant virtue of the republic; it concerned itself with the humanity of people of color, too, but only in-

[50] "An Act to prevent the Slave-Trade, and to encourage the Abolition of Slavery," last Monday in October, 1787, in "Acts and Resolves . . . of Rhode Island," p. 4; "An Act to prevent the Slave-Trade," second Thursday of October, 1788, in "Acts and Laws . . . of Connecticut," p. 368; "Acts and Laws . . . of Massachusetts," May 31, 1787–February 27, 1788, pp. 672–73, all in *Early American Reprints*.

[51] "An Act in addition to an Act, entitled, 'An Act concerning Indian, Mulatto and Negro Servants and Slaves,'" p. 462, and "An Act to repeal certain paragraphs of an Act, entitled, 'An Act concerning Indian, Mulatto, and Negro Servants and Slaves,'" p. 477, second Thursday of October, 1797, in "Acts and Laws . . . of Connecticut," *Early American Reprints*.

strumentally—that is, only to the extent that their humanity tested the humanity of whites. In most cases, legislative initiatives swept into acceptance in a burst of pietistic or republican sentiment were quickly followed by provisions that limited their economic impact and minimized the degree to which they made any effective change in the relations of slaveholders, slaves, and their communities. Statutes that eroded slaveholding nonetheless preserved slaveowners' property rights in slaves and sought to minimize the losses that abolition might entail.

Public interest in resolving the slavery problem never included a willingness to expend public monies. Theoretical support for public compensation to slaveowners, as widely discussed before the Revolution in proposals such as Levi Hart's, faded quickly in the face of actual experience with programs that offered compensated emancipation in exchange for slave enlistment. Later resistance to public support for the children of slaves proved that repugnance for public complicity in slaveholding was only a small part of the opposition to public compensation. Even though whites in increasing numbers refused moral responsibility for slavery, they had no interest in taking on financial responsibility for its dissolution—or for its residual consequences.

The statutes uniformly assumed the inevitability of dependency for all but a narrowly defined group of youthful, healthy, adult persons of color. The likelihood that even members of this group would fall into a condition of dependency was strongly implied by the persistent attention of the statutes to limiting the indemnification of slaveowners who wished to manumit their slaves. The assumption that former owners would retain financial responsibility for adults who were unrelated free persons worked to minimize the distinction between slavery and freedom. Because it sustained the convention of membership of slaves (and former slaves) in their owners' families, this assumption also undermined any claim to citizenship that black male heads of household might otherwise have been able to make in a society where each independent family had representation in the polity through its male head.

The language of the abolition statutes may be read as a map to assist white Americans to negotiate a heretofore unexplored terrain: the no-man's-land between the clearly marked territory inhabited by slaves of color and white free citizens (with native peoples at the margins) and the speculative ground occupied by a multitude of free persons whose respective status was as yet not fully differentiated. There were blank spots as well as mismarkings on the map; its final contours would be determined in practice partly by the way the map was read but chiefly by actual encounters along the path.

Amid the host of contradictory assumptions embedded in state constitutions and gradual abolition acts in the New England states, how would the passage out of slavery actually be negotiated?

The gradual abolition statutes did not legislate slavery out of existence; they were not designed to do that. Slaves were included in the population schedules for New England states through the 1840 federal census.[52] Acts finally and specifically banning slavery were not passed in Rhode Island until 1843 and in Connecticut until 1848.[53] Meanwhile, passage of the abolition bills encouraged some white slaveowners to manumit some of their slaves; as for the rest, their slaves began to give birth to a new generation of persons of color whom they continued to hold in an indeterminate status of noncontractual, uncompensated servitude. It was not slavery, because it was of finite length. These children of slaves were a kind of oxymoron: they were born free into servitude.

The judicial interpretations of the Massachusetts and New Hampshire state constitutions, ambiguous as they were, may have been intended by their authors to end slavery definitively, but they did not. The ambiguity was never resolved in Massachusetts. After 1783 some white slaveowners sent their slaves away, or began to pay them wages, or sold them out of state (breaking the law, or acting in ignorance of it), or did nothing; some of their slaves simply ran away. Slavery was declared to have ended in Massachusetts when no slaves were reported there in the first federal census, although there may well have been a few remaining. In New Hampshire, much the same scenario ended more formally with the passage of a final abolition bill in 1857.[54] Abolition in New England was gradual indeed.

By the mid-1780s the practice of slavery for nearly a century and a half had burdened white New Englanders, whether they individually approved of slavery or not, with a set of assumptions that naturalized the role of people of African descent as a presumptive enslaved class. Until the 1780s the great majority of people of African descent were slaves in fact, formally classified as items of property; free Africans were rare, anomalous cases. Freed people of color did give birth to children who were thus "freeborn." But enslaved women produced enslaved children; by statute, the condition of

[52] Bureau of the Census, *Negro Population, 1790–1915,* p. 57.

[53] The 1843 Rhode Island state constitution, art. 1, sec. 4, stated, "Slavery shall not be permitted in this State." Yet *a year later* sec. 1 of the state's revised Poor Law provided that "all persons who are holden in servitude or slavery who have not been emancipated" shall be supported at the expense of "their owners." In Connecticut, "An Act to prevent slavery," which was passed in 1848 and became sec. 1 of title 51 of the 1849 Revision of the General Laws, stated "that no person shall hereafter be held in slavery in this State." See John Codman Hurd, *The Law of Freedom and Bondage in the United States* (Boston: Little, Brown, 1865), 2:50 and 2:47.

[54] "An Act to secure freedom and the rights of citizenship to persons in this State," 1857, in Hurd, *Law of Freedom and Bondage,* 2:36.

children followed the condition of their mother. The principal political characteristic of this presumptive enslaved class of people of color, including its odd "free" members, was its permanent removal from any possibility of power in any sphere, especially participation in citizenship.

The abolition statutes required whites to adjust to the new concept of "freeborn people of color" as a class. The problem facing white New England in attempting to free itself from slavery was threefold: to establish a space in the imagination for the new collective conceptual category "free black"; to create a fresh or adaptive set of practices with which to deal with this new class; and to invent a language in which to enact these new practices and power relations. Whites found this transformation virtually impossible. Their collective imagination had been severely circumscribed by the experience of slavery, and their expectations of dependency on the part of any person of color limited their vision, for the most part, to little beyond the anticipated result. Most important, the mechanics of gradual emancipation itself fostered the mapping of the habitual language and practices of relations with slaves onto relations with this new category, "freeborn people of color."

Nothing better illustrates the persistence of slave relations in the context of emancipation than the *post nati* "freedom" that was the birthright of slaves' children under the abolition statutes: the status of involuntary, uncompensated servitude that would presumably prepare slaves' children for free adulthood. We can usefully contrast this form of service with the practice of public indenture, whereby indigent, (mostly) white children were bound out to service until their majority. Like *post nati* service, public indenture was an involuntary form of servitude insofar as the very young child was concerned (older children were often encouraged to select a master or, very rarely, mistress).[55] It was a form of coercive assistance appropriate for poor white children who might be expected to achieve, in adulthood, at least limited economic independence as heads or members of independent families. In sharp contrast, the expectation for the adult status of a slave's child—always until then a member of a presumptive enslaved class, always until then categorized as property—was dependency.

Although indenture was primarily a solution to a social problem—providing temporary economic support as cheaply as possible—poor, free white children were bound out also to acculturate them to community values and to train them for independent citizenship. The relationship of

---

[55] The practice of public indenture in Rhode Island and its comparative use for people of color and whites are discussed thoroughly in Ruth Wallis Herndon, "To Live after the Manner of an Apprentice" (paper presented at the annual meeting of the American Studies Association, Boston, November 7, 1993). The practice was similar in Massachusetts and Connecticut.

indenture was formal and contractual. The contracts spelled out the obligations of each party: on one side, to be obedient, work diligently, and learn
a trade; on the other, to provide instruction in reading, writing, arithmetic
to the rule of three (this last to boys), sewing and other household skills
(to girls), and a "freedom suit" of clothes. When poor children were indentured by town councils or selectmen, the contract was made and enforced by that public body, which assumed a guardianship position for
such persons. Indenture contracts enabled caretakers of children and of
those temporarily in the status of dependent childhood to be compensated for their efforts, but they required those caretakers to train, or retrain,
such persons to assume responsibility for themselves as adult citizens.

Before 1784 the children of (still anomalous) free persons of color who
became indigent were subject to public indenture along with indigent
white children, but this was an adaptation of a system not intended for
them. They were never envisioned as potential citizens, and their indenture contracts reflected different expectations and usually included fewer
obligations on the part of the caretaker than were provided in contracts
for whites. For example, indenture contracts for children of color usually
did not specify any educational requirement; when they did, they required
training only in reading, not writing or arithmetic even for males, and
rarely did they require training in a specific skill.[56]

As the antislavery impulse gained public approval, indenture was also
used occasionally as a transitional status for groups of enslaved persons
who for some reason came under the supervision of a public body unwilling to maintain them as slaves but reluctant to release them into a status of
freedom that might require town support. For example, in May 1774,
when Jacob Shoemaker of Providence died intestate and his six slaves, four
of whom were infants, became town property, the Providence Town Meeting voted that "it is unbecoming the Character of Freemen to enslave the
said Negroes." But after the force of moral argument had compelled the
freemen of Providence to "give up all Claim of Right or Property in them
the said Negroes under their protection," fiscal prudence asserted itself.
Their next act was a vote to "bind the small children to some proper Masters and Mistresses" and to "bind out one or both of the adult Negroes" if
"there should not be personal Estate of the said Jacob Shoemaker sufficient to pay his Just Debts."[57] Here, indenture of "free" persons of color
was a straightforward labor sale in payment of a white man's debts; training of the individuals involved for independence or citizenship was clearly never imagined to be part of the bargain.

[56] Ibid., pp. 13–14.
[57] Providence Town Meeting Records, 6 (1772–83): 16.

The system of indenture could thus be adapted to solve individual problems of social control and poor relief for free children—and sometimes
adults—of color, but it was not designed to cope with a permanent and
growing class of such persons. Even though the gradual emancipation
statutes created an entire category that was conceptually new—freeborn
persons of color—their eventual citizenship remained inconceivable. Personhood, yes—the relation of slaveowners to their slaves, and of slaves to
the social order, had always been strained by the person/property ambiguity inherent in the slave relation—but citizenship, never. Effectively, the
statutes institutionalized the problems of social control and the cost of support during the collective childhood of freeborn persons of color.

To cope with these problems, however, the statutes also institutionalized
an alternative to indenture in a form of "freedom" quite different from the
freedom of whites (or even children born to persons of color who were
themselves already free) who might be indentured. This special "freedom"
appropriate to children of slaves—noncontractual, uncompensated service to the owners of their parents, or statutory servitude—extended the
expectation of literal dependency inherent in the slave relation. The statutory servitude mandated by *post nati* emancipation was not, and was never
intended to be, training for independent citizenship. What the gradual
abolition statutes offered was a framework within which whites could enjoy abolition and slavery at the same time—just as they had always enjoyed
personhood and property together in their slaves. *Post nati* emancipation
hardly provided the context for the kind of transformation in imagination,
practice, and language that freedom demanded.

Most important, a profound contradiction lay at the heart of the gradual emancipation statutes: they might provide for the creation of a new
class of free persons of color, but their promise of the ultimate extinction
of slavery contained within it, as an indivisible element of the rhetoric of
abolition, the expectation of the eventual absence of those who had been
enslaved. This worked to stymie the development of new practices, new language, and fresh expectations about free people of color; it also led many
whites to perceive the new and growing class of free persons of color with
frustration and outrage.

"The Privilage of Freemen": Blacks' Expectations of Freedom from Slavery

A hundred and fifty years of slavery had not naturalized a condition of
servitude for most persons of color in their own eyes, however. The prob-

lem facing free people of color in the 1780s was the same problem they
had had all along: to enact their conception of themselves as heads and
members of families, as community leaders, as workers, lovers, parents,
and friends within a structure of formal regulation and informal custom
and expectation maintained by people who took their status of servitude
for granted.

As the formal structure governing people of color shifted away from slavery during and after the Revolutionary crisis, the dominant rhetoric of antislavery and republicanism offered free people of color a misleading set
of expectations. Whereas to whites it clearly supported the informal structure of expectation and practice by which they defined people of color as
dependent, disorderly, and soon to disappear from the republic, its manifest message to the people of color was a revitalizing promise of independence, enfranchisement, and incorporation—the "privilage of freemen,"
as a 1780 petition of seven free men of color from Dartmouth, Massachusetts, put it.[58] How were two such radically different readings possible?

Revolutionary rhetoric defined "liberty" as the exercise of natural rights,
and "slavery" as the political condition resulting from the loss of liberty as
a consequence of the exercise of power, or perhaps a corruption of will. In
Bernard Bailyn's words, slavery meant "the inability to maintain one's just
property in material things and abstract rights, rights and things which a
proper constitution guaranteed a free people." Revolutionary leaders thus
understood slavery to be an "absolute political evil" and saw in England's
measures to tax and strengthen control of the judicial, ecclesiastical, and
representative affairs of the colonies a clear attempt to enslave them, since
these were "just property," and they were clearly a "free people."[59]

People of color saw their own situation clearly depicted in this argument.
For them, slavery was not a prospective political condition but a present
state of physical and material disempowerment. They had already been deprived of "just property": "We have no Property! We have no Wives! No
children! We have no City! No Country!" declared one Revolutionary-era
freedom petition. And they too were a "free people": another petition insisted, "We are a freeborn Pepel . . . unjustly dragged by the cruel hand of

---

[58] In Herbert Aptheker, ed., *A Documentary History of the Negro People in the United States*
(New York: Citadel Press, 1951), p. 15.

[59] I am using rather simple and straightforward definitions from Bernard Bailyn, *The Ideological Origins of the American Revolution* (Cambridge, Mass.: Harvard University Press, Belknap Press, 1967), pp. 56–57, 234, 232. The revolutionary pamphlets annotated and published by Bailyn in *Pamphlets of the American Revolution* (Cambridge, Mass.: Harvard University Press, Belknap Press, 1965) demonstrate the finer points of a spectrum of Revolutionary
thinking.

power . . . to be made slaves for life in a Christian land!"[60] To people of color the increasing fervor of attacks on British "slavery" in the years just before the Revolution fairly screamed for alleviation of their own plight; they were quick to adopt virtually identical language in their own petitions to drive this point home. Four Boston slaves made the analogy quite explicit in 1773: "The efforts made by the legislative of this province in their last sessions to free themselves from slavery, gave us, who are in that deplorable state, a high degree of satisfaction. We expect great things from men who have made such a noble stand."[61] In fact, the condition or potential condition of each group served as a metaphor for the other, a metaphor that seemed to gain substance with every passing day. As the Revolutionary crisis deepened, whites became increasingly uncomfortable with the implications of the republican argument for slaveholding, and many joined the antislavery campaign. At the same time, people of color found English "enslavement" of the colonies to be such a convincing threat that at least three thousand of them enlisted and fought on the American side in the Revolution.[62] These developments suggested to them that an unmistakable convergence of interest and purpose was taking place.

What people of color failed to recognize was how their dual identity as property and persons in the eyes of whites complicated the meaning of "just," "property," and "free." At some level of consciousness, whites—even many of those who recognized slavery theoretically as the Achilles heel of their Revolutionary logic—understood slaves to be part of the "just property" to which their own natural rights entitled them. Whites reasoned that even if Africans had once had entitlement to themselves as free people, such entitlement did not extend to slaves born and raised in white families—persons never free, raised at the "expense" of their owners. But this reasoning implied that emancipating one's slaves conferred freedom upon them as a gift to which they were at best theoretically but never actually entitled. And in the view of most whites, since even the act of being freed represented the exercise of the owner's power over the slave, an emancipated slave could never become a "free" person but only a "freed" one—a person acted upon, not acting. Freed slaves, as well as slaves' children freed by reaching their majority, could thus be considered categorically depen-

[60] Petition of "Felix," to the Governor, Council, and General Court of Massachusetts Bay, January 6, 1773; and petition to the Governor and General Court of Massachusetts Bay, in Aptheker, *Documentary History*, pp. 6–7, 8–9.
[61] Petition of Peter Bestes, Sambo Freeman, Felix Holbrook, and Chester Joie, in Aptheker, *Documentary History*, pp. 7–8.
[62] Greene, *The Negro in Colonial New England*, p. 190. Some of these slaves bought their own freedom by their service, but at the end of the war many petitioned the legislature for their freedom.

dent—not simply because they had been dependent upon their owners throughout their enslavement but also because their very emergence from the condition of enslavement was a dependent, not an independent, act. This chain of reasoning, although seldom articulated, provides the only conceivable rationale for whites' simultaneous acknowledgment of the natural rights of slaves in the abstract and their denial of autonomous identity to actual freed persons of color. But because it rested upon assumptions utterly foreign and repugnant to people of color themselves, it was not easily accessible to them. Comfortably inhabiting their own unqualified personhood, they found it incomprehensible that the obvious fiction of property in persons could be so potent as to code an alternative set of meanings in the clear and unmistakable language of freedom and entitlement.

To people of color, Revolutionary natural rights and antislavery rhetoric clearly promised an unambiguous state of freedom identical to that of persons who had never been enslaved. Slaves anticipated that once they were emancipated, they would be *free*, not merely "freed." To them, Revolutionary rhetoric promised not only autonomy but also prospects for civic participation and even leadership. After all, one of the most profound changes in social beliefs effected by the Revolution was the erosion of unquestioning faith in the hierarchical social order.[63] Revolutionary natural rights rhetoric was already undermining traditional notions of authority based in rank by 1766, when Richard Bland wrote, "Rights imply equality in the instances to which they belong and must be treated without respect to the dignity of the persons concerned in them."[64] In 1776 a Pennsylvania pamphleteer wrote that "no reflection ought to be made on any man on account of birth, provided that his manners rises decently with his circumstances, and that he affects not to forget the level he came from."[65] People of color understood such arguments as promising the opportunity to remake themselves and to participate in the civic order as free citizens, able to rise as far as their abilities would take them.

Nor did they doubt that they would be capable as free citizens of the degree of virtue required to sustain their liberty according to classical republican theory. Indeed, insofar as republican theory suggested that virtue flourished in simplicity and foundered in luxury, people of color might

[63] Bernard Bailyn, *Ideological Origins*, pp. 301–19, discusses the transformation in attitudes toward authority during the Revolutionary period.

[64] Richard Bland, *An Inquiry into the Rights of the British Colonies . . .* John Harvard Library 17, (Williamsburg, Va., 1766), in Bailyn, *Ideological Origins*, p. 307.

[65] *Four Letters on Interesting Subjects,* John Harvard Library 69 (Williamsburg, Va., 1766), in Bailyn, *Ideological Origins*, p. 308.

well have regarded themselves as especially qualified republicans.[66] Whereas whites assumed that any virtues demonstrated by slaves resulted only from judicious management by their owners and simply suppressed a disorder that would emerge in freedom, people of color assumed precisely the opposite causal relationship. As one petitioner wrote, "Although some of the Negroes are vicious, . . . there are many others of a quite different Character, and who, if made free, would soon be able as well as willing to bear a Part in the Public Charges. . . . and may it not be said of many, that they are virtuous and religious, although their Condition is in itself so unfriendly to Religion, and every moral Virtue except Patience."[67]

The gradual emancipation statutes that were finally passed after the Revolution seemed to offer an opportunity, at last, for people of color to realize the promises of antislavery rhetoric. Slowly, as more and more slaves were emancipated and ever greater numbers of slaves' children released from bondage at their majority, free people of color began resolutely trying to enact their expectations.

So did whites.

[66] Bailyn, *Ideological Origins,* pp. 65, 83.
[67] Petition of "Felix," in Aptheker, *Documentary History,* p. 6.

3

"Slaves of the Community":
Gradual Emancipation in Practice

People of color did not celebrate gradual emancipation anywhere in New England. The ambiguity of constitutional interpretations "ending" slavery in Massachusetts and New Hampshire might have been sufficient to discourage celebration in those two states, but even the statutes specifically enacting gradual abolition in Connecticut and Rhode Island were largely ignored by people of color. Their lack of response does not necessarily imply that they were unaware of the statutes, although awareness of legislative actions was not uniform even among the most literate members of the white elite. Later, people of color responded immediately to the end of the legal slave trade and the abolition of slavery with widespread festivals and celebrations—but not to gradual emancipation in southern New England. The reason seems clear: the statutes effectively preserved the status quo, delaying the freedom of newborn "free" children until their twenties, denying the possibility of freedom to most slaves over forty (and later, thirty) years of age, ignoring the situation of those between. What, after all, had changed?

Two public notices that bracket the gradual emancipation period in southern New England reveal at one and the same time a great transformation in the formal requirements for relations between most whites and most blacks and a slippery remapping of some of the meanings of "Negro," "slave" and "of color" during the gradual abolition period.

At the end of May 1783 the *Connecticut Journal* alerted its readers: "Take Notice! A great Bargain! To be Sold (if applied for soon) A Family of Negroes now in the town of New Haven, consisting of a very likely Negro Man, a Woman, and Two Children who can be well recommended, and a good title given.—They are sold for no fault. If any person should chuse to purchase them, a reasonable time will be allowed for payment."[1] Interested buyers were told to inquire of the printers for further particulars. Advertisements like this were still very common as late as 1783, at the peak of active debate over the still-thriving institution of slavery in southern New England.

Nowhere in the notice did the advertiser find it necessary to state that the "family of negroes" was enslaved; conceptually, "negroes" were still slaves unless specifically identified otherwise in 1783, and whites in New England stubbornly continued to consider anomalous each instance of the growing number of free African Americans in both Connecticut and Rhode Island. The printer could assure the buyer of "a good title" to this family; he as a private agent was brokering a contract between two presumably white citizens regarding a set of third parties who were private property. The "title," or bill of sale, would state the price and terms of payment, if any, but no contractual relation between the new owner and the third parties would be imagined, and their obligation would not be documented or understood to be reciprocal. The wording does suggest that the seller saw some value in offering an intact family as a useful unit of production, if not for more humane reasons.

A decade and a half later, everything and nothing had changed. The language of the *Connecticut Journal* advertisement still resonated clearly in some instructions given by the Providence, Rhode Island, Town Council to the clerk of the council in November 1800, some sixteen and a half years into the gradual abolition process. The clerk was ordered to compose an advertisement for the *Providence Gazette.* "That a number of black Men—Women and Children now here and others expected are to be bound out by this Council, men and women for a term of years—male children until they are 21 years old and females until they arrive to the age of eighteen. All persons desirous of taking indentures of such people to apply to this Council as Soon as may be."[2]

In 1800 the council as a municipal institution was offering an opportunity for presumably white citizens to enter into a formal contract with the

[1] *Connecticut Journal*, May 29, 1783, p. 3.
[2] Providence Town Council Records, 8:6, November 28, 1800.

council for the labor of people of color as individuals. A fixed term was specified and reciprocal obligations for good behavior on the part of the laborer and appropriate treatment on the part of the master were spelled out. The council was selling the time of the laborers, not property in them; they had gained sufficient agency that the person contracting for their labor must now promise something in return.

We can also see that in referring to "a number of black Men, Women, and Children now here and others expected," the council had come to perceive free African Americans as a growing class of persons, rather than a set of particularities or anomalies. The order to the clerk to produce a notice of availability of blacks for indenture followed the council's decision two weeks earlier to identify "all transient white people in poor circumstances, as also of the blacks of all descriptions."[3] By 1800 the Providence Town Council took for granted the power to assign arbitrarily a status of dependency to that category of persons on grounds of their color alone.

Finally, although the two notices offer a strikingly similar conception of people of color, enslaved and free, as somehow publicly available or "on the market," the private agent for the transaction in the first instance, the printer, had become a public agent in the second—an elected public body. This transformation illustrates Frederick Douglass's shrewd observation that emancipation laws in the North had merely transformed people of color from slaves of individuals into "slaves of the community."[4]

But the assumptions and conventions depicted in the advertisement of 1800 do not reflect a simple extension of the oppressive practices of whites and the condition of dependency of people of color associated with the institution of slavery, during and after the expiration of the institution itself. On the contrary, the particular conditions of gradual emancipation in New England generated a new conception of "racial" difference on the part of whites in which the characteristics of availability, dependency, and instrumentality associated with slave status were redefined as uniquely innate and permanent biological traits in persons of color, irrespective of their status. The ideology and language of the antislavery movement produced and shaped this redefinition.

The assertion that postabolition "freedom" for people of color was severely circumscribed has been made repeatedly. Analyses have ranged from the "two freedoms" notion—that "freedom" was experienced differ-

---

[3] Ibid., 7:575, November 4, 1800.
[4] Frederick Douglass, "An Address to the Colored People of the United States," *North Star*, September 29, 1848, in Philip S. Foner, *The Life and Writings of Frederick Douglass: Early Years, 1817–1849* (New York: International, 1950), p. 333.

ently by whites, as a category in opposition to "enslavement," and by people of color, as a continuum of unfree statuses[5]—to the "degrees of freedom" position, which suggests that people of color were freed into a set of constraints imposed by a belief, already in place as developed in the course of slavery, in the permanent inferiority of people of color.[6] The implication has often been that after some moment at which people of color were technically freed, whites imposed upon them a set of discriminatory social and political practices that restricted their freedom, limited their earnings, and so forth, erecting a new framework of law and practice that substituted for the old one, institutional slavery. But this interpretation seems to derive from the much more closely studied abolition of southern slavery, in which one set of institutional practices was dismantled and another put in its place—a template that has been incorrectly laid over the New England experience. I suggest that the process of gradual abolition in New England actually inscribed the practices of slavery itself in what was quite arbitrarily defined as the "free society" to which it gave birth. The fact that New Englanders began extolling their "free society" the minute the ink was dry on the gradual emancipation statutes does not mean that the statutes inaugurated a state of being that differed materially from the one that existed before the statutes were passed. Rather, in the ideology of the abolition movement "free" had developed a set of meanings ready to be mapped definitively onto the specific geographic space defined by the passage of abolition statutes and the rendering of judicial rulings and constitutional interpretations in 1783 and 1784—"free" New England. These meanings could then be amplified and fine-tuned in the nineteenth century in reference to an opposing concept, the "enslaved" South.

The meaning of "free" as it had developed in the ideology of the abolition movement was a category that existed paradoxically in two apparently contradictory semantic domains: "absence" and "availability." The language of abolition framed the possible meanings of "free person of color" as a category to include a state of being for whites along with people of color: "free" always included the state of being "free of slavery," which included a presumption of freedom from slaves themselves—that is, the promise of the ultimate absence of the humans occupying that category—as a desirable status for whites. This accommodated and reinforced the nonhuman (nonexistent in the sense of human presence) aspect of the on-

[5] Jane H. Pease and William H. Pease, *They Who Would Be Free: Blacks' Search for Freedom, 1830–1861* (1974; Urbana: University of Illinois Press, 1990), pp. 3–5.

[6] See, e.g., Leon Litwack, *North of Slavery: The Negro in the Free States, 1790–1860* (Chicago: University of Chicago press, 1961), p. 15: "No statute or court decision could immediately erase from the public mind, North or South, that long and firmly held conviction that the African race was inferior and therefore incapable of being assimilated."

tological category "slave." At the same time, the language of abolition preserved and indeed strengthened assumptions about the ultimate availability, dependency, and instrumentality of "free" persons of color as a class,
everywhere and always constituting an indivisible element of their presence, which nonetheless remained undesirable and ultimately to be removed. This contradiction was embodied, literally "fleshed out," in the real
relations of whites with "free" people of color, enacted in a set of practices
that in turn inscribed this contradictory set of meanings into the broader
language of post-Revolutionary republicanism.

Slavery had provided a fixed role, status, place, and identity in the social
structure for persons of color: within the white household and, by that
means, in the polity. Emancipation—either gradual or immediate—offered a kind of expulsion from this structure without providing a new place
or a new structure to accommodate the new category of free persons. The
state of being "emancipated" was an empty category, referential only to the
state of being that had preceded it (and had literally given birth to it, in
the case of children freed by birth under *post nati* provisions). In this sense,
the state of being "freed" or "freeborn" drew its essential meaning from
conceptions of availability and absence with reference to a former enslaved
condition. Former slaves, once infinitely but exclusively available to their
masters, were now freed from that limited and proprietary availability to
become, in a sense, publicly available to everyone (white). Free persons of
color were no longer formally a part of the coherent social structure constituted by the interrelationships of household, community, and polity. In
whites' minds, formally and conceptually, free people of color had no place
at all, even though they were physically still present as day or contract laborers. Whites felt little obligation to devise new language and a new set of
practices for establishing relations with a new class of persons, a class whose
existence they could imagine only with reference to the former enslaved
status of its members.

The ways in which whites treated "free" children born after passage of
the statutes—whom I call "statutory slaves"—illustrate the difficulty or,
more properly, the resistance of whites in coming to terms with the concept of free persons of color as a new class requiring a new set of relations.
Precisely because these statutory slaves were not indentured or contracted
for in any way, records clearly identifying them are rare. Some are undoubtedly included among various "boys" and "girls" mentioned in Connecticut and Rhode Island letters and diaries, but they are not distinguished from other servants in these documents. Their very invisibility is
significant: whites made no manifest effort to distinguish statutory slaves
from slaves, because there was no effective difference in their treatment or

employment. In fact, there is evidence that some slaves' children born after passage of the gradual emancipation statutes considered themselves
slaves. James Mars, for example, born in Canaan, Connecticut, to slave parents on March 3, 1790, six years after passage of the statute, called his narrative, "Life of James Mars, A Slave Born and Sold in Connecticut," despite
his awareness that "until they were twenty-five . . . was as long as the laws of
Connecticut could hold slaves."[7]

Even though most slaveowners and other whites seem to have adopted
the term "freeborn" for such children, there is compelling evidence that
they resolutely continued a set of practices that failed in every way to acknowledge the children's legal or ontological status as free persons.

Estate inventories offer a fascinating glimpse into the persistence of assumptions of entitlement to "free" children. The inventory of George Hazard of South Kingstown, proved in August 1788, lists six children valued at
between £6 and £20, including James, a "Negro boy 2 years old" at £6. The
inventory of the personal estate of Henry Gardner, also of South Kingstown, proved in January 1796, lists three adults and a young adolescent,
valued at between £12 and 5 shillings, and three children: Robey, seven
years old, and Patience, two years old, each valued at 6 shillings; and Jack,
no age given, a gift to Samuel Champlin, also valued at 6 shillings (he was
probably between two and eight years old, given his value and listing with
other children of that age group).[8]

All four of the children named as property in these inventories were
legally free; James, Robey, Patience, and Jack were all born after passage of
the *post nati* acts. The great difference in the relative value of James in 1788
and the other three in 1796 may reflect the growing recognition that the
institution of slavery had a short future, diminishing the value of children
born to slaves. It probably does not, however, reflect an adjustment to the
distinction between property in a person and property in a portion of that
person's time. Since the consciousness of the distinction is explicit in other wills and inventories—for example, the year before Hazard's death,
John Rose of South Kingstown left his wife "my Mustee boy called James
Mue what time I have in him"[9]—it seems that, whether by oversight or design, George Hazard and Henry Gardner were simply blind to the freedom
of the children they left as property, illustrating the resistance of many
white Rhode Islanders to the new category "freeborn black."

[7] In Arna Bontemps, *Five Black Lives* (Middletown, Conn.: Wesleyan University Press,
1971), esp. pp. 35, 46.
[8] South Kingstown Town Council and Probate Records, 6 (Wills 1772–1800): 209, August
5, 1788; 6:255–57, January 11, 1792.
[9] Ibid., 6:168, October 7, 1787.

Sometimes a determination to evade the consequences of *post nati* provisions is very clear. In Stonington, Connecticut, on June 9, 1784 (three months after the effective date of the gradual emancipation statute), a failing Nathan Smith made a will leaving his one Negro woman, Zine, to his wife. Nathan's four pages of instructions for the distribution of his worldly goods are detailed down to the last spoon, and Zine is the only slave included. Yet the inventory of his personal estate barely seven months later includes Zine, valued at £30, and "1 Negro boy about 2 years old—£10." It is not very likely that this sick, elderly man acquired a new two-year-old slave in his last months. Nor is it likely that the meticulous Nathan forgot to mention the child in his will seven months before. What is likely is that Zine, pregnant at the writing of the will, gave birth shortly thereafter to a boy who, had he been represented at his true age of under a year, would have been a freeborn child whose time would be considerably reduced in value.[10]

Even more compelling evidence is provided in the 1792 sale of a slave named Cleona by John Payson Child of Pomfret, Connecticut, to one John McClellan. Two signed bills of sale, documenting two different versions of the transaction, both survive. The first describes Cleona as "about eight years of age," gives her price as £7 and 7 shillings lawful money, and indemnifies the new owner for sores on the girl in the event "they may prove of bad consequences"; if so, McClellan can return her within one year, and Child will reimburse him cost plus interest plus any expense "said McLellan may be at taking care of said Negro." The second document gives Cleona's price as £8. It says nothing about the girl's disease, but in it Child agrees "to warrant and defend the said McClellan his heirs and assigns in the property of sd Girl against all claims whatever and that she is now more than Eight years of Age." Both documents are dated April 11 and witnessed by the same persons, Nathaniel McClellan and Mary L. McClellan (probably brother and sister-in-law of the buyer).

It seems apparent that the second document superseded the first. The original bill of sale was probably drafted before McLellan had actually seen Cleona, and it was the face-to-face encounter of the buyer with his new property that changed the terms of the sale; at least, this interpretation seems to fit the evidence. One can imagine the encounter: Cleona is small, perhaps, or unusually shy, and McClellan is suddenly possessed of the conviction that she is less than eight years old. To be a slave for life on April 11, 1792, Cleona would have to have turned eight before March 1. Her skin disease quickly loses its value to McClellan as a bargaining chip; clear

[10] Stonington Probate Journal and Record, 4:450, June 9, 1784; 4:453, January 12, 1785.

title for life becomes everything. Child offers assurance—for a higher price. Neither party apparently considers modifying the agreement to reflect the sale of time instead of property, to accommodate Cleona's entitlement to eventual freedom. The deal is struck.[11]

Some children born to slaves after passage of the *post nati* statutes may have been kept in ignorance of their entitlement to freedom by never being told exactly when they were born, as suggested by the surprising number of men and women of color examined as transients who stated that they did not know their own age. It is true that most of these individuals clearly could not have fallen within the *post nati* provision: Coley Yates, for example, who "cannot say how old he is," had been born in Africa and brought to Rhode Island from the coast of Guinea; Philis Page alias Sarl said she was born a slave in Cranston and "does not know her age but supposes herself to be about forty" in 1804, placing her well beyond the reach of the *post nati* provision. Phebe Niles, who "does not know her own age" in 1802 and was characterized as "a freed slave," might have been an underage statutory slave who had been released from service, but lack of birth knowledge could only have supported the conflation of these statuses in practice.[12] It would be dangerous to take transient testimony entirely at face value as evidence of victimization (some people of color clearly had no idea when they were born; others may have claimed such ignorance as a strategy, resisting the right of town authorities to know their personal histories); further, the absence of a large body of legal cases in which the age of majority of a statutory slave is the focus of dispute suggests either that, when ignorance of age extended a statutory slave's period of service unfairly, the ruse was successful or that it was infrequently used. Nonetheless, it lurked as another in the slaveowner's bag of tricks for assuring continued control and dependency under gradual emancipation.

Vagueness in general about the origins of children of color rendered them subject to simply materializing into service. In 1785 the Providence Town Council learned from Dr. John Chace that "he hath a Mulatto Child called Betsy Richmond about Ten Years old who has no parents living and it being probable that said Child may become chargeable to the Town," he would be "willing to take her as an Apprentice by Indenture." The Council indentured her to him forthwith.[13] Dr. Chace "hath" Betsy—but where did she come from? Did she have other family relations? No one asked, because Betsy was assumed to be both dependent and available for service,

---

[11] Slavery Documents (microfilm), Connecticut Historical Society.

[12] Providence Town Council Records, 6:12, July 9, 1787; 8:363, February 22, 1804; 8:169, June 29, 1802.

[13] Ibid., 5:312, May 2, 1785.

and these assumptions were part of the very unspecificity of her origins.

The remarkable tenacity and longevity of the conventions of slavery in Rhode Island are apparent in the language and intent of William Dyre's 1791 sale of two-year-old Violet to Prince Dyre and his wife, Violet, who were obviously the child's parents and slaves of William Dyre. (Slaves were able to own property throughout New England.) Violet's price was "forty Shillings silver money," in return for which Prince and Violet Sr. were "to have and to hold the said Negro child, Violet, . . . for the full Term of twenty years next ensuing the date hereof," who "from and after said Term of twenty years, shall be forever absolved manumited and discharged from the bonds of slavery and servitude . . . and . . . from and after said twenty years, shall be to all Intents and purposes free and as such entitled to all the priveliges of a Freed woman."[14]

Of course, Violet, born five years after the *post nati* statute went into effect, was not a slave. William Dyre's awareness of the statute is manifest in his sale of her time "for the full term of twenty years"; he obviously knew he could not convey a lifetime right in Violet Jr. as property. Nonetheless, he explicitly defined her as a slave and used the conventional language of property transfer: "Give, Grant, bargain sell and Confirm"; "to have and to hold." His assumption that he must prospectively "manumit" Violet so that she could be free at the conclusion of her term of service completely ignored the *post nati* effect of the statute, which was to endow Violet with the ontological status of "free person" at the moment of her birth and the functional agency of freedom at twenty-one years of age. It is impossible to tell whether William Dyre was unable to grasp the concept of "freeborn" enacted within the provisions of the *post nati* statute or was cynically manipulating Prince and Violet Sr. After all, in his sale of the time of the child Violet to her parents, William Dyre had managed to find an ingenious way of implementing the effect of the original statutory provision for reimbursement to slaveowners of the cost of raising the "free" children of their slaves: he had passed the cost on to the enslaved parents.

Many whites just could not grasp the practical meaning of "freeborn" even when they clearly acknowledged it, especially in the earliest years of the abolition period. In 1789, for example, the clerk of the Providence Town Council noted, "Amos Atwell Esq. appeared and manumitted his Negro Woman named Esther of 18 years of age . . . and her Child Ulania 4 years old born free, approved by this Council." The council members acted to free the "free" because nothing had altered their habitual assumption that only action on their part could transform the unit of property that

[14] William Dyre, September 4, 1791, Miscellaneous Manuscripts, Rhode Island Historical Society.

was a slave's child into a free person.[15] Even when it was acknowledged, the legal status of freedom was often suspect. An inventory of the personal estate of Silas Church of New London, made in June of 1786, noted "Negro man Cato & Negro wench Jenny both poor & old & Jenny supposed to be free"—valued at 10 shillings.[16]

And freedom was reversible, too. Lucy, slave of Daniel Stillwell, was manumitted with authorization from the Providence Town Council in September 1787. But one month later Stillwell was back before the council, complaining that at the previous meeting he had "supposed . . . that the law exempted such Persons as freed their slaves under Forty Years of Age from maintaining such slaves if they became paupers" but that he had since been informed of the amendment to the gradual abolition act reducing that age to thirty. Since Lucy was under forty but over thirty, she would remain his responsibility even if freed; therefore, he asked the council to rescind her manumission. Because the council members did not see Lucy's freedom as representing any kind of real transformation of identity before the law, they saw no problem in reenslaving her; after one month of freedom, Lucy again became a slave.[17]

Slaveholders seemed oddly confident of their power to control their slaves even as the gradual emancipation period progressively reduced that power to illusion. They left runaways in their wills; they petitioned to free certain slaves they had not seen in months.[18] Assumptions originating in real, physical, day-to-day exercise of practices that subordinated slaves physically and maintained their subordination by force had become categorical and idealized long before 1800, rendering actual practical arrangements irrelevant to many slaveholders and to some slaves, whose obedience was read commonly as "loyalty."

Certain practices continued unchallenged in direct violation of the abolition statutes, so taken for granted even by lawmakers that they seemed somehow to exist outside the context of gradual emancipation. Although the 1784 statute made it explicitly illegal to bring slaves into the state of Rhode Island, travelers arriving on passenger and merchant ships were often accompanied by "servants" who, given their listing by first name only and their place of origin, may be assumed to have been slaves. At least twenty-five individuals of questionable status arrived in Providence between 1798 and 1807, including Shusteen, a female from Africa who came with

[15] Providence Town Council Records, 6:80, June 1, 1789.
[16] New London Probates 1 (1781–83): 210, June 7, 1786.
[17] Providence Town Council Records, 6:18, September 3, 1787; and 6:22, October 1, 1787.
[18] South Kingstown Town Council and Probate Records 6:216, September 14, 1789; Providence Town Council Records, 8:272, July 29, 1803.

Susannah Mumsille on May 1, 1803; Fortune, from Batavia, with Samuel
Snow on July 13, 1801; James, born in Nevis, and Mary, born in Africa, with
Alexander Lawrence on November 12, 1804; and Jupiter, with an un-
named master from the Dutch East Indies on April 30, 1807.[19] These arrivals seem to have occasioned no comment. Even more telling is an act of
the Rhode Island General Assembly in November 1793, "Respecting the
Relief of the unfortunate Exiles from Hispaniola & other Territories of the
Republic of France who have arrived in a destitute Condition in this State,"
and the response of local officials to its provisions. The Providence Town
Council, citing this act, provided ten shillings a day and clothing to support seven families—totaling thirteen exiles and their slaves—and de-
frayed the travel expenses of three exiles: a Mrs. Janin, for "her own & her
Negros passage to New York," and a Mr. Dumorier and a Mr. Gilmore, passage to New York "with their two Negro boys."[20] Thus the council recorded the ownership of "Negros," and their arrival in the state, without
comment. The persistence of such arrangements served to bolster whites'
assumptions of entitlement to ownership of people of color and to undercut progress toward developing new kinds of relations with them in the
context of their emancipation.

Gradual abolition appears to have sustained paternalistic assumptions
about the obligations of slaveholding, as well as its entitlements to the persons and labor of people of color and their perpetual availability as objects of exchange and appropriation. The grip of convention seems the
only explanation for the curious failure of most Rhode Island slaveholders to seek compensation, under the reimbursement provision of the abolition statute, for raising the children of their slaves in their first year.
Repealed in October 1785, this provision offered a twenty-month window
of opportunity following the effective date of statute in March 1784. Yet
the only clearly documented instance of a slaveowner actually taking advantage of this provision involved John Smith of Providence, mentioned
above, who appeared before the town council on August 1, 1785, exactly
a year after the birth of a child to one of his slaves, to claim reimbursement for his expenses.[21] The records of other town council clerks list payment requests and authorizations for the relevant time period, but it is not
clear whether any of these payments were made to slaveowners for sup-

[19] "Providence Passenger Lists," manuscript compiled by Maureen Taylor, Rhode Island
Historical Society. I deeply appreciate Ms. Taylor's generosity in sharing her data and her insights.

[20] Providence Town Council Records 6:303–4, 308, November 9–10, December 2, 1793.

[21] Ibid., 5:323, August 1, 1785; 5:340, October 8, 1785; 5:356, December 13, 1785.

port of children. At any rate, the lack of persuasive evidence of a flood of requests for public support for slaves' children suggests the power of ideology to overcome even greed, even though fear of such demand led the General Assembly to repeal the reimbursement provision. Alternative strategies on the part of slaveowners to obtain compensation for supporting their slaves' infants, such as William Dyre's "sale" of the child Violet to her own enslaved parents, did not emerge until the gradual abolition process had been under way for several years. One can speculate that it may have taken some time for slaveowners to begin to regard the slave relation critically and to demand economic sense of it in a new way that made infant support, with slavery itself, less the unexamined assumption it had been in 1784.

Similarly, there is little evidence that town councils actually acted to bind out the children of slaves after their first year, as provided under the 1784 reimbursement provision. Here, the window of opportunity was smaller; only children born during the first seven months following the effective date of the statute would have reached a year old before the provision was repealed. John Smith's slave's child would have qualified, being a year old in August 1785, but the Providence Town Council took no action to bind out this child. Few if any other children of slaves were bound out under public auspices, most likely because it was distinctly to the financial advantage of the slaveowner to employ the children of his own slaves as statutory slaves.

It was not only the particular form of *post nati* abolition prescribed under the Rhode Island and Connecticut statutes that undermined the substance of "freedom" and continued to confirm whites' assumptions about black servility by sustaining old practices under a new name. In Massachusetts, where the 1783 judicial interpretation of the state constitution in the last Walker-Jennison case might have been expected to produce an immediate change in status for all enslaved people of color at once, the ambiguity of the decision rendered the results the same: whites ignored and evaded (and may on occasion have acted in genuine ignorance of) the abolition of slave status for people of color.

It is clear that many enslaved persons in Massachusetts knew of the *Commonwealth v. Jennison* decision. Sam Sharp, born in Warwick, Rhode Island, but sold to a Massachusetts slaveholder, told the Providence Town Council in 1789 that "he was made free by the Constitution of Massachusetts & that he came to this Town in January last." Pink Williams, born in Scituate, Massachusetts, reported that she lived with her owner till she was twenty-four years of age, at which time "her father, Cuff Williams, alias Stoddard, told her she was free, on which she left her Master and went to Boston."[22]

Massachusetts slaveowners employed a variety of techniques to preserve the property value of their slaves and to ignore or circumvent the intent of the Walker-Jennison decision after 1783. Notices for runaway slaves continued to appear in local newspapers; for example, in June 1784, a year later, Thomas Tripp of Dartmouth advertised for the return of fifteen-year-old Jonathan White, described as "a Mustee Boy," and offered a four-dollar reward—sizable enough to suggest that Tripp anticipated more from White than six years' value remaining on an indenture contract; it seems likely that Tripp still considered White a slave for life.[23] Sales of slaves also remained brisk. Elisha Brewster of Worthington sold "my Negro family Consisting of the following Persons, Viz my Negro man named Peleg and his wife Lucy, and their son Peter & Daughter Peggy," to Jeremiah Wadsworth of Hartford at the end of August 1784.[24]

Other arrangements were clearly intended to sidestep the implications of Walker-Jennison. In 1789 John Ashley Jr. of Sheffield in Berkshire County purchased Mary, who "before this Time of Making this agreement was a Slave or Servent for Life," from "her said Master," William Venniss of Cloverock, New York, "in consideration whereof the Said Mary Doth hereby bind and oblige himSelfe [*sic*] faithfully and honestly to Serve the Said John Ashley Junr Esquire and his heirs for the term of ten whole years from the Date hereof as Indented Servent of the Said John Ashley Junr and in all things to obey and Serve him as Such." The indenture was made and signed in Sheffield.[25] In this case, Ashley apparently conspired with Venniss to bring Mary as a slave into Massachusetts (though she was technically free upon setting foot in the state) and, in the same day, purchased and freed her into indenture. Under Massachusetts law Ashley was not empowered to place a free person under indenture against her will (only indigent or disorderly persons could be indentured against their will, and only by town selectmen and councils acting in a guardianship position), and the fact that the indenture contract was made between Ashley and Mary herself suggests that Mary "agreed" to the arrangement. But Mary's agreement would almost certainly have been made under duress on "free" ground in Massachusetts as the only way out of continued enslavement in New York. This

[22] Ibid., 6:92, August 5, 1789; 6:165, July 14, 1791.

[23] *Newport Mercury*, July 3, 1784.

[24] Bill of sale, 23 August, 1784, from Elisha Brewster to Jeremiah Wadsworth, Wadsworth Papers, Massachusetts Historical Society.

[25] Indenture in two parts between J. Ashley and Mary, Miscellaneous Manuscripts [Theodore Sedgwick] Bound Addition, Massachusetts Historical Society.

kind of pressured service, whose legality seems dubious at best, was obviously calculated to extend the slave relation rather than to mitigate it.

Throughout New England the mapping of dependency from the category "slave" onto the category "person of color" was achieved by a range of practices that insisted upon a slavelike status for people of color in freedom. Slaveowners in Connecticut and Rhode Island continued to make wills giving slaves to other slaves or freeing them under specified terms and conditions that effectively assumed the owner's continuing control from the grave. Elisha Reynolds freed Lydia and gave her the time of her daughter Genny till Genny turned eighteen, when she too would be free. Jeffery Champlin gave "my three Negro girls to wit Patience Unice & Sarah unto Pero Potter (so called) their Father he not to take them nor the profits of them nor either of them until after the death or second marriage of my said wife." By leaving lifetime servitude in place even as they introduced a new category of *post nati* servitude for a limited term, the gradual emancipation statutes thus reinforced old conceptions of the appropriateness of long-term, dutiful service by people of color, conceptions that continued to be reflected in slaveowners' wills. As late as 1790, when twenty-one had been established as the age of emancipation from statutory slavery for children born under the *post nati* statute, Rhode Island slaveowners were still making wills that freed their slaves at thirty or thirty-three.[26] It seems that slaves, after all, were slaves, their terms of service to be defined entirely on an individual basis by the whim of their owners, without regard to the legally established age for terminating the services of new (statutory) slaves as a class.

Some slaveowners did provide for the emancipation of a slave immediately upon their deaths, usually in language like that of William Dyer, who, "in consideration of the faithful services performed by my Negro man Prince," manumitted him by will probated in 1788.[27] But these beneficiary emancipations further reinforced the conception of freedom for persons of color as a reward to be earned by diligent labor and good behavior, rather than an entitlement.

The manumission provisions of the gradual emancipation statutes were a source of persistent conflict over the support of ex-slaves, drawing public attention to cases of dependency on the part of people of color and serving to conflate their status with that of slaves. When Rhode Island slaveowners sought to employ the provision giving them the right to manumit slaves without further financial responsibility, with town council approval,

[26] South Kingstown Town Council and Probate Records, 6:241, December 7, 1790; 6:393–95, April 9, 1798; 6:231, June 28, 1790; 6:263–64, December 7, 1790.
[27] Ibid., 6:205, entered April 18, 1788.

resistance of the councils grew as the abolition process continued. Assumptions that manumitted slaves would be dependent and thus require relief, and would surely disturb the public peace by being disorderly and riotous, became more powerful and widespread with each passing year. South Kingstown, with the largest proportion of persons of color, stubbornly refused to authorize manumissions of individuals who clearly fell within the requirements of the statute, directing the clerk to engage counsel to defend the town against slaveowners' lawsuits rather than be "put in jeopardy of expense." In one such suit the aptly named Patience waited two years while Elisha Gardner, her owner, went through session after court session until the Supreme Judicial Court for Washington County finally ordered her manumission in October 1808.[28]

Manumissions had clear-cut results only for whites. Authorized and documented ones did unambiguously free whites from further obligation to their former slaves but, as we have seen, did not end the obligation of former slaves to former owners, which could on occasion be reinstated arbitrarily. Undocumented and beneficiary manumissions (which did not always observe the age restrictions imposed by statute) had ambiguous consequences for both parties; often they resulted in bitterly contested claims and counterclaims of financial obligation on the part of a variety of former owners, heirs of owners, and town governments. In either case, the persons manumitted became suspended in a complicated legal discourse of obligation and dependency, which they themselves frequently endeavored to shape to their advantage but which, ultimately, trapped them in circumstances defined by their former status.

Sometimes protracted legal wrangles over responsibility for persons of color whose status was ambiguous left free people of color and slaves in the same limbo of uncertainty and destitution. The Newport Town Council magnanimously agreed that Tom Hazard, apparently an elderly slave who "belonged" to the estate of the late Enoch Hazard, Esquire, "may remain on sufferance" in Newport "with the family till the 20th of October next, and if he does not remove at that Time to be removed by an Order." But Tom was part of the movable property in Enoch Hazard's estate inventory, which was not proved before the Town Council until October 6, 1788—two years later. Still enslaved yet without a responsible owner, Tom could neither legally leave nor legally stay in Newport for two years; the records are silent on his status and well-being during that time. In 1800 Newport Tew, a seventy-five-year-old ex-slave freed by the will of his last owner, Paul

---

[28] E.g., ibid., 7:22, August 13, 1804, and 7:23, September 12, 1804; Rhode Island Court Archives, Records of Supreme Court 226 (1797–1810, Supreme Judicial Court for Washington County, October session, 1808): 397.

Tew, of Providence, reported "that Paraclite Tew [Paul's heir] is to Maintain him if he becomes chargeable." On these grounds, he was allowed to stay in Providence.

In the 1780s and early 1790s the families of former slaves quite commonly provided financial assistance for them even where, as in Massachusetts, there was no longer a legal obligation to do so. For example, Mrs. Love Lawrence of Groton, Massachusetts, made a payment of £3, 18 shillings in 1787 and another of more than £36, 7 shillings in 1789 on behalf of Bode or Body, "a negro man" left to be supported by her in her husband's will.[29] Although such assistance was humanitarian and at the very least a form of reparation to which all former slaves were surely entitled, nonetheless the continuing support and responsibility of former owners for free persons of color tended to blur the boundaries between slave and free.

By 1813, however, when many of the families of former slaveowners had distanced themselves effectively from the institution of slavery, the reflexive machinery of paternalistic obligation seems to have broken down almost completely. Official action to compel former owners and their heirs to care for old and indigent slaves became commonplace. This was the situation of Quam Peckham, born blind, who was left as part of the late Benjamin Peckham's estate to his son, Josephus Peckham, a minor. Benjamin Peckham's will, proved in 1792, had left "use and improvement of my Negro boy Quam" to his wife "while she is my widow," then to "my daughter, Mary Perry if she wants him or son Josephus if she doe not." Twenty years later Benjamin's wife had died, and neither Mary nor Josephus had assumed any responsibility for Quam, who had been reduced to "a Suffering State." Josephus too had died, having a minor child—a second Josephus— as *his* heir. In response to a formal complaint, the South Kingstown Town Council authorized the clerk "to write to the Guardian of said Josephus Peckham to provide for Said Black Man out of the Estate of Sd Josephus Peckham."[30] Ironically, the necessity of intervention of town governments on behalf of slaves and former slaves served to make most visible the least self-sufficient persons of color and to support assumptions about their inability to function as independent members of the community.

Other practices too tended to extend, reinforce, legitimate, and institutionalize the differential treatment of free people of color as dependent

[29] Newport Town and City Council Records, September 15, 1786; Providence Town Council Records, 8:7, December 8, 1800; Receipt from Isreal Hobart, March 14, 1787, and Receipt from James Prescott, July 17, 1789, Groton [Mass.] Manuscripts 6:89 and 6:90, Massachusetts Historical Society.

[30] South Kingstown Town Council and Probate Records, 7:106, December 30, 1813.

and in need of extended supervision. Public indenture, which had been used to control and provide support for indigent children and adults since the 1750s, became a much more frequent tool of control of free children of color after 1780.[31] Indenture contracts, which had customarily required up to thirty years of service from persons of African descent and had imposed fewer obligations on their masters, gradually became somewhat shorter but still remained longer than comparable contracts for whites and in fact often obligated children of free people of color longer than statutory servitude would have bound them had their parents been enslaved. As late as 1794, for example, the South Kingstown Town Council voted that "Fisher a Negro Boy about Six Years old be bound as an apprentice to William Potter Esq. until he be 24 years of Age."[32] Born in 1788, Fisher could have been required to serve only until twenty-one if he had been the child of slaves.

In fact, there was some disagreement over whether, under the abolition statute, the age of majority for "freeborn" statutory slaves might not also terminate or even categorically invalidate involuntary indenture for persons of color. Moses Brown thought this was the case. In 1810, in the course of assisting a female black indentured servant who had run away from her master and sought his help, Brown declared that he believed the abolition statute in Rhode Island "limits the Age of females at 18 Beyond which they could not be held Either as Slaves since 1784, or by Indenture."[33] Brown's position was not widely shared, however.

Even more significant was the appearance in the 1790s of apprenticeship and indenture contracts that explicitly outlined ways of extending and replicating the conditions of slavery. In 1790, when Jacob Dresser of Thompson, Connecticut, apprenticed "a Negro Girl Named Peggy" (apparently the child of his slave) to Darius Parkhurst of Pomfret, he wrote, "During the aforesd term Sd Dresser Doth fully impower Sd Parkhurst to Control, order & comand said Peggy in all Respects, and to all Intents &

---

[31] Public indenture was a solution to the social problem of Poor costs, not a means of providing labor or skills training, according to Ruth Wallis Herndon, "'To Live after the Manner of an Apprentice': Public Indenture and Social Control in Rhode Island, 1750–1800," (paper presented at the annual meeting of the American Studies Association, Boston, November 7, 1993), p. 3. I would argue that it was an apparatus for socializing poor people of all descriptions to labor and training them for their quite different social roles: for white males, economic, social, and political independence—i.e., citizenship; for white females, economic independence but social and political dependence; for males and females of color, economic independence but social and political nonexistence.

[32] South Kingstown Town Council and Probate Records, 6:206, March 10, 1794.

[33] Moses Brown note, verso of letter from Mary Vinton, September [October] 12, 1810, Moses Brown Papers, Rhode Island Historical Society.

Purposes as though She were born his Servant."[34] In the 1797 indenture of Sophia Havens, a woman of color, to David and Mary Vinton of Providence, recorded on a standard, printed apprenticeship contract form, the word "Apprentice" was methodically crossed out wherever it appeared and the word "Servant" inserted.[35]

Another practice that dissolved the distinction between indenture and slavery of persons of color was the repeated sale of their indenture contracts. The experience of Maria Slade, a mulatto woman freeborn in Swansea, Massachusetts, was quite typical. Bound out at four years of age to Samuel Nial of Rehoboth, she reported that her time had been sold to five different masters before she was twenty years old, when she finally ran away about a year before her indenture would have been completed. The only unusual aspect of her experience was that her next to last master in Attleborough, Massachusetts, was "a Negro Man."[36]

As gradual abolition continued and the inevitability of the eventual disappearance of slavery became obvious, slaveowners frequently attempted to recoup their investments by selling their slaves to new owners in states that had not yet acted to restrict slaveholding. William Venniss of Cloverock, New York, was probably trying to cut his potential losses on Mary in the face of abolition agitation in his own state by selling Mary to John Ashley of Massachusetts under the guise of indenture (above). Other entrepreneurs who were not themselves slaveowners saw a similar business opportunity in the growing number of free black children and adults. Nothing so clearly demonstrates how freeborn and manumitted people of color remained a form of property in the eyes of many if not most whites— everywhere available for transfer and exchange, seizure and sale—as the widespread practices of kidnapping and sale out of state.[37]

[34] Indenture contract, January [2]6, 1790, Slavery Documents (microfilm), Connecticut Historical Society.

[35] Providence Town Papers, 28:48, August 7, 1797. Children bound out by public officials were not routinely considered servants. The intention was to train children in useful labor, and the standard public indenture contract used the term "apprentice" throughout. See "Indenture to Bind Out a Poor Child," pp. 34–35 in Samuel Freeman, *The Town Officer; or, The Power and Duty of Selectmen, Town Clerks, . . . and Other Town Officers. As contained in the Laws of the Commonwealth of Massachusetts. . . .* (Portland, Maine: Benjamin Tiscomb Jr., 1791), first edition of a handbook that was reissued periodically and used by town clerks throughout New England until the 1820s.

[36] Providence Town Council Records, 6:145, January 28, 1791.

[37] Carol Wilson, *Freedom At Risk: The Kidnapping of Free Blacks in America, 1780–1865* (Lexington: University Press of Kentucky, 1994), describes at length the practice of abducting and selling free people of color into slavery (children and impoverished adults were most vulnerable), a pervasive practice throughout the United States, but most prevalent in states contiguous to slave states (pp. 9–39, esp. 9–11). She also devotes a chapter (pp. 40–66) to the

Legislative action to curb these practices in several states was largely in-
effective. Rhode Island slaveholders had begun to sell off slaves during the
Revolution in anticipation of gradual abolition, and passage of an act forbidding the practice in 1779 probably had little effect.[38] In Connecticut
kidnapping had become enough of a problem to be included in the 1788
act prohibiting the slave trade, and selling slaves out of the state was explicitly prohibited in 1792.[39] In 1788 Massachusetts, too, found a need to
restrict the sale of "divers peaceable inhabitants . . . privately carried off by
force, or decoyed away under various pretences, by evil minded persons,
and with a probable intention of being sold as slaves."[40] Many of these "inhabitants" were undoubtedly persons of color purchased as slaves before
the 1783 Walker-Jennison decision, and their offspring, in whom the pur-
chasers still claimed property rights. Others were simply "available" free
persons of color.

Moses Brown of Providence, prominent Quaker businessman and abolitionist, regularly received correspondence concerning free persons of
color who had been kidnapped or decoyed back into slavery; he and the
Providence Abolition Society worked diligently to obtain their release.
Brown's assistance was sought in cases involving attempts to enslave or
reenslave free individuals and families seized in a wide range of environments, from Providence to Maine, Trinidad, and the Cape Verde Islands.[41]
Most appeals came from other antislavery supporters, often fellow members of the Abolition Society, as when Stephen Hopkins of Newport reported that "a Capt. Moses Smith of Providence shipped two free Negroes
as seamen on board his vessel: and when he arrived in this place [New-
port], he, instead of paying them their wages, according to agreement, sold
them for slaves." Although they had been redeemed, Hopkins believed
that "such iniquity ought not to go unpunished, if any law will take hold of
it."[42] Another case, which Brown called "a renewed and very Exercising Oc-

---

ways in which kidnappers exploited uncertainties of status and identity in operating "legally"
under the Fugitive Slave Laws of 1793 and 1850.

[38] "Act of the Rhode Island Assembly," October, 1779, in "Acts and Resolves . . . of Rhode
Island," pp. 5–7, *Early American Imprints.*

[39] "An Act to prevent the Slave-Trade," second Thursday of October, 1788, and "An Act
in addition to an Act, entitled an Act, to prevent the Slave Trade," second Thursday in May,
1792, in "Acts and Laws . . . of Connecticut," pp. 368–69, 423–24, *Early American Imprints.*

[40] "An Act to prevent the Slave-Trade, and for granting Relief to the Families of such unhappy Persons as may be kidnapped or decoyed away from this Commonwealth," February
27, 1788, in "Acts and Laws . . . of Massachusetts," pp. 672–73, *Early American Imprints.*

[41] Examples are David Barnes to Moses Brown, Providence, August 5, 1796; Moses Brown
to James Pemberton, Providence, July 20, 1784; Obadiah Brown to Moses Brown, Providence,
January 26, 1794; John Taber to Almy Brown, Portland, Maine, n.d., 1803, all from Moses
Brown Papers, Rhode Island Historical Society.

[42] Stephen Hopkins to Moses Brown, Newport, March 9, 1787, in ibid.

cation of controversy," involved his own brother, John, lifelong slaveowner and trader. As Moses Brown wrote to his friend John Pemberton, John Brown was prosecuted for "forceably sending a Negro Man on board one of his Vessels, after the [abolition] society's Committee had agreed to support the man in his Right to Freedom." Moses wearily noted that Brother John continued to insist "we had as good a right to Claim his Coat on his Back as his Negro &c."[43] Both the enslavement and the freedom of people of color pitted white elites, even brothers, against each other.

Sometimes former slaveowners appealed for the help of known abolitionists to recover their own former slaves and slaves' children who had been kidnapped for reenslavement, demonstrating the responsibility they continued to feel. Philip Slead of Somerset, Massachusetts, asked Moses Brown for help in 1793 regarding "a Negro Boy Named John Richman that was Bornd in my house & I Bound him to Silvester Richman Til he be Came Twenty one years old before that Time was Expired he was Clandistantly Sold, by Enformashon at Cape Francois and Is Know Taken up and Put in Gail at Newprovidence and I Desire you would Take Som Methard to Releve Him by Appliang to the Govener of That Island or Som other way as you Shall Think most proper." Brown noted on the letter that he had written for notarized confirmation of the facts, preparatory to interceding.[44] This exchange is instructive on several counts. While Slead's ongoing interest in Richman's freedom was no doubt admirable, the fact that his involvement remained essential to sustaining that freedom confirms the extent to which, for many free persons of color, the state of freedom in the present remained in a kind of perpetual bondage to the unfree past, contingent on the continuing and vigilant good will of former owners. Slead's letter to Brown, in its diction, spelling, and general level of sophistication, also reveals that neither the practice of slaveholding itself nor its residual noblesse oblige was confined to educated elites.

In Connecticut, too, the perception of children and adults of color as "available" for kidnapping and sale out of state seems to have been widespread. The Connecticut Society for the Promotion of Freedom enlisted prominent citizens and even the governor of the state to make inquiries and otherwise intercede in kidnapping cases.[45] After the 1788 act prohibiting the slave trade empowered citizens at large to bring damage suits

[43] Moses Brown to John Pemberton, Providence, April 26, 1790, in ibid.

[44] Philip Slead to Moses Brown, Somerset, December 26, 1793, in ibid.

[45] E.g., Governor Samuel Huntington got involved in an attempt by the society and its agents to recover Aaron, whose name was apparently changed to Bristol by those who decoyed him away from New Hartford for sale into slavery in the Carolinas; see Jonathan Edwards and David Daggett to Samuel Huntington, Governor, New Haven, March 4, 1793, Miscellaneous Manuscripts, Connecticut Historical Society.

against kidnappers, less disinterested individuals also became involved in the retrieval of reenslaved persons of color though the activities of plaintiffs in some of these suits were suspect, accusations of profiteering in human misery brought angry denials.

One document provides an unusually rich source of information on virtually every aspect of the practices of kidnapping and recovery: the crosscurrents of public opinion surrounding them; the conflicting values of disinterested benevolence and pecuniary opportunism that provided the social context in which these issues were debated; the lead-footed judicial process through which they were arbitrated; the bedrock assumptions about slaves and free persons of color themselves as available commodities, which fueled kidnapping and recovery alike. This sixteen-page defense of an eight-year career of recovery activities in Connecticut was published around 1797 by one notorious freelance agent. Isaac Hillard offered his text as a rebuttal to unnamed persons who had attempted to "prevent me from prosecuting those who kidnapped, sold, and sent free Negroes out of the State by insinuations that I had no principle, but did it purely because I expected to be rewarded."[46]

Hillard opened with a poignant narrative of the incident that initiated his involvement in the recovery business: in 1789, in Virginia, "I saw with my eyes, two poor helpless children [whom he later defines further as 'young, helpless girls'], thus stolen or kidnapped from Derby, in the county of New-Haven, and sold as slaves for life." He then described his long and costly legal battle to prosecute the case: from the Court of Common Pleas in 1790; to Superior Court for a rehearing, where he won two judgments; to the Supreme Court of Errors, which heard defendants' appeals but finally in 1797 sustained the lower court's rulings in his favor. Eventually the perpetrators were forced to repurchase the two children in Virginia and return them to Connecticut. Hillard complained that his expenses totaled $800 over seven years of litigation. Later in the document, however, he noted that the recovery provision of the statute mandated a fine of $334 for the sale of a slave out of state, half to go to the state and the other half to the private prosecutor; presumably Hillard would have received half of the state's bounty of $668 as the statute provided. In addition, the "little children" recovered were each awarded £40, suggesting that Hillard may have received additional "bounty" money. That he in fact made a profit is argued by the indignation his success apparently aroused and the fact that he was willing to take on additional cases, although he said he accepted

---

[46] Isaac Hillard, "To the Public" [1797?], p. 1, Miscellaneous Manuscripts, Connecticut Historical Society.

them only "provided I did not make too great a sacrifice." He reported a few details of a second case—"one boy, a slave, sold in the State of New-York, [was] likewise repurchased and brought back"—and referred to "other actions not yet determined."[47]

In his final argument, Hillard made a very telling distinction between two different kinds of recovery which apparently elicited somewhat different public responses. With respect to his recovery of free children of color, as in the two cases he had recounted in detail, he offered a long appeal for moral vindication based in his own good citizenship: "Have I done good to these poor helpless children? That is the question. Have I not done what the legislature meant to have done? Have I not done what every good man must say is the duty of every good citizen to do?" With respect to his recovery of slaves sold out of state (as opposed to "free" children of slaves born under *post nati* statute), he responded to a different question: "I . . . have been asked, what good that would do? It would not, say they, relieve them from slavery." He answered by defining the position of slaves under gradual abolition as completely transformed: "Those poor unfortunate creatures had no law privilege, any more than the beasts, their masters will was their law: the hon. General Assembly entered them on the list of human creatures, and gave them a privilege, . . . that their masters nor any other person should send or sell them out of the State; and further that their children should be free." He listed miscellaneous benefits slaves could expect from their continued residence in the state of Connecticut, including the comfort they could take in the assurance that "any one who should attempt to send or sell them out of the State, should pay 334 dollars." Hillard concluded this astonishing document with a final slap at his accusers, noting that people had approved of him when he stood to lose nearly a thousand dollars in a good cause but became disgruntled at the prospect that he might get his money back and "some pay for his trouble."[48]

On one level, Isaac Hillard's defense of his recovery activities is evidence of the sheer magnitude and common currency of the kidnapping and sale of persons of color, both as actual events and as topics of public debate. It also demonstrates that free persons of color continued to share the commodified status of slaves, experiencing the same vulnerability to seizure, removal, and sale; this presented an ongoing practical, not theoretical, problem. Most important, the "bounty" provision of the 1788 statute confirms the commodity status of persons of color after their slavery had ended in freedom: they could be bought back for a price, their recovery

[47] Ibid., pp. 2–3, 8.
[48] Ibid., pp. 8–9, 15–16.

framed in the language of "repurchase" from the perpetrators rather than "release" from flatly illegal confinement, accompanied, perhaps, by confiscation of the monies that had changed hands in the illegal exchange. Hillard's narrative of struggle can be interpreted as mirroring the struggle going on in the broader society of New England to reconcile the values of virtuous, disinterested republican citizenship with the pursuit of the opportunities offered in a rapidly expanding commercial society. His perception of the inherent contradiction—indeed, hypocrisy—in public expressions of approval for his activities only when they succeeded at personal cost did not prevent him from framing his own argument in the same terms—minimizing his profit, exaggerating his costs, and redefining his real reward as fulfilling his moral obligations to God and the Connecticut General Asssembly. But for all these people, the benevolent as well as the greedy, kidnapped free persons of color fulfilled precisely the same objectified role as contraband.

Both kidnapping and recovery practices, then, reinforced the commodity status of free people of color. Yet these were only the most blatant of a host of practices that effectively reenslaved them in other ways by asserting control over their actions, confiscating their freedom, and appropriating their goods and real estate. James Davis, "a Negro man" of Charlestown, Rhode Island, recognized quite clearly that this was the intent of the petition of Jedediah Browning, grandson of Davis's former master, Jedediah Davis, asking the General Assembly to place him under a restrictive guardianship "necessary for the good of said negroman" and to rescind his physical possession of two-thirds of a farm and its profits, bequeathed to him—along with his freedom—by his former master. "And as to Giving my guardians Greater Power So as to Put me in slavery again," he beseeched the assembly in a counterpetition, "your memorialist Begs you Honour's protection against Such Proceedings." Not surprisingly, however, Browning prevailed.[49]

In a host of ways less complicated than by petition to the state legislature, free persons of color were often denied access to land and property to which they were entitled. James Davis explained in his petition that he had waited ten years to take possession of the two-thirds of the farm his master left to him because the executors had failed to divide it as required by the will and had simply let it out to strangers. Only when Davis lost patience and moved into a small corner of the house did Browning take action to evict him. Eber Hopkins, "a Mustee or Mowlatto Man" of Hartford,

---

[49] Jedediah Browning Petition, Petitions to the General Assembly (1792–93), 27:6, Rhode Island State Archives, Providence; James Davis Petition, General Assembly and Town Council Legal Papers, 1730–1798, Newport Historical Society.

Connecticut, testified that he had been bequeathed some land in the will of his former master but "was never put in Possession of it."[50] In a series of cases in 1786 regarding land legally belonging to them, Job, Elisabeth, Samuel, and Mary Sambo—fatherless children under the guardianship of James Austin of North Kingstown—filed suit to evict Ezekiel Hunt and his family, who had apparently moved to take possession of the Sambos' land. Depositions attesting to the legal marriage of Job Sambo, deceased, and "Margary Broadfoot (so called)" before the birth of any of the children suggests that the Hunts were making a counterclaim of bastardy to try to nullify the Sambos' ownership of their land.[51]

Among other strategies by which whites were able to wrest control of what little real and personal property persons of color were able to amass, some town councils and selectmen seem to have moved quite quickly to take possession of land owned by those who died intestate, paying somewhat less than scrupulous attention to finding legal heirs.[52] Further, councils routinely appointed white persons, often former masters, to be administrators of the estates of deceased persons of color, even when adult family members were available to perform this task.[53]

In all these ways, whites evaded the emerging necessity of creating a new set of relations with free people of color and, instead, transferred to them their old assumptions about slaves as publicly available commodities in permanent need of direction and control. The effect was to undermine any possibility of a shared entitlement between people of color and whites to real freedom and its fruits which might otherwise have taken root as slavery withered. Given whites' assumptions of entitlement to the labor of people of color and to blacks' acceptance of whites' authority, the material effects of these practices in turn confirmed the assumptions on which they rested. Still, the steadily diminishing numbers of slaves forced whites to be-

[50] Browning Petition, Davis Petition, and Providence Town Council Records, 6:20, September 7, 1787.

[51] Miscellaneous Court Papers, April and June 14, 1786, Rhode Island Court Archives.

[52] E.g., the South Kingstown Town Council moved to take possession of thirteen acres left by Joshua Watson, "a man of Colour," in 1814 and an unspecified number of acres left by Cesar Northup in 1826, in each case less than three months after the man's death (South Kingstown Town Council and Probate Records, 7:10, March 10, 1814; 7:235, December 11, 1826).

[53] See, e.g., the appointment of William Rodman to administer the estate of Prince Rodman, of Joseph Hazard (white) to administer the estate of Jacob Hazard, "a Negro Man," and so forth. An interesting exception is a letter of administration voted to Rexom Mumford, "an Indian Woman," on the personal estate of her son Isaac Michael (South Kingstown Town Council and Probate Records, 6:102, March 25, 1784; 6:108, June 14, 1784). Such practice began during the Revolution; see, e.g., Providence Wills, 6:185–86, May 31, 1977; and 6:259, January 4, 1779,

gin to acknowledge in some ways that slavery was becoming obsolete as a system of labor and social control. The most visible sign of their grudging acceptance of this fact was the diminishing value assigned to slaves in estate inventories, and the appearance of appraisers' comments on the subject, beginning on the eve of passage of the statutes and increasing in frequency throughout the 1780s and 1790s.

Even before the passage of the statutes, antislavery fervor had begun to be reflected in estate appraisals. In 1782 Jonathan Arnold and Nathan Waterman, Appraisers, listed as part of the estate of William Brown of Providence two slaves named London and Nancy "Who did We consider them in the Rank of irrational and [?] natures of property (which we conceive to be repugnant to Religion and forbid by every Principal of Humanity and Natural Right) We should adjudge to be of no Value but rather an Incumbrance to said Estate."[54] As gradual emancipation progressed, however, the principles of human rights disappeared while the notion of "Incumbrance" appeared more and more frequently. Some inventories listed slaves without assigning any property value to them at all. The inventory of Caleb Gardner's estate includes "Negros Nancy Gardner, George Dyre, Stephen Gardner," valued at "Worse than nothing"; Archibald Young's inventory lists "3 Negro boys—the one Runn Away, the others loth to stay" along with "1 Negro Woman—no value."[55] The slow devaluation of slaves and the naturalizing of valuelessness for people of color in general can be read in a corresponding devaluation of objects associated with them in estate inventories. For example, in South Kingstown, Rhode Island, "1 bedstead & Negro beding" were valued at £2.6s in early 1787, whereas by October 1794 "1 old Negro bed & bedstead" were listed at "no value."[56]

This devaluation was also reflected in the insidious transformation of whites' assumptions about people of color as workers. During the peak of slavery, persons of African descent were deemed to be "natural" slaves and, of course, slaves were "natural" workers. But emancipation radically altered the equation: if, as slaves, Africans were "natural" workers, then outside of slavery they could become "natural" nonworkers; hence they could be expected to be unproductive, and this tendency would only compound their fundamental dependency and need for external discipline and control—views around which the gradual emancipation proposals of Levi Hart and other abolitionists had been constructed in the first place. In 1783, on

[54] Providence Wills, 6:337–40, March 29, 1782.

[55] South Kingstown Town Council and Probate Records 6:365, December 15, 1796; Providence Wills 6:33, August 12, 1782.

[56] South Kingstown Town Council and Probate Records 6:85, 304. The same usage and slightly lower value appear in 1786 in New London Probates, 1:203–6, where "5 different Beds and their furniture used by Negroes" were valued at £4, 10 shillings.

the eve of the gradual emancipation period, items such as William and Samuel Helms's ad in the *Connecticut Journal* offering a year's employment to "a stout able MAN, (either white or black)"—suggesting a general interchangeability of black and white labor—could be found with some frequency.[57] By 1800 they were almost nonexistent.

Many whites continued to hire persons of color specifically for "Negro jobs," usually heavy, unskilled labor in agricultural and domestic settings—not coincidentally, the jobs frequently done by slaves at an earlier time. For example, between June 1790 and early December 1792, Timothy Shepherd of Medfield, Massachusetts, took "into my service" three men, one boy, and one woman, whom he identified as "black," to perform such work.[58] Outside slavery, people of color continued to be seen as inherently "available" for heavy work but as usually unwilling to perform it unless coerced; hence their availability was forcibly enacted by means of public indenture as a legal penalty for various offenses, notably indebtedness and noncompliance with court orders. When Jupiter, "alias John Potter," was jailed for failure to support his bastard child as ordered by the Justice Court, John C. Nightingale was able to apply to the Providence Town Council to have Potter bound out to him for seven years. Nightingale agreed to pay $10 per month, half of which would go to Potter and the other half to the town to support the child and pay off accrued unpaid support "plus costs." Retroactive and weekly child support over seven years would total $273.32, leaving "costs" amounting to $146.68 in the town coffers. While Potter would receive "wages" on this contract in return for the labor extracted from him, the town would also receive a handsome return for supervision that was very likely nominal.[59]

Only occasionally did circumstances require the active intervention of councils and boards of selectmen in indenture arrangements because of the extreme dissatisfaction of the master; much less frequently, because of complaints of abuse made by or on behalf of the indentured person; or because of the master's death. For example, in 1825 Amos Morris communicated repeatedly to the selectmen of Guilford, Connecticut, concerning a "Negro Boy" named Eli Bailey who had been indentured to Morris's father at the time of the elder Morris's death. Because the indenture contract terminated at the death of either party, Morris was concerned that "the heirs of the Deceased can have no controll over said Boy," who had taken the opportunity to run away. Morris wrote to the selectmen

[57] *Connecticut Journal*, December 31, 1783.

[58] Timothy Shepherd's Report, December 1, 1792, Adams Morse Papers, Massachusetts Historical Society.

[59] Providence Town Council Records, 7:424, December 13, 1799.

"trusting that they will feel themselves under the obligation to take the charge of sd boy—and provide of or Dispose of him as they may see fit."[60] There is no evidence that the selectmen bothered to take action in this case, but the language of the petitioner makes clear that the unlimited prerogative of the public, in the persons of its officials, to order the affairs of persons of color was a widely shared assumption. Although whites were sometimes bound out in like fashion, such arrangements far more commonly involved indigent, indebted, and incarcerated persons of color, sustaining the convention of their public ownership.

An extensive machinery of surveillance and interrogation also reinforced assumptions about the entitlement of white officials, acting in the public interest, to the personal histories as well as the time and labor of people of color. Town bodies throughout New England closely monitored their presence, enacted requirements that employers and landlords report their arrivals and departures, enumerated them separately on a fairly frequent basis, and conducted personal examinations to determine their place of legal residence and warn them out of town as "transients" if they did not meet criteria for suitability as inhabitants. These measures gave towns at least the illusion of controlling people of color.[61] Even when it was clearly the case that most of the adults were engaged in some form of useful, if menial, labor, the equation of emancipation with "natural" dependency and indiscipline rendered people of color everywhere a magnet for surveillance and a presumed problem requiring the management of white leaders.

By the end of the first decade or so of the nineteenth century, whites in New England had made a reluctant adjustment to the slow disappearance of slaves and the inexorable growth in the numbers of free people of color. But that adjustment consisted in large measure of reinscribing the practices of slavery and transferring their assumptions about the dependency and incapacity of slaves to free persons of color. Therefore, the new entitlement of blacks to freedom was everywhere circumscribed by the persistence of whites' imagined entitlement to control.

An 1810 case of disputed indenture, documented by the records of a series of examinations of her family members as "transients" in Providence,

[60] Amos Morris to selectmen of Guilford, 26 December 1825, written in East Haven, Miscellaneous Manuscripts, Connecticut Historical Society.

[61] In the gradual emancipation period, many New England towns passed regulations that strengthened long-standing colony laws requiring that residents report the presence of strangers, especially persons of color. See, e.g., "Acts and Resolves . . . of Rhode Island," 1767, 228–29, *Early American Imprints;* and Hopkinton Town Council Records 2:311, order of January 4, 1790.

Rhode Island, provides an unusually detailed and textured view of the nature of "freedom" and control within the framework of gradual emancipation, as perceived by its friends as well as its foes and as negotiated by its
subjects. In October 1810 an indigent black apprentice arrived on Moses
Brown's doorstep seeking asylum and assistance. She remained unnamed
both in Brown's extensive notes on the case and in an angry letter to Brown
from her putative mistress, Mary Vinton, but from Providence Town Council records authorizing her indenture in 1797 we know that her name was
Sophia Havens.

Havens wanted to know "if blks could be bound Out Longer than they
were 18." She said that she had been indentured in 1797 by the Providence
Town Council—presumably because her mother was indigent—to David
Vinton, a local shopkeeper, until she reached twenty-one years of age.
Sophia had served Vinton for thirteen years when her mother, who apparently lived in Boston, visited her and informed her that "she was Twenty-one Years old last Mo. that she was bound without her Knowledge and
had a right to her freedom." She had immediately left Vinton, but he "had
overtaken her and brot her back and taken her cloaths from her." Brown
suggested that she had "better return and live with him if he would pay her
Wages," but she insisted "she had become very Unhappy in her Scituation
and wanted her freedom." At some point the Vintons had promised her
three shillings a day for working but had failed to pay her. Brown suggested that she seek day employment with his friend Thomas Arnold.

A couple of days later, Brown went to the city clerk's office to check the
council record authorizing her indenture, which he found, and the actual
indenture contract, which could not be located; he also went to see Vinton, who "shewed me the indenture which was for 15 years." Brown told
Vinton he should pay the girl wages because "the Council had no right to
bind her Longer than till she was 18." Vinton sweet-talked him, as he later
realized: "There we Set down and Talked Matters all Over quite Satisfactorily as far as I knew; he thanking me on parting for my attention, Saying,
the Blacks had rights and it [was] a happy Circumstance that the [Aboli-
tion] Society took Care of them." But "as to this his Wife Seem'd More
despotic" and insisted "by the Indenture, they had 2 years service in her
[Sophia]. She wished me to Impress that Idea on the Girl that She was to
be their Indented Servant during that Time tho they agreed to pay her a
Dollar a Week if She would Live with them." Brown agreed to "Advise her
to go back." Subsequently, Mary Vinton sent Brown a stiff note:

> Sir, Will you be so obliging as to inform me, on what principle, & by what
> authority, you have thought proper to alienate my Servant girl from me,

& introduce her into another Service?—Reflecting on this procedure, & the active part you have taken in the business, I find it irreconcilable, either to law, equity or Christianity. I hope, Sir, your explanation will shew the justice of your Conduct, & satisfy me to acquiesce in a privati[o]n, which causes to devolve on me, the entire drudgery & concern of my family, consisting of nine persons, one of whom is sick, another an infant, & all of them too small to be usefull. With due respect, Mary Vinton.

Finally, Vinton offered to sell his claim to Sophia's time for $10.04, plus her clothes and "Some Earrings & breastpins he said he had given her but were added for her good behaviour. But as She had left them he should keep them and a little change among her things." Moses Brown paid Vinton and obtained a discharge on the young woman's Indenture, "Expecting the Girl to Work Out the 10 Dollar Advanc'd."[62]

This situation, as outlined in Brown's account and Vinton's letter, is a rich source of insights into the persistent vulnerability especially of women of color to a variety of exploitive maneuvers rooted in assumptions about their continuing availability and whites' continuing entitlement to their services within the framework of "emancipation." Brown's account of Sophia's growing discomfort with her master, her vehement resistance to suggestions that she return, Vinton's gifts of earrings and breastpins for "good behaviour," and possibly his taking of her clothes suggest that he may have pressed unwanted sexual attention on Sophia, although she herself apparently did not make this accusation to Brown. In fact, from what we know of Brown, if confronted with an unambiguous tale of rape or near-rape, he undoubtedly would have been outraged, would have noted it in his meticulous record, and certainly would not have continued to press Sophia to return to Vinton's service. But Brown seems to have been deaf to any such implications in Sophia's story. Mary Vinton, too, seems to have been unaware of any sexual tension in her husband's relationship with Sophia; at least, her determination to reestablish domestic help must have overridden such concerns, if they existed.[63]

Sophia's anonymity in both Mary Vinton's letter and Brown's notes suggests that her identity as an individual person was unimportant to either of them, but for quite different reasons. For Mary Vinton, the particularity of "my Servant girl" rested entirely in Vinton's entitlement to her; she was ful-

---

[62] Brown's detailed account of this case is carefully penned on the back of Mary Vinton's letter of September [October] 12, 1810, Moses Brown Papers, Rhode Island Historical Society.

[63] Although these suspicions seem plausible, there is no way of knowing whether they have any basis in fact, since Sophia (perhaps out of shame, fear, or resignation) made no such accusations.

ly named, from Vinton's point of view, by the proprietary "my." For Moses Brown, Sophia had only circumstantial individuality; his notes refer six times to "the Girl" and once to "the Woman." In his extensive records and correspondence concerning other victims of kidnapping, reenslavement, and unjust bondage, Brown routinely used generic terms such as "boy," "man," girl," and "woman" to refer to them; for him, they were all humanitarian projects, distinguishable only by the their particular victimization, which he detailed minutely even though frequently leaving their identities unspecified. The language of Vinton and Brown demonstrates the way the gradual emancipation process produced two overlapping discourses that rendered free people of color categorical rather than individual: abolitionist discourse, which identified them with slaves as a class of undifferentiated objects of compassion and charity; and master/employer discourse, which also identified them with slaves as a class of undifferentiated objects of ownership and entitlement.

Brown and Mary Vinton shared basic assumptions about the implicit availability of persons of color for labor, differing only in their formulation of the Vintons' entitlement to it. Mary Vinton's indignation at her own sudden responsibility for "the entire drudgery & concern of my family" (which actually must have represented quite a stunning change after her reliance on Sophia for thirteen years) as a violation of "law, equity or Christianity" rested on her assumptions of categorical as well as contractual entitlement to Sophia's labor. Brown's observation that Mary Vinton did not seem to share her husband's affirmation that "blacks had rights" reinforces this reading. But Brown, too, saw Sophia as a "natural" laborer who should "naturally" be working for the man who originally contracted for her labor—*even though* he acknowledged that person to be detaining her illegally; *even though* he knew Vinton had broken previous agreements to pay her; *even though* Sophia's emphatic resistance to returning to Vinton's employ under any terms whatsoever strongly hinted at some form of abusive behavior on Vinton's part. Brown saw Sophia's situation as an extension of slavery made illegal by the 1784 abolition statute and, at the same time, sought to extend and naturalize the relations within which that situation had developed. The actual indenture, a copy of which has survived, suggests that assumptions about people of color as natural servants were widely shared. Everywhere the word "apprentice" appeared on the printed contract, the word it was crossed out and replaced with the word "servant."[64]

Mary Vinton's letter, read against Brown's account, also reveals the com-

[64] Providence Town Papers, 28:48, August 7, 1797.

plicated gendering of work relations across "racial" lines during gradual emancipation. The letter calls Sophia "my Servant girl," one employed in "drudgery & concern of my family" under Mary Vinton's direct supervision, performing tasks that, without Sophia's presence, "devolve on me." When Brown visited David Vinton's shop, Vinton would not resolve the problem alone with Brown, insisting he "wait till I see his Wife." But in her husband's presence, Mary Vinton's assertions became plural: "They had 2 years service in her"; "She was to be their Indented Servant"; "She would live with them." On the other hand, Sophia, according to Brown, limited her references to David Vinton alone. She told Brown "she had lived with Vinton 13 years," a further indication that his conduct was her major concern. And it was David Vinton who had taken away her clothes, who had given her gifts, and who negotiated the discharge of her contract. Clearly, Sophia was subject to David Vinton's whim and ultimate power, and Mary's deferral to her husband implies that Sophia could seek no protection from Mary. At the same time, Mary, the "more Despotic" of the pair, according to Brown, directed Sophia's daily work life. These relations were completely continuous with those established under slavery.

Providence Town Council records, documenting a series of encounters between the council and Sophia's family over the course of a dozen years, frame Sophia's narrative within a longer and more complex story: a twelve-year struggle within one family of color to negotiate the transition from slavery through the bondage of involuntary indenture to some form of freedom. This additional evidence amplifies and enriches the narrative; though not really clarifying Sophia's situation and claims, it offers an alternative voice for Sophia and makes possible plural readings of aspects of her story.

In March 1785 one Deliverance Havens, "a Negro Girl" about sixteen years old, born a slave in the family of William Havens of North Kingstown and manumitted around 1784, was examined by the Providence Town Council as a transient person likely to become chargeable. With no claim to legal residence in Providence, she was rejected as an inhabitant and ordered removed to North Kingstown. Eight years later, in October 1793, a Patience Havens, fifty years old, also raised and manumitted around 1784 by William Havens and therefore almost certainly the mother of Deliverance, was examined by the Providence Town Council. With her were her three minor children: Deborah, eighteen years old; Ruth, seventeen; and Simon, seven. Patience stated that she and her children had been born in North Kingstown and had arrived in Providence a week before. The council determined that their legal residence was North Kingstown (to which they would be sent should they in fact become chargeable). No mention was made of the existence of a child of Deborah at that time. Two years later Ruth Havens was also examined and ordered removed to North Kingstown.[65]

On August 7, 1797, Deborah Havens was listed as the mother of Sophia Havens when the council directed the clerk to bind out Sophia to David Vinton "on the usual Terms, and conditions, till she arrives to the age of twenty-one years."[66] Clearly, little Sophia had become a public charge; less than a month later, her mother, Deborah Havens Greene, and her grand-mother, Patience Havens, were examined before the council and rejected as inhabitants (Patience for the second time). Deborah's examination list-ed Sophia as seven years old (born before her mother's marriage) and her brother George as eighteen months old. The council merely ordered Pa-tience to depart for North Kingstown (possibly because by that time she was fifty-three years old); Deborah, at twenty-three still producing children by a husband who was, by her account, "at sea," was ordered removed by warrant.[67]

At first glance, these pieces of evidence, together with the information Sophia gave to Brown, would seem to provide an unusually rich and co-herent twelve-year narrative of a free black family. At the very least, one would expect them to confirm Sophia's age and thus her right to be re-leased from indenture, which was the problem that brought her to Brown in the first place. But the several stories that Sophia and her mother told to Brown and to the town council cannot be reconciled on this point or, possibly, on others.

The council's instructions to the clerk and the indenture itself suggest that Sophia should have been six years old in 1797, at the time of her in-denture, in order to become twenty-one in fifteen years. Her mother's tes-timony at examination suggested that she was seven. But if she had existed to the council's knowledge as a two- or three-year-old in 1793, when her mother left North Kingstown and arrived in Providence, Sophia's legal res-idence would have been in North Kingstown, as was her mother's, and the Providence Town Council would merely have sent her there when she be-came chargeable instead of taking the trouble to bind her out (which they would have lacked jurisdiction to do, in any case). On the other hand, if she was born after October 1793, an indenture binding her out in 1797 for fifteen years would have released her at nineteen, short of the council's

[65] Providence Town Council Records, 5:302–3, March 7, 1785; 6:299, October 23, 1793; 7:69, December 17, 1795.

[66] Providence Town Papers, 28:48, August 7, 1797.

[67] Providence Town Council Records, 7:155, August 7, 1797; 7:67–168, August 31, 1797; 7:212, December 15, 1797.

mandated age of twenty-one. And by this reckoning, Sophia would have been seventeen at the moment in question, making irrelevant Brown's insistence on the illegality of the council's indenturing women of color past the age of eighteen. Even more confusing, Sophia's own mother seems to have told her in 1810 that she was twenty-one, according to her story to Brown; in that case she would have been four years old in 1793 and chargeable to North Kingstown rather than to Providence.

Why are these stories contradictory? Did Sophia invent an age of twenty-one because it made her freedom certain, regardless of the efficacy of Brown's claim that free women of color couldn't be indentured beyond the age of eighteen? In 1797, when it indentured her for fifteen years, the council evidently thought Sophia to be six, although her mother when examined three weeks later told them she was seven. Who gave them that idea? When Brown saw Sophia's indenture, clearly requiring her to serve till 1812 to fulfill fifteen years of service, did he notice that her original age claim and the indenture seemed at odds? Was Sophia in fact nineteen in 1810, making her inquiry concerning indenture past eighteen more logical? But then, where was little Sophia in 1793, when the Council established her mother's legal residence as North Kingstown? Did her mother Deborah or her grandmother Patience send her to live with someone else before they came to Providence?

Public indenture of whites and the body of information generated by the examinations of white transients were seldom so ambiguous and contradictory as this and other cases involving the public indenture of persons of color during the quarter-century of gradual emancipation. The system of transient examination was designed to elicit information from people who knew their personal history and were known in some other community to which they rightfully "belonged." But people like Patience Havens, born into slavery, had a problematical relationship to their birth communities. Although nearly every ex-slave and child raised by enslaved parents reported being raised "in the family" of the slaveowner, the great majority also reported leaving the community upon emancipation. This reflected that fact that the desirable consequence of emancipation, a movement framed in the language of removal and absence, had always been and continued to be the elimination of the person of the slave. Freed slaves regarded themselves quite realistically as having been emancipated out of that family and community of which they had been a part. Then, too, some persons of color who reported having been manumitted may in fact still have been slaves by law; as the gradual emancipation period continued, an increasing number of slaves just walked away from owners less and less concerned with hunting them down. Others simply did not know when or where they had been born. For all these people, "legal settlement" was either an empty concept or a threatening one. Often they must have shaped their stories sufficiently to gain some small control over their lives, or told different stories in various circumstances to achieve different ends, as Sophia seems to have done.

Sophia and her family, then, had slippery identities fashioned in slavery and ill-suited for systematic processing into and out of the institutions of indenture and legal settlement that formed a part of the larger structure of social participation and citizenship. These women managed to maintain their desired residence together in Providence for at least twelve years by reshaping their stories, ignoring rejections of their legal settlement, resisting orders for removal, and, possibly, hiding the existence of at least some of their children. But their achievement was a contingent and temporary solution to the enduring problems of maintaining continuity between past and present, of achieving permanence, of establishing a "home."

The last appearance of the Havenses in the official Providence records occurs in a payment notation made only two months after the last examination of Patience and Deborah as transients following Sophia's indenture. At that time the town treasurer paid Thomas Pigging $1.50 to dig a grave for Patience Havens, dead of "the malignant [yellow] fever."[68] Possibly the loss of Sophia and Patience within two months shattered the fragile family cohesion completely; perhaps Ruth remained with Deborah. In any case, sometime after August 1797 Deborah probably left Providence for Boston, since Sophia said her mother had come from Boston to visit her in 1810. In any case, the Havens women appear no more in the Providence records.

Sophia's case demonstrates that as late as 1810, both public policy and private interest were rooted in and in turn sustained assumptions about the "natural" availability of the time, labor, and personal lives of people of color for use and control as public resources by whites, and that public officials in Providence in 1810 construed these assumptions and practices to constitute the common interest of the citizens of Providence—a common interest that by definition excluded the interests of people of color, especially women and children. It also demonstrates that the racial perspectives of a passionately committed abolitionist such as Moses Brown, a basically indifferent businessman such as David Vinton, and a deeply prejudiced homemaker such as Mary Vinton were in fact systematically related, shar-

---

[68] Providence Town Papers, 28:90, October 25, 1797.

ing a common vocabulary and resting on shared assumptions. Their seem-ingly divergent perspectives were outgrowths of one common experience: the enslavement of people of color. And the assumptions on which they all rested had been mapped onto free people of color in the course of grad-ual emancipation.

4

A "Negro Spirit":
Em-bodying Difference

More ominous in some respects than the mapping of servility and
dependency, once thought to derive from the state of being enslaved, onto free people of color generally was the developing
perception by whites of this new amalgam, "free" and "of color," as a problem, a dangerous embodiment of disorder and disruption that represented a threat to the stability of the republic. The emerging status of people
of color as a "free" people appeared as both a symptom and a catalyst of
disorder. By 1835 many whites probably agreed with J. Jacobus Flournoy
that "the every riot at Electional meetings, attest[s] the pervadence of a
negro spirit," and that "[negroes] are, as I believe, a direct agent of Satan,
to the destruction of order and the distracting of the mind."[1]

Several factors contributed to the power of this idea. First, the very
wrenching apart of two halves of a seemingly indivisible term, "negro slavery"—and the recombination of the first, long a virtual synonym for slave,
with a term heretofore principally reserved for white, male, republican citizens—challenged the accustomed social order as reflected in conventional language. In colonial new England, "free" was commonly associated
with "men" in "freemen" to identify that 40 to 75 percent of adult white
males who were eligible to vote in town meetings: owners of freehold

---

[1] J. Jacobus Flournoy, *An Essay on the Origin, Habits, Etc. of the African Race: Incidental to the
Propriety of Having Nothing to Do with Negroes: Addressed to the Good People of the United States* (New
York, 1835), p. 42.

estates of a certain size, eldest sons of such owners over the age of twenty-one, men who paid sufficient rent on real estate.[2] The very terms "free negro" and "free person of color" were hybrids that reconstituted the social order. Thus free people of color formed a disruptive element of the community by their constitution as a category of being.

Second, "free" seemed to be synonymous with "uncontrolled" when it applied to people of color, "self-controlled" when it described white citizens. Slaves were by definition persons controlled by others; emancipation freed them from external control, but did not ensure the development of self-control in its stead. Whites believed that free people of color, lacking a history of self-control, could be expected to behave in socially disruptive ways.

Abolitionists, too, had seen the problem as a matter of managing the adjustment of a formerly enslaved people to freedom, not one of encouraging (or legislating) the adjustment of a slaveowning people to an inclusive expansion of their franchise. But leaders such as Levi Hart had argued strenuously against the expectation of slaves' becoming "more vicious & disorderly, & in particular, more given to stealing by being made free. . . . There is no apparent want of capacity in the Negros in general to conduct their own affairs & provide for themselves but what is the natural consequence of the Servile state they are in, & the treatment they receive." Hart and others had insisted that "common interest with others in the support of good order & preservation [of] private property" and "gratitude to the white people for procuring their liberty would tend strongly to unite them to our interest." In this view, emancipation would strengthen the social order.[3]

But the emergence of a class of free people of color, beginning as it did in the 1780s during a period of intense postwar economic hardship and political and social uncertainty, proved to be a disruptive phenomenon. A decade into gradual emancipation, (twenty years after Hart had made his arguments), abolitionists' expectations that it would enhance social order were unfulfilled. Eager to take credit for saving white society from itself by

[2] Requirements of freemanship varied, but Rhode Island's were typical: owners of freehold estates in excess of £40 ($134 after 1798), eldest sons of such freemen when they reached twenty-one years of age, and those who paid in excess of 40 shillings ($6.75) in annual rent on real estate could be admitted as freemen. Ruth Herndon reviews these rules and the sources of the estimates of eligibility in "Governing the Affairs of the Town: Continuity and Change in Rhode Island, 1750–1800" (Ph.D. diss., American University, 1992), pp. 89–91.

[3] Levi Hart, "Some Thoughts on the Subject of freeing the Negro Slaves in the Colony of Connecticut, humbly offered to the Consideration of all friends to liberty & Justice" (c. 1775), p. 4, Miscellaneous Manuscripts (typescript by Doris E. Cook, manuscript cataloguer), Connecticut Historical Society.

eradicating a sinful institution, abolitionists moved to assert leadership in the efforts to manage free people of color—in a sense, to assume the role being vacated by slaveowners—by attempting to replace coercion with moral guidance.

A broadside issued a little over a decade into the emancipation process by the national Convention of Delegates from the Abolition Societies in the United States, addressed "To the free Africans and other free People of color in the United States," offers considerable insight into the discourse of gratitude and betrayal, obligation and entitlement, disorder and control in which the "problem" of free people of color unfolded at the turn of the nineteenth century.[4] Issued in May 1797, it resonates with disappointment and frustration at the failure of the freed people to behave as Hart and the other abolitionists had promised they would. The statement of the president of the convention, Joseph Bloomfield, opens with a self-description of the convention delegates "assembled for the purpose of promoting your happiness" as "your sincerest friends." It urges "strict and faithful observance" of the advice of the preceding year, reviewed in the second half of the broadside, in order to "justify the solicitude and labors of your friends in your behalf." This message constructs free people of color as indebted to the abolitionists for their freedom and bound to behave virtuously in order to pay off their debt, evoking Hart's earlier expectation that gratitude would motivate free people of color to behave in socially acceptable ways. The message notes that "many of you have evinced, by your prudent and moral conduct, that you are not unworthy of the freedom you enjoy," implying reproachfully that many others have not evinced such worthiness. Far from a natural right, freedom here is to be earned; the implication for children born after passage of the 1784 statute (the oldest of whom would have been thirteen) is that after working for eighteen or twenty-one years to repay the slaveholder for raising them, they could anticipate a lifetime of further repayment to abolitionists in the form of constrained behavior.

Besides adding one new admonition against gambling, the message then restates the specific "advice" originally provided in the message from the convention of a year earlier: nine injunctions concerning many of the areas of "disorderly" behavior that would be the target of escalating condemnation and legal action during the first three decades of the nineteenth century throughout New England. In addition to (1) regularly attending public worship services (to "evince gratitude" yet again, this time to "your CREATOR"), free people of color were encouraged to (2) ac-

---

[4] The Convention of Delegates from the Abolition Societies in the United States [Joseph Bloomfield, President], "To the Free Africans and other free People of color in the United States," Broadside Collection, Boston Public Library.

quire education in "useful branches" and also (3) learn "useful trades"; (4) be diligent, simple and frugal; (5) abjure drinking and (6) "frolicking and amusements" that "beget habits of dissipation and vice," these in turn leading to "deserved reproach amongst your white neighbours"; (7) contract legal marriages and register all births and deaths; (8) save money and invest it; and (9) be "civil and respectful" to "remove every just occasion of complaint," since "it is by your good conduct alone that you can refute the objections which have been made against you as rational and moral creatures, and remove many of the difficulties, which have occurred in the general emancipation of such of your brethren as are yet in bondage."[5]

Here are identified virtually all the standards of conduct by which free people of color would be judged worthy or unworthy of the freedom they had received: usefulness, controlled sexuality, public and private passivity and invisibility—in other words, behavior appropriate to well-disciplined slaves. By failing in sizable numbers to meet these standards, they would betray a crucial aspect of the covenant made between Revolutionary-era abolitionists and white citizens: that once free, well-managed people of color would preserve the public order of white citizens by becoming just like them and remaining nothing at all like them simultaneously—in short, by remaining ideally slavelike.

Accusations of "disturbing the public peace" and "disorderly conduct" against people of color increased dramatically between 1784 and 1830. Repeatedly, called before town councils for "riotous behavior in the Street" were individuals such as "a young person of color who calls himself Samuel Crawford," or "the mulatto woman called Boston Nance who conducts herself in a riotous disorderly manner."[6] Their disorderly behavior was sharply defined by gender, however: women of color were characterized as disorderly in terms of sexually transgressive behavior; men, in terms of an alleged propensity for violence. The sources of this gender distinction lay less in the actual differences in the behavior of males and females than in the way those differences resonated with the conception "free negro" or "free person of color" as the embodiment of miscegenation.

The earliest concern of colonial legislators regarding the slave trade was the fear of "race" mixing, expressed clearly in the 1705–6 Massachusetts bill taxing the importation of "Negroes" for the "Preventing of a Spurious and Mixt Issue."[7] "Race" mixing in the context of slavery involved an in-

---

[5] Ibid.
[6] Providence Town Council Records, 7:442, March 28, 1800; 7:419–20, December 25, 1799.
[7] *Acts and Resolves, Public and Private, of the Province of the Massachusetts Bay, 1692–1704*

terconnected set of transgressions against community standards of propriety and the property rights of white citizens, acts seen as extremely disruptive of the social order. This perspective is reflected in the earliest colonial ordinance that addressed such mixing, published in New Netherland in 1638: "Each and every one must refrain from Fighting, Adulterous Intercourse with heathens, Blacks, or other persons, Mutiny, Theft, False Swearing, Calumny and other Immoralities."[8] All those proscribed behaviors were seen as potentially disruptive of community peace, either because they were violent in and of themselves or because they challenged the claims of rightful authority and ownership (over wives, children, slaves, other property) that undergirded the social order.

In the context of slavery, "mixt issue" initially seemed to represent a straightforward problem of managing investments. Colonial New England custom dictated that the "mixt issue" of a white woman and a male slave would be free, following the condition of the mother, and thus would constitute in some sense a value lost to the owner that might have been gained had his slave impregnated another of his slaves. Conversely, the child of a white male and a slave woman would represent an increase in the slave-owner's property.[9] The 1705–6 act of the Massachusetts General Court that taxed slave imports to prevent "race" mixing also provided punishments for fornication in an apparent attempt to prevent contractual relationships from interfering with established property rights in slaves. It prescribed sale out of the province for any "negro or molatto" man who should fornicate with an English woman or a woman of any other Christian nation, and severe whipping for both offenders; here, the slave's action could result in the direct loss of the slave's value to the owner. If the man were English or of another Christian nationality and the woman "negro or molatto," he would be whipped and fined, she sold out of the province (but not whipped); here again, "race" mixing would result in substantial loss to the slaveowner. (Failure to prescribe whipping for the transgressive female slave suggests recognition of her vulnerability to coercion.) The act further required a white father to maintain the child, a white mother either to maintain the child independently or to be bound out for the child's maintenance. Finally, the act also prohibited anyone English, Scottish, or of an-

(Boston: Wright and Potter, 1869), I:578, 579, in Lorenzo Greene, *The Negro in Colonial New England* (New York: Columbia University Press, 1942), p. 51.

[8] *Laws and Ordinances of New Netherland, 1638–1674*, comp. and trans. by E. B. O'Callaghan (Albany, 1868), p. 12, in David H. Fowler, *Northern Attitudes toward Interracial Marriage: Legislation and Public Opinion in the Middle Atlantic and the States of the Old Northwest, 1780–1930* (New York: Garland, 1987), p. 33.

[9] Fowler, *Northern Attitudes toward Interracial Marriage*, pp. 33–100, discusses the legal development of the growing distinction between the races in American law.

other Christian nationality from contracting matrimony with any "negro or molatto." Like the others, this last provision can be interpreted as protection of private property.[10]

These regulations may also be read as attempts to police the female body in general, black and white, as the site of "race" mixing, and David H. Fowler argues that in fact it was the specter of the white female body as the source of "mixt issue" that provoked passage of the act: several cases of bastardy involving sexual relations between white men and women of color had produced no legal response, whereas the 1705–6 act was passed immediately following two cases involving illicit sexual relations between white women and men of color which were tried in the Massachusetts Court of General Sessions (Fowler may be mistaking sequence for causation here, however).[11] The willingness to impose whipping sanctions on free white females but not on enslaved black ones might suggest greater outrage at the notion that white women could actively prefer the sexual attentions of men of color to those of white men; on the other hand, it might merely suggest recognition of the powerless position of female slaves or the desire to protect property. In any case, laws of this kind were only formal measures reinforcing the more common, everyday institutional arrangements that discouraged "race" mixing: the patriarchal social order among white colonists, which served to contain the sexual behavior of white women to some extent within the boundaries of (at least prospective) marriage; and slavery itself, which provided a set of behavioral codes and restrictions for enslaved women of color.

As long as slavery existed primarily in the context of the family, the rigid patriarchal order of the New England household served to restrain "race" mixing (although sexual relations across "race" were certainly not unknown within family households). Once substantial numbers of persons of color were no longer confined within white family households, however, relations across "race" became ungovernable, a manifest threat to the con-

---

[10] *Acts and Resolves . . . of Massachusetts Bay,* 1:578, in Fowler, *Northern Attitudes toward Interracial Marriage,* p. 50. Fowler and others have read southern prohibitions on miscegenation as evidence of early racial antipathy. I think that such readings impose a twentieth-century notion of "race" on a phenomenon that predates it and underestimate the degree to which relations within slavery, North and South, were conditioned by the economics of the institution. Bastardy, regardless of the "race" of the actors, was as much an economic as a moral issue in the colonies, as the careful assignment of responsibility for support in this and similar legislation attests. See Richard Burn, *The Justice of the Peace, and Parish Officer,* 12th ed., 4 vols (London: Strahan & Woodfall, 1772), a compilation with commentary of the entire development of English Law to the date of its publication. American town councillors, selectmen, justices of the peace, etc., used this as a guide to implementing American colonial law well into the nineteenth century. American laws of bastardy and settlement were modeled on British law throughout the colonial period; see esp. 1:305–13. I am indebted to Ruth Herndon for recommending Burn to my attention.

[11] Fowler, *Northern Attitudes toward Interracial Marriage,* p. 51.

ventional social order. The body of the free woman of color, cast out of the white family's patriarchal institutional structure and no longer constrained by the bonds of slavery, constituted an uncontrollable site of potential race mixing. After 1780, as the number of free people of color and children of mixed "race" as well began to increase dramatically, the number of women of color accused of "disorderly behavior" rose significantly.

By 1800 it was not unusual for women of color to be charged before the Providence Town Council with "disorderly behavior," behaving "in a very disorderly manner," or being "a disturber of the Public peace"; they included "a Certain black Woman a transient Person known by the Name of Crazy Cate," "Betsy Stanton a black woman," and "Mary Keene, transient Mulatto." In April and May alone, six different women of color were removed from Providence as "disorderly." Sometimes the accusation was slightly more explicit: Lydia Morgan was removed to Newport for being "a person of bad fame"; Betsey Sisco, a "mulatto girl about fourteen whose conduct is represented to this Council to be such as to make it improper She should be at Large," was incarcerated and, nine days later, bound out to the age of eighteen.[12]

The charge of moral disorder adhered to liaisons between black men and white women as well, but to a lesser extent and often with less severe consequences. Bristol Rhodes, a Revolutionary veteran with a $60 annual pension, was removed from Providence to Cranston, his birthplace, on the grounds "that said Bristol keeps a house of bad fame and reputation, and that he is an unsuitable person to reside in this town" because "he keeps a white woman of lewd character in his house" but "is not married to the woman aforesaid, and has no children by her." Sally Hutson, a sixteen-year-old white woman, was ordered to depart Providence for East Greenwich, her father's home, within twenty-four hours after she explained that she had "no home except at the Houses of black People." When one Mrs. Manuel made two poignant appeals in 1822 to the Providence Town Council "with a soriful heart" to remove a girl named Hannah Johnson, who was "distressing my family daly by taking the Suport they ought to have" (apparently by having distracted Mr. Manuel from his family duties), she characterized Hannah as "a ridiculous Charicter" who "lives in a hous with one Laskill a Colourd man."[13] Evidently Mrs. Manuel believed that Hannah Johnson's living arrangements constituted the key bit of damning evidence needed to push the council into removing her.

The "moral disorder" of white men of means who lived equally uncon-

[12] Providence Town Council Records, 8:14, December 15, 1800; 8:16, January 1, 1801; 7:511, September 3, 1800; 7:453–54, April–May, 1800; 8:263, June 20, 1803; 8:22, January 19, 1801.

[13] Providence Town Papers 111: 52, August 26, 1822; and 111:53, October 7, 1822.

ventional lives and who likewise consorted with women of color could be more easily ignored. A good example of an upstanding citizen whose reputation seems to have remained unblemished by the irregularity of his personal life was the prominent Benjamin Bowen of Providence, whose 1783 will distributed a large estate among his natural children by two named women and one unnamed one, another child who also may have been his offspring, and his slave Sylvia, apparently his current mistress, whom he also freed. Bowen's will was probated without objection or comment, Governor Arthur Fenner serving as executor.[14]

The patterns of "race" mixing that developed after the passage of the emancipation statutes were viewed by whites as alarming even though they actually represented a slow withdrawal of people of color from their relative integration within the communities of the whites whose slaves they had been into more solidly black communities on the margins of white neighborhoods. In fact, whites paradoxically found dense communities of color to be as disturbing as mixed communities, since in neither case were the people of color any longer reliably under white control. Whites developed new strategies to contain and control the spaces used and inhabited by people of color and the activities that took place there, especially those that mixed the "races."

From the earliest years of slavery, when slaves lived in white households and could find occasional refuge from constant surveillance only by slipping away to private spaces to enjoy gatherings and entertainments, whites had attempted to police the recreational choices of people of color. Beginning in 1693 in Massachusetts the New England colonies had passed a series of laws forbidding licensed innkeepers and private housekeepers alike from entertaining combinations of whites and slaves, or Indians and slaves, or free persons of color and slaves—all thought to be volatile mixtures of unlike kinds of persons. Some of these laws also sought to prevent the sale of liquor to free white minors and free and enslaved persons of color—that is, people assumed to lack self-control, whose consorting and drinking together were construed to be disruptive of the public peace. For example, in the early 1750s, complaint was made in South Kingstown that "one Jacob a M[ul]atto man keepeth a Disorderly house frolicking entertaining Servants &c"; the case was dismissed, "he having promised to Suffer no Disorders For Future." A year later, also in South Kingstown, complaint was made against Christopher Fowler, a white tavern owner, "for Keeping a Disorderly house allowing people to play Cards and Entertaining Indeons Negros &c"; this case was dismissed when no one appeared to press the

---

[14] Providence Town Council Records, 8:173, July 12, 1802; 8:395–96, August 13, 1804.

complaint. In Boston the selectmen ordered retailers not to "sell or deliver rum and other spiritous liquors to Negro and Mullatto servants, not bringing certificates from their masters" and not to "allow [such] persons to sit tippling in their houses." These efforts to restrain the disorder thought to be associated with the free use of liquor, lack of supervision, and unrestrained mixing of free and enslaved, white and nonwhite people continued after 1784, as more and more people of color themselves became able to provide opportunities for such behavior. In 1785 the Newport City Court heard the case of Thomas Ferguson, "a Negro man" accused of "entertaining slaves in his house and permitting them to dance there." His case was dismissed. But by 1822 the formal licenses issued by the City of Providence "to retail strong liquors" often included a clause forbidding the grantee from allowing "any person of colour to take charge of his store."[15]

Drinking and "frolicking" in taverns and private homes in the neighborhoods of free people of color was seen as even more threatening when it spilled out into public spaces in the very late evening. In an earlier time, slaveowners could be counted on to help enforce laws such as those in Boston forbidding "Negroes and mulattoes" from carrying sticks or canes in public places and from being on the streets at all after nine o'clock at night.[16] By the turn of the century, in an attempt to curb what they saw as the increasing threat to the public welfare presented by disorderly free people of color and mixed groups in the streets late at night, town councils were ordering night watchmen to detain, question, and incarcerate people committing "disorderly" acts. For example, in November 1799 the Providence Town Council ordered the night watch to "suppress riotous conduct in the streets, to commit all refactory persons to Bridewell" (a detention facility); the order did not target a specific group, but four of the next six individuals so detained were persons of color. Four months later, apparently after the night watch reported instances of resistance to their questioning, the council stretched the definition of disorderly conduct to include unresponsiveness and voted that anyone walking around in the streets after eleven o'clock who should refuse to give his name to a night watchman should be deemed disorderly and detained. The next detainee was "a Person of Color who calls himself Samuel Crawford," accused of "Ri-

[15] Greene, *The Negro in Colonial New England*, pp. 134–37, offers a litany of laws governing consorting and drinking in public houses and private homes in Massachusetts, Connecticut, and New Hampshire. South Kingstown Town Council and Probate Records, 4:22, February 10, 1752, and 4:224, February 12, 1753; *Records of the Boston Selectmen, 1754–1763* 19 (1887): 7 (August 12, 1761); Newport City Court Records, January 11, 1785; Providence Town Papers, 111:142.

[16] Greene, *The Negro in Colonial New England*, p. 299.

otous behavior in the Street." Samuel was fortunate enough to be discharged.[17]

These measures sought to regulate spaces usually controlled by men, where men gathered. The form of disorder whites feared from men of color, and from the mixing of enslaved and free men of color with white men and boys in taverns and in the streets, was violence, or violent resistance to authority. Until the advent of gradual emancipation, virtually all persons of color lived in white-dominated households, and thus domestic spaces were not seen as potential sites of disorder on the part of people of color. But by the 1780s, as independent communities of free people of color inevitably grew in size and steadily edged away from white presence and authority, residence itself began to attract attention as the perceived locus of disorder. As white officials tried to regulate the living situations of free people of color, a gendered distinction emerged: moral disorder was the province of women in the activities of the household and, more particularly, the bedroom; civic disorder was the province of men.

Women of color were often accused of running "a disorderly house," frequently a euphemism for a brothel but often merely a boardinghouse that catered to a mixed clientele. Public officials only reflected private sentiment; as early as 1782 a mob pulled down the house of Margaret Bowler, alias Fairchild, who had rented the old jail in Providence five years earlier for $1,400 (paper money) a year to use as a boardinghouse. Upon examination by the town council, Margaret listed the occupants of her house as Phebe Bowen, Betsy Bowen, "another white woman called Debby," Black Bets, and "a Molatto girl of eighteen or nineteen years." Even though Margaret's yearly rent qualified her for legal settlement and she had been an unfortunate victim of illegal mob violence, the council had her removed to Newport. Again in 1783 and in 1784, Providence mobs destroyed "disorderly" houses of black women. Likewise, the Reverend John Eliot reported in 1795 that relations between blacks and whites in Boston were generally harmonious "except in houses of ill-fame where some very depraved white females get among the blacks," which had resulted in "the pulling down of such houses at times."[18] The riots of white mobs against people of color which flared in Providence, Hartford, Boston, and elsewhere in the 1820s and 1830s were foreshadowed by the violence of the 1780s and 1790s surrounding the emergence of free people of color as a visible and disturbing class.

[17] Providence Town Council Records, 7:419–20, November 25, 1799; 7:440, March 3, 1800; 7:442, March 28, 1800.

[18] Ibid., 7:442, March 28, 1800; 8:138, January 10, 1802; 5:212–13, July 24, 1782; 7:453–54; 5:231, May 5, 1783; 5:293, November 1, 1784; Newport Town and City Council Records, City Court of Newport Minutes, January 11, 1785; *Massachusetts Historical Society Collections*, 5th ser., 3 (1891):383.

Often, public officials actively undermined the independence of women of color, and especially the independence of their sexuality, in their efforts to control spaces in which "race" mixing might take place. For example, in January 1802 Margaret Simons, a woman of color, was confined to Bridewell for disorderly conduct and only released "provided she goes to work in some family and does not set up the Keeping of a House in this place." Margaret may have submitted to wage work for a time, but in 1804 she was again running a boardinghouse, according to Sarah Babcock, a transient woman of color who testified that she lived there.[19] The sexual activity of people of color was construed to be disorderly even when it did not involve "race" mixing, in that it often ignored or defied community rules and conventions. Legal marriage, legitimacy of births, legal settlement—all these were tests of suitability for community acceptance, tests that people of color frequently failed. Although whites too often failed to marry legally and to gain legal settlement, people of color were publicly questioned on these matters and suffered punishments as a consequence in grossly disproportionate numbers.

Women of color, and sometimes men as well, were frequently required to give explicit evidence of the legitimacy of their family arrangements to public officials. Sylvia Taylor, "a Mulatto Woman" of South Kingstown, Rhode Island, insisted to the Providence Town Council in 1795 that she had been married to James Helme, but the clerk reported that she was "ignorant of the person who married her, has no marriage certificate, has a female Child of the Age of Nine Months"—clearly responses to skeptical questioning. Sylvia was removed to South Kingstown forthwith. Five years later, when the marriage of Robert Lovett, "a black man born in Guinea," was questioned, he was able to name a "Mr. Waldo of Attleborough" as the man who had legally married him to Maria Mends of Mindon, Massachusetts, eight years before.[20]

The spaces occupied by people of color began to be seen as threatening to the civic order when the density of independent black households on the margins of white neighborhoods increased after the 1780s. At the first federal census, in 1790, nearly 64 percent of free people of color were living in independent households in Boston, at least 65 percent in Providence and in New Haven.[21] Because census takers in these towns and cities

[19] Providence Town Council Records, 8:138, January 20, 1802; 8:140, January 28, 1802; 8:355, January 27, 1804.

[20] Ibid., 7:66–67, December 17, 1795; 8:1, November 12, 1800.

[21] The source for these numbers is the following series of volumes by state: Bureau of the Census, *Heads of Families at the First Census of the United States Taken in the Year 1790* (Washington, D.C.: Government Printing Office, 1908), Rhode Island, Providence Town, pp. 33–37; Massachusetts, Boston Town, pp. 183–95; Connecticut, New Haven City, pp. 102–5. Because the totals given for "all other free persons" (free persons of color) for "Hartford Town" can-

recorded household information as they moved physically through neighborhoods, names listed consecutively can be assumed to represent physically contiguous households; on this basis the census lists suggest that 27 percent of free people of color in Providence lived in proximity to at least two other households of color, and more than 16 percent lived in groups of four households or more. In Boston nearly 23 percent of free people of color lived in groups of four households or more and over 12 percent in proximity to at least six other black households. (Lack of nearby black households did not necessarily isolate individuals: five of the black households isolated in white neighborhoods in Boston each had ten or more members.) In New Haven, with a much smaller population of free people of color, none lived in groups of four or more black households and less than 16 percent in three, but 38 percent lived next to at least one other household of color.

Black residential neighborhoods began to attract increasingly negative attention as sites of disorder after 1800. Boardinghouses continued to arouse the wrath of white leaders for attracting transients, sailors (many of whom were persons of color), and "loose" women. In October of that year, for example, Jenny Rhodes, a white woman, was given a week to depart from Providence because she was running a boardinghouse for black sailors; when she had failed to leave in a month's time, she was bound out to service.[22] But a new problem began to emerge at the same time: complaints about "tenements" housing black residents began to appear in public records as an even greater threat to the public welfare. For example, on February 7, 1800, the Providence Town Council voted to empower the town treasurer, Samuel Nightingale, to hire a lawyer to prosecute a white doctor, Thomas Greene, "for admitting into one of his Tenements to reside, certain transient black people." Two of these residents, Jacob Hull and Katy Holden, appeared before the council to testify that they indeed lived together in Greene's tenement, quarters rented by Katy's mother, Margaret Holden, who now lived "in" as a servant to a Captain Page else-

---

not be generated by adding numbers of persons in columns so headed (i.e., the totals do not tally), Hartford is not used as an example here. Robert J. Cottrol, *The Afro-Yankees: Providence's Black Community in the Antebellum Era* (Westport, Conn.: Greenwood Press, 1982), states that only 26.8 percent of all blacks were living in independent black households in 1790 and that "only 44 of 276 blacks listed in the census were slaves" (pp. 47–49). But since the 1790 census for Providence accounts for 48 slaves and 427 "other [nonwhite] free persons," I am at a loss to explain his figures or his conclusions. A calculation of the percentage of all people of color, free and enslaved, who lived in independent households would yield 58.3 percent in Providence, 40.1 percent in New Haven, and 63.2 percent in Boston (where no slaves were reported). Of course, I am using the numbers here to make a point somewhat different from Cottrol's.

[22] Providence Town Council Records, 7:568, October 28, 1800; 8:6, November 28, 1800.

where in Providence. A week later Greene appeared before the council, to beg that he not be prosecuted, and charges were dropped upon payment of costs. But a year later the council was still warning out black transients such as Margaret Simmons, "who said she lived in a house belonging to Doct. Thomas Greene." In the meantime, one Stephen Harris had also come under fire for renting a tenement he owned to James Merrit, "a black man."[23] Efforts to prosecute whites who rented to transients of color subsided after a couple of years, probably because the landlords were so frequently prosperous and well-known citizens, but tenement dwellers themselves continued to be targets of official surveillance and interrogation.

The growing concern on the part of Providence officials over disorder in black neighborhoods was exacerbated by outbreaks of yellow fever, which had raged intermittently since the 1790s. The epidemic of 1800–1801 focused new attention on living conditions in the tenements as a threat to public health as well as to peace and safety, attention that continued after yellow fever had subsided as a specific threat. Since established medical opinion linked noxious smells with disease, the special health committee assigned to patrol the streets to identify nuisances paid particular attention to low-lying areas with poor drainage and to crowded conditions that produced large amounts of garbage and overflowing necessaries—in other words, the areas along the river where the tenements had been built.[24] A report of the council's Committee on Nuisances in 1821 is typical: "Where there are four black families crowded into a small house as in this instance having no other means of disposing of their filth, except laying it in the Street there will all ways be a nuisance evented in a few days." Tellingly, the same committee also complained soon after about the yard and privy of "John Brown Keeper of the sailor boardinghouse."[25]

Another consequence of the yellow fever epidemic of 1800 was the worsening economic conditions it created. According to a letter drafted by the Providence Town Council, although the disease was confined principally to the south part of town, "the alarm occasioned thereby has induced about one third of the Inhabitants (comprising the most wealthy) to leave their abodes, this with the Stoppage of the Coasting trade and the Suspension of the necessary Supplies from the Country, and the general stag-

[23] Ibid., 8:431, February 7 and 15, 1800; 8:46, March 17, 1801; 8:450, April 26, 1800.

[24] Ruth Wallis Herndon, "Clearing the Public Ways: Animal Pollution and Animal Control in 18th Century Rhode Island" (paper presented at the annual meeting of the American Studies Association, Nashville, Tennessee, October 28, 1994), describes the evolution of the late eighteenth-century efforts of Rhode Island officials to beautify and sanitize urban environments.

[25] Providence Town Papers, 111 (1821–22): 30, 60.

nation of business has operated greatly to the disadvantage of the laboring poor who are destitute of employ." As a precautionary measure, the council put on a special watch in the affected area "to prevent looting."[26] Here, the "laboring poor" themselves were considered a kind of secondary infection, threatening to invade and destroy terrain already ravaged by yellow fever. This particular letter makes no overt reference to people of color, but their concentration in the waterfront tenements in the south part of town suggests that they were part of the perceived threat. Indeed, a month after the letter was drafted the council ordered that a census of all blacks, as well as transient whites in poor circumstances, be undertaken, and four months later it voted to pay one Henry Alexander for "reporting the number of blacks in the south part of Town."[27] And once more, in June 1822, the Providence Town Council ordered a written census of people of color on the pretext of notifying them that "if they receive into their Houses or Possessions any transient white persons or colored people to reside . . . they will be prosecuted." On this basis the council secured, ostensibly as evidence that "such persons have been duly notified," a written list of names of "all Coloured people in this Town who are Housekeepers" and adult family members, an enumeration of their children, and an identification of the "Owners of the Houses & Tenements wherein they reside."[28]

By the early 1800s, then, "disorder" had come to characterize free black people as a collectivity partly as the imaginative reconstitution of their dependency: whites saw them as unmanaged, incapable of self-management, and thus requiring management by whites. But this characterization was also in part a response to the actual forms of their resistance to continued efforts to subordinate them. The examinations of transients and other sources reveal that as whites ignored or failed to grasp the meaning of black freedom, many people of color refused to engage or acknowledge whites' institutional frameworks such as "legal settlement" and "racial identity." People of color *were* disorderly: that is, they refused (or failed, as whites often saw it) to order themselves according to institutional rules that disadvantaged them.

People of color flagrantly disregarded the statutory requirements for obtaining "legal settlement" in towns and cities, living where they chose and returning to their desired places of residence repeatedly after being warned out, even when threatened with whippings or confinement in a

---

[26] Providence Town Council Records, 7:543, September 29, 1800; and 7:547, October 1, 1800.

[27] Ibid., 7:575, November 6, 1800; 8:41, March 11, 1801.

[28] Providence Town Papers, 112 (1821–22): 118.

workhouse. For example, Zelph Carpenter, warned out of Providence in 1784, returned in 1787 and was confined to the "cage" in the workhouse and then whipped ten stripes. Notwithstanding, she returned in November of the same year, winning permission to stay for a week if she would then depart, on pain of twenty stripes if she did not. Seventeen years later Zelph was back before the council. Jacob Hull was examined and warned out sometime before 1800 and again in February, April, and November of 1800. Four years later he appeared before the town council yet again concerning his legal settlement; a new set of council members, apparently unaware of his previous visits, merely warned him out again instead of escalating his punishment.[29]

The resistance of free people of color to the requirements of legal settlement suggests more than simple determination to flout rules for the sake of doing so. The towns in which free people of color had been born, many as slaves or statutory servants, offered relatively few employment opportunities and represented associations of dependency that many were anxious to leave behind. There were few reasons for free people of color to remain at "home," and many reasons to leave. Some transient blacks representing themselves as free had never been legally emancipated. In any case, port cities such as Boston and Providence offered employment opportunities unavailable elsewhere. Large numbers of men of color became sailors, the most "racially" mixed occupational group in the early antebellum period.[30]

The presence of free people of color was merely the most visible and, to whites, irritating symptom of the growing disjuncture between the traditional New England community—organized around such concepts as legal settlement—and the ever more mobile and fractured, commercially oriented society of 1800 and after, to which community leaders tried vainly to continue to apply the old rules. The whole notion of legal settlement was predicated upon stasis: the idea of maintaining internal stability within communities as relatively closed systems by repelling external elements that might disturb the fragile balance of need and resources sustained by interdependent people enacting roles transmitted relatively unchanged

[29] Providence Town Council Records, 6:13, July 7, 1787; 6:28, November 7, 1787; 7:443, April 1, 1800; 8:358, January 27, 1804.

[30] James Oliver Horton, *Free People of Color: Inside the African American Community* (Washington, D.C.: Smithsonian Institution Press, 1993), pp. 25–39, discusses black migration to Boston. The Providence Town Council Records and Town Papers provide compelling evidence of the migration of people of color to the city from outlying Rhode Island towns as well as from Connecticut and Massachusetts towns. W. Jeffrey Bolster, *Black Jacks: African American Seamen in the Age of Sail* (Cambridge, Mass.: Harvard University Press, 1997), documents the considerable presence of African Americans in the New England maritime trades.

through generations. The rapid transformation of a class of dependent, subordinated workers within a system of household production into a class of free, independent wage workers could not be accommodated by communities in which there was not as yet a substantial demand for industrial wage labor; the shrinking availability of unsettled land was forcing numbers of whites, too, into outmigration or wage labor. Free people of color constituted an element of disorder merely by virtue of being a new category in a system with no space to accommodate it. Then, too, this new category emerged during the particularly disabling and disruptive period of economic hardship that followed the Revolution in the mid-1780s, when the economy was less able to absorb either new workers or the newly destitute, and former slaveowners were less able to pay wages to former slaves than they might have been a decade earlier and would be a decade later.

Tenement dwellers and "transients" eking out a living as day laborers or threatening to become public charges, however, were not the only groups of people of color to constitute a disruptive element. By 1800 a stubbornly achieving black working class and tiny middle class, located most visibly in cities such as Hartford, Boston, and Providence, represented disorder in quite a different way. Their measure of success in inserting themselves into the economic structure constituted yet another of the paradoxes represented by the very existence of free people of color. In communities still bound by the conception of economic, social, and political position as constituting one's integrated status—one's "place" in society—the appearance of free people of color as independent players was revolutionary. It seemed a forcible entry, a violent overthrow of assumptions about the neat configuration of citizenship, virtue, and economic success embodied in "free men," who as late as 1780 could be assumed to be white.

Before 1780 the few, anomalous free persons of color could be construed as exemplars of that old chestnut, the exception that proves the rule. The rare painter, poet, mathematician, or entrepreneur of color could be "taken up" as some sort of prodigy, often regarded as a product of white philanthropy or at least sufferance. Phillis Wheatley, Benjamin Baneker, and Paul Cuffe were thus understood and applauded. It could be argued that the attention paid to such unique black "geniuses" in the eighteenth century served principally to demonstrate the unbridgeable chasm between them and the multitude of people of color, for whom such achievements were unthinkable. But by 1800, considerable numbers of "free men" were people of color, people onto whom the characteristics previously associated with the status of slave had been unquestioningly mapped, as we have seen. How, then, could whites interpret the rising numbers of people of color whose relative prosperity could not be discounted as a result of their peculiar genius, but who instead represented a collectivity—of citizens?—intruding into an economy where there was no imagined space for them?

Occupational data on free people of color in major New England cities before the Civil War is spotty, but available information suggests that between 4 and 14 percent of men of color were engaged in professional or skilled occupations. According to the *African Repository,* of 408 persons of color whose occupations were reported in 1830, 69 percent were either mariners or laborers; another 20 percent were barbers, waiters, and shopkeepers; but the remaining 11 percent worked in twenty-one different skilled or professional occupations.[31] The Committee upon the Condition of the Colored People reported to the 1843 National Convention of Colored Citizens in Buffalo that thirty-five skilled and professional workers among free people of color held total assets of $100,000 in New Bedford.[32] More detailed, statewide estimates of the business assets, occupational characteristics, and employment status of free people of color were made in a report to the Colored National Convention of 1855, held in October in Philadelphia, by the Committee on Mechanical Branches among the Colored People of the Free States. According to this committee, free people of color "in active business" in Massachusetts, Maine, Rhode Island, and Connecticut had assets worth $2,000,000 in 1855. Further, on the basis of its own occupational census, the committee estimated that there were 448 skilled workers and professionals among free people of color in Maine, Vermont, Massachusetts, and Connecticut and that three out of four of these were currently employed in nearly fifty separate skilled professions. (The committee received no returns for Rhode Island and New Hampshire.) Although there is no way of assessing the accuracy of these figures, this information demonstrates that *people of color themselves* believed that 4.5 percent of their adult populations in four New England states were skilled workers or professionals, more than three-quarters of whom were successfully employed.[33]

[31] *African Repository* 13 (March 1837): 90, in Lorenzo J. Greene and Carter G. Woodson, *The Negro Wage Earner* (1930; New York: Russell & Russell, 1969), p. 5.

[32] "Minutes of the National Convention of Colored Citizens" (Buffalo, August 1843), pp. 38–39, in *Minutes of the Proceedings of the National Negro Conventions: 1830–1864,* ed. Howard Holman Bell, (New York: Arno Press and the New York Times, 1969). Various national and local conventions were organized by free black leaders during the antebellum period as forums for discussion of issues crucial to improving the "condition"—the social well-being and political status—of free people of color.

[33] I have used the populations of people of color in Maine, Vermont, Massachusetts, and Connecticut as reported in the federal census of 1860 to make this calculation; see Bureau of the Census, *Negro Population, 1790–1915* (Washington, D.C.: Government Printing Office, 1918), table 6, "Negro Population, Slave and Free, at Each Census by Divisions and States:

The federal census of 1850 tabulated statewide occupational data for men of color in Connecticut (alone among New England states). Of a total of 1,973 men of color, employed in a wide range of occupations, nearly three-quarters were listed as either laborers or mariners and almost 10 percent as servants, cooks, or barbers. Nonetheless, over 7 percent were reported to be farmers (and thus presumably independent producers); nearly 2 percent were merchants, ministers, or shopkeepers; skilled craft occupations such as blacksmith, gunsmith, carriagemaker, shoemaker, and ship's carpenter accounted for another 5 percent, and skilled personal services such as tailoring and clerking accounted for nearly 2 percent.[34] The notes accompanying the table sneered that "in Connecticut there are only twenty individuals [of color] engaged in occupations requiring education, or one in one hundred of the whole."[35] Assuming that the number of professionals is correctly reported, however, a more illuminating approach might be to note that 9 percent of adult males of color were professionals or owned their own businesses and farms, and another 5 percent were skilled craftsmen—a visible minority. And even the unskilled employment of the vast majority, involving independently contracted day labor, must have occasioned envy and resentment on the part of increasingly proletarianized working-class whites, subjected to ever more regimented factory work. (The fact that people of color for the most part did not choose to avoid factory work but rather were excluded from most such jobs does not alter the impact of their visible freedom from factory discipline.)

Data from several sources, then, document the presence in New England in the early nineteenth century of a small class of skilled and professional people of color, and a much larger group of men of color who continued to work as unskilled laborers largely outside the encroaching factory system. The 1855 estimates presented to the Colored National Convention demonstrate the consciousness of black leaders that such a class was growing and constituted a potent source of pride, strength, and power among people of color as a whole. Moreover, independent households headed by persons of color suddenly warranted inclusion in city directories: those of Boston in 1828, Providence in 1832, and Hartford in 1843.[36]

1790–1860," p. 57. I have assumed half of each total population to be "adult," (over nineteen), using age distribution calculations based on table 3, "Negro Population Classified by Sex and Quinquennial Age Periods: 1910 and 1900," p. 164.

34 J. D. B. DeBow, Superintendent of the United States Census, *Statistical View of the United States, . . . being a Compendium of the Seventh Census; to which are added the resuts of every previous census, beginning with 1790. . . .* (Washington, D.C.: Government Printing Office, 1854), table 70, pp. 80–81.

35 Ibid., p. 81.

36 *Directory of Boston, Massachusetts* (Boston: Hunt & Simpson, 1828); *Directory of Providence,*

Nevertheless, it seems clear that to whites this emerging class represented a disturbing and much-resented element. Just as the earliest awareness
of "free people of color" as a category in New England had taken shape
during a period of extreme economic dislocation in the 1780s, the class of
independent, skilled workers and professionals of color emerged during
the economic instability and rapid change of the 1820s, a period that
brought hard times to many white families. The rise of manufacturing,
spurred by the Embargo and Non-Intercourse Acts and the War of 1812,
was moving production out of households and independent shops into fac-
tories; the growth of commerce was fostering specialization and deper-
sonalizing the exchange of goods. These changes were transforming
preindustrial life for whites by restricting their independence, regiment-
ing their use of time, and altering the nature of work, especially women's
work. Whites clearly found the adjustment difficult; at the same time, they
could see that many free people of color appeared able either to negotiate
the new order successfully or maintain some degree of independence from
it. Whites found any degree of success among blacks—any evidence of free
people of color *living like white people*—to be as disruptive of the social order as the presence of indigent, dependent, transient, or publicly rowdy
ones.

Emancipation enacted its disturbing transformation of a previously
fixed and safely stable identity—black/slave—in the larger context of post-
Revolutionary instability. The hierarchical social order in the colonial period had always been somewhat more fluid in American than in British
practice, yet it remained a constant and reassuring ideal until republican
rhetoric and post-Revolutionary economic and political turmoil destabilized it. Ordinary citizens, wondering how Revolutionary social change
might affect their previously secure role and status, watched the transformation of slaves into free people of color with its two quite different kinds
of consequences, both very visible: a disruptive and dependent poverty on
the one hand, an upstart and intrusive prosperity on the other. As part of
this transformation, whites also saw a theretofore reliable "marking" system for identifying persons as enslaved or free by their physical characteristics break down and become inoperative. Males of color were becoming
free men; could they also become freemen?

Widely held environmental theory explained servile demeanor, condition,
and even physical attributes as environmental effects. Comte de Buffon,

Rhode Island (Providence: H. H. Brown, 1832); *Geer's Directory of Hartford, Connecticut* (Hartford: Elihu Geer, 1843).

Samuel Stanhope Smith, and others argued that the physical characteristics of Africans were associated with their equatorial origin and would change over time to become more similar to those of the white European.[37] At the same time, antislavery advocates insisted that the negative social and psychological characteristics generally attributed to slaves—lack of mental acuity, laziness, dependency, and so forth—were consequences of enslavement. Persons of color had become slavelike in slavery; emancipation and firm guidance on the part of whites would diminish, if not eradicate, those characteristics over time. Environmental theory promised qualitative transformation as well as physiological adaptation.

Although this argument had reassured white colonists contemplating the possibility of emancipation sometime in the future, it gained troubling implications in the post-Revolutionary climate of anxiety over the uncertain outcome of revolutionary social change. The disassociation of "slave" and "negro" in the course of emancipation also resulted, inevitably, in the wrenching apart of the previously unchallenged correlation "free" and "white," leaving open all possible permutations of the four terms. "White" and "slave," "negro" and "free" emerged, floating and unanchored, available as an explanatory and metaphorical language that had great utility in the unstable post-Revolutionary environment for investigating and describing the disruptive political, social, and perhaps biological consequences of democracy as well as emancipation. People of color served as a kind of case study or reference point, but such investigations implied the possible transformation of whites as well.

Many scholars have noted the heightened interest in issues surrounding people of color in post-Revolutionary America, but most, such as Winthrop Jordan, have viewed this development as a fairly straightforward element of the ongoing debate over the role that blacks and slavery would play in the new republic, itself part of the developing construction of a national identity.[38] David R. Roediger has explored the debasement of black culture as a key element in the formation of post-Revolutionary working-class identity, but he focuses on the distancing of whites from the continuing association with slavery that people of color represented.[39] The link between

[37] George Louis Leclerc, Comte de Buffon, *Histoire Naturelle,* trans. in *Barr's Buffon: Buffon's Natural History, containing A Theory of the Earth, A General History of Man . . . &c. &c. from the French with Notes by the Translator,* vol. 3 (London: H. D. Symonds, 1797), pp. 324–25, 334–40, 348–52; Samuel Stanhope Smith, *An Essay on the Causes of the Variety of Complexion and Figure in the Human Species. . . . ,* 2d ed. (New Brunswick, N.J.: J. Simpson, 1810).

[38] Winthrop Jordan, *White over Black: American Attitudes toward the Negro, 1550–1812* (Chapel Hill: University of North Carolina Press, 1968), pp. 334–35.

[39] David R. Roediger, *The Wages of Whiteness: Race and the Making of the American Working Class* (New York: Verso, 1991), esp. pp. 43–60.

northern emancipation and new modes of "racial" discourse has been noted much less frequently.

Shane White, examining the connection between emancipation and racial attitudes in popular media in the middle Atlantic states in the 1780s and 1790s, finds a "curiously disembodied quality" in most of the discussion of the place of blacks in America during this period.[40] One could also argue exactly the opposite position from his evidence: that the almost pornographic portrayal of slaves as commodities and objects of abuse in the magazines and newspapers of elites, on the one hand, and, on the other, sympathetic portrayals of free blacks in rural-oriented almanacs, using distinctive physical and linguistic traits rather than slavery as the source of humor, served to embody, not disembody, the discussion about free people of color. But almanac humor is just a small part of an extensive literature of black/white role reversal that suddenly appeared after 1780. This literature seems clearly linked to whites' interpretation of the emergence of free people of color, whether dependent or successful, as a disruptive factor, somehow not merely symptomatic of but actually engendering the disordering of society, with implications or possibly direct consequences for the role, status, and even "nature" of whites.

Role-reversal literature, constituting a new mode of "racializing" discourse in the early republic, seemed to consist of two distinct but related types whose development overlapped somewhat. The first comprised journalistic, "scientific," and autobiographical accounts, some fictionalized, which explored the literal possibilities of transformation posed by the application of an environmental theory of difference to actually occurring phenomena. Although these accounts diminished in number after 1810, references to them continued to appear in polemical literature on "race" through the 1830s.

The second type explored the appropriation of traditionally white social roles by people of color and involved the ventriloquistic production of fictional persons of color as objects of humor or derision, beginning with the almanac dialogues of the 1780s and 1790s. This fictional genre reached its zenith between 1815 and 1830 with elaborate burlesques in which people of color were ridiculed as inept poseurs imitating the public performances and practices of citizenship in outlandish ways. Just as the journalistic and autobiographical literature responded to actual situations and natural phenomena, the humorous anecdotes and burlesques responded to real events—for example, the establishment of an alternative

---

[40] Shane White, *Somewhat More Independent: The End of Slavery in New York City, 1770–1810* (Athens: University of Georgia Press, 1991), pp. 61–75.

Independence Day celebration on July 14 by people of color to commemorate the closing of the slave trade. But whereas the journalistic and autobiographical accounts of the 1780s and 1790s tested the mutability of the blackness and whiteness of real, living persons in the face of extreme alterations in their conditions and social roles, the humorous anecdotes and especially the burlesques of the early 1800s treated this question as resolved; in them, blackness and whiteness had become rigid, immutable categories, and the humor lay in placing highly stylized caricatures of free persons of color in citizenship roles to which they were "naturally" unsuited. In other words, in its second phase, role reversal replaced real, diverse people of color with imaginary ones who were predictably, and "naturally," alike. In this respect, the anecdotes and burlesques, although clearly a response to anxiety over the social disorder produced by emancipation and revolution, were also part of a much larger discourse of removal—attempts to realize the promise of Revolutionary antislavery to eliminate "the problem" of slavery (that is, slaves/people of color)—which animated New England in the second and third decades of the nineteenth century. (Close examination of the burlesque literature is reserved for the next chapter, which focuses on removal.) In the 1780s and 1790s, though, with mutability questions not yet resolved, much of the early role reversal literature was an attempt to work through and resolve them and, in so doing, to restore order to the Republic.

Two actual situations that engendered extraordinary interest and anxiety in this period and produced extensive literatures of role reversal were the apparent transformation of black skin into white (instances of albinism and vitiglio) and the protracted captivity and enslavement of whites, especially Americans, in the so-called Barbary States of North Africa. These situations suggested that environmental theory might have disturbing implications. If the "markings" of enslaveability were indeed mutable and could disappear gradually in freedom, might the relationship be inverted? Could enslavement transform whites into a servile people, as dependent and instrumental as black slaves? If so, physical characteristics might not be a reliable indicator of "aptitude" for enslavement. Underlying these questions was a profound anxiety over the unmanageability of revolutionary social change; the literature of role reversal posed questions about the "nature" of citizenship in terms of the "nature" of enslaveability and the permanence of its signs.

Many scholars have noted the intense public interest generated in the mid-1790s by the case of Henry Moss, an American-born man of African descent whose dark skin turned white in his early middle age. Ronald Takaki, Shane White, and others have read Moss's case as illuminating whites' concern about the role or "place" of blacks in the new republic. White also has suggested that interest in Moss was part of a broader "curiosity about freaks."[41]

While it is true that the public fascination with physical anomalies embraced "freaks of nature" of all kinds, human and otherwise, it might be useful to place both interests within the larger context of the Enlightenment enthusiasm for classification, observation, and experiment and, more specifically, for analytical physiognomics: seeking systematic correspondences between the external characteristics or markings of living creatures and innate truths about their nature and condition, and classifying them according to the differences perceived. In the preceding half-century a host of scientific discoveries and inventions such as the microscope had altered human perspective and seemed to offer a window on previously inaccessible inner structures of the natural world. American philosophers such as Samuel Stanhope Smith (1787) and leading European naturalists such as Comte de Buffon (1797) attempted detailed ethnographic descriptions of the world's human populations, classified by "races"[42]—fol-

---

[41] Ibid., p. 66; Ronald T. Takaki, *Iron Cages: Race and Culture in 19th-Century America* (Seattle: University of Washington Press, 1979), pp. 16–35; Benjamin Moss, "Acount of Henry Moss, a White Negro: together with Reflections on the Affection called, by Physiologists, Leucaethiopia humana; Facts and Conjectures relative to the White Colour of Animals, and Observations on the Colour of the Human Species," *Philadelphia Medical and Physical Journal* 2 (1806): 3–18. To Takaki, the importance of Moss's case was its role in Rush's diagnosis of blackness as leprosy, and his understanding of both slavery and blackness as contradictions that "sickened" the new republic by undermining its virtue. Takaki used the well-worn demographic argument to distinguish Rush's proposals for isolation and "cure" of blackness from Jefferson's proposals for its removal by means of colonization. Takaki argues that the small numbers of people of color in Rush's North made ultimate assimilation possible, whereas in Jefferson's South only removal was feasible (pp. 49–50). I would argue that Rush's solution must be read as *part* of the broader northern discourse of removal (see Chapter 5).

[42] It is my position that the word "race," both as a colloquial term and in its technical use by eighteenth-century philosophers and naturalists to distinguish one group of humans from another on the basis of perceived physical and cultural differences, was synonymous with "category of human," lacking the ideological content it gained in the course of gradual emancipation. I argue that one consequence of gradual emancipation in the northern United States was an anxiety over the mutability of difference, and that this anxiety was resolved in the late eighteenth century and early nineteenth by "naturalizing" difference, locating it within the body and defining it as innate and permanent—in other words, "racializing" it (producing the ideological construct "race"). Like David Roediger (*The Wages of Whiteness*, esp. pp. 43–92), I see this process as motivated by anxiety about the stability of whiteness; unlike him, I locate it not within white workers' struggle to distinguish themselves from southern slaves but rather within their struggle, and that of the emerging white middle class, to stabilize their role as citizen workers in opposition to "dependent and disorderly" ex-slaves emerging as a visible class in their own region.

lowing Linnaeus's 1735 model in *Systema naturae* or a subsequent alternative classification—and then by named groups or tribes.[43]

The very act of classifying human groups or tribes necessarily emphasized differences in cultural practices, clothing, food, environment—and
skin color. Buffon, for example, carefully differentiated "very brown"
Egyptian women, "very tawny" Moroccans, "brown and tawny" people of
the Barbary Coast, "brown, or olive-coloured" Ethiopians, "exceedingly
black" Nubians, "very black" Faloffs (peoples to the south of Senegal), and
Moors "so tawny that they appear almost black," emphasizing differences
in their cultures and small variations in their native climates.[44]

By suggesting that explanations for previously unaccountable variety in
human appearance and behavior might lie in the body's response to its environment, science seemed to hold out the possibility of rationalizing revolutionary social change. The permanence of Africans' skin color, at first an
evidentiary issue in the scientific and religious controversy over the unity
of the human species, seemed to have less abstract implications as well. In
the context of gradual emancipation and revolution, the physical transformation of a "negro" into a white person or vice versa, or the birth of one
to the other, demanded a scientific explanation that would also constitute
a political explanation; these events raised questions about the meaning of
both categories and where precisely, or if, identity—black, white, slave, citizen—could be located in an individual human being. They tested environmental explanations of difference against hypothetical inner (or
innate) and fixed ones, and they probed the validity of external, physical
markers in locating essential human identity. Moss's was only one of more
than a dozen cases of anomalies of skin color that were publicized and discussed between 1788 and 1810 in an attempt to explore and resolve these
questions. While some of these individuals were exhibited, or exhibited
themselves, as marvels (see Figure 1), their definitive categorization as
freaks—as opposed to products of systematic transformations that could
be explained and reliably replicated—represented a conclusion reached
after more than two decades of scientific and philosophical debate, a conclusion that served political imperatives at least as much as it satisfied scientific ones.

Henry Moss was not the first "Negro" or "African" to achieve fame for
being or becoming white. Among earlier accounts the best known may be
Jefferson's description in 1781 of "a negro man within my own knowledge,

---

[43] On the genealogy of scientific arguments over the origin and nature of diversity of
"races," see William Stanton, *The Leopard's Spots: Scientific Attitudes toward Race in America,
1815–59* (Chicago: University of Chicago Press, 1960).

[44] Buffon, *Barr's Buffon*, pp. 250, 254, 280, 272.

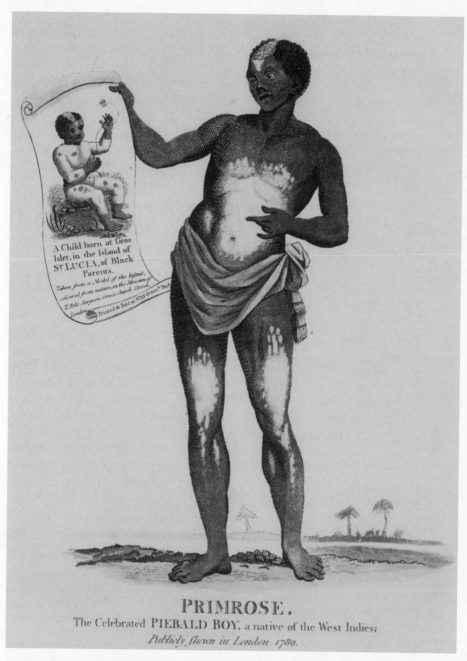

A Child born at Gros Islet, in the Island of St LUCIA, of Black Parents.

Taken from a Model of the Infant, coloured from nature, in the Museum of T. Pole, Surgeon, Grace-church Street, London. Printed & Sold at N.º 33 Grace-ch Str

PRIMROSE.

The Celebrated PIEBALD BOY, a native of the West Indies:

Publicly shewn in London 1789.

Figure 1. Courtesy of the Library Company of Philadelphia

born black, and of black parents," who developed a white spot on his chin in boyhood that "continued to increase till he became a man, by which time it had extended over his chin, lips, one cheek, the under jaw, and neck on that side," without accompanying disease. Jefferson also described seven instances, four of which he knew personally, of what he suggested was "an anomaly of nature, taking place sometimes in the race of negroes brought from Africa, who, though black themselves, have, in rare instances, white children, called Albinos."[45] In 1788 James Bate, a Maryland surgeon, published an account of a forty-year-old cook-maid whose skin, "originally as dark as that of the most swarthy Africans," had begun fifteen years earlier to turn white "in the parts next adjoining to the fingernails" and gradually became white "over the whole body. . . . In her present state, four parts in five, of the skin, are white, smooth, and transparent, as in a fair European." This story had originally been recounted in a private letter in 1759, which the recipient had held until the topic gained currency nearly thirty years later. A shorter version, "Account of a Negro-Woman who Became White," was published, unattributed, in 1796 in the *New York Weekly Magazine.*[46] Also, in 1788 Charles Willson Peale described a man about fifty years old named James, born in Maryland around 1741, who was "of a black or very dark mulatto colour until he was about fifteen years of age, when some white spots appeared on his skin, and which have since gradually increased; so that, at this time, his skin is entirely white from head to foot, excepting some brown specks like moles, and some blotches of a dark mulatto colour on his cheekbones." His account appeared in the *New-York Magazine; or Literary Repository* and the *Universal Asylum, and Columbian Magazine* in 1791 as "An Account of a Person born a Negro, or a very dark Mulatto, who afterwards became white." It was also published the same year in the *Massachusetts Magazine* under the slightly altered title "Account of a NEGRO, or a very dark MULATTO, turning WHITE." According to Benjamin Rush, Peale displayed a portrait of "James, the White Mulatto," in his museum.[47] And in 1789 a doctor named James Parsons published "Account of a white negro" in the *American Museum.* This, like Bate's story, had

[45] Thomas Jefferson, *Notes on the State of Virginia* (1781; New York: Harper & Row, 1964), pp. 70–71.

[46] James Bate, "An Account of a remarkable alteration of colour in a negro woman: in a letter to the Rev. Mr. Alexander Williamson of Maryland, from Mr. James Bate, Surgeon in that Province, 1759," *American Museum* 4 (December 1788): 501–2; "Account of a Negro-Woman Who Became White," *New York Weekly Magazine* 2 (August 31, 1796): 71.

[47] Charles Willson Peale, "An Account of a Person born a Negro, or a very dark Mulatto, who afterwards became white," *New-York Magazine; or, Literary Repository* 2 (November 1791): 634–35, and *Universal Asylum, and Columbian Magazine* 7 (December 1791): 409–10; Charles Willson Peale, "Account of a NEGRO, or a very dark MULATTO, turning WHITE," *Massachusetts Magazine* 3 (December 1791) 744; Rush, "Account of Henry Moss," 7.

been written much earlier, in 1765, and only published more than two decades later when the subject had become newsworthy.[48]

Thus, the issues of "Negroes turning white" and "white Negroes" had already received considerable public attention when Henry Moss became a celebrity around 1796. His case achieved greater notoriety than many others at least in part because Henry apparently had a considerable talent for public relations; one physician, Charles Caldwell, reported that "Moss procured a comfortable subsistence by exhibiting himself as a show."[49] Caldwell and Benjamin Rush both examined Moss in Philadelphia sometime in 1796. Rush featured him in a paper on the causes of skin color in "Negroes," read before the American Philosophical Society in 1797 and published in the society's *Transactions* in 1799.[50] Caldwell apparently discussed his examination of Moss widely among colleagues, notably Benjamin Smith Barton, professor of botany and natural history at the University of Pennsylvania, but failed to publish his conclusions until 1855, when he discussed Moss at length in two different sections of his autobiography and bitterly accused Barton of stealing his ideas.[51] In 1798 a writer signing himself "D.W." published a lengthy account of Moss in the *Weekly Magazine* entitled, "Account of a singular change of color in a negro." Moss visited Rhode Island antislavery activist Moses Brown in 1803, who also conducted a careful physical examination before writing a letter certifying Moss's condition as "an evidence of the sameness of human nature," he being "a man who appears to our senses, both black and white."[52] In 1806, Rush as editor of the *Philadelphia Medical Medical and Physical Journal* published a very long and detailed article about "Henry Moss, a White Negro."[53] By 1810, Samuel Stanhope Smith's much-expanded second edition of his *Essay on the Causes of the Variety of Complexion and Figure in the Human Species* could cite Henry Moss, without introduction or elaboration, as the obvious proof of Smith's contention that "difference of color does not demonstrate diversity of origin."[54]

[48] James Parsons, M.D., "Account of a white negro," *American Museum* 5 (March 1789): 234.

[49] Charles Caldwell, *Autobiography of Charles Caldwell, M.D., with a Preface, Notes, and Appendix by Marriot W. Warner* (Philadelphia: Lippincott, Grambo, 1855), p. 269.

[50] Benjamin Rush, "Observations intended to favour a supposition that the black Color (as it is called) of the Negroes is derived from the LEPROSY. Read at a Special Meeting July 14, 1797," *Transactions of the American Philosophical Society* 4 (1799): 289–97.

[51] Caldwell, *Autobiography*, pp. 163–64, 268–69.

[52] D.W., "Account of a singular change of color in a negro," *Weekly Magazine* 1 (February 24, 1798): 109–11; Moses Brown, "To all whom it may concern," 1803, Moses Brown Papers (Antislavery File), Rhode Island Historical Society.

[53] Rush, "Account of Henry Moss."

[54] Smith, *Essay* p. 52.

In the meantime, public interest in Henry Moss generated stories of similar cases in the popular literature and also produced lay contributions to medical periodicals. In October 1800, for example, the *Monthly Magazine and American Review* picked up an article published earlier in the year by the *Medical Repository:* "Another instance of a Negro Turning White" was the story of one Maurice whose "sable cloud is plainly disappearing on his shoulder."[55] A year later the *Medical Repository,* under the headline "ANOTHER ETHIOPIAN TURNING TO A WHITE MAN," published a letter to the editors from a Mr. A. Catlin of Lichfield, Connecticut, who reported proliferating and enlarging white spots on "Pompey, a very healthy negro," and evinced "the fullest belief that a very few years will complete the total change."[56] IN 1809, an *American Magazine of Wonders* article largely recapitulated Jefferson's litany of known African albinos but included an additional case of "a female of this kind born of black parents, married to an Englishman, whose children were mulattoes. The woman was exhibited as a show, but her children were the greatest curiosities" (presumably because both parents appeared to be entirely white).[57]

Interest in Moss's case and others coincided with the gradual emancipation process, peaking in the 1790s and dissipating by 1810. Such intense interest reflected whites' anxiety about the stability of their own as well as blacks' emerging role as citizens in a rapidly changing political and social environment. Although these accounts posed the possibility of radical metamorphosis, their language ultimately served to reassure white readers that even seemingly extreme types of transformation of human identity could be understood, controlled, placed within the limits of science, and, finally, revealed to be superficial rather than essential. By emphasizing the authenticity of the transformed person's original blackness, the accounts secured a permanent association of a visibly altered individual with her or his "real" identity as a "negro."[58] Several accounts certified Henry Moss's original blackness. Joseph Holt, who had enlisted with Moss in the Continental Army, stated in writing that "from the first of my acquaintance with him, till within two or three years past, he was of as dark a complexion as any African.[59] In his letter, "To all whom it may concern," an authenticating document relying on its author's reputation, Moses Brown noted, "He

[55] "Another Instance of a Negro Turning White," *Monthly Magazine and American Review* 3 (October 1800): 391–92; *Medical Repository* 3 (1800): 199–200.

[56] A. Catlin, "ANOTHER ETHIOPIAN TURNING TO A WHITE MAN," *Medical Repository* 5 (1801): 83–84.

[57] *American Magazine of Wonders* 1 (1809): 220.

[58] In this respect, these accounts resemble slave narratives in which testimonials from whites legitimate the writers' "real" identity as former slaves.

[59] D.W., "Account of a singular change," p. 109.

needs no cirtificate that he has been a black man."[60] Buffon, too, confirmed two "white negroes" on his own reputation, noting that "one of the two I saw myself."[61]

These accounts sought to map the location of difference deep within the body, where heredity alone rather than skin color could provide a valid marker for it. Not a single account refers to a "loss of former color in a white woman" but rather to an "alteration of color in a negro woman"; never to "negroid whites" but always to "white negroes"—even though several of the subjects came to public attention after they had become, or were born, entirely white. In this way, these reports distinguished between appearance and essence: these individuals were certified to be substantially "negroes" and only accidentally "white."

The metaphor of mapping is extraordinarily apt in these disturbingly detached explorations of living human bodies, which rendered the contours of the subjects literal objects of study. James Bate's original account of his examination (made in 1759 but published in 1788) of a forty-year-old female cook included his observation that "her head, face, and breast, with the belly, legs, calves, and thighs, are almost wholly white, the *pudenda . . . ,* party coloured" (subsequent reprintings left this section out). Bate also reported trying to raise a blister on her skin, without success.[62] Bate was a surgeon, but Moses Brown, a Quaker businessman, reported an even more intrusive examination of Henry Moss in 1803: "His back below his shoulders is mostly as white as white people of his age, as are parts of his breast and even his nipples. The white parts of his skin and especially his anus are so transparent as to show the vains [*sic*] as distinct, as a white mans." Moss told Brown that he had also "been examined and viewed by President Washington, Secy Jefferson, Docr Rush &c," whether with a similar thoroughness in the first two cases one can only wonder. According to Moss's memory of the third examination, Brown reported, "the Docr apprehending he could cause his [Moss's] skin to change, he blistered him &c, but to no purpose, the black skin whereon they were put returned, til the Doc gave up further experiment."[63] Although "D.W." apparently observed some decorum when he examined Moss (with women present), noting that "the whole of his breast, arms, and legs, so far as it was decent to expose them to a mixed company, were of a clear European complexion," his propriety did not keep him from poking at his subject: "Upon pressing his skin

---

[60] Brown, "To all whom it may concern."

[61] Buffon, *Barr's Buffon,* p. 324.

[62] Bate, "Account of a remarkable alteration of colour," p. 501; for shorter version, see, e.g., *New York Weekly Magazine* 2 (August 31, 1796): 71.

[63] Brown, "To all whom it may concern."

with a finger, the part pressed appeared white; and on removal of the pressure, the displaced blood rushed back, suffusing the part with red, exactly as in the case of an European, in like circumstances."[64] The very nature and matter-of-fact reporting of these examinations confirms the examiners' view of the intrinsic chattel nature of the subjects, despite the fact that not one was described as a slave. Some of them, including the two subjects of letters written at least twenty years before they were published, may have been slaves in fact; but it was their whiteness, not their status, that generated interest in the age of emancipation. Henry Moss, the most widely discussed, was in fact born a free man.[65] Nonetheless, the discursive exploration of the limits of transformation was ultimately essentializing.

A few commentators did see the interesting implications of these cases for the continuation of southern slavery, especially since enslaveability still rested on the marker of skin color in the South. Noting first the importance to the zoologist of cases like that of "Maurice," the unnamed writer of "Another Instance of a Negro Turning White" in 1800 ended with this comment: "How additionally singular would it be, if instances of the spontaneous disappearance of this sable mark of distinction between slaves and their masters were to become frequent! They would then be no less important to the moralist and political economist."[66] D.W., too, saw the antislavery implications of Henry Moss's case, carrying the analysis a step farther:

> Such is the history . . . of the change of a negro to a white man—a change, which, had Henry Moss happened to have been a slave, would have furnished an irrefragable argument for annihilating his owner's claim. Now as . . . a black colour so clearly authorises the extreme degradation of a considerable portion of the human race; and as the change from white to black must be admitted as equally possible with the reverse above stated, it may be well for the white slave dealers, and their fair abettors . . . to consider how far they may be personally interested in perpetuating such a criterion; as by it, they may ultimately be doomed.[67]

One commentator read the "negro turning white" phenomenon as the vanguard of a wholesale transformation to white of all people of color in

[64] D.W., "Account of a singular change," pp. 110–11.
[65] Stanton (*The Leopard's Spots*, p. 6), claims that Moss was born a slave in Virginia; however, both Joseph Holt's certification of 1798 (in D.W., "Account of a singular change," p. 109) and Rush's 1806 "Account of Henry Moss," p. 5,—detailed accounts that agree with each other—state that Moss was born free in Virginia.
[66] "Another Instance of a Negro Turning White" (*Medical Repository*), p. 200.
[67] D.W., "Account of a singular change," p. 111.

the hospitable American environment. Samuel Stanhope Smith concluded in 1810:

> It is evident to every eye capable of comparing an American, with an
> African negro, that the change of climate, and of their manner of subsis-
> tence, has already produced in the posterity of the Africans, all the alter-
> ation in their appearance which, in so short a period of time, could justly
> be expected. . . . I do not hesitate to apply this remark to the American
> slaves, in general; but is applicable especially to the domestic slaves of opu-
> lent families in the southern states, and the free blacks who are found in
> considerable numbers in the northern portion of the union. . . . I repeat,
> and I repeat it with the most perfect confidence, because the fact is open
> to the observation of every American, that, in the United States, the physi-
> ognomy, and the whole figure and personal appearance of the African
> race is undergoing a favorable change.[68]

Smith proposed a hierarchy of transformation in which the entire population of free northern blacks stood poised on the brink of becoming
white, proof positive of the efficacy of the environmental theory of human
difference. But his analysis was distinctly out of step with the growing conviction of many more northerners that the differences distinguishing free
people of color from whites could not be located in superficial, and mutable, skin color, any more than they could be located in the assimilable religious and cultural differences that had seemed to distinguish Africans
from Europeans in the early years of British colonial slavery. Skin color was
only a sign—a variable, unreliable sign—of innate and permanent difference.

The last articles on albinism and vitiglio in persons of color appeared in
the *Medical Museum* and the *American Magazine of Wonders*, two magazines
devoted largely to sensational stories about freaks and curiosities. The concluding paragraph of one article asserted, "These facts fully ascertain, that
this [albinism] is a variety only of the Negro race."[69] By 1835 J. Jacobus
Flournoy, in his effort "properly to expose the true nature of the blacks,
and to disabuse our countrymen of a partiality to them, *free* or *bondmen*,"

---

[68] Smith, *Essay*, pp. 152, 155. George M. Fredrickson, *The Black Image in the White Mind: The Debate on Afro-American Character and Destiny, 1817–1914* (New York: Harper & Row, 1971), pp. 72–73, and Stanton, *The Leopard's Spots*, pp. 3–14, discuss Smith's ideas.

[69] See, e.g., "Account of two Albinos," *Medical Museum* 2 (1806): 284–86; "Account of a Negro Woman Who Became White, *American Magazine of Wonders* 2 (1809): 312–13; "A Curious Account of the Albino Negro," *American Magazine of Wonders*, 1 (1809): 218–20 (quo-tation, p. 220).

could dismiss out of hand Samuel Stanhope Smith's assertions about "the gradual change from black to white in certain negroes," insisting confidently, "May it not have been that nature sometimes plays pranks on the grown person as well as the foetus in the womb; that the sudden circular whiteness in a negro is such a freak; and entirely disconnected with the long link of millions accounted for in the Bible—made black as suddenly, to discriminate the once fallen from the twice fallen—the white man from the negro?"[70]

Transformations of skin color could, of course, occur in either direction. D.W. was probably not the only person who thought the real significance of the Moss case lay in the implications of the mutability of color for the enslaveability of whites.[71] Although Buffon might insist that abrupt change in color or an anomalous birth coloration such as albinism "never happens but from black to white," his environmental theory of diversity and long-term change convinced him that "many ages might perhaps elapse before a white race would become altogether black; but there is a probability that in time a white people, transported from the north to the equator, would experience that change, especially if they were to change their manners, and to feed solely on the productions of the warm climate."[72] Under radically different conditions, enslaved in a tropical climate by a "savage" people of color, could free white Americans become . . . something else? Slaves? And how profound and permanent would such a change be? Was whiteness part of some stable, essential nature, or did the conditions of their existence have the power to transform the "nature" of Americans and Europeans too, as Buffon and Smith suggested?

An ongoing diplomatic crisis that coincided with the peak of the emancipation period posed these questions, and the enormous popularity of the literature it generated suggests that many Americans found the questions compelling and looked to this literature for answers. The crisis involved the enslavement of white Americans by an African people of color. Beginning in 1785 the so-called Barbary States of North Africa (Morocco, Algiers, Tunis, and Tripoli)—mounted a persistent threat to United States commerce in the Mediterranean—which before the Revolution had represented as much as one-sixth of the American colonies' exports of wheat and flour and one-quarter of their exports of preserved fish and rice—by preying on American shipping.[73] The Americans negotiated a series of

70 Flournoy, "*Essay on the Origin, Habits, Etc. of the African Race,* pp. 3, 13, 15.
71 D.W., "Account of a singular change," p. 111.
72 Buffon, *Barr's Buffon,* pp. 324, 306.
73 The most recent monograph on U.S. relations with the Barbary States is Robert S. Al-

treaties with each of the Barbary States, trying to accommodate or finesse escalating demands for tribute, often in the form of naval stores, arms, and jewels. Disruption or delay of payment, or efforts to renegotiate terms more favorable to the United States, resulted in the periodic seizure of American vessels by Barbary corsairs—especially those of Algiers—and the capture and imprisonment of the American crew members, many of whom spent eight or more years in captivity before negotiation and payment of ransom effected their release.

Between 1785 and 1795 thirteen American ships were seized by the Algerines, and about 130 crewmen were captured; a treaty with Algiers approved by Congress in 1795 ransomed the 85 American prisoners who remained alive.[74] Eight years later another 307 American crewmen were captured off the coast of Tripoli, two years after a formal declaration of war by Tripoli on the United States. When the war ended after a U.S. naval victory in 1805, 297 of the 302 surviving crewmen were ransomed (the remaining five had adopted Islam and elected to remain in Tripoli). During the same period a number of American ships, and vessels of foreign registration carrying American citizens, foundered on the North African littoral, and their crews and passengers were also imprisoned in Barbary.[75]

The common term for this captivity of Americans (and other Europeans as well: in 1786 there were at least 2,200 foreigners imprisoned in Al-

lison, *The Crescent Obscured: The United States and the Muslim World, 1776–1815* (New York: Oxford University Press, 1995). Allison focuses on ideological aspects of the war with Tripoli; he explores the meaning for Americans of the victory of the United States, as a Christian and free nation, over an Islamic one seen as mired in sexual, religious, and political despotism. See his chap. 4 for the connections Americans made between U.S. and Algerian slavery. Michael L. S. Kitzen's *Tripoli and the United States at War: A History of American Relations with the Barbary States, 1785–1805* (Jefferson, N.C.: McFarland, 1993), pp. 10–11, is a straightforward diplomatic history, offering little analysis of popular American perspectives on the captivity of American seamen or insight into the effects of cultural or "racial" factors. Earlier though relatively infrequent antecedents of the crisis in U.S.-Barbary relations dated back to the 1690s; e.g., in 1693 Benjamin Fletcher, governor of New York, solicited contributions to redeem New York City sailors from slavery in Morocco (Broadside Collection, American Antiquarian Society).

[74] The eleven American vessels captured by the Algerines in October and November 1793 are listed in *Naval Documents Related to the United States' Wars with the Barbary Powers*, vol. 1, *Naval Operations including Diplomatic Background from 1785 through 1801* (Washington, D.C.: U.S. Navy, Office of Naval Records and Library, 1939), p. 56, giving the number of men captured as 105. The same list, as recorded in *A Journal, of the Captivity and Suffering of John Foss; Several Years a Prisoner at Algiers,* 2d ed. (Newburyport, Mass.: Angier March, n.d.), gives the number captured as 109, plus 21 from two earlier seizures of July 1785; it also lists 35 crewmen as having died but does not make clear whether they were killed in the encounter with the Algerines or died early in captivity. See Kitzen, *Tripoli and the United States,* pp. 19–21.

[75] Kitze, *Tripoli and the United States,* pp. 96, 166.

giers)[76] was "slavery." This was not a hyperbolic or allusive term. Captured Europeans and Americans were sold in slave markets; they were forced to perform heavy physical labor and to beg monies from their friends and families abroad to provide anything above the barest subsistence level of food and clothing; they were regularly beaten and chained for the slightest infractions; and, because their eventual ransom was uncertain at best, unless they converted to Islam they could expect only death to liberate them from bondage. A letter to a U.S. State Department official from Samuel Calder, former captain of the American schooner *Jay* out of Gloucester, Massachusetts, described the treatment he and his crew received following their capture in October 1793:

> On our landing we were all put into Chains without the least distinction and put to hard labor from daylight until night with only the allowance of two small black loaves and Water & close confined at night. . . . we think ourselves happy if we escape through the day being beat by our driver, who carries a stick big enough to Knock a man down. . . . we have no Reason but to expect but that the Plague will in the course of a year take off many of us, as the last Plague took away 800 out of 2000 Slaves. . . . I would if it was in my power forward you a regular Protest, but you know its impossible in this Country & I suppose one from a Slave would be of no importance.[77]

The American public was deeply concerned with the fate of the American slaves in Algiers, a concern extending beyond prayers and editorial letters to raising subscriptions in Boston and Norfolk for relief of the captives. The later, and shorter, Tripolitan captivity also aroused international interest and support for the crew of the captured *Philadelphia*.[78] But what really seemed to seize the popular imagination were the personal narratives of the captivity experience and literary simulations of such narratives—some in poetic and dramatic form—which appeared between 1794 and 1820, many reprinted five and six times.

The narratives of the Algerine captivity share some characteristics with those of the captivities of whites by Native American peoples, and their popularity undoubtedly stemmed from some of the same fascinations. Both depended for their appeal on the terror of sudden loss of aegis, es-

---

[76] The Algerines also attacked the merchant shipping of Russians, Spaniards, Neapolitans, and others (ibid., p. 13).

[77] Letter to David Pearce Jr. from Samuel Calder, Slave, Algiers, December 4, 1793, *Naval Documents*, pp. 57–58.

[78] Kitzen, *Tripoli and the United States*, pp. 18, 102–4.

trangement from everything familiar, and submission to the seemingly irrational whim of people distinguished from the captive by alien appearance, religion, and culture; both became increasingly stylized and sexualized around 1800. In addition, the characterizations of Arabs, Moors, and Algerines in the one genre and American natives in the other drew upon strikingly similar imagery. June Namias notes what she terms "the overtly racist and bloodthirsty" character of American captivity narratives in the Revolutionary and early republican era, which suggests that one element of their project, like that of the Algerine narratives, may have been to test environmental theory (here, limited to the effects of alien cultural practices) and the stability of whiteness.[79]

Nonetheless, there were telling differences. Whites captured by Native American were called "prisoners" or "captives," never "slaves," even when the work their captors demanded formed a significant part of their narratives. Conversely, the imprisonment of Americans in Barbary was always termed "slavery." White Americans' captivity in a continent that had been, and continued to be, the source of America's own slave labor offered a context so rich in irony that the reversal of roles simply could not be ignored. Nearly all the Algerine narratives include a detailed description of the geography, climate, and history of North Africa and the customs of its various peoples—elements absent from the narratives of white captives of American natives. Captivity on American soil reduced the potency of the transforming effect of imprisonment, since environmental theories emphasized climate as the factor most productive of variety in humans. Native American tribes were perceived in static rather than historical terms, for no written history of their migration, change, or encounters with Europeans, Arabs, or other literate peoples could be referenced. They could also be seen as relatively "pure" (partly because Americans collapsed tribal distinctions into the all-encompassing term "Indian"), whereas written histories of North African peoples recognized the intermixing that had resulted from migration and conquest and minutely catalogued the multitude of mixed and "degraded" peoples of color that had resulted.

Since the 1780s, white Americans had become familiar with ethnographic descriptions of the peoples of North Africa that clearly depicted them as people of color. Although North Africans' allegiance to Islam represented another element of difference, "heathenism" had receded in importance since sixteenth- and seventeenth-century Europeans encountering Africans and North American natives had regarded it as a critically

[79] June Namias, *White Captives: Gender and Ethnicity on the American Frontier* (Chapel Hill: University of North Carolina Press, 1993), pp. 23, 24.

important, if not defining, difference.[80] Late eighteenth-century philosophers counted colors, not saints. Buffon cited an earlier observer, who had declared that "the sea coast people of Barbary are brown and tawny"; that Capex, a city in Tunis, was populated by "poor people exceedingly black" and that those in the kingdom of Morocco "are very tawny."[81] Smith described north Africans as an elaborate melange of colors:

> In passing above the river Senegal we enter on a lighter shade of the negro colour; after which, as we advance towards the North, and before we arrive at the kingdom of Morocco, we find the darkest copper of the Moorish complexion. But all this tract is filled with various tribes of wandering Moors and Arabs, and often with a mixed breed, the offspring of unions formed between these, and the native blacks, among whom the negro complexion predominates; but their features bear a greater resemblance to those of the Moors, and make some approach to the European face.[82]

The "savagery" of North Africans was also emphasized. Buffon observed the "state of lawless independence" of the Arabs of North Africa, Persia, Turkey, and Arabia and their tendency to "glory in their vices."[83] Again, savagery was now evaluated in terms of personal and social practices, in contrast to the seventeenth-century association of savagery with paganism.

The people of Algiers were not, then, "negroes," but were characterized as "savage," "lawless," and "tawny"—language quite similar to that used to describe the native peoples of North America. "Savages will always be discoloured, even in temperate climates, by different shades of the tawny complexion," said Smith in a section on American natives that directly followed the one on Africans.[84] He believed that the coloration of both North Africans and Native Americans supported his contention that "manners" (degree of civilization) and climate and food jointly produce human variety.

[80] See Jordan, *White over Black*, pp. 20–24, 92–94. Allison (*Crescent Obscured*) emphasizes religious factors in Americans' distaste for and fear of the inhabitants of Tripoli, Algiers, and Tunis and discusses the view of Islam not only as a false and dangerous belief but also as a source of political tyranny (pp. 35–59). He does not really explore European and American representation of Muslims as peoples of color, however, although he does note the "color line" between white and black captives as a factor both in their treatment by Arab captors and their solidarity as prisoners (pp. 121–26).
[81] Buffon, *Barr's Buffon*, p. 254.
[82] Smith, *Essay*, pp. 136–37.
[83] Buffon, *Barr's Buffon*, p. 246.
[84] Smith, *Essay*, p. 140.

Thus, when personal stories of enslavement by "tawny" Arabs and "dusky" or "swarthy" Moors of unbridled savagery began to surface in the United States, Americans were prepared to read these stories as tests of the durability of republican whiteness, much as an earlier generation had read narratives of the captivity of colonists by native peoples as tests of the durability of Christian faith. The experiences of slavery in Algiers and Tripoli thus represented tests of the ability of free white Americans to resist being degraded to the moral, cultural, and even physical level of the people who enslaved them. In other words, the Algerine captivity provided an environment in which enslavement might in fact transform white Americans into slavelike persons, as instrumental and dependent as black slaves. This potential mutability of whites into slaves/people of color in Africa offered as great a symbolic challenge to the American social order as the actual mutability of blacks into freemen/whites at home; both could be read symptomatically to evaluate the potential political, social, and perhaps biological consequences of democracy and emancipation.[85]

American interest in ethnography encouraged nearly every narrator of Algerine captivity to include a classification of the Barbary inhabitants. They described them variously as mixtures of several different peoples— Moors or Morescos, Levantines, Turks, Cologlies, Arabs—although the proportions and identifications differ from account to account. Virtually every writer on the subject attempted to describe the precise colors of the North Africans. Robert White, enslaved for four years and nine months in Algiers, referred to them as having "a black, swarthy complexion"; Mathew Carey, too, called them "swarthy." But a Mr. Brooks, a former captive, reported to James W. Stevens that the inhabitants of the Barbary Coast exhibited a "pretty fair complexion"; only those in the interior, particularly the Arabs, were "swarthy." Robert Adams, three years a slave, described the Moors as "straight haired but quite black," the Arabs as "a deep but bright brunette, essentially unlike the sallow tinge of the mulattoes," and the "Arabs of the Desert" as "more or less swarthy according to their proximity to the Negro states." John Foss, enslaved for four years and one month, found the Turks "not unlike Americans" in complexion, the Cologlies "more tawny," and the Arabs "of a much darker complexion than the

---

[85] Allison reads the ideological import of the Algerine captivity narratives quite differently, regarding them as significant and popular because they presented an analogy between American slavery and Islamic tyranny that forced Americans to confront slavery as the potential worm in the apple of their political liberty (*Crescent Obscured*, pp. 87–106). He sees the imprisonment of Americans in the Barbary States as presenting a test of the character of Americans in the face of severe restrictions on their liberty; absent a "racial" dimension, however, he does not see implications for the nature of citizenship and its qualifications for American whites (Chap. 5, esp. p. 126).

Moors, being darker than the Mulattoes." To Maria Martin and Lucinda Martin, six years enslaved, all the Algerines were "tawny" or "very tawny."[86]

Most accounts also emphasized the savagery and inhumanity of the Algerines. Nearly every account included graphic descriptions of punishments meted out to white slaves, including being bastinadoed, burned, roasted alive, impaled, and cast over the walls to catch and dangle for days on iron hooks. [87]

The sexual practices and moral character of the Algerines were deplored as particularly degraded.[88] To John Foss they were "cursed with all the vices of mankind"; Foss's and James Stevens's narratives stated in identical language that the Algerines had adopted "the very worst parts of the Mahometan Religion," which "countenances all their vices."[89] Some of the narratives described the sexual exploitation of small Christian boys in relatively explicit terms. John Burnham told the *Rural Magazine* that the Dey (governor) would always review newly captured "boys or good-looking young men," of whom he would select "such as he pleases for his own do-

[86] Robert White, "A Curious, Historical and Entertaining Narrative of the Captivity and almost unheard-of Sufferings and cruel Treatment of Mr. Robert White, Mariner," in *Bickerstaff's Boston Almanack, or Federal Calendar for 1791* (Boston: Bickerstaff, 1790); Mathew Carey, *A Short Account of Algiers, containing a Description of the Climate of that Country, of the Manners and Customs of the inhabitants. . . .*(Philadelphia: J. Parker, 1794), p. 2; James W. Stevens, *An Historical and Geographical Account of Algiers; Comprehending a Novel and Interesting Detail of Events Relative to the American Captives* (Philadelphia: Hogan & M'Elroy, 1797), p. 143; Robert Adams, *The Narrative of Robert Adams, An American Sailor, who was Wrecked on the Western Coast of Africa in the year 1810; was Detailed Three Years in Slavery by the Arabs of the Great Desert. . . .* (Boston: Wells & Lilly, 1817), pp. 31, 186; John Foss, *The Algerine Slaves: A Poem, by a Citizen of Newburyport* [with] "A Journal, of the Captivity and Suffering of John Foss; Several years a Prisoner at Algiers; Together with . . . Observations on the Manners and Customs of the Algerines," 2d ed. (Newburyport, Mass.: Angier March, 1798), p. 74; Maria Martin, *History of the Captivity and Sufferings of Mrs. Maria Martin, who was six years a slave in Algiers: . . . To which is Annexed, A History of Algiers, a Description of the Country, the Manners and Customs of the Natives. . . .* (Boston: W. Crary , 1806), p. 27; Lucinda Martin, *History of the Captivity and Sufferings of Mrs. Lucinda Martin, who was six years a slave in Algiers. . . .*(Boston: Lemuel Austin, 1810), p. 43. The American Antiquarian Society catalogue lists Lucinda's as a second edition of Maria's, and in fact the historical material (pp. 4–38), is identical, as are the details of imprisonment in a small apartment in an old castle (pp. 61–65); but the rest is completely different. Parts of the later narrative are obviously "borrowed" from the earlier one; similarly, the historical accounts of both are "borrowed" in substantial part from Stevens. The Carey and Stevens accounts are quite similar on some points as well, especially in their descriptions of punishments carried out in Algiers; either these matters were singularly memorable to all observers, or both writers borrowed liberally from earlier sources.

[87] Stevens, *Historical and Geographical Account*, pp. 161–64; Carey, *Short Account of Algiers*, pp. 16–17.

[88] In chap. 3 of *Crescent Obscured,* "A Peek Into the Seraglio: Americans, Sex, and the Muslim World" (pp. 61–85), Allison discusses at length the portrayal of Muslim sexuality as tyrannous and debased.

[89] Foss, *The Algerine Slaves*, pp. 64, 66; Stevens, *Historical and Geographical Account*, p. 164.

mestics, and they remain always in his house"; he said that "the Dey hath always a particular boy, one of the fairest among the number, for attending in his bed-chamber, with whom, it is said, he is guilty of the most horrid of all crimes." James Stevens generalized the practice to all the Barbary elite: "Sodomy is so extremely fashionable among them, and so little are they disposed to keep this foible a secret, that it is the subject of their most plaintive songs, and they will spare no pains in procuring the gratification of their infamous love."[90]

Many narratives equated the Algerines with animals or used animalistic descriptive terms. Robert White described them as "those *Beings*, who have only the shape and appearance of the human race"; they "fell on us like ravenous wolves," he wrote, and their stronghold was a "nest of vermin." Mathew Carey said it was their custom that "the family and domestic animals, lie promiscuously in the tents together."[91]

The reports of cruel, depraved, and bestial behavior raised serious questions for American readers: would enslavement by such people degrade white American freemen to a similar level? John Burnham, commander of the ship *Hope*, taken in 1793, wrote of the housing conditions of the slaves that "in many places of the building are Christians, monkeys, apes, and asses altogether." Reduction to the condition of animals was, after all, only a metaphor, but it was the central metaphor of slavery: systematic eradication of personhood, debasement to the status of chattel. The Algerines commonly called their white slaves "dogs," Stevens reported.[92]

James Stevens said that each public slave was forced to wear an iron ring around one ankle "as evidence of his belonging to the public," while private slaves sold into the country must carry burdens to market, work naked in the fields, tend cattle, drag ploughs, and "do all other kinds of the most servile drudgery." John Burnham reported forced work at trades such as sailmaking, carpentry, and smithing, along with periodic labor hauling rocks from the mountains to the "mole," or breakwater, protecting the harbor of Algiers. He was forced to carry "a burden of at least 250 weight" and, after falling under it, had to be carried to the hospital. Yet his rations were only "three small black loaves a day." John Foss wore a "25–30 pound chain from leg to shoulder," performed forced labor on the mole, and summed up his experience in verse: "Slavery, more abject than the mind can

---

[90] John Burnham, "The Curses of Slavery: Treatment of the American Prisoners at Algiers," *Rural Magazine; or, Vermont Repository*, March 1795. Stevens, *Historical and Geographical Account*, p. 216.

[91] White, "A Curious, Historical and Entertaining Narrative"; Carey, *Short Account of Algiers*, p. 11.

[92] Burnham, "The Curses of Slavery"; Stevens, *Historical and Geographical Account*, p. 215.

trace, / the pen pourtray—or human tho't embrace." Robert White complained that he and seventeen shipmates were chained to the oar of a galley, where he survived for four years and nine months; others, he said, were "weltering under their chains in the mines, and dragging out a miserable existence, scarce worth possessing."[93]

Yet the narratives represented the Algerines' arbitrary and despotic exercise of power as complemented by a cringing servility. Narrators blamed both extremes of Algerine behavior on their own crushing oppression by the Turks, representing them as a kind of partial paradigm of environmental transformation: subjected to despotic power, they had themselves become despots; made to submit, they had become servile. As James Stevens put it, "in consequence of the violence that is exercised over them, and their total subserviency to the rapacious views of their Turkish oppressors, . . . [e]very spark of political liberty is totally extinguished, and the government has now attained to the very acme of the most horrible despotism."[94]

If Algerine behavior could be understood as a consequence of extreme oppression, and if the servile behavior of slaves of African descent in America could be understood that way as well, then perhaps Americans in slavery would likewise become servile and even depraved. Many narratives seemed to confirm these fears. The daily existence of the American slaves was "scarce worth possessing"; a Christian, after a long captivity, appeared "exceedingly stupid and insensible"; some "turned Turk (adopted Islam)." In *The Algerine Captive* (1797), a convincing imitation of a captivity narrative, Royall Tyler included an incident obviously intended to dramatize just this problem of potential transformation. At the outset of his imprisonment the narrator, Dr. Updike Underhill, resists a whipping and tries to incite his fellow prisoners, long enslaved, to help him bind their overseer and escape: "But I called in vain . . . I spoke to slaves, astonished at my presumption."[95]

Unlike most of the earlier "true story" narratives, however, Tyler's novel proposed an answer to the transformation question. So did several other highly stylized and embellished narratives, some manifestly fictional,

[93] Stevens, *Historical and Geographical Account*, pp. 240, 242; Burnham, "The Curses of Slavery"; Foss, *The Algerine Slaves*, pp. 20–40, 180–84; White, "A Curious, Historial and Entertaining Narrative."

[94] Stevens, *Historical and Geographical Account*, pp. 208–9.

[95] White, "A Curious, Historical and Entertaining Narrative"; Adams, *Narrative*, p. xviii; William Ray, *Poems on Various Subjects, Religious, Moral, Sentimental and Humorous. To which is added, a brief sketch of the Author's life and of his captivity and sufferings among the Turks and barbarians of Tripoli* (Auburn, Mass.: U. F. Doubleday, 1821), p. 235; Royall Tyler, *The Algerine Captive; or, The Life and Adventures of Dr. Updike Underhill, Six Years a Prisoner Among the Algerines* (Walpole, N.H., 1797), 2:23–24.

and a number of plays and poems that with few exceptions were published after the return in 1796 of all of the surviving Americans captured by the Algerines (although some appeared before the 1805 return of the crew of the *Philadelphia* from slavery in Tripoli). This second wave of captivity-based works frankly proclaimed the triumph of republican whiteness over the enslavement experience.[96]

These works, in a number of ways, naturalized and embodied for the first time the differences between Algerines/Arabs/Moors/Turks and Euro-Americans. Some transformed the captivity experience into highly sexualized tales of romance and rescue. Unlike the earlier narratives, in which females had virtually no role at all,[97] many featured female characters, both Algerine and American (or sometimes British). Here, for the first time, virtuous whiteness often took the shape of a woman.

For example, in John Vandike's 1801 account ostensibly of his own captivity, the hero risks his life and comfort to save a beautiful English woman who has run from rape in an Algerine captain's seraglio. Before meeting her the hero had spent three apparently secure years in Algiers, during which he had won a position of trust with a wealthy Algerine captain, converted to Islam, and agreed to marry an Algerine lady of fortune. Although he describes his behavior as a ruse to ensure eventual escape, it is only the intervention of the white woman who has risked death to fend off intercourse with an Algerine (in a graphic bedroom scene) who prevents his consummation of a marriage with a woman of color.[98] In other words, even an uncertain whiteness, wilfully submerged and weakened, could be redeemed by a resolute whiteness strengthened by the battle to preserve it. In Susanna Rowson's *Slaves in Algiers*, Fetnah, favorite concubine of the Dey, is actually English but has been raised as a Moslem Algerine; she learns "the love of liberty" and resistance to both the Dey and Islam from Rebecca, who "came from that land, where virtue in either sex is the only mark of superiority.—She was an American."[99] Here, whiteness and virtue

---

[96] Allison does not distinguish early from later narratives with respect to the responses of Americans to their captivity; he sees resistance to submission as a nearly universal position (*Crescent Obscured*, pp. 118, 125–26).

[97] Only Stevens discussed the role and behavior of Algerine women, which he cited as evidence of Algerine depravity. He simultaneously condemned Turkish men for believing women to "have no souls" and judged Turkish women to be lascivious, indolent, and tasteless. (*Historical and Geographical Account of Algiers*, pp. 230, 220–22).

[98] John Vandike, *Narrative of the Captivity of John Vandike, who was taken by the Algerines, in 1791. An Acount of his Escape, bringing with him a Beautiful Young English Lady Who was taken in 1790. . . . Translated into English by Mr. James Howe, of Holland* (Leominster, Mass.: Chapman Whitcomb, 1801). Here the hero's unusual susceptibility to the "good life" in Algiers can probably be accounted for by the fact that he was not American but Dutch.

[99] Susanna Rowson, *Slaves in Algiers* (Philadelphia: Wrigley & Berriman, 1794), pp. 9–10.

are unmistakably republican characteristics that can be resurrected because, no matter how submerged, they are innate.

In all these fictionalized and romantic works, proud and virtuous whiteness is portrayed as triumphant over oppression and slavery because it is inborn in all whites, especially Americans. The imagery of descent, linking country and family, appears everywhere. Tyler's Dr. Underhill concludes, "I had been degraded to a slave, and was now advanced to a citizen of the freest country in the universe. I had been lost to my parent, friends, and country, and now found, in the embraces and congratulations of the former and the rights and protection of the latter." Rowson proclaims, "Nor *here* alone, Columbia's sons be free, / *Where'er* they breathe there must be liberty. / —There *must* there *is,* for he who form'd the whole, / Entwin'd blest freedom with th'immortal *soul.*"[100]

Some of the captivity literature, especially the later, fictionalized narratives, also offered a straightforward indictment of American slavery. But this argument, too, depended for its power on a threat to republican whiteness—a threat from a different quarter. Analogies between American and Muslim slavery had been made by some antislavery leaders before the introduction of gradual emancipation As early as 1775, for example, Samuel Hopkins had suggested, "The Mahometans enslaving Christians, and their cruel treatment, . . . might afford matter of reading and declamation suited to awaken people, and make them feel fear[;] tis easy to shew that our treatment of negroes is of the same kind."[101]

After the commencement of northern emancipation, when numbers of Americans had joined Europeans enslaved in Algiers in the 1780s, several newspapers and magazines sympathetic to the antislavery position followed Hopkins's advice. In 1795, the *Rural Magazine; or, Vermont Repository* slyly followed "The Curses of Slavery," subtitled "Treatment of the American Prisoners at Algiers," with "Treatment of the African Slaves in America," subtitled "Intelligence from Africa." Royall Tyler's novel bore an explicit antislavery message, and as late as 1847 Charles Sumner was reciting the history of white slavery in the Barbary States as a compelling antislavery argument before the Boston Mercantile Library Association.[102] These works emphasized the threat to republican virtue more than to whiteness per se, however: slaveholding might turn Americans into debauched tyrants.

The Algerine captivity, then, questioned the meaning of slavery for re-

---

100 Tyler, *The Algerine Captive,* pp. 226–27; Rowson, *Slaves in Algiers,* p. ii.

101 Samuel Hopkins to Levi Hart, 15 January 1775, Miscellaneous Manuscripts, Connecticut Historical Society.

102 *Rural Magazine; or, Vermont Repository,* March 1795, pp. 118–24; Charles Sumner, *White Slavery in the Barbary States. A Lecture before the Boston Mercantile Library Association, Feb. 17, 1847* (Boston: William D. Ticknor, 1847).

publicanism and whiteness in two different ways. The power of its implications for slaveholding, directed at the South, gained intensity in the second wave of largely fictionalized narratives, which at the same time confirmed the stability of whiteness and blackness in the face of enslavement. They proclaimed the whiteness and virtue of true republicans—northern, free, white citizens—to be innate and inherited, as was the slavishness and dependency of people of color.

The literatures of role reversal, then, not only posed questions about the mutability of "black" and "white," "slave" and "free citizen" but, especially after 1800, provided clear answers calculated to reassure whites. In every case the answers challenged environmental theory, proposing a radically different conception of human difference: that whiteness and citizenship, savagery and servility were innate characteristics; that there was indeed an immutable human nature that was not subject to substantial change by external experience—a fixed nature to which the somatic or physiognomic could after all provide reliable clues.

The popular conclusion about the stability of whiteness paralleled the direction of scientific thought, which increasingly turned away from environmental explanations in the early nineteenth century. Physicians and philosophers began to offer new physical proofs of essential and permanent "racial" difference and attempted to reconcile such difference with the unity of human descent. Dr. Charles White in England and Drs. John Augustine Smith and Samuel George Morton in the United States were among the earliest of a growing body of critics of environmentalism who argued from anatomical structure and skull shape that there was a biological basis for permanent "racial" difference.[103]

Thus science affirmed what politics demanded: that the instrumentality and dependency of slaves, in fact mapped onto free people of color by the persistence of pre-Revolutionary practices during gradual emancipation, could be understood instead as characteristics innate to "Negroes." People of color could never become citizens; they were not equipped by nature for the role. Similarly, republican whiteness would persist through temporary enslavement, impoverishment, and other degrading experiences (in-

---

[103] Charles White, *An Account of the Regular Gradation in Man, and in Different Animals and Vegetables; and from the Former to the Latter* (London, 1799); John Augustine Smith, "A Lecture introductory to the second Course of Anatomical Instruction in the College of Physicians and Surgeons for the State of New-York," *New York Medical and Philosophical Journal and Review* 1 (1809): 84–96; Samuel George Morton, *Crania Americana; or, A Comparative View of the Skulls of Various Aboriginal Nations of North and South America, to which Is Prefixed an Essay on the Varieties of the Human Species* (Philadelphia: J. Dobson, 1839). See Stanton, *The Leopard's Spots*, pp. 15–44, on the developing argument against environmentalism.

cluding post-Revolutionary social dislocation) because it too was an innate and "natural" quality.

The discourses of science and role reversal thus became mutually reinforcing. Together, they located stable and virtuous republican citizenship in the essential nature of whites; at the same time, they constituted free people of color as essentially and immutably servile, "naturally" unsuitable for citizenship, and fated to remain a permanent element of disorder and a persistent obstacle that whites would need to ignore, overcome, or eliminate in the course of building their new republic.

5

"To Abolish the Black Man":
Enacting the Antislavery Promise

The promise of freedom as it had developed in the context of the New England antislavery movement had always been ambiguous, its fundamental contradiction replicating the one at the heart of slavery itself. "Freedom," like "slavery," encompassed quite different constellations of meaning for the parties involved. To slaves, the freedom promised by antislavery rhetoric meant release from white ownership and enactment of independent agency. To white slaveholders, freedom meant release from the sin of slaveholding, from the heavy responsibilities of owning and managing slaves, and from the daily presence of slaves. To whites who did not themselves hold slaves, whether opposed to slavery or indifferent to it, emancipation promised cessation of the shrill controversy this issue provoked and, ultimately, an end to the presence of slaves in their society. In other words, to whites, regardless of their personal relationship to slavery, "freedom" meant the absence of slaves.

But because it was easy to conflate the elimination of slaves as a category with the elimination of the humans occupying that category, the prospect of an end to slavery undoubtedly had meant to many whites the end of a troubling black presence. The constitution of the Foster Moral Society, a Baptist group in northern Rhode Island, neatly illustrates this point: in it, the members announced themselves determined "to array ourselves against Slaves Papacy and all other great evils of the day."[1] More than clumsy diction is revealed in the substitution of "slaves" for "slavery." Emerson's perceptive if simplistic observation about abolitionists of the 1850s applies as well to eighteenth-century antislavery activists: "The abolitionist wishes to abolish slavery, but because he wishes to abolish the black man."[2] Many whites had imagined that gradual emancipation would ultimately restore New England to an idealized original state as an orderly, homogeneous white society. A free New England would be a white New England. But gradual emancipation had merely redefined slaves as freemen; their numbers, and certainly their visibility, had not decreased.

The hardening ideology of "race"—innate, permanent difference, located within the body as part of each person's essential nature—effectively contained and managed people of color, as had the old institution of slavery. But slavery had controlled them inclusively; that is, slaves had occupied a naturalized place within the structure of family household and community, as the testimony of both slaves and their owners makes clear, and they had been represented thereby in the polity (in the same sense in which women were represented) through the male household head. "Race," on the other hand, controlled people of color as an excluded category, a presence-in-absence with no representation and no new system of reciprocal bonds of obligation, of affection, or of any other kind. Thus, as the social uncertainty of the post-Revolutionary period subsided, a new institutional order took shape in which free people of color, "naturally" inferior, not only had no predetermined place but seemed to be unwelcome survivors of an emancipation process that was supposed to have eliminated them. In this new order, the conception of people of color as "strangers," which had been evoked as an initial justification for enslaving them almost two hundred years earlier, reemerged as a potent argument for their isolation and removal. An extraordinary range of antebellum responses in New England to issues and events involving people of color can be read as attempts to fulfill the implied promise of antislavery rhetoric—to effect the removal of people of color.[3] These efforts took highly symbolic as well as quite literal forms.

[1] In Edward Mathews and Andrew T. Foss, *Facts for Baptist Churches* (Utica, N.Y.: American Baptist Free Mission Society, 1850), p. 156.

[2] *The Journals and Miscellaneous Notebooks of Ralph Waldo Emerson*, ed. William H. Gilman et al. (Cambridge: Harvard University Press, Belknap Press, 1960–82), 13:198.

[3] Many scholars have discussed the rising white nationalism of the 1840s and 1850s and consequent efforts, notably of the American Colonization Society, to eliminate people of color. See, e.g., George Fredrickson, *The Black Image in the White Mind: The Debate on Afro-American Character and Destiny, 1817–1914* (New York: Harper & Row, 1971), esp. pp. 131–32. Here, however, I stress Revolutionary antislavery rhetoric and the process of gradual emancipation as sources of a distinctly regional white nationalism; I also argue that one of the most im-

Symbolic removal included the production of graphic and literary representations of people of color as preposterous extremes of the stupid, the evil or the saintly, and often the alien or foreign, thus substituting totally imaginative constructions for depictions of existing persons. Representing people of color as the singularly "expendable" element in games and stories was another form of symbolic removal, as was spiriting away their corpses for experimentation or sport. Some of these measures were exercises in wishful thinking on the part of whites longing to eliminate "the problem" of people of color who had somehow survived emancipation. Others, especially those that systematically portrayed people of color as defective and dangerous ersatz citizens, served to stimulate and authorize other strategies of removal that promised to achieve more tangible results.

Literal attempts to reduce the black populations in New England cities and towns included targeting people of color for "warning out" as undesirables under the legal settlement laws; taxing their presence; advocating their wholesale transportation to Africa under the aegis of the American Colonization Society; and, finally, conducting terroristic, armed raids on urban black communities and the institutions that served them.

Inseparable from both symbolic and literal attempts to eliminate the "problem" were efforts to constitute free people of color imaginatively as removable or to idealize them in a setting far removed from New England. The two kinds of efforts functioned dialectically: imaginative representations of people of color as personifications of evil or absurdity or even saintly tractability validated the various strategies of literal removal and actually carried them out in the symbolic sphere; the discourse of removal in turn projected an ever more distorted identity of alienation and anomaly onto people of color.

A crucial step in effecting the removal of people of color from New England was the imaginative construction of a crude set of caricatures that could capture the public imagination as representing the "true" nature of free blacks. Whites could then substitute these easily understood, static representations, which fulfilled whites' assumptions about the limitations of people of color and the problems they presented, for the complex and ever changing reality of free people of color struggling to build lives and communities in the chaotic environment of post-Revolutionary America. In the sense that this substitution effaced actual people of color for perhaps a majority of whites, it not only represented a preliminary step in the removal

---

portant consequences, the ascendancy of "race" as a defining and controlling ideology of exclusion, activated removal efforts.

of people of color but constituted a form of removal itself. This "imaginary negro" was popularized in a genre of humorous and (often savagely) satiric anecdotes, cartoons, and broadsides which began to appear in the 1780s and 1790s as gradual emancipation unfolded. This fictional exploration of role reversal represented people of color as "naturally" ineligible for the role of "true" republican citizen.

The earliest examples merely depict free people of color as a kind of earnestly silly curiosity. Humorous blacks first appeared in almanacs, a literature written largely for rural workers and their families. Shane White sees almanac humor as acknowledging and often applauding black agency and thus as evidence of working-class whites' receptivity to the inclusion of free people of color in mainstream culture. It is important, however, to interpret almanac humor about people of color within a larger discourse of role reversal ridicule: the long and evolving effort by whites to embody free people of color in print, not merely to speak for and through them in a ventriloquistic mode but also to gauge the extent to which they might plausibly enact equality, and to demonstrate the aspects of black character and behavior that would operate to limit or obstruct such a transformation.

For example, an anecdote in Daniel Sewall's 1794 *An Astronomical Diary, or Almanac* describes a scene in which four "negroes" carry a corpse to a grave "at a place where it was a custom to give the bearers gloves; but those four were not presented with any." Cuffee asks Caesar, Cato, and Toney in turn, "You got e gruv!" When each confirms he has no gloves, Cuffee says, "Well then, fring he down, and let he *go heself.*"[4] Here, blacks (probably free?) who are not given equipment appropriate to their task even the score by refusing to do the work. The humor, however, comes from the apparent relish with which Cuffee satisfies his outrage by mistakenly asserting his authority over a dead man instead of the appropriate target, his employer. The employer is not only unidentified but universalized to all whites by the use of the passive voice in describing the withholding of gloves from a particularized "those four"; thus the anecdote sets up an equivalency between the rights of dead whites and live "negroes," leaving the rights of living whites—universal owners/employers—as intact and inviolable, above any arithmetic of reciprocity that might include people of color. Although the black protagonist asserts equality and "wins," the victory is not merely hollow but inherently laughable.

Other examples, such as those in David Everett's 1799 *Common Sense in Dishabille; or, the Farmer's Monitor,* test the limits of equality across color more explicitly. In a much longer and more sophisticated story, "a gentleman"

---

[4] Daniel Sewall, *An Astronomical Diary, or Almanac* (Portsmouth, N.H.: John Melcher, 1794), n.p.

who is "fond of French fashions" decides to introduce democratic practices into his family governance: "A council was called, and Sambo was invited among the rest." (Although Sambo's precise status is unstated, he is clearly a servant of some sort.) The father announces to his assembled family members, "Hereafter I will lay aside commands and punishments, the instruments of tyrants, and you shall be governed by reason. Your own judgment, instead of my severity, shall correct your faults." Sambo responds, "You berry good, master; I tanka you, master." Mother and daughter immediately object to Sambo's sitting at table for dinner, and one son who "foresaw Sambo would soon rule the roost" proposes that he exchange the right to sit at table for his obligation to serve the meal to the white members; he agrees, and the family members serve themselves. A series of incidents ensues in which Sambo asserts his rights. When his master wants his boots blacked, Sambo is busy blacking his own boots; when the master's boots are finally ready, a son has ridden off with his horse. The next day, when the master invites people to dinner, Sambo has already invited his own friends, and "the sooty tribe had taken possession of the kitchen just before his master's party entered the parlour." When the master reverts to "high words and hard blow's," then "liberty and equality" are "echoed from each corner of the kitchen by the blacks." In the end, the master reestablishes patriarchal authority, shaking his head at "liberty and equality" and noting that "he believed that if they were allowed to run at large in our country, they would do more mischief than sword and famine."[5] Here, Sambo takes full advantage of the equality offered to him; the story is funny only because the underlying assumption is that such equality is inherently absurd. Making choices on equal terms with a white male adult is understood to be as absurd for an adult person of color as it is for a white child; exercising equality is an effort to "rule the roost" when the inherently unqualified attempt it. Sambo is as unqualified as a child for equal status as a citizen.

Part of the humor of some anecdotes lies in the incongruousness of situations in which a "false" citizen of color bests the "true" white citizen. These passages invite the reader to marvel at instances of superior wisdom emanating from a source generally thought to be incapable of it. In this sense, the black characters follow in a long tradition of "wise fools," a role whose effectiveness depends upon the general acceptance of the negative assumptions to which it proves exceptional.

Free people of color were featured as counterfeit citizens in other forms

[5] David Everett, *Common Sense in Dishabille; or, the Farmer's Monitor. Containing a variety of Familiar Essays, on Subjects Moral & Economical. To which is added, a Perpetual Calendar, or Economical Almanack* (Worcester, Mass.: Isaiah Thomas, 1799), pp. 45–48.

Cuffey near him
grasps his hand!
Page 66. ECHO 10.

Figure 2. Courtesy of the Library Company of Philadelphia

of humorous writing as well. For example, an untitled satirical poem attributed to one of the "Connecticut Wits" (probably Richard Alsop) which appeared in the *American Mercury* in January 1793 ridiculed "the celebrated Equality Ball given to the Negroes of Boston by Massachusetts Governor John Hancock." The poet calls Boston a land of "motley scenes" and "a mixture strange of various things," where people of color "loud to anarchy their voices raise / in hallelujahs and in hymns of praise, / to the sweet Tune of Freedom born anew." In an accompanying illustration, Hancock is pictured at the ball where "the noble sons of Afric call," delighting in "their graceful tricks, and winning ways," their "toones enchanting," and the "fragrant air" they exude (see Figure 2). Then,

> While CUFFEY near him takes his stand,
> Hale-fellow met, and grasps his hand—

> With pleasure glistening in his eyes,
> "Ah! Massa Gubbernur!" he cries,
> "Me grad to see you, for de peeple say
> "you lub de Neegur better dan de play."[6]

Having characterized Boston as a locus of disorder, of "motley" and "mixture," the poet then identifies people of color as the cause—people who sing to anarchy and who can be identified by the inappropriateness of their language to the station to which Hancock has elevated them. Here again, people of color are represented as enacting a preposterous imitation of the forms of a citizenship whose substance eludes them.

The nature and uses of the dialect in which black speech is represented in these examples must be critically examined. Shane White sees the use of dialect in the almanac dialogues as a strategy for affirming black cultural distinction which renders people of color as sympathetic characters, and he returns to these examples in his later discussion of the development of creolized dialect as an element of New World black culture.[7] It can also be argued, however, that dialect serves an estranging and delimiting function. A black speaker may outwit a white citizen, but he (speakers in these dialogues are invariably male) cannot aspire to citizenship; he remains safely imprisoned within his speech, which is as much an indelible sign of his ineligibility for true citizenship as his skin color or his former enslaved status. The dialect can thus be interpreted as working to establish the "racial" boundaries of citizenship and the foolishness of black aspirations to its ranks.

The latter interpretation does not rest upon the assertion that the form of speech used by black characters is a figment of white imagination. There is no doubt that the dialect represented in almanac humor is drawn from the actual speech of large numbers of people of color living in New England. This language may have been a creolized pidgin or trade language, with an English vocabulary, spoken widely by slaves in North America. J. L. Dillard, the best-known scholar of Black English, suggests that it probably developed on the West Coast of Africa in the course of the English involvement in maritime trade, specifically the slave trade. He and others have thoroughly discredited early attempts to define "Negro dialect" in literary works as pure invention. Except for "eye dialect," in which distortion is merely visual and does not reflect actual patterns of

---

[6] *The Echo, with Other Poems* (Hartford, Conn.: Porcupine Press, 1807), p. 65, rpt. from *American Mercury,* January 1793.

[7] Shane White, *Somewhat More Independent: The End of Slavery in New York City, 1770–1810* (Athens: University of Georgia Press, 1991), pp. 166–73, 88–192.

pronunciation (e.g., *wuznt* for *wasn't*), he sees most literary representations as faithful attempts to reflect the language actually spoken by slaves and free people of color.[8]

Yet Dillard somewhat overstates the verisimilitude and transparency of literary versions of black dialect and underestimates the extent to which it could be, and frequently was, strategically employed as a kind of code for blacks' incompetence and impoverished imitation of the language, and personhood, of whites. It worked as a code in this way precisely because white Americans were so familiar with the English of African and African American speakers. In New England the influx of slaves imported directly from Africa during the 1760s must have produced a generation of speakers of African-influenced pidgins who would have been in their fifties and sixties at the turn of the nineteenth century.[9] Chloe Spear, a native African enslaved about 1750 and brought to Boston, was recalled as speaking in this way: "I say, O massa, I poor creature, I no fit for baptize," and "Cesar, house to sell [there is a house for sale]."[10] Peter Cooper, a free person of color of New Haven, was recalled in 1827 as having told a story some years before about Heaven's gatekeeper: "He take de book and he look de book, and at last he finda Peeta Coopa in lilly, lilly [little] corner."[11]

But as a host of other sources make clear, many people of color did not speak pidgin or creole. Certainly, members of the literate middle class did not. Prince Hall, founder of the African Masonic Lodge, denounced discrimination in Boston in 1797 as follows: "We may truly be said to carry our lives in our hands, and the arrows of death are flying about our heads."

[8] J. L. Dillard, *Black English: Its History and Usage in the United States* (New York: Random House, 1972), pp. 6, 21. Dillard's insistence that Black English was an entirely separate language with a deep structure quite different from that of standard English has been hotly debated; see, e.g., Walter A. Wolfram and Nona H. Clarke, eds., *Black-White Speech Relationships* (Washington, D.C.: Center for Applied Linguistics, 1971), p. 156. Most linguists now would probably agree with William Labov that Black English exhibits significant differences in surface structure (which Labov claims are increasing in a process Edgar W. Schneider calls "neocreolization") but few in deep structure. See Labov and Paul Cohen, "Systematic Relations of Standard and Non-Standard Rules in the Grammar of Negro Speakers," in *Language, Society, and Education: A Profile of Black English*, ed. Johanna S. De Stefano (Worthington, Ohio: Charles A. Jones, 1973), p. 153; and Schneider, *American Earlier Black English: Morphological and Syntactic Variables* (Tuscaloosa: University of Alabama Press, 1989), pp. 4–41, esp. 18–22, 16.

[9] Ira Berlin, "Time, Space, and the Evolution of Afro-American Society on British Mainland North America," *American Historical Review* 85 (February 1980): 51–54.

[10] [Mary Webb], *Memoir of Chloe Spear, A Native of Africa, who was enslaved in Childhood, and Died in Boston, January 3, 1815 . . . Aged 65 Years. By a Lady of Boston* (Boston, 1832), pp. 39, 57. See Schneider, *American Earlier Black English*, pp. 223–24, on the use of the "dummy subject" in its zero form.

[11] "Black Man's Dream," *Connecticut Journal*, September 11, 1827. See Schneider, *American Earlier Black English*, pp. 65–69 for use and nonuse of verbal -s morpheme in its zero form.

Lemuel Haynes, a black Congregationalist minister to mostly white churches in New England, composed his sermons in language such as this: "He that would infringe upon a mans liberty may reasonably Expect to meet with opposision. . . . Liberty is Equally as pre[c]ious to a Black man, as it is to a white one, and Bondage Equally as intollarable to the one as it is to the other."[12] Even the writing of many poor and nonliterate persons of color who are somewhat phonetic spellers reflects little if any pidgin/ creole influence. Jeney, wife of Ceser, wrote to Moses Brown in 1800, "Mr. Brown Ceser is left me and my tou children without Vittels or drink he sase you must maintain him and he is a coming. . . . he has gave the house up and if you Dont assist me I shall be Turn out adoors."[13]

Free people of color, then, exhibited a variety of styles of speech and writing, depending on their experience as African- or American-born, their age and gender, their level of literacy, and their economic position. Educated black speakers of standard English may have engaged in "code-switching"—or altering their patterns of oral language toward the pidgin/ creole in what might be termed "street speech"—in predominantly black company, but they would have been much less likely to do so in the hearing of whites.[14] Thus, urban whites in particular would have been exposed to a wide range of black speech patterns. In this context, the use of pidgin/creole dialect as a code for "black" can be read as an effort to establish an undifferentiated social identity for free people of color as a group, to distance or estrange that group from whites' social identity, and to establish its unbridgeable mental difference.

By 1815, representations of black dialect had been elaborated and combined with eye dialect to produce a stylized, exaggerated language manifestly constructed as an instrument of estrangement and ridicule. It was a source of vicious humor in a series of satirical broadsides, most if not all published in Boston, which first appeared around 1816 and remained popular until about 1828. Whereas the almanac pieces had undertaken to represent people of color in third-person narratives, the broadsides were ventriloquistic impersonations of them. Much more elaborate productions than the brief almanac pieces, these broadsides directly ridiculed the life-

[12] Hall quoted in William C. Nell, *The Colored Patriots of the American Revolution* (1835; New York: Arno Press, 1968), p. 63; Ruth Bogin, "'Liberty Further Extended': A 1776 Antislavery Manuscript by Lemuel Haynes," *William and Mary Quarterly* 40 (1983): 95.

[13] Jeney to Moses Brown, November 1800, Brown Papers, Rhode Island Historical Society. See Schneider, *American Earlier Black English*, pp. 81–82, on the formation of the past tense with the zero form of *-ed*, and pp. 145–47 on the use of the prefix *a-* before a present participle.

[14] Dillard, *Black English*, p.31, briefly discusses code-switching among contemporary speakers of Black English.

styles and manners of people of color in New England who "presumed" to take on the social and cultural characteristics of middle-class whites.[15]

The broadside literature can be interpreted as a quite specific response to several linked aspects of the changing role of free people of color which many whites interpreted as their disruptive intrusion into the accepted social order: their growing visibility as they withdrew from white households and formed dense communities at the margins of white society; their independence from the increasing regimentation of industrialization (because, ironically, for the most part they were excluded from factory employment); their public display of a separate institutional life.

The broadsides were usually issued in response to some public event in which people of color figured prominently. Many satirized the annual July 14 celebrations, held by Boston's black community beginning in 1808, of the closing of the Atlantic slave trade (see Figure 3).[16] After 1828 another series of single-sheet, colored etchings and lithographs, published in Philadelphia but apparently widely distributed elsewhere in the northern states, offered a somewhat more general (and vicious) satirical attack on the manners and pretensions of well-to-do people of color, replacing the extensive text of the earlier broadsides with cartoonlike punch lines (see Figure 4). The popularity of the series outside Philadelphia is evidenced by the rapid appearance of a similar series in New York and, in the 1830s, an even more elaborately executed one in London (it seems significant that the popularity of the British series, "Tregear's Black Jokes," coincided with the parliamentary debate over emancipation in the colonies).[17] That the Boston "bobalition broadsides" were prototypes for the new forms of

[15] The broadsides of the early 1800s do not represent the first combination of pidgin/creole forms with eye dialect to ridicule people of color; Alan W. C. Green notes that in *The Candidates; or, The Humors of a Virginia Election* (1775), by Robert Munford, the character "Ralpho is distinguished not by his dialect but by foppishness, ostentation and a ludicrous misuse of language." The characterizations of African Americans in formal dramatic and literary productions were varied and not as relentlessly derisive as those in the broadsides, although after 1780 they too tended to emphasize black pretensions to white social status, as is clear from Green's article "'Jim Crow,' 'Zip Coon': The Northern Origins of Negro Minstrelsy," *Massachusetts Review* 11 (Spring 1970): 385–88.

[16] *Columbian Centinel*, July 6, 1808.

[17] Shane White, "'It Was a Proud Day': African Americans, Festivals, and Parades in the North, 1742–1834," *Journal of American History* 81 (June 1994): 35–38, discusses "Bobalition" broadsides parodying July 14 marches. Henry Louis Gates describes three and characterizes them as racist "signifyin(g)" parodies in which whites demonstrate critical familiarity with black dialect; see *The Signifying Monkey: A Theory of African-American Literary Criticism* (New York: Oxford University Press, 1988), pp. 90–95. Alan Green, "Jim Crow," p. 388, briefly mentions one as "exploiting the grotesqueries long associated with Negro speech." Philip Lapsansky discusses them as the progenitors of a genre of "consistent and coherent antiblack caricature," focusing on their graphic elements; see his "Graphic Discord: Abolitionist and Antiabolitionist Images," in *The Abolitionist Sisterhood: Women's Political Culture in Antebellum America*, ed. Jean Fagan Yellin and John C. Van Horne (Ithaca: Cornell University Press, 1994), pp. 216–19. I am deeply indebted to Philip Lapsansky, research librarian at the Library Com-

antiblack caricature that rapidly appeared throughout the so-called free states can be argued from the elements they share. Some of their differences, such as the greater elaboration of graphic images in the later series, probably reflect technological advances in printing. Others, notably the reduction of what was frequently a full hundred square inches of text, usually in a three-column format, in the New England broadsides to punch-line captions and dialogue balloons in the Philadelphia, New York, and London series may have had more substantive ideological implications.

The New England broadsides were typically headed by an announcment of an event or celebration, rendered in dialect, usually accompanied by a depiction of elaborately dressed people of color engaged in an activity that is inappropriate in some way. Three columns of text, also in a broad dialect, followed, often in the form of letters or dialogues attributed to individuals whose names combined common slave names with words lampooning physical attributes or actions. Toasts and song lyrics are also regular features.

A good example exhibiting all these characteristics is an 1827 broadside headed "GRAND JUBELUM!!! Order 12f Annebersary ob Affricum BOBALITION. Copy of a Letter from CEZAR BLUBBERLIP to his Brother CUFF CROOKSHANK, in the Country." The graphic image (see Figure 5) portrays five men and one woman of color gathered around a table on which sit three glasses and two overturned bottles, one pouring its contents onto the floor unnoticed by the party. The men are well dressed, with one sporting striped pants and a cane. Another man is lying under the table, obviously drunk, and a third is dancing off balance, possibly about to hit the floor as well. The woman, whose facial features are greatly exaggerated, is wearing an overly large beplumed bonnet and neck ruffle. The man to her right has his arm across her shoulder with his hand at the back of her neck, and her head appears to be leaning back on his wrist; yet she is at the same time raptly staring at the man on her left, against whose shoulder she is tightly nestled.[18]

In the letter that follows, dated "Bosson, Augus Tre 180027," "Cezar" re-

---

pany of Philadelphia, for generously sharing his personal collection of these broadsides and making available the graphic series, "Life in Philadelphia," "Life in New York," "Tregear's Black Jokes" (1834), and related materials from the collection of the Library Company, as well as his thoughts on their genealogical relationship to the more textual broadsides. I am also indebted to John Saillant for informing me of the 1817 "Bosson Artillerum Election" broadside (the earliest one I have located) in the collection of Sturbridge Village (Mass.) Research Library.

[18] "GRAND JUBELUM!!! Order 12f Annebersary ob Africum BOBALITION," 1827, Broadside Collection, John Hay Library Brown, University, Providence. Figure 5 is actually reproduced from a different broadside on which the print is clearer but the image is the same: "Grand Celebration of the Bobalition of African Slavery," 1825, Broadside Collection, Boston Public Library.

SQUANTUM FESTIVAL!
Or, Bobalition No. 2.

A DIALOGUE between Scipio Smilax, Barber, & Mungo Meanwell, Bootblack.

SCENE—BELKNAP STREET.

Mungo.—Ah! Misser Smilax, how you do, sir—hope to see you berry well sir.

Scipio.—Why tollyble, tank you—hope you much better as I am.

Mungo.—Well, sir, what you get for news now; any ting berry splent and speshal turn up lately? you know cherry ting what come out in de paper, besides good deal what you find out down in town.

Scipio.—Why yes, I hab good chance to hear de news as mose my body. I take all de paper in my shop to suit de customer, and mose always read um through, sept dat half of um which fill up wid long story bout quack medicine and other vegetable what cure folks when dey half dead, and bring um to life again afterwards.

Mungo.—Ha! ha! ha!—I believe so, when I find out how de moon made of green cheese. But is dere any ting new to day, sir?

Scipio.—Why no, not zackly any ting new—cause be no more dan what I spect, and jiss what happen lass year, little fore dis time afterward.

Mungo.—Well, sir, what be um? Hab de Boston folks take up some of deir old nation cause dey no got time to find new one?

Scipio.—No, he hab only nudder long talk wid old Missy Squantum what berry de broad axe tree four year ago. I tought after so much fuss about one ting an mudder, dey better mind he own business, and let de old Squaw alone one year.

Mungo.—It be no more dan what I spect, Scipio; but seem to me he put off dis bobalition good while mose as he use to. What you spose was de reason of dat, sir?

Scipio.—Why I tell you all bout um. You see, Mungo, dey hab so many sellyorabum altogedder, dat de feel shame to keep frolic all de time, so dey put of Missy Squantum till mose de lyss of um.

Mungo.—A berry good reason too Misser Smilax—and I guess some of um want time to earn money to pay for what he hab frolic mose all summer into de fall of de year.

Scipio.—Yes, you hove half right dere. But less count up how many time he hab frolic day. In de fuss place he hab two beeshum same as commonsensam de fourt of Uly—tou hove a week whim de Cadet Soger come from de West side of de Point, and dey come up right and dis. Den dey hab de mincement two tree days round now to day dey go nex Id Squantum. In de next place, dey go to hab gran trainin on de common week after nex—and I guess, on dey make out till tanksgiving, spose de Sea Serpent no come, and dey all go down to Nahant to count how many tickle he carry on his back, and measure how long his tail be nudderd foot under water.

Mungo.—And yet Scipio, dey brackguard us cause we hab one bobalition day, and dey all leave deir work to run and see our pocashum too.

Scipio.—Yes, dat jiss like um. Nudder ting I like to forget—Dey spend whole afternoon, jiss to Misser Guille five minutes way up in de air in he balloon out of sight, chasing a thunder shower over to Charlestown. However, I no blame for dat so much. cause I go myself and see um. But dey needent holler so when he fuss start—how dey know but what dey scare de man so he no able to stir himself, and no tumble overboard toward foot high, and break he neck?

Mungo.—Sure nuff, I guess so, but I say, Scipio, you know how de white people disrepresent our procesdum. spose you and I go to de printer, and get um to print song and toue bout deir Squantum Bobalition. It be no more dan fair—and de Printer glad of de jub, so he get pay for um.

Scipio.—Why I was tinking bout dat myself. So lass night I set down and write parcel of toue and song. If dey make fun of our good dinner, and de bottle of Madeira, I no see why we hant got a right to laugh at deir clam chowder and strong water as he call um.

Mungo.—stil thak so too. But less hear some of de toue you make for um. I guess dey look mad when dey see um in print.

Scipio.—Well, den, I read some of um to you.
(Scipio reads.)

De Squantum lobster—We no see he got bigger claws dan what dey sell in Tate-treet.

De Squantum clam—Good deal better dan dem up by de rope-walk.

Missy Squantum—Hope she no get so drunk as no tell which way to go back to he wigwam.

De big Sachem—He look no more like Indian dan my old fiddle like a gate post.

De town of Shaumut—Some great wigwam, and good many little um—some half Indian, and some no tell what to make of um.

De great broad-axem—Guess he mose want new handle by dis time.

Tate treet—Some beard-shaver dare, but de noteshaver cut de closest.

De Boylston market—Wonder how much time it take to clean um up dis fall.

De Long wharfem—How long you spose he take to go from Squantum to de end of um, spose you no start for five o'clock dis arternoon.

De President of de Noted Tate—Wonder whedder he like clam chowder—Guess better send him some by de Steam-Boat.

Tom cole he Sachem—He little tink in de mornin he get so merry fore sun-down.

De big Stone Hospital—Wonder if de corner rock dey lay two, tree, four year ago, and make such fuss about um, lay still now.

De 'Convention' what try to mend de old Constitushum—He jiss like tinker, try to stop one hole, and make half dozen more; gess he want nudder job. and get two dollar a day for um.

De Cadets—Now dey get home, gess dey laf good good deal bout Boston folks action.

De man in de moon—Gess he laf too if he see how dey carry on here.

De day we sellybrate—We gut him off good while, but he come long full fass nuf dese hard time.

De Bosson Theatre—Guess de Manager keep Keea look out dis year, and no get catch like a weazel asleep again.

De Bosson Banks—Much better dan de Squantum clam bank.

De town of Charlestown—Wonder how many hog constable dey go to choose nex March meetum.

Wess Bosson—He great sore on de city, as Massa Jefferson say. Guess he take big plaster to cover um.

De Mill Dam—Guess some folks d—— him up hill and down, fore dis time.

Old time in de Primer—No such time now adays.

Cambridge Bridge—Since dey build big mill-dam, he look sour on tother side de mout.

De Brighton Cattle Show—He berry fine place for de modest lady to go to.

De late storm—He jiss like us to day—he hab a regular blow-out.

De old Rebolutionary Pensioner—Fore dey gib him, dey make him swear he poor as Job's tu'key's.

De memory of Major Andre, who die quick good many year ago—Why dey no let de dead rest, and no sturb um to make fuss bote tide de water?

Scipio. Well Mungo, how you like dese tose, sir?

Mungo.—Spose my word, Scipio, I no tink you reach Poet-maker before. Now I tell you what, you gib me tose and de song, and I ge right down and make bargain wid de Printer, spose I have to pay de whole myself. Well see den whedder de white people brackguard our Bobalition again.

Scipio.—Ay, so do, Mungo—I pay half de spence, and I guess we sell nuff to make up tudder tree quarters— So I wish you berry good day, sir.

Mungo—Good bye sir. I fetch you de proof-sheet to morrow morning by sun-rise, and haps dis arternoon. Member my specks to your lady, and de rest of de family.
(Exeunt severally.)

Mungo. Yes, sir, I like um berry well, cause I tink dere jiss as much and good deal more trute in um, dan in dem dey make bout us. But, sir, I should like to hear de song what you make for um. I hope be better dan de one he make for in lass Bobalition Day.

Scipio. Why to tell de trute, Mungo, I no confess to be much of poet; but now and den I scrabble little for de newspaper, and tell de printer he put um in if he like.

Mungo. Yes, all dat right nuff; but now for de song.

Scipio. Well den, here be; now you mind and keep bote ear open.
(Scipio reads.)

DE SQUANTUM FEAST.

Tune—"Great way off of cez."

JOLLY blades and all,
Who are fond of frolic,
Join with us to-day,
It will cure de cholic.
How we dash along,
Full of mirth and glee, sirs,
Here are " waters strong,"
Both for you and me, sirs.

CHORUS.
Lobster, Chowder, Clam,
For de lads who want 'em,
Brandy, Gin and Rum,
All are found at Squantum.

II.

Here upon de rock
As we view de ocean,
Tom-cods to the shore,
To haul we have a notion.
Now slice up the pork,
And we'll soon be trying
All our cocks at work
To have a glorious frying.

CHORUS.
Lobsters, Eels and Clams,
For de lads who want 'em,
Fried and boil'd and stew'd,
All are found at Squantum.

III.

Push about de can
With strong waters flowing,
Let the song go round,
We shall soon be going;
Let us, while we stay
Spite of wind and weather,
If we do get high,
All get drunk together.

CHORUS.
Lobsters, tom-cod, clam,
He no longer want 'em,
Brandy, Gin, and Rum,
Flow full fast at Squantum.

IV.

Now the sun declines,
We must all be moving,
Farewell, Squantum, now,
Good old Squaw so loving:
When we come next year,
Into this your quarter,
We will never fear,
Bring plenty of strong water.

CHORUS.
Lobsters, eels and clams,
We no longer want 'em,
Now good night ad once,
Fine old Madam Squantum.

Figure 3. 1821 Broadside. Courtesy of Brown University Library

Figure 4. Courtesy of the Library Company of Philadelphia

Figure 5. Detail of 1825 broadside. Courtesy of the Trustees of the Boston Public Library

counts "de magnanumus doing in dis town lass Uly de eleben." He exclaims,

> O! 'twoud make your heart jump for joy and miseration to see by 9 o'clock horror and convality depict in ebery countenance, much as to say "take care yoursef you brack b—ch and you little sheldrens, dare will be de debble to pay fore night!—At 10Q.M. de moss spiceable brack folk ob stinkation gan show he head from ebery treet and ally, like so many Mohe-choah Mink in a mud-bank—at eleben precise, or little arter, de Common was fill to oberflowing, and fifty more lady in a mud-scow.

He describes the procession of marshals "wid role ob sheep skin," guards "in plete uniform," a "Torator in scarlet robe ob lambs wool," and last, "great many white and yallur folk, who bring up de rear, some to honor us, but more to hurl brik bat and rotten egg at our head." He concludes, "in dis order we peaceably proceed" and then details the ensuing dinner celebration. He reports fifteen toasts, all in dialect, several of which comment sharply upon political issues national and local. He concludes with the lyrics of a song sung by "Pomp," the "Vice Preseden":

> When I was a Picanniny,
> I was brot away from Guinea,
> Tore away from my poor Modder,
> Farder, granny, sisser, broder.
> My cruel Massa hard did treat me,
> Starve me, kick me, cuff and beat me,
> Call me tick-skull, wool-head mink,
> And say I lousy, rotten—stink!
> But now 'tis better time for me,
> Pomp little bigger man den he.
> I have pig, and wife, and child,
> He grow poor, despise, and wild,
> While he sorely now repent,
> *He honor Pomp, Vice-Prezedent!*[19]

The overall strategy of such broadsides was to ridicule the public activities of free people of color as imitation citizenship—ridiculous and pathetic efforts to assume the forms of civic participation and a public identity whose substance they were incapable of understanding. Clearly,

[19] "GRAND JUBELUM!!!" 1827, John Hay Library.

whites found the public role and "place" of free people of color in ante-bellum Boston to be galling and incongruous. The anonymous promulgators of the broadsides viewed their public behavior in celebrating the closing of the slave trade as a kind of encapsulation of everything objectionable about their "intrusion" into the public life of the community, especially their appropriation and debasement of "white" institutions and practices such as patriotic celebrations of events of public significance.

The dialect invented for these broadsides enacted this intrusion by disrupting the orderly grammar and diction of standard English, imitating "high style" in truncated or otherwise distorted rhetorical flourishes and juxtaposing grandiloquent words with ungrammatical constructions and mispronounced words.[20] This language embodies misrule, naturalizing "false whiteness" and counterfeit citizenship as innate characteristics of free people of color. It is a language that depends for its effect on the punning oppositions it generates by altering words to resemble other words with a contrary meaning, achieving an unintended (by the speaker) self-derogation: For example, "de moss spiceable brack folk ob stinkation" represents a garbled attempt at "respectable" and "distinction," yielding, instead, something closer to "despicable" and a vernacular neologism for the state of "stinking." Thus the broadsides show people of color as debasing and barbarizing the practices of citizenship while trying to employ them in the service of aristocratic pretensions that are not only false but also unrepublican.

Occasionally broadsides expressed sympathy as well as ridicule for the celebrations of people of color, as Shane White has pointed out.[21] "Reply to Bobalition," for example, represents two black figures criticizing whites for misrepresenting the behavior of people of color at July 14 celebration and reporting on the public misbehavior of whites at one of their own celebrations. Yet the dialect and names (one speaker is named "Mungo Meanwell") suggest that even if people of color deserve sympathy because their desire to speak and participate in civic life is well-intentioned, they lack the capacity to do so.[22]

The song that concludes the text of "GRAND JUBELUM" offers a particu-

[20] I am treating the language forms represented in all the broadsides as one invented dialect because they exhibit more similarities than differences. E.g., grotesque misspelling is a common characteristic, although variations in spelling occur between and even within broadsides: "de," "dat," "dose," and so forth, are common, but "the," "that," and "those" may appear alongside them; "xcellum" in one may be "exellunt" in another, but the effect is the same. It is precisely their invented nature and common purpose that constitute the broadside languages as a single dialect for analytical purposes.

[21] See White, "It Was a Proud Day," p. 35.

[22] "Reply to Bobalition," 1821, Broadside Collection, American Antiquarian Society.

larly clear example of the ambiguity and complexity of whites' perception, and ultimate rejection, of blacks' claim to the role of citizen. The slaves' experience of capture and brutal treatment is depicted starkly and with obvious sympathy, which is nonetheless undercut by an appeal to ridicule inherent in the choice of derogatory concepts, such as "tick-skull, wool-head mink." The reversal of fortune of "My cruel Massa"—celebrated as "He grow poor, despise, and wild, While he sorely now repent, He honor Pomp, Vice-Prezedent!"—seeks to inspire revulsion and disbelief by the juxtaposition of civic office with a slave name and the ersatz officeholder's equation of civic achievement with the acquisition of a pig, a wife, and a child in that order of priority.[23] The graphic image too, in a calculated appeal to white outrage, emphasizes the juxtaposition of class pretension and debasement in the behavior of free people of color. The participants in a scene of public drunkenness are attired in exaggerated finery. The woman advertises her indiscriminate sexual availability by allowing herself to be groped by two different men at once.

Another popular image that adorned a number of "bobalition" broadsides depicts a company of black foot soldiers with exaggerated facial features, attired in elaborate uniforms and tricorn hats with outsized plumes. The soldiers at the front carry cudgels angled upward at the groin level. Two carry spears, while three at the rear play a drum, a horn, and a fife. Another carries the company flag bearing the image of an African elephant. This military image appears in two versions: in one, used in at least two broadsides, the company is led by a black officer wearing epaulets, bearing a curved sword, and mounted on a white horse (Figure 6). In the second version, used in at least three broadsides, the procession appears to be led by the cudgel bearers; the cudgel of the man slightly in the lead extends beyond his groin in an unmistakable allusion to an erect penis (Figure 7).[24] Evidently, whites regarded military formations of men of color as oxymoronic. The broadsides ridiculed their claims of eligibility to participate in such civic, and civilized, activities, stressing their barbaric origins and animal urges by means of the spears, the elephant, and the suggestive placement of the cudgels.

The African Society of Boston, a mutual aid society founded in 1796 which spearheaded the annual July 14 celebrations in Boston, was a special target of the broadsides.[25] Whites apparently found the established

[23] "GRAND JUBELUM!!!" 1827, John Hay Library.

[24] An example of the first version is "Grand Bobalition of Slavery," n.d. [1820?], Broadside Collection, John Hay Library; an example of the second is "Grand Bobalition, or 'Great Annibersary Fussible,'" 1821, Broadside Collection, Boston Public Library.

[25] See James Oliver Horton, *Free People of Color: Inside the African American Community* (Washington, D.C.: Smithsonian Institution Press, 1993), p. 49.

Grand Bobalition of Slavery

Grand and most helligunt Selebrashum of de Bobalition of Slabery in de Nited Tate ob Neu Englunt, and commonwet of Bosson in de country of Massa-chuse-it.

Order of de Presidum of de day, to de Shief Marshall, and all de rest of he understraper.

DEAR SIR—You GREAT RASCAL!
I haking been compinted de President of de day,

marshall, company wid de music of de band, and dischaige of a popgun.

De Day—May he be sellymate long as de Fourt of July, and seben year arter all lates posterity.

How sweet be de rum, and de sugar and water, When enuf you can get in de belly to fill, But sweeter he Cato more booutiful daughter, De lubly Miss Phillis, de Rose of de Hill.

2. She blush like a blanket wid hole in de corner

Figure 6. Detail of broadside, n.d. [1820?]. Courtesy of Brown University Library

leadership and middle-class constituency of the society especially rankling. For example, "Grand Bobalition of Slavery," bearing the illustration of the black military company with its mounted leader, begins with a letter from "Cato Cudjoe, Presidum of de day" to the "Shief Marshall," announcing, "To day, by virtue of de autority of de Shocietee, I knock you down if I like. . . . Tomorro, I shake hand wid you, help you sweep de street, or brack de boot and do noting at all almos besides: and Massa Monro when he done being President, hab no more authority at all as I do, ebery bit and grain."²⁶ This speech mocked the society as a pretentious bunch of boot-blacks and street sweepers whose equation of the presidency of a street festival (conferred by their institution) with the national presidency (con-

²⁶ "Grand Bobalition of Slavery," [1820?], John Hay Library.

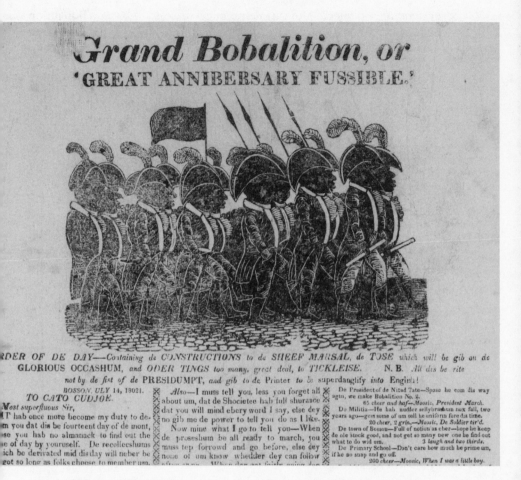

Figure 7. Detail of 1821 broadside. Courtesy of the Trustees of the Boston Public Library

ferred by the electoral process provided in the Constitution) revealed their utter incomprehension of the meaning of citizenship. Another broadside ridiculed the society for being confused about the exact nature of an event that had been celebrated "since de Africum Shocietee become independent, and set he whole race at liberty, sept dem who still be kept slave at de sout."[27]

Another common feature of the broadsides is reflected in an addled defense of the frequent observance of the July 14 anniversary on a day oth-

[27] "Grand and Spendid Bobalition of Slavery," 1822, Broadside Collection, John Hay Library.

er than July 14, selected for various practical reasons. In "Grand Bobalition of Slavery," "de Presidum of de day" reminds "de Shief Marshall . . . please to recolleck that de *fourt* of July cum on *fif*—so in consequence de four-teent muss be on de fifteent—derefore, take notice, dat cordin to de same rule, Wensday will be on a Tursday, as Shakespole say. I telle you dis to lette you see what a fine ting logic be to find out de day of de mont."[28] The point is obvious: people of color, and especially those inflated by their associa-tion with the African Society, aspired to logical argument and Shakespeare without a hint of awareness that both were completely beyond their grasp.

The strategy of ventriloquism achieved a special effect because it was a compound ventriloquism; that is, whites impersonated people of color im-personating white citizens.[29] This strategy called attention to itself as the product of superior whiteness by forcing readers to make a comparison be-tween the two ventriloquisms demonstrated: whites' ability to know, sub-sume, and reproduce blackness in its "essence," and blacks' manifest failure to know, subsume, and reproduce whiteness (especially its most im-portant feature, citizenship). The texts constituted a vehement denial of environmental explanations of difference by demonstrating that the forms and practices of social interaction and citizenship—environmental fac-tors—had failed to transform people of color into citizens, and that the dif-ference between their poor imitation and the "real" thing remained invisible to them. At the same time, the successful act of ventriloquism seemingly rendered the opacity of difference transparent to whites, re-vealing it to be vast and safely unbridgeable, yet at the same time knowable and manageable. The ventriloquistic strategy located this fatal inability to reproduce and enact citizenship within the bodies of people of color them-selves by invading and inhabiting those bodies, constituting them as agents of disorder and misrule.

The graphics that accompanied the texts reinforced these effects, but the broadsides' principal tool for locating difference in the collective body of free people of color was language, a language manufactured for the pur-pose. By contrast, in succeeding series of comic illustrations lampooning black community life in New York and Philadelphia—which also derided pretentious language and manners and ridiculed ostentatious dress—the focus shifted to the graphic image, and the text was reduced to a single cap-tion. These images can be read as a kind of shorthand for the earlier, more elaborate constructions; they did not so much define free people of color

[28] "Grand Bobalition of Slavery," [1820?], John Hay Library.
[29] On ventriloquistic black dialect, see also John Wood Sweet, "Bodies Politic: Colonial-ism, Race, and the Emergence of the American North, Rhode Island, 1730–1830 (Ph.D. diss., Princeton University, 1995), p. 452.

as refer to an already existing conception of them. They depended less on malapropisms and other linguisitic effects and more on visual detail to depict black pretensions to upper-class life-styles. It is as though whites employed the broadsides to sharpen the image of free people of color, still blurred by gradual emancipation: to distinguish them clearly from whites, to define those distinguishing characteristics as innate, and to fix the location of that innate difference in the black body (and mind) in estranging language manufactured for the purpose. Once constituted by whites in this way, the conception "free negro" was available for endless reference and replication in cartoons and, later, in minstrelsy: ritualized performances that extended the broadsides' ridicule of "defective" citizenship and their mockery of both the successes and the failures of free people of color in industrialized America into the domain of theater and the purview of the working class.[30]

Another mode of imagining free people of color which became popular in the 1820s and 1830s was, on its surface, quite antithetical to the vicious caricatures of the broadsides. This mode invoked the vocabulary of Christian piety to claim that certain exemplary people of color were natural Christian saints. But the sainthood of the imaginary few, of course, foregrounded the human frailties of the majority and served further to distort whites' view of the complex reality of black lives.

Although stories of exceptional people of color had appeared periodically since the early 1700s, until 1800 such tales usually stressed remarkable talents and accomplishments—Phillis Wheatley's poetry being perhaps the best known—and suggested that these gifted persons of color, who became quite famous public figures in the process, could equal whites in intelligence and achievement. Yet they also served to confirm the singularity of such individuals among the vast majority of people of color, who could safely be assumed to be relatively unintelligent and incapable.

After gradual emancipation had begun to increase the numbers of free people of color and raise their visibility as an element of disorder in New England society, stories appeared describing not the singularly gifted but

[30] David R. Roediger argues that antebellum minstrelsy in the northern states masked tensions between classes and within the working class and, citing George Lipsitz, that it offered an opportunity for workers subjected to industrial discipline both to experience and reject the "natural self." It also served to homogenize ethnic identities into one general "white" identity in opposition to a "black" identity. Roediger points out that minstrels for the most part supported proslavery positions and ridiculed "bobolashun." See his *The Wages of Whiteness: Race and the Making of the American Working Class* (London: Verso, 1991), pp. 116, 118, 124. Eric Lott, *Love and Theft: Blackface Minstrelsy and the American Working Class* (New York: Oxford University Press, 1993), p. 6, sees minstrelsy as characterized by a "mixed erotic economy of celebration and exploitation," fueled by cross-racial desire as well as revulsion.

rather the extraordinarily "good." Stories of black saints—individuals far superior to most whites in their piety, humility, and moral courage—began to emerge around 1820 in many different guises. Some of these purported to be narratives of actual children; Frederic Swan, for example, had visionary and prophetic dreams steeped in apocalyptic imagery and "fell asleep . . . in the arms of Jesus." Others were fictions in which acts of piety or heroism were performed by children of color: eight-year-old "Little Amos," whose pious attention in Sunday School enabled him to achieve "an early and happy death"; the ten-year-old "Heroic Negro," who saved a drowning white toddler.[31] Still others featured adults, often but not always women. In *The Praying Negro* an unnamed woman serves as a model of undemanding love to a traveler who overhears her praying to God to "make me more glad for what thou has done for me, a poor negro" and to forgive her for "not submitting with more resignation" to the repeated whippings she has received from her master.[32] Such works substituted for the complex and diverse reality of antebellum people of color a one-dimensional, perfectionist model representing the only type of "negro" that whites wished to encounter in "their" landscape. It might be argued that these characters closely resemble the white "saints" of the didactic literature; after all, how does "Little Amos" differ from the "Little Eva" of *Uncle Tom's Cabin?* The difference, of course, lies in the twin, naturalizing assumptions of "race": that white is the standard from which black deviates; and that this deviation is itself limited and monolithic, whereas the white standard is diverse and complex. Amos's piety is astonishing because it so far exceeds what can be expected of most people of color, whereas Eva's piety represents exactly what can be expected of every white person who chooses Eva's path of faith. Although ostensibly a model, the tale of Amos contained a powerful subtext that perversely reinforced the desirability of eliminating the vast majority of people of color who so manifestly did not and could not behave like Amos.[33]

[31] *Remarkable Visionary Dreams, of a Mulatto Boy, in Northfield, Massachusetts, by the Name of Frederic W. Swan, Aged Thirteen Years, Together with a Sketch of his Life, Sickness, Conversion, and Triumphant Death* (Chesterfield, N.H.: Joseph Meriam, 1822), pp. 3–19 (I am indebted to John Saillant for this source); "Little Amos," *Children's Magazine* 7 (1835): 143–44; "The Heroic Negro," *Parley's Magazine* 3 (1835): 171–72.

[32] *The Praying Negro. An Authentic Narrative*, Tract no. 92 (Andover, Mass.: New England Tract Society, 1818), pp. 2–3. In New York in 1818 gradual emancipation was under way, but this adult woman would most likely still have been a slave (although her status is not stated); in any case, the object lesson, intended for New Englanders, derived from her "Negro" nature.

[33] Fredrickson, *The Black Image in the White Mind*, pp. 102–10, 125, dates the emergence of what he calls "romantic racialism" at 1837–38, but the examples cited above suggest that it began more than a decade earlier. Whereas he calls these representations "anomalous" and "benevolent in intent," I find them thoroughly consistent with other forms of symbolic displacement and rather more malevolent than not. Such imaginative constructions may have

Whites symbolically acted out the removal of "Negroes" in countless veiled ways. Some of them are shocking in the very commonplace nature of their insertion into ordinary lifeways. For example, the classroom workbook of Sarah Durand, a student at Stamford Academy in Connecticut, preserves an apparently unremarkable antebellum arithmetic problem: "How to seperate [sic] blacks from whites." The problem, apparently copied verbatim from the teacher's dictation, involves a long-becalmed ship with a crew of thirty men, half of whom were blacks, whose provisions had begun to run low. "The Captain, being satisfied that if their numbers were not greatly diminished, all would perish of hunger before they could reach any friendly port, he therefore proposed to the sailors, that they should cast lots, that every 9th man should be cast overboard, till half of the crew was thus destroyed. He then placed them on the deck, and the lots were cast. To the astonishment of all, every 9th man was found to be a negro. Consequently, the whites were all saved, and the blacks were all destroyed. Can you tell me how he placed them?" The students were asked to draw a circle, placing x's for blacks and o's for whites around its perimeter so that every ninth letter, counting clockwise around the circle as the number of letters slowly diminished, would be an x.[34]

Other kinds of practices, still largely symbolic but more immediately and materially threatening, derived from and contributed to the discursive project of "Negro" removal. Exclusionary practices were by no means unprecedented; by statute or custom since the inception of slavery, people of color had been excluded from, or required to participate separately in, many kinds of activities. For example, they had been routinely excluded from juries, their worship restricted to the "Negro gallery" and "Negro pews" in churches, and so forth. But with gradual emancipation came a new wave of exclusionary efforts that, in some ways, paralleled the voluntary withdrawal of free people of color from white households to independent communities. Reading these new concentrations of people of color, with their visible independence and unmanageable growth, as threatening, whites initiated new practices to segregate both the living and the dead from white society.

For example, whereas slaves had often been buried next to or near their masters, free people of color were nearly always excluded from burial among whites and were interred either in separate sections or in completely separate cemeteries. More disturbing still, beginning around 1780

---

represented wishful thinking, but wishing persons to be substantially different from their actual selves in ways unattainable except in the imagination is not a generally benevolent exercise.

[34] Arithmetic workbook of Sarah Durand, Stamford, Connecticut, Miscellaneous Manuscripts, Connecticut Historical Society.

the corpses of people of color seem to have become a target of graverobbers and, from the outset of gradual emancipation through the 1820s at least, particularly vulnerable to theft from burial places for purposes of dissection (and, perhaps, sport).[35] The Enlightenment enthusiasm for the study of anatomy by means of dissection led to a general upsurge in the demand for corpses; the bodies of white criminals and indigents were frequently spirited away to the dissecting room along with those of people of color. But black bodies seem to have been particularly desirable, perhaps because they seemed perfectly suited for the investigation of two questions of obsessive interest to the Enlightenment: explaining the origin of human diversity, and finding systematic correspondences between external characteristics and inner qualities. A simpler explanation might be the expectation that because they were often relatively powerless and marginal members of their communities, people of color would be unlikely to attempt to prosecute cases of graverobbing.

Some did make such attempts, however. In 1782 in Boston, at the outset of emancipation, Anthony Frederick, a free man of color, brought an action of trespass against one Doctor Curtis for digging up and dissecting Frederick's deceased wife, Jenny. Israel Keith, judge of the Massachusetts Court of Common Pleas, responded to Frederick's unidentified advocate with frank comments on his lack of sympathy for Frederick's case. Judge Keith reluctantly acknowledged that "there is great reason to believe there was some dead creature brought into a room under Doctor Curtis' roof, and there dissected," and he was willing to "suppose for the sake of argument" that it was Jenny. But he went on to argue that it was not "an impiety or disobedience to any divine law . . . because it is no where said that thou shalt not dig up or dissect a dead negro." Nor was it a violation of the rights of the dead, "for a dead body has no rights," and "though dissections have been performed in this town for two or three years past without secrecy, yet no one complained till Anthony Frederick." Keith listed other cases in which the dead had been dug up for dissection in Boston; since all of them apparently involved unidentified wanderers and convicted criminals, however, he took some pains to explain why Jenny's case should not be distinguished from these.

> But it may be said that these cases are not parallel, that Jenny was no stranger or malefactor, but the wife of Anthony, and though she has suffered no injury, yet the feelings of an affectionate husband have. . . . But

[35] On the frequency of illicit dissection of the bodies of people of color in New York, see Stephen Robert Wilf, "Anatomy and Punishment in Late Eighteenth-Century New York," *Journal of Social History* 22 (1989): 511.

where are the scales, where is the balance that shall way [*sic*] the feelings of Anthony Frederick? Have you [the advocate] not repeatedly affirmed that Jenny was a whore, a slut, and a drunkard, and that you was glad she was dead? Did you not tell me in my office with a laugh that Doctor Curtis had got his pay for tending Jenny while alive by converting her to his own use when dead? Are these the feelings that are valued at a thousand pounds?

The judge concluded by addressing questions of law. He pointed out that no law could give Frederick "a right or property in the body of Jenny of a longer duration, than that expressed in the marriage covenant—'Until death does them part.'" As to the statutory basis on which Frederick might be awarded relief for an action of trespass, Keith triumphantly concluded, "And what do our Statutes say upon this Subject? Nothing! They are as silent as the negro that is dissected."[36]

The tone as much as the content of Judge Keith's comments illuminates the estranged position of freed people of color in their native communities and demonstrates how emancipation functioned as a kind of expulsion from the fabric of community life in a (still) slaveholding society. Jenny's status as a free woman of color left her liable to hearsay "conviction" as a "a whore, a slut, and a drunkard," which then enabled Keith to classify her with "strangers" and "malefactors" who might be dug up and dissected with impunity, since they either lacked or had forfeited any claims to community membership. Anthony Frederick was similarly liable to hearsay conviction as a fraud whose "feelings of an affectionate husband" could be dismissed as spurious and worthless on the basis of his advocate's apparent hypocrisy; it did not occur to Judge Keith that Frederick might have independent, and legitimate, feelings of his own. Put simply, neither Anthony Frederick in life nor Jenny in death was fully present as a legally constituted individual to Judge Keith; in his legal view their "race" truly reduced them to the status of strangers.

In a similar case in 1823–24, the Providence Town Council appears, at first glance, to have acted more compassionately. John Thompson, a person of color, complained to the council that the body of his child, between three and four years of age, and also the body of a black woman, both of which had been deposited in the family vault of Dr. Stephen Randall preparatory to burial, had disappeared. The council officially resolved to offer a $100 reward to "any person who will prosecute to final conviction" the perpetrator or perpetrators, but it apparently never advertised this re-

[36] "Case of Doctor Curtis and Anthony Frederick, 1782," Israel Keith Papers 2 (1767–1803), Massachusetts Historical Society.

ward, as was customary.[37] Despite Thompson's naive conviction that "the Vault must have been forced by means of false Keys—as the true Key was in the possession of Dr. Randall and had not been out of it," the disappearance of two black corpses from a doctor's vault seems suspicious.[38]

One can easily imagine Dr. Randall as the perpetrator in this case, a man of education and substance with the humanitarian rationale of advancing his medical knowledge, marshaling in his own mind a set of common assumptions to defend an action indefensible if its target had been a white resident: that people of color were possessed of limited resources and limited emotional range, and thus would be unlikely to go to the trouble and expense of purchasing a burial plot for a mere dead child; that people of color were, after all, like strangers and criminals, members of a dispossessed class that could be dispossessed of their own bodies with impunity. John Thompson's intervention disputed these assumptions, but his own assumptions of Dr. Randall's good faith—perhaps because Randall was a doctor—prevented him from taking Anthony Frederick's position. The council, though it humored Thompson by resolving to offer a reward, did not in fact offer it in any way that might have brought results. And it is by no means clear what the formal charge would have been in any case. Perhaps the council suspected Randall, perhaps it did not. In any case, no charges were brought or reward paid.

These cases and others suggest that by jettisoning people of color from the conventional matrix of mutual obligation and regard that had defined pre-Revolutionary community life, emancipation *did* enact a kind of erasure of them from the landscape, just as the voices of antislavery had promised.

Measures to restrict the participation of free people of color in civic institutions also fall within the rubric of "negro" removal. In one obvious example, as the movement to make at least some public schooling available to every child spread throughout New England after 1800, children of color were routinely excluded from most schools. Where some *were* allowed to attend classes with whites, their treatment elicited strenuous complaint. Sporadic participation in town or district schools slowly gave way to establishment of separate, publicly funded schools for children of color—in 1820 in Boston, 1830 in Hartford, 1838 in Providence.[39]

[37] Providence Town Papers 119 (1824): 8, original complaint; Providence Town Council Minutes (from original clerk's notes at Rhode Island Historical Society), 170:282–83.

[38] Ibid.

[39] Boston's African School was established in the late 1780s but did not receive public funding until 1820. See Horton, *Free People of Color,* p. 43; David O. White, "Hartford's African Schools, 1830–1868," *Connecticut Historical Society Bulletin* 39 (April 1974): 47–53; Irving

Another obvious example was the restriction of black suffrage. In New England, although only Connecticut and Rhode Island voted outright to rescind the franchise of people of color (in 1818 and 1822, respectively), the issue was debated everywhere, and in many towns people of color were discouraged by custom from voting.[40] Discussions of the emerging hostility to black suffrage usually place it within the context of the expansion of political democracy in the early nineteenth century and the movement to eliminate property requirements, which ultimately achieved "universal white manhood suffrage." Imposing new voting restrictions on people of color has often been naturalized as simply a part of the "growing racism" of the antebellum period, often explained as a hostile response to the threat of disunion posed by abolitionism. Newer arguments also link black disfranchisement to the competitive hostility of white workers.[41] But these reasons fail to explain how the discursive construction of "free people of color" as a category initially made their eligibility to vote a nonissue, and how that construction evolved to produce such a violent reaction. Certainly the fact that the numbers of free people of color were very small before 1780 was one factor. The transformation in the conception of free people of color in the process of gradual emancipation was much more significant, however. Their increasing visibility as disorderly elements, juxtaposed with a persistent conviction of the desirability of their disappearance—the failed promise of gradual emancipation—strengthened the determination of many whites to seek their physical removal.

It was this sentiment at least in part that fueled widespread public disapproval of Isaac Hillard's efforts to recover kidnapped people of color and slaves for bounties in Connecticut (see Chapter 3). In his 1797 defense of his activities, Hillard observed how frequently he was questioned about the desirability of such efforts: "It is hard to find one man in Connecticut, but who professes to disapprove of, and openly bears testimony against kidnapping, and sending those called slaves out of the State; but I have been asked such questions, and so often, that [I have concluded] they are liars,

---

H. Bartlett, *From Slave To Citizen: The Story of the Negro in Rhode Island* (Providence: Urban League of Rhode Island, 1954), p. 37; Leon F. Litwack, *North of Slavery: The Negro in the Free States, 1790–1960* (Chicago: University of Chicago Press, 1961), p. 115.

[40] Emil Olbrich, "The Development of Sentiment on Negro Suffrage to 1860," *Bulletin of the University of Wisconsin,* History Series no. 477, 3 (1912): 24. See also James T. Adams, "Disfranchisement of Negroes in New England," *American Historical Review* 30 (October 1924): 543–47. In 1841 people of color regained the franchise in Rhode Island as one consequence of the failure of Dorr's Rebellion; they had supported the Legal Party against the Suffrage Party of Thomas Dorr, representing whites who wished to broaden the franchise to include all white men but to exclude people of color.

[41] E.g., see Litwack, *North of Slavery,* pp. 74–79; Roediger, *The Wages of Whiteness,* pp. 56–60.

and are willing to have free children stolen and sold."[42] By 1797 the rhetoric of emancipation had obviously become the dominant discourse of polite, civic-minded whites. Nonetheless, a critical component of that discourse, the imminent absence of people of color, remained a latent desire, discernible in the ambivalence surrounding the kidnapping and recovery of free blacks. Whites seemed to find it unfair that men who, like Hillard, engaged in admittedly virtuous efforts to return unjustly kidnapped people of color to Connecticut be rewarded. The demand for disinterested benevolence at the surface of this response seems to mask a latent hostility to the results: restoration of the physical presence of people of color.

Explicit strategies to remove people of color physically from communities, states, and nation were already well under way by 1800 and entered a new and more intense phase around 1820. One of the most effective means of achieving this end was the examination and "warning-out" of transients, an old practice aimed generally at eliminating impoverished and otherwise undesirable strangers who might become a public expense if allowed to remain in a given town. Strangers were defined as people who had not qualified for "legal settlement" in the town where they were living, by either birth; residence of indenture; ownership of real estate of a certain value or the generating of rents or other income of a certain value; payment of taxes for five years within ten years' residence; or successful completion of one year of residence without having been warned out.[43] Persons of color, along with unmarried mothers and elderly persons, had always been disproportionately represented among people examined as transients, but after 1780 the legal settlement requirement clearly began to be used explicitly to maintain control of local black communities. In one of the few quantitative studies of this issue, Ruth Wallis Herndon has shown that in Rhode Island, though only 5 percent of transients were designated as people of color in the 1750s, that number had grown to 22 percent in the 1790s and 50 percent by 1800. She points out that the increase was due to greater precision in recordkeeping and a greater representation of people of color in the transient population—both consequences of a heightened attention to "race."[44]

Transient examinations provided the legal ammunition to achieve what

---

[42] Isaac Hillard, "To the Public," (1797?), p. 8, Miscellaneous Manuscripts, Connecticut Historical Society.

[43] *The Public Laws of the State of Rhode Island and Providence Plantations* . . . (Providence: Carter & Wilkinson, 1798), pp. 345–58. The value of real estate or income required to establish legal settlement changed over time; in 1798, the minimum was real estate valued at $200 or generating annual revenue of $20.

[44] Ruth Wallis Herndon, "Women of 'No Particular Home': Town Leaders and Female

abolition could not—removal—and were an effective means of reducing the numbers of people of color residing in a given New England town. Charges of "disorderly behavior" were also grounds for warning out and hence instruments of potential removal wielded by town councils. The ever more frequent appearance of people of color "with no legal settlement," "likely to become chargeable," and "behaving riotously" reinforced the growing public conception of them as a naturally dependent and disorderly group of permanently estranged aliens, leading in turn to further examinations and warnings-out.

The records of the Town Council of Providence, Rhode Island, provide a particularly rich source of information on one town's campaign for removal. After 1785 the council frequently conducted what can only be termed periodic roundups of people of color who were "likely to become chargeable" and who, if found to lack a legal settlement, could be warned out of Providence. Although whites too were examined, whole meetings would frequently be devoted to the examination of people clearly identified as persons of color.[45] The records reveal that their construction as "strangers" was true only in the sense of whites' estrangement from any comprehension of their reality. Of sixty-five examinations between 1782 and 1800 of people who can clearly be identified as persons of color and whose length of residence in Providence is clearly discernible, 37 percent had lived in Providence for five years or more, and 26 percent for ten years or more (interim warnings-out not having been enforced, presumably). Median length of stay in the city was three years. These people were not strangers.

Nor were they "likely to become chargeable"; even those who did hardly represented a disproportionate drain on the public treasury. In the early 1820s, at one peak of antiblack sentiment in Providence, the reports of the Overseer of the Poor demonstrate that people of color received an extremely small proportion of the town's financial support for the indigent. In 1823 and 1824, for example, 16 of 154 cases and 9 of 157 cases, respectively, involved persons of color. The average amount of support received by whites was $33.33 in 1823 and $44.84 in 1824; by people of color, $11.24 and $11.93, respectively.[46] Again, the menace was imagined.

After 1820, efforts to remove residents of color were augmented by

Transients in Rhode Island, 1750–1800," in *Women and Freedom in Early America*, ed. Larry D. Eldridge (New York: New York University Press, 1997), p. 272.

[45] E.g., Providence Town Council Records, 6:27, November 7, 1787; and 6:97, October 1, 1789. Two such meetings were held August 31, 1797, when seven people of color were called, and again on October 13, 1797, when twelve were examined (Providence Town Council Records, 7:66–71; 7:195–200).

[46] "Report of the Overseer of the Poor for 1823," and "Report of the Overseer of the Poor for 1824," Providence Town Papers 118 (1823–24): 125; and 122 (1824): 36.

strategies to discourage the immigration of new ones, and anti-immigration statutes were debated in nearly every state. Massachusetts is representative; an 1821 ad hoc legislative committee concluded that a proposed anti-immigration bill was necessary to prevent people of color who were fleeing restrictive legislation in other states from seeking haven in Massachusetts. The committee warned that such an influx would necessarily swell the population of criminals and indigents and take jobs away from whites. The bill was narrowly defeated. The next year a second committee agreed with all the sentiments of the first but recommended against passage of the bill, citing the interests of "humanity" as a reason both for needing some kind of restriction and for rejecting the proposed bill.[47]

The only widespread, organized, institutional effort to enact literally the promise of abolition to eliminate the slave/"Negro" from the new republic was the colonization movement. Expatriation as a solution to the presence of people of color after their emancipation had been advocated by many prominent Americans, including Jefferson, since the 1780s, but no sustained effort to implement such a program materialized during the next thirty years. Some scholars, notably Lawrence Friedman, have found this slow development strange.[48] Within the context of gradual emancipation, however, the determination to organize a removal effort seems a logical outgrowth of the newly fixed, "racialized" perception of free people of color as permanently estranged and inherently unequal noncitizens which had developed slowly over the course of more than three decades.

The American Colonization Society (ACS), organized in 1816 to resettle free people of color in Liberia, represented several seemingly disparate interests. Chesapeake slaveholders feared the potentially disruptive influence on slaves of free blacks, especially after Gabriel's revolt in 1800, and sought to safeguard the institution of slavery. Northern Federalists, Protestant evangelicals, and moral reformers were motivated by a complex set of interrelated and sometimes conflicting goals: many Federalists saw free people of color as a particularly galling element of disorder in an increasingly egalitarian and unruly Jacksonian America; many evangelicals and reformers saw them as agents of moral laxity; some evangelicals who were interested in the conversion of the "dark continent" to Christ (sometimes the very individuals who feared free people of color as a "degraded element" in America) saw them as agents of African redemption. Still other antislavery reformers regarded colonization both as a means of enabling

---

[47] Litwack, *North of Slavery*, p. 66; *Niles Weekly Register* 20 (July 14, 1821): 311–12; and Massachusetts House of Representatives, *Free Negroes and Mulattoes* (Boston, 1822), in Litwack, *North of Slavery*, p. 68.

[48] Lawrence J. Friedman, *Inventors of the Promised Land* (New York: Knopf, 1975), p. 183.

free people of color to escape from their oppression in the United States, which they considered inevitable, and as a conservative approach to eventual abolition which might be acceptable to the South.[49]

The ideal of African colonization as espoused by the American Colonization Society gained nearly universal support in the northern states between its inception and the mid-1830s. William Lloyd Garrison, initially a supporter of colonization but later its fiercest opponent, observed that "wherever I turned my eye in the free states, I saw nothing but unanimity; wherever my ear caught a sound, I heard nothing but excessive panegyric. No individual had ventured to counteract the influence of the scheme."[50] In New England the ACS was enormously popular; by 1830 state auxiliaries had been established everywhere but in Rhode Island.[51] New England clergy led widespread efforts to raise funds, especially by means of annual Fourth of July collections that were solicited in conjunction with sermons on colonization preached on the Sunday nearest the Fourth.[52] The popularity of the concept also spawned other detailed schemes for emancipation and removal which, in their authors' opinions, represented improvements in speed, efficiency, or scale, over the Colonization Society's program.[53]

[49] On northern support for the ACS, see Fredrickson, *The Black Image in the White Mind*, pp. 6–30, and Friedman, *Inventors of the Promised Land*, pp. 185–87. Fredrickson locates the principal impetus for its founding among evangelical Protestant clergy and Federalists who sought a conservative strategy to end slavery. He downplays the influence of southern slaveholders, suggesting that historians have mistakenly accepted abolitionist claims that ACS promises of noninterference with slavery constituted an affirmative effort to strengthen the institution (pp. 8–10). Friedman attributes its founding to a "multi-interest constituency" of Chesapeake slaveholders, Federalists, and evangelical clergy and moral reformers, to whom he gives more or less equally distributed weight. He suggests that the northern groups were motivated only by a desire to restore social and moral order, completely ignoring their claims that colonization would promote eventual abolition. I find Friedman's position on the influence of southern slaveholders persuasive, but I also accept as sincere, although misguided, the conviction of at least some northern ACS members that colonization would ultimately end slavery. The most thorough treatment of the ACS is still P. J. Staudenraus, *The African Colonization Movement, 1816–1865* (New York: Columbia University Press, 1961). Superseded by Staudenraus but still useful is Early Lee Fox, *The American Colonization Society, 1817–1830*, Johns Hopkins University Studies in Historical and Political Science (Baltimore: Johns Hopkins University Press, 1919).

[50] William Lloyd Garrison, *Thoughts on African Colonization* (1832; New York: Arno Press, 1968), pt. 1, p. 4.

[51] *Annual Report of the American Society for Colonizing the Free People of Colour of the United States* (Washington, D.C.: American Colonization Society, 1838), app.

[52] Fox, "The American Colonization Society" pp. 63–64.

[53] E.g., "a New-England Man" proposed a program for slave redemption and removal that provided economic incentives he felt the ACS program lacked. According to *An Attempt to Demonstrate the Practicability of Emancipating the Slaves of the United States of North America, and of Removing Them from the Country, without Impairing the Right of Private Property, or Subjecting the Nation to a Tax. By a New-England Man* (New York: G. & C. Carvil, 1825), the U.S. government

Curiously, support for colonization in the New England states seems to have been inversely related to the actual proportion of free people of color in each state's population. For example, Vermont, whose black population represented slightly under 0.4 percent in 1820, had the most active ACS chapter, whereas Rhode Island, with the highest proportion (4.5 percent), had no auxiliary at all.[54] This odd correlation strongly suggests that the imagined menace of free people of color aroused far greater fear and antipathy where the more complex reality in day-to-day community life was seldom confronted (although simplistic demonizing, as in the Boston broadsides, was by no means absent in areas with diverse populations as well).

Whereas the ventriloquistic broadsides used outrageous exaggeration and cruel humor to ridicule and belittle people of color, the colonizationists adopted a tone that ranged from gravely reasonable to apocalyptic, depicting the growing population of people of color in their midst as dangerous rather than ridiculous. Baxter Dickinson, for example, predicted that the black population would double every twenty years, a "manifest evil" that would produce seventeen million people of color by 1889: "Who can foretell those scenes of carnage and terror which our own children may witness, unless a seasonable remedy be applied?" The remedy was removal: "We can stop their increase; we can diminish their number; we can in thirty years entirely remove the race, and that without any sacrifice."[55] Relatively few colonizationists made such undisguised pleas to white Americans to rid themselves of an unwanted menace as did Calvin Yale in 1827, when he forthrightly defined the first and most immediate object of the American Colonization Society as an effort "to relieve our nation from an

---

would issue stock equal in value to all existing slave contracts, making slaves "free" redemptioners who would then be sent to farm "huge tracts of uncultivated land" in St. Domingue and Spanish America. Their wages would be fixed by the government, and the produce they generated would constitute a sinking fund for redemption of the debt incurred by the issue of stock. This scheme would accomplish immediate emancipation and removal of all slaves. With respect to free people of color, "no special measures" would be necessary, but to satisfy others who thought their removal desirable, the writer suggested, possibly with tongue in cheek, that the U.S. government "let a bounty be offered for their self-expatriation, and give the largest sum to the most worthless object" (p. 9). J. Jacobus Flournoy, dismayed at the lack of progress made by "the slow and imbecile Colonization Society" by 1835, proposed his own society, "The Efficient Instantaneous Expulsion Association of Philosophic and Fearless Patriots" with a goal of "a ready and sudden practicable expulsion of every Negro and Mulatto from this Country, back to their own Africa" (*An Essay on the Origin, Habits, Etc. of the African Race: Incidental to the Propriety of Having Nothing to Do with Negroes: Addressed to the Good People of the United States* [New York, 1835], p. 4).

[54] Bureau of the Census, U.S. Department of Commerce, *Negro Population, 1790–1915* (Washington, D.C.: Government Printing Office, 1918), p. 45.

[55] Baxter Dickinson, *Sermon Delivered at Springfield, Mass., July 4th, 1829, before the Auxiliary Colonization Society of Hampden County* (Springfield, Mass.: S. Bowler, 1829) p. 17.

onerous burden, the free coloured population."[56] The cleverest and most persuasive offered assessments that seemed to balance the costs of heterogeneity and the benefits of homogeneity for whites and for people of color, and to express concern for the futures of America and Africa as parallel entities.

All, however, cast people of color squarely in the role of strangers. "In short, are they not, in the estimation of the community and in their own consciousness, aliens and outcasts in the midst of the people?" Leonard Bacon asked a Connecticut audience in 1825.[57] Few whites of any persuasion, could imagine people of color as numbering among "the people." For them, as John Wheeler put it, "an introduction to all the rights of citizenship is impossible. You must alter the whole man; you must take from him the very feature and colour of nature, if you would advance him to equal privileges with our common population."[58] Neither Wheeler nor most other whites could conceive of altering the *white* man—his assumptions, his habits of thinking and acting—to achieve this result.

The sober, Christian solution to the presence of these permanent strangers was to colonize them in their "native" land. Colonizationist tracts and the sermons delivered at meetings of ACS auxiliaries in New England stressed the "natural" relationship between each distinct people and its "native" environment, the negative consequences to both groups of maintaining a population of "strangers" within a population of "natives," and the benefits to the two respective populations of restoring their homogeneity in their "native" lands. Whites were represented as native to North America, people of color to Africa. "Among us is a growing population of strangers," Baxter Dickinson declared in his 1829 address to the Auxiliary Colonization Society of Hampden County, Massachusetts. "Rise to their relief. Restore them to their proper home."[59] Daniel Dana emphatically agreed: "This is not their country. . . . O let them breathe the air of the land of their fathers. . . . Send them home."[60] In effect, since the ancestors of most people of color then living in New England had been taken from Africa from 70 to 140 years earlier, colonizationists erased nearly a centu-

[56] Calvin Yale, *A Sermon, Delivered before the Vermont Colonization Society at Montpelier, October 17, 1827* (Montpelier, Vt.: E. P. Walton, Watchman Office, 1827), p. 3.

[57] Leonard Bacon, *A Plea for Africa, Delivered in New-Haven, July 4, 1825* (New Haven, Conn.: T. G. Woodward, 1825), p. 13.

[58] John Wheeler, *A Sermon, Preached before the Vermont Colonization Society at Montpelier, October 25, 1825* (Windsor, Vt.: W. Spooner, 1825), p. 14.

[59] Dickinson, *Sermon*, p. 16.

[60] Daniel Dana, *A Discourse Addressed to the New Hampshire Auxiliary Colonization Society at Their First Annual Meeting, Concord, New Hampshire, June 2, 1825* (Concord, N.H.: Shepard & Bannister, 1825), p. 10.

ry and a half of the American history of people of African descent. "Children of Afric! . . . Ye shall return in peace / To your own land—Your natal shores," poet Ann Evans promised earnestly in 1826.[61]

A few colonizationists believed people of color to be degraded everywhere, even "at home." Africans are "a very ignorant and miserable race of men in their own country; very indolent, and very wicked," claimed a pamphlet published by the American Tract Society to explain to children "why the colored people in Africa let the white people come and steal them."[62] In his 1825 sermon, curiously titled *A Plea for Africa,* Leonard Bacon told a New Haven audience that Africans "combine all that is degrading in human imbecility, and all that is horrible in human depravity, unrefined by civilization and unrestrained by the influence of Christian truth. . . . Wherever they are found they are partakers in the misery of one common degradation."[63] John Hough, a professor of languages at Middlebury College, may have offered a Montpelier audience in 1825 the most thorough condemnation of American free people of color (under the rubric, "Sermon"!) ever made by a New England colonizationist:

> The state of the free colored population of the United States, is one of extreme and remediless degradation, of gross irreligion, of revolting profligacy, and, of course, deplorable wretchedness. Who can doubt . . . the blacks among us are peculiarly addicted to habits of low vice and shameless profligacy? They are found in vast numbers in the haunts of riot and dissipation and intemperance where they squander in sin the scanty earnings of their toil, contract habits of grosser iniquity and are prepared for acts of daring outrage and of enormous guilt. . . . Squalid poverty, loathsome and painful disease, fell and torturing passions, and diversified and pitiable forms of misery are to be found [there].

Although Hough limited his analysis to an American context, he left its application open-ended, concluding that "these disabilities are the result of complexion."[64]

But most colonizationists agreed that the degraded condition of people of color in America resulted principally from their status as "strangers" in the midst of whites; in Africa, their "native" land, they were destined for re-

[61] Ann Evans, *Africa, A Poem* (Andover, Mass.: Flagg & Gould, 1826), p. 13.

[62] *Children's Friend,* no. 4 (April 1826), published by the New York State Branch of the American Tract Society (Albany: Webster & Wood, 1826).

[63] Bacon, *A Plea for Africa,* p. 10.

[64] John Hough, *Sermon Delivered before the Vermont Colonization Society at Montpelier, October 18, 1826* (Montpelier, Vt.: E. P. Watton-Watchman Office, 1826), pp. 8–10.

publican greatness. "We can plant them on a distant coast, where they will thrive, and in sixty years become a powerful Republic," Baxter Dickinson insisted.[65] The implication was that blacks might be natural republicans, as Jefferson had believed,[66] and many colonizationists saw this characteristic, if confirmed, as a source of great danger to the American republic. Dickinson made this insinuation when he remarked, "Almost as numerous are [people of color] now, was our whole population when this nation stood forth for freedom in a context with the mightiest power of the civilized world."

The belief that people of color were at the same time a hopelessly degraded population in the American environment and a force for establishing a virtuous republic in Africa appears on its surface to represent a return to "racial" environmentalism. But the most common colonizationist argument was not that "degraded" people of color would be transformed by a change in environment but that the "fit" between the essential nature of a group of people and its "natural" environment was determinative of the maximum level of development and attainment of virtue they might achieve. This was an argument of essence, not environment.

Some colonizationists sought to strengthen the contention that people of African descent belonged in Africa and could achieve greatness there by evoking a glorious African past lost in antiquity. Ann Evans, for example, rhapsodized:

> Populous and powerful kingdoms rise to adorn
> Thy far-extending sceptre.—With fix'd gaze
> Departed ages, in their mighty march,
> Have marked thy greatness. On thy land arose
> Cloudless and beautiful, the glorious smile
> Of star-crown'd Science, empress of the mind. . . .
> The Lofty walls and towers of royal Carthage!
> Rival of spendid Rome.[67]

Such images made the prospects for the success of Liberia more credible in the face of unremitting propaganda about the "degraded condition" of free people of color.

Other colonizationists vigorously denied the claims of prior achieve-

[65] Dickinson, *Sermon,* p. 17.

[66] *The Writings of Thomas Jefferson,* ed. Andrew A. Lipscomb and Albert Ellery Bergh (Washington, D.C.: Thomas Jefferson Memorial Association, 1903), 1:72–73, cited in a discussion of Jefferson's insistence upon colonization for people of color by John D. Saillant, "Race and Revolutionary Ideology: Lemuel Haynes's Black Republicanism and the American Republican Tradition, 1775–1820," *Journal of the Early Republic* 14 (Fall 1994): 317.

[67] Evans, *Africa, A Poem,* pp. 3–5.

ment. Leonard Bacon, for example, could "tell of no distant and shadowy antiquity, when Africa was the cradle of the human race, and the seat of science and arts and Empire. I cannot compare the darkness that is now resting on those tribes with some period of ancient glory. . . . There are no lighter shades to variegate the gloom."[68] Such denials had the same effect, perversely, as recitals of ancient African glory: they effaced the actual struggle of people of color to survive slavery and emancipation in America, a struggle that had generated vital and heterogeneous communities. For this complex story they substituted a uniform and continuous history of "degradation" that spanned several centuries, a "story of simple, unalleviated, unromantic wretchedness"[69] whose focal point was not the United States but Africa.

The rhetoric of colonization constituted the dominant discourse of "race" in New England and elsewhere for over a decade. Denounced by people of color almost immediately and nearly universally, it finally began to be discredited among New England whites after 1832 by the wide circulation of William Lloyd Garrison's condemnatory *Thoughts on African Colonization,* by the subsequent unremitting opposition of the New England Anti-Slavery Society, and also by the growing awareness that the project was logistically impossible. Nonetheless, during its brief period of ascendancy, colonizationist rhetoric shaped "racial" thinking in New England in critically important ways.

First, colonizationists effectively telescoped the class structure of free people of color—which had in fact grown ever more complex as a consequence of their diverse economic and social experiences during the years of gradual emancipation—into a single monolithic, "degraded" condition which, in light of the dimming recollection of New England slavery was represented as the natural result of an essential and permanent inferiority. Second, by consistently representing people of color as a permanent class of strangers, native only and always to Africa, it contributed to the effacement of their local history of enslavement and undermined their claims of entitlement to citizenship. In so doing, it further encouraged whites to regard the nineteenth-century presence of people of color in New England as anomalous and unaccountable. By the time the zeal for actual expatriation had abated in the face of its sheer impracticality and persistent abolitionist attack, this rhetoric had made a major contribution to naturalizing the undesirability of free people of color and thus of fostering their civic and cultural segregation—especially in the cities.

[68] Bacon, *A Plea for Africa,* p. 9.
[69] Ibid.

"Signals, styles, systems of rapid, highly conventionalized communication are the lifeblood of the big city. It is when these systems break down—when we lose our grasp on the grammar of urban life—that [violence] takes over."[70] In *Soft City,* Jonathan Raban was speaking of London at a moment almost two centuries later, yet his observation might apply also to the 1820s and the breakdown in previously clear-cut systems of social meaning that had occurred in Boston, Hartford, Providence, and other New England towns and cities as a consequence of the Revolution and gradual emancipation. A critical element of the grammar of urban life in the eighteenth-century New England city had been the system of signs by which elites, members of the middling classes, workers, servants, and slaves could be distinguished at a glance—by their skin color and physiognomy, their demeanor, their clothing and possessions. If the Revolution had blurred this system, gradual emancipation had dismantled completely the aspect of it that had made dark skin color and a specific set of physiognomic characteristics virtually infallible signs of a formal status of servitude. The resulting uncertainty over the meaning of "race" was an important factor in the upsurge of violence against people of color in New England and elsewhere that began in the 1780s and reached its zenith in the 1820s and 1830s.

By the early 1820s whites had begun to apply a strategy for their physical removal—assaulting their communities, burning down their homes, and attacking their advocates. The characterizations of actual people of color as disorderly and dependent, and the literary and graphic invention of imaginary people of color who were upstart, savagely ridiculous, and demonic fueled this outpouring of frenzied anger and resentment. So, for that matter, did the counterimage of the imaginary "good negro," a saint against whose model every living person of color must necessarily fall woefully short. Saints or sinners, free people of color became targets of periodic violence that erupted out of whites' simmering frustration and anger at the "problem" that refused to disappear.

Although antebellum violence against free people of color has conventionally been treated as part of, and subordinate to, the antiabolitionist sentiment that was widespread in the North, that reading oversimplifies a more complex situation. The conventional explanation for the crescendo of mob violence against people of color and abolitionists in the 1830s used to be that it represented a reaction against Garrisonian immediatism.[71] In

[70] Jonathan Raban, *Soft City* (London: Hamilton, 1974), quoted in David Harvey, *The Condition of Post Modernity: An Enquiry into the Origins of Cultural Change* (Cambridge, Mass.: Blackwell, 1989), p. 6.

[71] The principal architect of this position was Gilbert Hobbes Barnes, *The Antislavery Impulse, 1830–1844* (New York: Harbinger Books, 1964).

1970, however, Leonard L. Richards, in his influential *"Gentlemen of Property and Standing": Anti-Abolition Mobs in Jacksonian America,* pointed out the importance of existing northern racism, especially virulent with respect to projects for "Negro" uplift and prospects of amalgamation. He minimized the effect of "Garrisonism" per se as a catalyst for violence, arguing that it was the effectiveness of Garrison's New England Anti-Slavery Society that sparked mob violence after 1832.[72] But Richards devoted only brief attention to selected incidents of violence against people of color as evidence of a "negrophobia" that predated antiabolition violence; his primary focus shifted quickly to attacks on abolitionists.

Some violent acts were indeed directed squarely at abolitionists; William Lloyd Garrison was dragged through the streets of Boston on the same day in 1835 that an antislavery convention in Utica was broken up by protesters—to name only two of several antiabolitionist mob actions between 1834 and 1837, characterized as the "high tide" of such action.[73] It is also true that dissension over the extension or abolition of southern slavery did threaten disunion, which most New Englanders opposed. And the focal point of the slavery issue, the slave, was indeed a person of color. These logical connections have led many historians to conclude that people of color aroused the hostility of northern whites because they functioned as personifications of the slavery issue.[74] That reading, however, depends on the potency of the mythology of a historically white New England: the presumption that white New Englanders had no independent, sustained relationship with people of color that could have generated its own antagonisms and violence; that people of color who somehow materialized in New England were fixed, blank screens upon which whites could suddenly project their hostilities against the rising agitation over the extension of slavery and the prospect of disunion. Putting slavery and the painful process of gradual emancipation back into the history of New England yields quite a different interpretation.

As described earlier, hostility to free people of color had been building steadily since the outset of gradual emancipation, independent of the vicissitudes of the antislavery movement. Free persons of color in northern

[72] Leonard L. Richards, *"Gentlemen of Property and Standing": Anti-Abolition Mobs in Jacksonian America* (New York: Oxford University Press, 1970), esp. pp. 20–27, 37–43.

[73] Ibid., pp. 64, 156.

[74] Richards conflates antiabolitionism and antiblack agitation in his discussion of the Prudence Crandall case and other acts of violence (*Gentlemen of Property and Standing,* pp. 38–40). Roediger describes white mob violence against free people of color as complexly motivated by attraction to and resentment of the cultural aesthetics and supposed preindustrial permissiveness of blacks, antiamalgamationism, and ease of attacking the relatively defenseless (*The Wages of Whiteness,* pp. 106–10). He uses the term "antiabolitionist mobs" without really attributing antiabolitionist motivations to mob violence against blacks (p. 109).

cities were attacked as precisely who and what they were, hardly as either surrogates for abolitionists or advertisements for antislavery. The fact that these violent acts predated antiabolitionist actions, persisted in concert with them, and continued after they had subsided supports the argument that the root cause of whites' anger was the presence of the "free Negro," and that abolitionists and printers of antislavery tracts were attacked principally because they were seen as advocates of the continuation and even growth of that presence. Richards's observations on the link between an upsurge in violence and Garrison's attacks on the Colonization Society—the only organized institutional effort to remove free people of color—support this argument.

There were dozens, possibly close to a hundred, violent incidents involving free people of color in New England between 1820 and 1840. In *Reaping the Bloody Harvest,* John M. Werner lists forty-one riots in the United States between 1824 and 1849—nine of which took place in the New England states—whose motivation involved "race" in one way or another. His list is somewhat arbitrary; he appears to exclude some incidents in which whites were attacked for sustaining or encouraging the black presence, such as the series of attacks on Prudence Crandall's boarding school for young women of color (described below), culminating in the near-destruction of her house by a mob in 1834. Richards notes a total of sixty-one "anti-abolition and anti-Negro mobs" in the six New England states alone between 1833 and 1837; elsewhere he finds 157 "Northern" mobs of this kind reported by the three leading antislavery papers—the *Liberator,* the *Emancipator,* and the *Philanthropist*—between 1834 and 1837.[75] Because Richards sees antiblack attacks as explicitly linked to abolitionist activity—specifically, the rise of immediatism—he excludes those that took place before 1833; hence his statistics cannot be compared with those of Werner. Nonetheless, from Werner and Richards, one can infer that New England locations may have accounted for one-fifth to one-third of all antebellum acts of mob violence against abolitionists and people of color. And the two sources together provide evidence of an enormous upsurge in violence against people of color and their advocates beginning around 1820.

These acts of intimidation and violence were recorded, studied, editorialized about, and lampooned widely in New England. The surviving literature makes it clear that a great proportion of this activity was animated by hostility to the *presence* of people of color, and the greatest animosity was directed at individuals and activities that seemed to foster the growth of

[75] John M. Werner, *Reaping the Bloody Harvest: Race Riots in the United States during the Age of Jackson, 1824–1849* (New York: Garland, 1986); Richards, *Gentlemen of Property and Standing,* pp. 40, 157.

that presence. Curiously, by the 1820s the discourse of strangerhood had become two-tiered. Many of the surviving texts differentiate between "our" people of color—strangers still and forever by virtue of behavior adjudged to be immoral and unproductive, but strangers who had become familiar and whose excesses, though deplored, could be (barely) tolerated—and "new" people of color: those newly arriving, or who might arrive, from distant places, whose numbers would exceed manageability and stretch toleration to the breaking point. Communities of color were seen as locations of prostitution, gambling, and other illegal activities that could be contained but never satisfactorily suppressed. Some of the concern over the manageability of such communities involved their appeal to "foreign" blacks and the threat that these communities would expand outside the limits of white control.

Another major concern was the appeal and availability of women of color to white men. Females of color who were strangers to the community might offer a particular threat, since they might be less likely to find work that would provide an alternative to prostitution. The famous 1833 case of Prudence Crandall, who opened her Canterbury, Connecticut, boarding school exclusively to black girls after the community expressed hostility to her admission of a single black day student, inflamed white anxiety on all these points.

A local press obviously sympathetic to the forces that opposed Crandall's school published *A Statement of Facts respecting the School for Colored Females, in Canterbury, Ct.,* highlighting the issues that so aroused the town fathers. According to this account, a "committee of the town" had interviewed Crandall twice. In the course of the second interview, when one committee member warned of the "danger of the levelling principles, and intermarriage between the whites and blacks," Crandall apparently alluded to Moses as having had a black wife, leading the committee to conclude that she approved of "amalgamation." Thereafter, Crandall followed the advice of abolitionist friends and made final preparations to open her school "exclusively for colored pupils, who were chiefly to be obtained from New York, Philadelphia, Boston and Providence." Her advertisement for the school listed about a dozen prominent supporters who were, the report stressed, "all Abolitionists, and with a few exceptions, residents of other States."[76] The complaint of the "impropriety" of her proposal, then, seemed to stem from the association of its author with principles of amalgamation, based on what seems to have been a fairly casual remark. This objection was also rooted in assumptions about the capacity of black fe-

[76] *A Statement of Facts, Respecting the School for Colored Females, in Canterbury, Ct.* (Brooklyn, Conn.: Advertiser Press, 1833), pp. 7, 6.

males to incite sober, white males into "amalgamating." The parallel complaint of the "injustice" of the proposal seemed to rest on the foreignness of the student body, a concern heightened by the endorsement of equally foreign outside agitators.

The townspeople, too, stressed the femaleness and foreignness of the proposed student body and, obliquely, its power to lure white citizens into amalgamation. The Canterbury Town Meeting denounced the proposed school on the grounds that it would "collect within the Town of Canterbury, large numbers of persons from other States, whose characters and habits might be various, and unknown to us, thereby rendering insecure, the persons, property and reputations of our citizens." When Crandall persisted, the town drafted a petition to the Connecticut General Assembly, requesting that it "draft some law by which the introduction of foreign blacks, might be regulated in a proper degree, by the feelings and wishes of the inhabitants of the towns."[77]

The state legislative committee appointed to study the matter made an even clearer distinction between local people of color and foreign ones. Its final report acknowledged that "the unhappy class of beings, whose race has been degraded by unjust bondage, are among us, and justly demand at our hands all which is consistent with the common safety, and their own best interest, for the amelioration of their state and character"; nonetheless, "*our* obligations as a *State*, acting in its sovereign capacity, are limited to the people of our *own territory*. . . . We are under no obligation, moral or political, to incur the incalculable evils, of bringing into *our own State*, colored emigrants from abroad." Although "colored people, in the midst of a white population, in all States and countries . . . are an appalling source of crime and pauperism," the committee conceded that their "degraded" condition in Connecticut was the legacy of slavery (a rare acknowledgement), which "imposes on us an imperious duty to advance their morals and usefulness," yet "the duty is not less imperative, to protect our own citizens, against that host of colored emigrants, which would rush in from every quarter, when invited to our colleges and schools."[78]

With hope fading that colonization would effect a significant decrease in the number of indigenous free people of color, legislators could resign themselves to their presence and work to contain it, encouraging efforts to curb the behavior whites found most unpalatable or dangerous. But they could not countenance the deliberate expansion of this population, especially the introduction of alien black females. For these reasons, the General Assembly enacted a statute—as an addendum, significantly, to "An Act

[77] Ibid., p. 8.
[78] Ibid., pp. 9, 10.

for the admission and settlement of Inhabitants of Towns,"—which prohibited any person from setting up or teaching in a school for "colored persons who are not inhabitants of this State" without the written consent of the selectmen.[79] As for Prudence Crandall, after vandals repeatedly defaced the school, sabotaged its operation, and finally attacked her house, she closed the school and went to Illinois.[80] It seems clear, however, that the real target of the physical violence was neither Crandall nor abolitionism but the threat of an expanding population of strangers of color.

Strangerhood, both categorical and specific, and the threat of amalgamation in the person of the black female, were linked issues that lay similarly at the heart of mob actions against people of color in Boston, Hartford, and Providence in the 1820s and 30s. In the fall of 1824 a white mob tore down a number of houses in a black community called Hard Scrabble in the northwest part of Providence. Hard Scrabble provided lodging for sailors, prostitutes, and poor whites as well as people of color and thus was, of course, a locus of sin and forbidden desire to the surrounding whites. The immediate cause of the riot was the refusal of several men of color to relinquish the inside path of the sidewalk to a group of white men, but subsequent discussion surrounding the trials of several accused white participants focused on the reputation of the community as a magnet for strangers and a sink of vice. As the *Hard-Scrabble Calendar,* a privately published report of the riot and trials, put it: "Here were held the revels and midnight orgies of the worst part of this class of the population of Providence. Owing to the difference in the severity of our Police and that of the neighbouring cities in relation to the blacks, the number had increased in this town, as ascertained by a recent enumeration, to upwards of 1200 persons. . . . the mass, as might be inferred, can hardly be considered a valuable acquisition to any community, and their return to the respective places from whence they came, probably would not be considered a public calamity."[81] In other words, Hard Scrabble was seen as a city of strangers.

It was also vilified as a source of vice and crime that tempted and corrupted the rest of the city. In his closing argument Joseph L. Tillinghast, the attorney defending one of the four white men actually brought to trial (two of whom were exonerated and the others freed on a technicality), essentially indicted the community itself for the crime committed against

---

[79] Ibid., p. 10.

[80] Richards, *Gentlemen of Property and Standing,* p. 40.

[81] *Hard-Scrabble Calendar: Report of the Trials of Oliver Cummins, Nathaniel G. Metcalf, Gilbert Humes and Arthur Farrier; who were indicted with six others for a Riot. . . .* (Providence, 1824), p. 4. See also Bartlett, *From Slave to Citizen,* pp. 27–30, for an account of this riot.

it: "The renowned city of Hard-Scrabble lies buried in its magnificent ruins! Like the ancient Babylon it has fallen. . . . The name of this celebrated city must give you some idea of its character, if you have not been sufficiently conversant with history to have become acquainted with it; . . . we must all agree that the destruction of this place is a benefit to the morals of the community."[82]

In a mock etymology of the name of the community, Tillinghast referred to "the zigzag movements of Pomp and Phillis, when engaged in treading the *minuet de la cour.*"[83] Shortly thereafter, someone who probably attended the trial or at least read an account of it published an anonymous broadside titled "Hard Scrabble, or Miss Philises Bobalition," which purported to be an account of the attack on a black couple named Pomp and Philis, written in the first person by Philis. Very much in the vein of the ventriloquistic broadsides lampooning black citizenship described earlier, this one blamed the riot on the presence of black strangers in Hard Scrabble and on the immoral conduct of the residents:

> I guess it best now for us brack folks be easy,
> And no longer live lives immoral and lazy,
> But gain honest living by sweat ob our brow;
> Depend on't de white folk won't den trouble or 'tack us,
> But de good people of Providence will always respec us,
> As they are wont to respec all good people now. . . .
> So Miss Boston keep home your lazy black rabble.
> Nor compel them seek shelter again at Hard Scrabble,
> For every maggot should stick to he core;
> For should they visit us gain they may find it foul wether
> We've plenty of Tar and de ground cover'd wid Fether
> And we've Pitch to pitch you all out of door.[84]

Through Philis, the writer seems to promise, rather ironically, that good behavior on the part of local people of color will earn whites' respect, in effect moderating their strangerhood. Then they can become the front line in the battle to keep people of color from other cities out of Providence.[85]

[82] *Hard-Scrabble Calendar,* p. 16.

[83] Ibid.

[84] "Hard Scrabble, or Miss Philises Bobalition" (1824), Broadside Collection, John Hay Library.

[85] The writer of this broadside does, however, reveal a certain sympathy for the victims of the riot and considerable disgust for the failure of the justice system to hold any of the perpetrators responsible: "But de damage 'twas judge was by some shock of nature, / Mr. Nobody

The idea of widespread depravity—sometimes identified as prostitution and other times as simply immoral behavior—as the nub of black stranger-hood seems to have prompted a number of the riots. A broadside pub-lished following a Boston riot in 1828, similar to the Providence one in that it recounted an attack on the home of a couple named Phillis and Pomp, identified the cause: "A great number of de white Truckerman get angry wid I spose so many bad girl who lib here."[86] After a Hartford riot in 1831 the *Liberator* published a letter in which J.K. of Hartford blamed the "strong connexion [that] exists between our colored women and white men, which has created all the riots in this place." J.K. went on to place the situation in quite a different light, however: "A few nights before the assault was com-mitted on the men who were much injured, no doubt part of that gang had some of our colored girls, who were as respectable in the community of color as those of a brighter hue in another circle, but who, through the in-fluence of a number of white profligates, have been made fit subjects for some House of Refuge. . . . The prey was taken from the clutches of these seducers, which gave them much offence, and they were determined to have their revenge."[87]

Strangerhood implied a lack of substantive claim to a residence, any property within it, or a community of such dwellings. It also seemed to im-ply a relinquishing of claims by black females to their own persons and by black men to any defense of such claims. Whites apparently invaded com-munities of color under the assumption that the admitted transiency of some of the residents extended to all its inhabitants. This idea was clearly fostered by the legal settlement statutes and the frequency of warnings-out of people of color under those statutes. Most whites did not comprehend that in the physical spaces occupied by communities of color whites were the strangers, and the predators. Neither did they fathom the degree to which black prostitution existed as a consequence of white men's demand for it and active effort to solicit it within the confines of largely black com-munities.

The Snow Town riot of 1831 in Providence illustrates how forays of white men into black communities were viewed as legitimate, whereas efforts of people of color to defend their own communities were understood as ille-gitimate acts of aggression in support of an immoral way of life. Snow Town was an area of rental properties owned by absentee landlords where, ac-

---

did it! O what a wile creature, / So de court find um No Guilty and tell um to go. / O dear what a Rogue Mr. Nobody."

[86] "Copy of a Letter from Phillis, to her Sister in the Country, describing The Riot on Ne-gro Hill" (1828), Broadside Collection, Boston Public Library.

[87] "The Late Riots," *Liberator*, June 4, 1831.

cording to a Providence paper, "the scum of the town and the out-scourings of creation, nightly assemble to riot and debauch."[88] It became the refuge of many people of color after the demolition of Hard Scrabble in 1824. In September 1831 a group of white steamboat men became involved in what the *Providence Journal* called "an altercation . . . at some houses of ill-fame." Soon they were joined by five white sailors who were, as one of them put it, "on a cruise" in Snow Town; the number of whites swelled quickly to about a hundred persons armed with stones and "ready for an affray." A black man with a gun met the crowd and, after warning them away twice, finally shot one white sailor dead, exclaiming, "Is this the way the blacks are to live, to be obliged to defend themselves from stones[?]"[89] This incident rapidly escalated into four days of rioting by a mob of "one or two thousand" whites.[90] The rioters were so determined to level all the dwellings in Snow Town that they assaulted the two militia companies called out to dispel them, finally provoking the militias to fire into the crowd. Four rioters were killed and fourteen were wounded. According to the report of an investigating committee, eighteen houses in and around Snow Town were seriously damaged or destroyed; however, "the Committee have not been able to ascertain that any houses occupied by respectable inhabitants, have been injured during the late riots."[91]

The committee clearly recognized that the actions of the rioters were illegal and wrong. Its report officially deplored "the very culpable conduct of many, even of our respectable citizens, who by their presence, and in some instances by open expressions of approbation, encouraged an unprincipled and sanguinary mob to the commission of deeds which never could be tolerated without an utter prostration of all law and order." Nonetheless, the committee seemed finally to pin the blame for the riots on the perceived shortcomings of the black community; its concluding remarks recommended that to prevent further outbreaks of such violence, "a vigorous and efficient Executive Magistrate is wanted in order that the decrees of the Council against idle and vagrant persons shall be rigidly executed."[92]

The Providence Town Council also condemned the "unlawful proceedings" but likewise seemed to allocate at least some measure of blame to the black community. It passed resolutions to maintain a citizen patrol of two

[88] Unidentified Providence paper, 1826, quoted in Bartlett, *From Slave To Citizen*, p. 30.
[89] *History of the Providence Riots, From Sept. 21 to Sept. 24, 1831* (Providence: H. H. Brown, 1831), p. 9.
[90] *Providence Journal*, September 23, 1831, cited in Bartlett, *From Slave To Citizen*, p. 31; Providence Town Council Records, 12: 422, September 23, 1831.
[91] *History of the Providence Riots*, p. 18.
[92] Ibid., pp. 6, 19.

hundred in the northern part of town (the vicinity of Snow Town) and to offer two $500 rewards: the first for the black man who had killed the sailor on the initial night of the riot; the second for miscellaneous other "persons involved." The equivalency and order of these rewards suggest that the council saw the black man not as a resident defending his dwelling and his community but as a perpetrator of an unjustified act of violence, on a par with the white rioters. Moreover, the council refrained from responding affirmatively to an outright appeal for protection on the third day of the rioting. When Edward Carrington, a prominent white attorney, sent a communication "expressing fears for the safety of a house in his neighbourhood belonging to Civil people of Colour, and Claiming protection for the same," the council merely ordered the clerk to file it—in effect refusing to endorse the right of people of color, even in principle, to obtain protection for property they owned.[93] Distinctions between "Civil" people of color (property owners) and so-called uncivil ones (tenants and boarders, for the most part), even when asserted by a powerful white advocate, evaporated in the face of mob hostility to people of color in general.

Efforts to reverse the tide of black bodies brought into North America in the course of the slave trade had grown with the trade itself. They had constituted perhaps the single most powerful motivation for ending the trade and continued long after its legal cessation. In New England, whites waged a persistent, if often masked, campaign to remove former slaves and their descendants from their landscape and memory and thus to fulfill the promise of the first generation of antislavery activists: to manage a gradual emancipation during which "Negroes" would slowly diminish in number until finally they would disappear altogether.

This project was facilitated by the reconception of the difference between whites and people of color that had taken place in the course of emancipation. Initially viewed as one element among many whose identity was in flux during the period of post-Revolutionary social instability and disorder, people of color had come to embody disorder itself, an innately and permanently inferior element in an otherwise perfectible world. Their removal could be justified by the endless evocation of them as permanently defective and alien elements who had been and always would be anomalous in white New England society.

The discourse of estrangement and removal legitimized a host of symbolic and material actions against people of color, ranging from warning

[93] Providence Town Council Records, 12:425, September 25, 1831; 12:422–23, September 23, 1831.

them out, to waging campaigns for their "return" to Africa, to mob destruction of their communities. Fear that abolitionists' activities would somehow empower existing black communities or increase their size was a contributing factor in persistent mob violence against abolitionists as well. Ironically, many of the most radical abolitionists themselves clung tightly to ideals of African repatriation, at least for a time, whether as an incentive for immediate emancipation or as a refuge from white racism. Although both the colonizationist enthusiasm and mob violence waned after 1840, to white New Englanders people of color continued to be anomalous and troublesome strangers.

6

"A Thing Unknown": The Free White Republic as New England Writ Large

The multitude of real and symbolic efforts to remove people of color from the narrative and landscape of New England must be understood as a crucially important aspect of a larger ideological process: the emergence of antebellum New England nationalism in the articulation of a regional identity morally and culturally distinct from that of the South. "Race" lay at the core of this ideological process.[1]

It was distinctly in New England's interests to lay claim to a kind of historical whiteness with both a moral and a "racial" dimension. Thus another element of the "negro removal" process was the shaping of a new historical narrative of New England in which the history of indigenous slavery was either suppressed entirely or revised to emphasize its extreme mildness and brevity and its triumphant early abolition. In turn, the myth of a historically free, white New England served to render the continuing presence of free people of color anomalous and disturbing and, absent a

[1] David Waldstreicher discusses the emergence of "nationalist regionalisms" in the antebellum period in "The Making of American Nationalism: Celebrations and Political Culture, 1776–1820," (Ph.D. diss., Yale University, 1995; to be published for the Institute of Early American History and Culture by the University of North Carolina Press), chap. Six, "Regionalism, Nationalism, and the Geopolitics of Celebration." He examines New England's claim to embody the nation and makes many of the arguments made here. He, too, sees a critique of the South as an important source of New England nationalism, although he does not find "race" per se an especially significant factor.

historical explanation, to naturalize their disadvantage as the result of inherent inferiority.[2]

Fashioning this narrative was at once an ideological process and a self-
conscious strategy for achieving political power. Its success as a political
strategy is evidenced by the fact that the northern states had, in many important ways, become New England writ large by the onset of the Civil War.
In southern as well as northern minds a certain "New Englandist" constellation of values, certain proprietary assumptions about the origins of
American history in New England's experience of it and thus about the
meaning of American history and the nature of American identity, had become embedded in the dominant ideology of "the North." Northern soldiers from Illinois and New Jersey as well as Massachusetts and Connecticut
marched south as Yankees.

In an elegant discussion of the relationship between antebellum New
England and the South, Lewis P. Simpson foregrounds this question of
New England nationalism. He describes the growing alienation between
New England and southern culture as the antipathy between "this national entity of New England, this [quoting Fisher Ames] 'northern confederacy of superior good order,' with its lofty spirit and destiny [and the]
'turbulent Parisian license of Southern Jacobinism.'"[3] Southern license, of
course, was rooted in the slave-master relationship, characterized by Jefferson as "a perpetual exercise of the most boisterous passions, the most
unremitting despotism."[4] But what was the origin of the "superior good order" of New England?

Simpson suggests that New England's claim to moral and cultural pre-
eminence lay in its foundation upon a "world-historical covenant with
God," a covenant rooted in liberty—uncoerced relations among free
(white) persons collectively building their City on a Hill.[5] That had been
the vision of the colonists in 1630, and it was the vision that New England
leaders carefully nurtured as the truth of the region's noble development
in the two centuries that had followed. In fact, of course, slavery had been
an entrenched social institution in New England for 150 of those years—

[2] John Wood Sweet discusses the transformation of "racial" hierarchies after "abolition"
and the construction of an imagined white North with a somewhat different emphasis in
"Bodies Politic: Colonialism, Race, and the Emergence of the American North: Rhode Island,
1730–1830 (Ph.D. diss., Princeton University, 1995), summarized p. 523.

[3] Lewis P. Simpson, *Mind and the American Civil War: A Meditation on Lost Causes* (Baton
Rouge: Louisiana State University Press, 1989), pp. 35, 52–53.

[4] *Notes on the State of Virginia,* in *Thomas Jefferson: Writings,* ed. Merrill D. Peterson (New
York: Library of America, 1984), p. 289.

[5] Simpson, *Mind and the American Civil War,* p. 44.

never the dominant mode of production, never the central organizing principle of the society, but nonetheless a widespread, persistent, and socially supported practice—until its protracted demise in the course of the last quarter of that two-hundred-year period. To nineteenth-century New England leaders the persistent presence of numbers of free people of color must have presented a troubling contradiction, offering visible evidence that New England, too, had exercised its own "unremitting despotism" in earlier times. Thus the strategies of removal described in the preceding chapter fit into a larger agenda of re-visioning a historically white New England that could stake a national political claim against the growing "Slave Power."

The revisionist thinking about slavery that would become such a persuasive element of antebellum New England nationalism is foreshadowed in Isaac Hillard's 1797 defense of his efforts to recover Connecticut slaves who had been kidnapped and sold South. Hillard proclaimed that the passage of the *post nati* statute in Connecticut had completely transformed life for slaves, contrasted with their prospects in the "slave states" of New York and Virginia; with this statute, "the hon. General Assembly entered them on the list of human creatures, and gave them a privilege, . . . that their children should be free." He listed the benefits slaves could expect from their continued residence in the state of Connecticut: having "a son in their old age, free, and able to support and assist them further than a cruel tyrant of a master would do"; being "secured" in the country where they were born, where "by law and custom they could justly expect to be fed and clothed comfortably" and where their children could "learn their duty to God and man, and be useful members of society."[6] Hillard was strongly implying that in Connecticut slavery was not really slavery at all, because the statute gave existing slaves their freedom vicariously by enabling them to enjoy their children's certainty of (delayed) freedom; and those children, though serving their masters until reaching their majority, could nonetheless begin at birth to savor the prospect of freedom. Thus, in Hillard's conception, *post nati* abolition did not simply begin to eliminate slaveholding gradually but inaugurated a new state of freedom immediately enjoyable by slaves and freeborn alike. It made Connecticut a "free state," unlike the "slave states" of New York and Virginia.

By 1820 the experience of New England slavery was rapidly disappearing as a frame of reference for discussing the "problem" of free people of color. No source of propaganda about a historically white New England was more powerful or more pervasive than the rhetoric of the American Colonization Society. Constituting people of color as not only undesirable but

[6] Isaac Hillard, "To the Public," (1797?), pp. 8–9, 15–16, Miscellaneous Manuscripts, Connecticut Historical Society.

also culturally and morally anomalous to northern life, colonization rhetoric in New England devoted nearly as much attention to distinguishing the "white" North, and particularly New England, from a fatally "colored" South as to the question of removal itself. Although the New England colonizationists failed to achieve the physical removal of more than a tiny fraction of the population of free people of color from the region, their enormously influential rhetoric, coupled with historical accounts of the early development of New England that erased the domestic institution of slavery, achieved remarkable success in the symbolic removal of people of color from their place in New England history.

Colonizationists' frequent debates over the origins of the endemic "prejudice" against free people of color provided one rhetorical context for the re-visioning of New England history. Although their portrayal of the "degraded" condition and "permanent" estrangement of free people of color could be represented as cause enough for their removal (claims discussed at length in the preceding chapter), the undeniable and irremediable prejudice against them was also cited frequently as a convincing removal argument. Historicizing "prejudice" allowed New England colonizationists to fashion a new narrative of their historical relations with people of color that could accomplish several important political tasks at once: it could further naturalize and legitimate feelings of antipathy on the part of New England whites; it could distance them from unwelcome associations with real, historical experiences and relationships that might account for those feelings; it could substitute for such experiences a limited and manageable degree of moral accountability that sanctioned their missionizing and commercial interests in Africa under the guise of obligation; and it could distinguish New England from the South without straining the essential alliance between northern and southern colonizationists.

Discussions among New England colonizationists on the sources of "prejudice" considered a range of possibilities. A few found the problem simply unfathomable; as Vermonter John Wheeler put it, "It is idle to speculate upon the origin of these feelings; they exist, and to that extent which will forever exclude a reciprocation in all the intercourse of life."[7] Many, however, acknowledged that whites had fastened upon blacks the prejudice they now saw as permanent and irremediable by enslaving Africans in the first place. Daniel Dana of New Hampshire was frank to admit that whites were responsible: "There are principles of repulsion between them and us, which can never be overcome" because, "by a law of human nature, I mean of human depravity, the man who has injured a fel-

---

[7] John Wheeler, *A Sermon, Preached before the Vermont Colonization Society at Montpelier, October 25, 1825* (Windsor, Vt.: W. Spooner, 1825), p. 13.

low being, becomes from that moment, his enemy," making it "harder to forgive a fellow creature we have wronged than one who wronged us."[8]

Placing this question of historical guilt for the sin of slavery on the rhetorical table enabled New England colonizationists to control its apportionment, to limit and circumscribe New England's responsibility in the sequence of events that had led to "the presence of a degraded and afflicted multitude in the bosom of a free, enlightened, and Christian land."[9] Several colonizationists were willing to acknowledge New England's role in the slave trade but not the practice of slaveholding itself. "From NEW ENGLAND have gone the ships and the sailors that have been polluted with this inhuman traffick," proclaimed Dana. "In NEW ENGLAND are the forges which have framed fetters and manacles for the limbs of unoffending Africans. In NEW ENGLAND are found the overgrown fortunes and proud palaces, which have been reared up from the blood and sufferings of these unhappy men." He did add, however, that "the guilt, both of the slave trade, and of slavery, is strictly national."[10] Silas M'Keen of Vermont agreed: "Let no one say that the Southern states only, are concerned in this guilt and danger, though some parts of the land are more deeply invol[v]ed in the evil than others, still the sin and peril are both strictly national." Yet even as he acknowledged that the region had been "most active of all our citizens in the slave trade," he could ask, "What part of our country is freer from the guilt of slavery than New England?" William O. Peabody of Massachusetts found New England guiltless thus far but poised dangerously on the brink of complicity, to be saved only by timely participation in the colonization scheme: "We are associated in our civil interests with the owners of slaves. . . . there is guilt at our doors as well as theirs, if something is not done to avert the threatened evil."[11]

Colonizationists who, like Dana, did acknowledge New England slaveholding, as opposed to slave trading, sought to minimize it (and its stubborn legacy). Leonard Bacon of New Haven insisted, "You would scorn the imputation, and justly, if I should suggest that there is anything here [in Connecticut] which subjects the African to peculiar disadvantages. On the contrary, it would seem far otherwise; inasmuch as slavery never existed

---

[8] Daniel Dana, *A Discourse Addressed to the New Hampshire Auxiliary Colonization Society at their First Annual Meeting, Concord, New Hampshire, June 2, 1825* (Concord, N.H.: Shepard & Bannister, 1825), p. 8.

[9] Baxter Dickinson, *Sermon Delivered at Springfield, Mass. July 4th, 1829, before the Auxiliary Colonization Society of Hampden Country* (Springfield, Mass.: S. Bowler, 1829), p. 4.

[10] Dana, *Discourse*, pp. 21–22.

[11] Silas M'Keen, *Sermon Delivered before the Vermont Colonization Society at Montpelier, Vermont, October 15, 1828* . . . (Montpelier, Vt.: E. P. Walter, Watchman Office, 1828), p. 11; William B. O. Peabody, *An Address Delivered at Springfield [Massachusetts], before the Hampden Colonization Society, July 4, 1828* (Springfield, Mass.: S. Bowler, 1828), p. 13.

here to any considerable extent, and for years it has been a thing unknown."[12]

By carving out a slice of guilt for enslavement that was limited in degree
and selective in kind, New England colonizationists effectively magnified
the distinction between New England and the South while appeasing
southern sensibilities. Such a delicate political balancing act was required
by the American Colonization Society's strange alliance of northern Federalists, reformers, and clergy with Chesapeake slaveholders. This alliance
generated contradictory opinions of the society's "real" agenda: did it want
to end slavery or to secure it? In the face of this hotly debated question,
both southerners and northerners could seize upon the eradication of the
"pernicious" influence of free people of color as a common objective, leaving deliberately vague their quite different reasons for endorsing the position. But moral questions remained. Many New England colonizationists
felt compelled to state their antislavery convictions yet had no desire to appear anti-South by pinning the blame for slavery and the residual presence
of free people of color on the southern states.

Another solution for a few New England colonizationists was to quote
southerners who extolled New England's supposed free labor tradition.
For example, the anonymous author of a pro-colonizationist article in the
Religious Intelligencer of 1825 who found New England blameless with respect to slavery chose as his spokesman the eminent southern colonizationist George Washington Parke Custis, a relative of George Washington.
In Custis's words, New England was "the favored portion of our country
where *virtute et labore florent Republicae* . . . that land of steady habits . . . the
essence of republicanism!" in contrast to the South, struggling under the
onus of a "deadly disease . . . entailed upon them by the fault of their fathers."[13]

Whether they resorted to southern compliments or selective historical
reconstruction, New England colonizationists skillfully fashioned a claim
to a kind of historical whiteness that highlighted the anomalous nature of
a resident black population and argued for a position of sectional superiority, even as it proclaimed the collaborative, national character of the enterprise. Colonization "has from the first obtained its most decided and
efficient support from the slave-holding states," effused Baxter Dickinson
of Massachusetts; it was an enterprise of universal appeal in which "the
Christian, the philanthropist, the patriot are united."[14]

[12] Leonard Bacon, *A Plea for Africa, Delivered in New-Haven, July 4, 1825* (New Haven,
Conn.: T. G. Woodward, 1825), p. 12.
[13] "Liberty and Slavery," *Religious Intelligencer* 10 (1825): 30.
[14] Dickinson, *Sermon,* pp. 4, 6.

The obsessive attention that colonizationists paid to guilt for slavery also served a second New England purpose. Acceptance of guilt, especially for the slave trade, laid the foundation for a recognition of America's debt to Africa, a debt that could legitimize American—and, in particular, New England—commercial as well as missionary interests there under the rubric of expiation. J. M. Wainwright of Hartford, for example, emphasized New England's direct debt to Africa as the rationale for a missionary program there. Wainwright was one of the few colonization supporters to acknowledge frankly that "slavery once polluted the now free and untrammelled states of New England." He was convinced that, "had the banks of the Connecticut been rice meadows, its uplands the soil for cotton, and its summer climate fatal to all but the African race,—the African race would, in all probability, still be in bondage among us." He argued further that the manufacture of cloth from slave-grown cotton and the consumption of slave-grown rice and sugar extended New England's complicity to his own day.[15] Wainwright's unusual frankness reflected his particular agenda: forming an African Mission School Society to train persons of color to become African missionaries.

New England colonizationists made an even more enthusiastic case for their debt to Africa in the context of opening up commerce there. They argued that free people of color, degraded in America, might, in their "natural" environment in Africa, be capable of commercial greatness; their dormant republican qualities, so dangerous in "strangers" in the United States, could be a source of considerable profit in trade representatives in "their own" land. Reuben Smith of Burlington, Vermont, envisioned a redeemed Africa in which "the energies of its children are turned to more rational pursuits" and the Nile, Congo, and Niger Rivers would "bear the rich burdens of commerce."[16] John Wheeler, taking as the text of his 1825 sermon the Golden Rule, "Do unto others . . . " (Matthew 7:12), which he apparently understood as an injunction to trade, happily described the founding of Liberia ("now secure against Africans") as "a mercantile company with two vessels regularly plying between this country and the Colony," which would shortly be "a place of extensive commerce."[17] Daniel Dana, in a footnote to the published text of his 1825 address to New Hampshire colonizationists, noted a little more delicately that although he wished to confine himself to "moral considerations" alone, "still, it may not

[15] Jonathan Mayhew Wainwright, *A Discourse, on the Occasion of Forming the African Mission School Society, Delivered in Christ Church, in Hartford, Connecticut on . . . August 10, 1828. . . .* (Hartford, Conn.: H. & F. J. Huntington, 1828), p. 18.

[16] Reuben Smith, *Africa Given to Christ: A Sermon, Preached before the Vermont Colonization Society* (Burlington, Vt.: Chauncey Goodrich, 1830), p. 15.

[17] Wheeler, *Sermon,* pp. 1, 6–8.

be improper to remark in this forum, that should the plan of Colonizing Africa from the United States succeed . . . it will probably be instrumental to open, in future time, a commerce between the two countries incalculably advantageous to both." His vision was far from reciprocal, however: Africa's "gold, her ivory, her beautiful dies [sic], her fragrant and precious gums, her healing plants and drugs, the varied produce of her now forsaken fields and lonely forests, will be brought by a joyous and grateful people, to the nations who, once their plunderers, will have at length become their protectors, friends and allies."[18]

In both its religious and its commercial possibilities, West Africa appeared to many New England colonizationists to be a prospective New England. William Peabody thought that Liberia would afford "at least as great a prospect as the infant settlement of New England, of laying the foundation of an enlightened, happy and religious people." Leonard Bacon, too, advocated that the ACS "train up and send to Africa such men as were the Pilgrims of Plymouth, or the Puritans of New Haven, . . . let there be erected one Christian African republic—powerful, enlightened, and happy, like ours."[19] According to this vision, New England might send forth its free people of color to bear Christian enlightenment, republican virtue, and sound commercial instincts into yet another New World—leaving the first one free of their presence.

In all these ways, the New England colonizationist discourse around "race," Christian mission, and commerce simultaneously distorted and minimized the history of indigenous New England slavery and strengthened New England claims to a uniquely white, uniquely moral, and enthusiastically commercial regional identity that could be contrasted sharply with the immorality, Africanization, and backward agriculturalism of a South fatally compromised by slavery. Southern writers, too, played into this dichotomous characterization in the course of their very defense of slavery. For example, writing as "Cecil" in 1850, Sidney George Fisher described the South as a "New Africa" in which "Negroes" have "destroyed all industry but their own. . . . they have thrown the administration of law throughout the South into lynch-law committees. . . . nominally slaves, they are really the masters of our destiny."[20]

As sectional controversy intensified, the mystique of a historically free, white New England provided a unique moral dimension to the Unionist position there, linking nineteenth-century Unionist redeemers with sev-

[18] Dana, *Discourse*, pp. 20–21.
[19] Peabody, *Address*, p. 14; Bacon, *A Plea for Africa*, p. 16.
[20] Cecil [Sidney George Fisher], *The Laws of Race, as Connected with Slavery* (Philadelphia: Willis P. Hazard, 1860), pp. 30–31.

enteenth-century Puritan ones. Thus, when Lewis Simpson invokes Emerson as the quintessence of the New England mind of the early nineteenth century, heir to Fisher Ames in having discovered by 1837 the "absolute cultural contrast between the South and New England," he locates the sources of this contrast in assumptions about a "whites-only republic of man" implicit in Emerson's rather abstract opposition to slavery. Simpson suggests that the governing mythology of this vision may be found in Emerson's musings that "the dark man, the black man declines. . . . It will happen by & by, that the black man will only be destined for museums like the Dodo."[21] But the "superior good order" of the New England nation-state had already come to be predicated upon the present *and historical* absence of slaves/people of color there, in contradistinction to the suffocating *and historical* presence of slaves in the South. Emerson's plan for a whites-only republic assumed the existence of a whites-only New England already in place. This assumption was not confined to Emerson, or to intellectuals, but was a fundamental element of a New England ideology that fueled and was fueled by a powerful sectional nationalism.[22]

New England had demonstrated a distinctly separate sectional interest—separate not only from the South, but also from the rest of the North—since the War of 1812, when conservative Federalists, the ascendant political party, had strongly opposed the war as inimical to their commercial interests and had toyed with secession, at least rhetorically, at the Hartford Convention of 1814. In his 1814 *Examinations of the Pretensions of New England to Commercial Pre-Eminence,* Mathew Carey, a Philadelphia Democratic-Republican, confirmed how widespread was the belief in New England's claims to unique sectional interest by that time, even as he attempted to demolish those claims:

> The Massachusettensian who makes the welkin ring with his bitter complaints of, and envenomed execrations against, the southern states for their hostility to commerce, is very little more than the wagoner who hauls their tobacco, and their cotton, and their rice, and their naval stores to

[21] *The Journals and Miscellaneous Notebooks of Ralph Waldo Emerson,* ed. William H. Gilman et al. (Cambridge: Harvard University Press, Belknap Press, 1960–82), 3:286. Simpson, *Mind and the American Civil War,* pp. 50, 67, 54, 53.

[22] Lawrence Buell has commented on the "overtly ethnocentric element underlying antebellum New England thinking," pointing out that "regionalism and ethnicity are homologous and sometimes coextensive formations." He argues, however, that New England did not develop a full-blown theory of philosophical "racism"—Anglo-Saxonism—until the late nineteenth century, and sees Emerson's "tribal consciousness" as an early sign of it ("The New England Renaissance and American Literary Ethnocentrism," in "Essays" section of *Prospects* 10 [1985]: 413–14).

market. . . . The senseless outcry about "the commercial states" is sickening as the croakings of a raven. New Hampshire a commercial state!— Vermont a commercial state! Connecticut and Rhode Island great commercial states! That this *soi-disant* enlightened age should be gulled and duped and deceived into these absurd opinions, is most lamentable![23]

The Hartford Convention left New England Federalists/National Republicans open to charges of disloyalty and accusations of fostering disunion, and they relentlessly worked to recover New England's political prestige over the next two decades, an effort that grew especially intense around the Missouri debates of 1819–21. Writing on sectional nationalism, Harlow Sheidley demonstrates a strategy on the part of the conservative elite leadership of Massachusetts that arguably could be extended to New England political and cultural leadership as a whole: an attempt to interpret American history as originating in the Puritan mission to revitalize the traditions of English liberty in the New England colonies, and to stabilize American identity around a set of cultural, moral, and political values drawn from New England and forged in the Revolutionary struggle led by New England patriots to preserve those liberties.[24] Sheidley shows how New England scholars and writers marshaled their cultural resources in the *North American Review,* established in Cambridge, Massachusetts, in 1815, to define their academic tradition as the source of a national American literature; and how Fourth of July orations, Bunker Hill commemoration speeches, and a host of other cultural productions supported the contention that "New England's history was the axis on which all American history turned."[25]

The self-conscious efforts of New England elites to foster an epic of cultural and historical preeminence were attempts to counter an actual decline in the region's relative demographic and political strength— punctuated by a brief resurgence in the election of John Quincy Adams in 1824. Adams himself, in a commemorative address on the bicentennial of the New England Confederation of 1643, claimed the Revolution for New

[23] Mathew Carey, *Examinations of the Pretensions of New England to Commercial Pre-Eminence To Which is Added, A View of the Causes of the Suspension of Cash Payments at the Banks* (Philadelphia: M. Carey, 1814), pp. *vi, ix.*

[24] Harlow Elizabeth Walker Sheidley, "Sectional Nationalism: The Culture and Politics of the Massachusetts Conservative Elite, 1815–1836" (Ph.D. diss., University of Connecticut, 1990). Buell looks at the invocation of Puritan rather than simply New England origins of New England literary nationalism: "The nineteenth century cult of Puritanism taught all America to look back upon the Pilgrim fathers as everyone's fathers" ("New England Renaissance," p. 409).

[25] Sheidley, "Sectional Nationalism," pp. 186–232, 329.

England in praising that confederation as "the model and prototype of the North American confederacy of 1774," even as he acknowledged that two hundred years later New England was "daily declining in her influence as a component part of the Union."[26]

Cultural arguments were paralleled by a New England boosterism of quite a different sort. A variety of economists, journalists, and visionaries, most of whom were not New Englanders themselves, found in the combination of agriculture, commerce, and industry of the New England countryside an economic model for the development of the rest of the nation, especially the West. Henry C. Carey, the influential Pennsylvania economist, saw the New England economy, in which each town operated as a center for manufacturing and served as a market for the produce of the surrounding farmland, as constituting the ideal American society.[27] The nature of the model society became a fiercely contested question in the debate over the extension of slavery in the territories. The *New York Tribune* concluded that barring slavery from the territories would "give them an opportunity to become what New England is now."[28]

But the issue of the extension of slavery racialized the question of the nature of the model society, and "what New England is now" comprised not only judgments about the superiority of small-town commerce and free labor over large-scale, slave-dependent agriculture in the present but also assumptions about the development of New England in the past as a region that was historically "white" as well as "free." In this context, efforts to remove free people of color from New England and to efface their history of enslavement there became critically important political maneuvers. A virtual amnesia about local slavery and a kind of perpetual, indignant surprise at the continuing presence of people of color became common ingredients in the epic of preeminent New England as it was shaped in the years after 1815. This narrative was convincing to many foreign visitors; for example, Henry Fearon, in his 1818 memoir of an expedition west in a wagon convoy with people from New Jersey, Maryland, Connecticut, and Massachusetts, told how he was able to distinguish residents of free and slave states: "The genuine Yankies (New Englanders) are ignorant of slavery; they have been necessitated to labour with their own hands; they have not been demoralized by familiarity with a system that establishes a barrier between fellow-beings on account of their colour; . . . they have relied

[26] John Quincy Adams, "The New England Confederacy of 1643," *Massachusetts Historical Society Collections*, 3d ser., 9 (1846): 219, 222.

[27] Henry C. Carey, *The Harmony of Interests, Agricultural, Manufacturing, and Commercial* (Philadelphia: Henry C. Carey Baird, 1872), pp. 47–48, 50.

[28] *New York Tribune*, February 20, 1854.

on their own resources, and the consequence is, that they are more enterprising, more healthy, more enlightened, and altogether better suited to cultivate the wilderness with success, than their slaveholding neighbours."[29]

The moral authority asserted by the idea of a free, white New England also served to rationalize the ambitions of many New Englanders and, ultimately, northerners—both intellectuals and entrepreneurs—to dominate the South commercially and culturally. This effect paralleled the way in which colonizationists' emphasis on Christian mission obscured and justified their commercial ambitions in Africa. Although colonization never met its supporters' expectations either for trade or for Christian conversion (and certainly not for the removal of large numbers of free people of color), the New England nationalism it fostered bore more satisfying fruit in the course of the Civil War and Reconstruction. As Emerson said in support of the confiscation of southerners' property at the end of the war, "You at once open the whole South to the enterprise & genius of new men of all nations, & *extend New England from Canada to the Gulf, et to the Pacific.*"[30]

When radical abolitionists—advocating immediate, uncompensated emancipation—began to gain adherents in the mid-1830s, they vilified the colonizationist argument, but their own position rested on quite similar assumptions about the superiority of Yankee blood and culture. The observation of Theodore Parker, leading Boston preacher and committed abolitionist, that "the Anglo-Saxon people . . . is the best specimen of mankind which has ever attained great power in the world"—although made later, in 1857—is quite typical of the thinking prevalent among New England abolitionists.[31]

The few abolitionists who acknowledged New England's indigenous history of slaveholding also minimized its extent and effect. For example, Garrison conscientiously reminded Massachusetts whites that they too were the descendants of slaveholders, publishing "The History of Slavery in Massachusetts" in several installments in the first volume of the *Liberator,* but the overall effect of the piece was more palliative than accusatory. The series reproduced a 1795 set of queries concerning Massachusetts slavery from St. George Tucker, a Virginia judge and colonizationist, and responses from Jeremy Belknap, eminent historian and founder of the Mass-

---

[29] Henry Bradshaw Fearon, *Sketches of America: A Narrative of a Journey of Five Thousand Miles through the Eastern and Western States of America with Remarks on Mr. Birkbeck's "Notes" and "Letters"* (1818; New York: Augustus M. Kelley, 1970), p. 188.

[30] Emerson, *Journals,* 15:445, quoted in Simpson, *Mind and the American Civil War,* p. 65.

[31] Letter to Miss Cobbe, December 4, 1857, in John Weiss, *Life and Correspondence of Theodore Parker* (New York: Appleton, 1864), 1:463.

achusetts Historical Society. Belknap explained, "The condition of our slaves was far from rigorous. No greater labor was exacted of them than of white people. . . . In the maritime towns, the negroes served either in families or at mechanical employments; and, in either case, they fared no worse than other persons of the same class. In the country, they lived as well as their masters, and often sat down at the same table, in the true style of *republican equality*."[32]

In short, abolitionists, like colonizationists (which many of them, such as Garrison, had previously been), frequently contrasted the brief life and mild nature of New England slavery with the longevity and brutality of the institution in the South. And both groups (as well as most black leaders) found the free black population in New England to be in a "degraded" condition. The *Liberator* article even suggested that "if a comparison be made between the former and present condition of this class of people in the New England states, it may be said, that unless *liberty* be reckoned as a compensation for many inconveniences and hardships, the former condition of most of them was preferable to the present."[33]

If the enslavement of Africans had been so brief and so tolerable in New England, why, then, were free people of color so "degraded" there? Belknap thought that "too many are improvident and indolent, though a subsistence for laboring people is here very easily obtained," because "having been educated in families where they had not been used to provide for themselves in youth, they know not how to do it in age, . . . having been accustomed to a plentiful and even luxurious mode of living, in the houses of their masters."[34] In other words, in Belknap's New England the slaveowners had toiled for the slaves' benefit; emancipation had released whites from this dreadful burden, leaving people of color dependent upon inner resources that were inherently inadequate to the task in most respects. The problem was internal, and irremediable.

Many abolitionists, however, concluded that the problem was not the innate inadequacy of northern free people of color but the continued enslavement of southern ones. As Garrison editorialized, "The toleration of slavery at the South is the chief cause of the unfortunate situation of free colored persons at the North."[35] This argument, embraced almost universally by New England abolitionists, made good sense as part of a strategy to heap blame for everything wrong with American society on southern slav-

---

[32] "The History of Slavery in Massachusetts: Judge Tucker's queries respecting slavery, with Dr. Belknap's Answers," pt. 2, *Liberator*, February 26, 1831.

[33] Ibid., pt. 4, *Liberator*, March 12, 1831.

[34] Ibid.

[35] *Liberator*, January 8, 1831.

ery, but it also had the advantage, to northern ears, of conveniently shifting accountability for a locally specific situation away from the indigenous institution from which it had evolved.

Abolitionists, then, like colonizationists, distanced and disconnected free people of color from their local history of enslavement, defining them, finally, as strangers. Whereas colonizationists linked them to Africa and worked to expatriate them, however, abolitionists linked them to the South, imagining them to be slaves *in absentia* and striving to free them by proxy.[36] Both arguments in their different ways sustained a mythology of a free, white, and godly New England and thus served both to intensify New England nationalism and, slowly, build support for antislavery. By the early 1850s large numbers of New Englanders were ready to find emotionally compelling an antislavery message couched in unabashedly nationalist terms—*Uncle Tom's Cabin*. Part of the genius and power of this novel as an antislavery tract undoubtedly lay in the clear contrast it offered between a southern hell and a New England heaven. In it, the only "good" slaveholder, Augustine St. Clare, has spent his formative years with an uncle in Vermont and been inoculated with New England compassion and love of justice before returning to his New Orleans plantation. By contrast, the most evil slaveholder of all, Simon Legree, has deliberately rejected a New England upbringing and the counsel of a northern Christian mother, fleeing to a life of uncontrolled debauchery on a decayed plantation deep in a Louisiana cypress swamp.[37] The Christ figure in the novel, Uncle Tom, is a native of Kentucky, a border state poised between these two value systems; by his steadfast choice of northern, Christian values over southern, despotic ones he earns a triumphant death and, presumably, a permanent place in heaven as a sort of honorary New Englander.[38]

A historically free, white New England, then, ever more favorably contrasted with a Jacobin, Africanized South, was the linchpin of a burgeoning antebellum New England nationalism. The formal strategies of "Negro removal" introduced in preceding chapters, including the colonization movement, appeared at more or less the same time, gathered force in the

[36] Many abolitionists also supported philanthropic efforts in northern black communities and inundated them with advice on changing their behavior (but not the behavior of whites toward them) with respect to education, temperance, steady work habits, frugality, faithful religious practice, chastity, and so forth. Abolitionists felt that these measures would improve the lot of blacks but that only the abolition of southern slavery could eradicate the persistent "prejudice" against them.

[37] Harriet Beecher Stowe, *Uncle Tom's Cabin; or, Life among the Lowly* (1852; New York: New American Library, 1981), pp. 168–69, 398.

[38] Ibid., pp. 358, 385–86, 442.

1820s, and had peaked by the mid-1830s. But the New England nationalism that may be considered in part their legacy remained a vital force
through the Civil War years. Indeed, by the outset of actual war in 1861 the
New England nationalist trope of virtuous, historical whiteness, clothed as
it was in a distinctive set of cultural, moral, and political values associated
with New England's Puritan mission and Revolutionary struggle, had come
to define the Unionist North as a whole.

This is not to say that the other northern states were innocent of anti-
South, antislavery, and antiblack impulses before being somehow infected
with these ideological viruses (benign or deadly) from New England. Obviously, the New England states were not alone among northern states in
their growing opposition to the so-called Slave Power in the years after
1815; after all, the ill-fated 1846 Wilmot Proviso, outlawing slavery in any
territory to be gained from Mexico, was authored by a Pennsylvania Dem-
ocrat. More important, the New England states were not alone in having
achieved widespread, if not total, abolition long before the war (some of
the others, notably Pennsylvania and New York, had also implemented *post
nati* statutes to accomplish it).[39] Neither were they alone in employing various efforts to remove their indigenous populations of free people of col-
or, in sustaining popular support for colonization, and in nurturing a
range of quite virulent antiblack sentiments. These other states, however,
do not seem to have experienced the kind of widespread, determined effacement of the historical experience of indigenous slavery, ranging from
resolute denial to mitigation and apology, which characterized New England's "racial" self-definition during and after its gradual emancipation of
slaves.

A quite different emancipation time frame accounts for the relative absence of amnesia or minimization of the slavery experience in some northern states outside New England. In New York and New Jersey, for example,
gradual emancipation statutes were not passed until 1799 and 1804. Colonizationist sermons in these states never touted a historically free, white
past or a distant, benign, and minimal experience of slavery. In his 1826
sermon in New York City in support of colonization, the Reverend James
Milnor clearly acknowledged the existence of slavery in New York, still ongoing under the gradual emancipation statutes: "We have among us an im-
mense population of the descendants of Africa. A part of them still endure
the galling chains of slavery. Under the influence of favouring circum-

[39] See Arthur Zilversmit, *The First Emancipation: The Abolition of Slavery in the North* (Chicago: University Press of Chicago, 1967), for the narrative history of emancipation efforts in
New York, New Jersey, and Pennsylvania. Ohio, Indiana, and Illinois had outlawed slavery in
their initial constitutions (1802, 1816, and 1818, respectively).

stances, in some of the States their fetters have been wholly, in others partially, broken. . . . A race of human beings is thus found among us, who, from their degraded origin, their complexion, their inferior means of instruction, . . . constitute a separate class, marked by many features of decided inferiority in public estimation, and, in the common course of things, doomed perhaps to occupy forever this degraded place."[40]

Theodore Frelinghuysen, addressing the New Jersey Colonization Society in 1824, used an even franker acknowledgment of his state's widespread use of slave labor to justify colonization as the fulfillment of an obligation to former slaves: "Citizens of New-Jersey—we appeal to you— survey your cultivated fields—your comfortable habitations—your children rising around you to bless you. Who, under Providence, caused those hills to rejoice, and those vallies to smile?—who ploughed those fields and cleared those forests? Remember the toil and the tears of black men, and pay your debt to Africa."[41]

In Pennsylvania, the one state outside New England which had initiated gradual emancipation before 1785, the pre-ACS discourse of colonization did reveal something akin to New England's amnesia as early as 1805.[42] But here the development of a progressively stronger assertion of being historically white as well as historically free was hindered by other factors. The location of Pennsylvania as a state bordering slave states and thus experiencing a steady influx of freed and fleeing slaves made the "racial" presence more visible and the connection between former slavery and the current "condition" of free people of color more manifest, even though in point of fact people of color constituted a percentage of the population only slightly greater than in Connecticut.[43]

In addition, Pennsylvania's border location seemed to render its inhabitants especially vulnerable both to the sensationalism of reports of atroci-

[40] James Milnor, *Plea for the American Colonization Society: A Sermon, Preached in St. George's Church, New-York, on Sunday, July 9, 1826. By the Rev. James Milnor, D.D. Rector of said church* (New York: John P. Haven, 1826).

[41] Theodore Frelinghuysen, *An Oration: Delivered at Princeton, New Jersey, November 16, 1824, before the New-Jersey Colonization Society, by the Honourable Theodore Frelinghuysen* (Princeton, N.J.: D. A. Borrenstein, 1824), p. 12.

[42] See Zilversmit, *First Emancipation*, pp. 124–37; and Gary B. Nash and Jean R. Soderlund, *Freedom by Degrees: Emancipation in Pennsylvania and Its Aftermath* (New York: Oxford University Press, 1991).

[43] Residents identified as "Negro" in the 1790, 1800, and 1810 censuses in Pennsylvania constituted 2.4, 2.7, and 2.9 percent of the population, respectively; comparable figures for Connecticut were 2.3, 2.5, and 2.6 (Clayton E. Cramer, *Black Demographic Data, 1790–1860: A Sourcebook* [Westport, Conn.: Greenwood Press, 1997], pp. 71, 68). On the influx of people of color into Pennsylvania, see Jean R. Soderlund, "Black Importation and Migration into Southeastern Pennsylvania, 1682–1810," *Proceedings of the American Philosophical Society* 133 (1989): 144–53.

ties associated with the Haitian Revolution and to fears of efforts to revive the slave trade. The about-face of longtime antislavery activist Thomas Branagan in 1805 illustrates both the amnesiac tendency and the countervailing fear of black immigration and its consequences which tempered it. Implying that southern, not indigenous, slavery was the source of a troublesome free population of color, Branagan noted that freed southern slaves "are of course exported to the North, where we have to provide for, and support them, with all their vices upon them. The negroes who have been most awfully contaminated by our Southern Fellow-citizens, are thus a grievous burthen to us. . . . They get the benefit, we get the trouble." He compared slavery to "a large tree planted in the South, whose spreading branches extend to the North; the poisonous fruit of that tree when ripe fall upon these states, to the annoyance of the inhabitants, and contamination of the land which is sacred to liberty." His solution was to send all free people of color to a part of the Louisiana Territory that might be set aside for the purpose.[44]

Branagan saw blacks in the North as "worse than the worst of tories" and stated flatly, "The sons of Africa in America, are the inveterate enemies of Americans." He conjectured that the free blacks of Philadelphia were very likely to join in rebellions with Delaware slaves. Following eight pages of horror stories regarding events in St. Domingue (the present Dominican Republic), which he obviously regarded as a harbinger of coming events in Delaware and Pennsylvania, he noted that "the blacks are jealous of their liberties and would wade through seas of blood, when an opportunity would offer, to vindicate their rights."[45] He quoted the argument that "if the negroes were properly informed they would become useful and respectable citizens, in a domestic as well as political point of view" only to deny it: "Such assertions are frequently made without a moment's previous reflection." Acknowledging his own change of heart regarding the potential role of free people of color in the American republic, he noted, "Indeed I have not only made a similar observation myself verbally, but also in writing, which I hereby acknowledge to be spurious and done without due reflection."[46]

Although Branagan thought slavery to be as foreign to Pennsylvania as

[44] Thomas Branagan, *Serious Remonstrances, addressed to the citizens of the Northern states, and their Representatives; being an appeal to their Natural Feelings and Common Sense: Consisting of Speculations and Animadversions, on the recent revival of the Slave Trade, in the American Republic, with an investigation relative to the consequent Evils resulting to the citizens of the Northern States from that Event. Interspersed with a Simplified plan for colonizing the free Negroes of the Northern, in conjunction with those who have, or may emigrate from the Southern states, in a distant part of the National Territory: Considered as the only possible means of avoiding the deleterious evils attendant on Slavery in a Republic* (Philadelphia: Thomas T. Stiles, 1805), pp. 33–34, 92, 36.

[45] Ibid., pp. 41, 43, 45, 47–54.

[46] Ibid., p. 112.

it was to New England, and liberty as native as to Boston, he could not claim a fundamental and historical condition of whiteness for Pennsylvania. Its contiguity with intransigent slave states led him to see its free people of color as a population of slaves in disguise, always newly replenished. The location of Pennsylvania defeated the very rationale of *post nati* emancipation and nullified its promise to end the source of new slaves and, eventually, the presence of all blacks. Unlike New England, buffered by other states themselves embarking upon gradual emancipation, Pennsylvania shared its southern borders with three states deeply committed to slavery. (Only one of these, Virginia, ever wavered in that commitment, flirting briefly with emancipation during debates inspired by terror following Nat Turner's revolt in 1831, long after slavery had ended in Pennsylvania.) Whites in Pennsylvania could never distance themselves sufficiently from the sights and sounds and smells of slavery to imagine themselves eternally free, white, and remote, as New Englanders could.

The midwestern states of Ohio, Indiana, and Illinois, bordered by Virginia, Kentucky, and Missouri, experienced a similar problem. Because slavery had been illegal since their organization as territories under the Northwest Ordinance (although slaves brought there prior to 1787 could be kept legally), a legitimate case could be made for a history devoid, or nearly devoid, of slavery.[47] But here, as in Pennsylvania, the proximity of slave states, coupled with a far more rapidly accelerating rate of growth in the black population, inhibited illusions of remote and unassailable whiteness.[48] By 1810 there were 3,310 persons identified as "Negro" in these three states, and in ten years the number had more than doubled to 7,517, most of the increase taking place in the southernmost counties.[49] Many midwestern colonizationists saw their southern regions as a reservoir into which poured free people of color from other areas and from which they were prevented from flowing onward. Ohio colonizationist David Christy offered a quite elaborate analysis of this phenomenon to the Ohio House of Representatives in 1849 and wove the many threads of his argument together in the following summation:

[47] Northwest Ordinance (1787), art. 6. But between 1803 and 1810 people of color could be brought into Indiana Territory under labor contracts for terms as long as ninety years and were thus bought and sold essentially as slaves. See Eugene Berwanger, *The Frontier against Slavery: Western Anti-Negro Prejudice and the Slaver Extension Controversy* (Urbana: University of Illinois Press, 1967), pp. 7–12; and Cramer, *Black Demographic Data*, pp. 14–15.

[48] Ohio's black population had grown especially fast, increasing by more than five times between 1800 and 1810, then doubling in each decade to 1830, and growing by 81 percent by 1840. See Bureau of the Census, U.S. Department of Commerce, *Negro Population, 1790 –1915* (Washington, D.C.: Government Printing Office, 1918), p. 45; Cramer, *Black Demographic Data*, p. 110.

[49] Bureau of the Census, *Negro Population, 1790–1915*, p. 45.

We cannot change the climate of the north-east, nor mold the African constitution so that it may endure the rigors of its winters, and much less can we impart to the colored man a spirit of energy and activity in business which shall enable him to compete with the New Englander; we are still less able to roll back the mighty wave of foreign emigration, which . . . drives the man of color from his employments [there], and compels him to wander to the west in search of bread. And it is still more impracticable for us to induce the slave states to repeal the laws and give up the prejudices which drive out the free colored man from amongst them. The colored people, if disposed, cannot extend westward and southward. The iron wall of slavery and the prohibitions in the new constitutions of Illinois and Iowa, will prevent emigration in that direction. They are, therefore, shut up, imprisoned among us, and instead of any diminution we must prepare for an increase of their numbers.[50]

Christy concluded by pleading for political support from the state representatives for the separation and eventual colonization of Ohio's black population.

In Ohio and other states of the Midwest, the steady influx of emigrants of color from the South and the looming presence of slavery on their southern borders made a claim of continuous historical whiteness impossible. Nonetheless, the antagonism toward their black populations was at least as virulent among residents of the mid-Atlantic and midwestern states as it was in New England. The sermons of colonizationists from these regions were indistinguishable in this respect from those of New Englanders. "Who does not perceive in the records of our courts, and in his daily walks, abundant proofs of the evils of an increased coloured population?" asked the Reverend Jay Milnor of New York. "Visit us with the plague, or any other *physical calamity,* rather than bring this *moral pestilence* into contact with our children," intoned David Christy of Ohio.[51]

The sources of this hostility were twofold. Obviously the discourse of "race," shaped as it had been in the New England states by the rhetoric and experiences of gradual emancipation and the emergence of free populations of color, did not remain sharply contained within those states but extended beyond them, especially as surrounding states began to debate and institute gradual emancipation legislation. Then, too, the experiences of

---

[50] David Christy, *A Lecture on African Colonization, Delivered in the Hall of the House of Representatives of Ohio. By David Christy, agent of the American Colonization Society* (Cincinnati: J. A. & U. P. James, 1849), pp. 25, 29.

[51] Milnor, *Plea for the American Colonization Society,* p. 14; Christy, *Lecture on African Colonization,* p. 26.

northern emancipation outside New England were themselves "race"-making, just as they had been in New England. The resulting "racial" conceptions and argument lacked that amnesiac component so distinctive to New England, and also the sense of beleaguered political identity that motivated New England's leaders to forge an imperialist cultural identity around its historic whiteness. Nevertheless, the "racial" hostility manifest in the sermons of the mid-Atlantic and midwestern colonizationists may have engendered a longing for effacement that made identification with New England's whiteness appealing to Americans in these regions in the same years that the fear of the Slave Power was becoming more and more compelling. And, of course, many New Yorkers and midwesterners were themselves transplanted New Englanders, making them sympathetic and susceptible to a resurgence of New England cultural and political leadership.

It is difficult to track the mechanics of the gradual identification of the entire North with New England nationalist ideology, whiteness at its core, during the antebellum years.[52] But one event can be seen as a kind of paradigm of this transformation: the famous Webster-Hayne debate which took place in the U.S. Senate over the course of six days—January 19–21 and 25–27, 1830—and culminated in what has come to be known as "Webster's Second Reply to Hayne."[53] In this debate, which originated in a resolution to limit the sale of public lands, Senator Daniel Webster of Massachusetts rebutted an attack on New England and its presumed hostility to the South

[52] John F. Berens, *Providence and Patriotism in Early America, 1640–1815* (Charlottesville: University Press of Virginia, 1978), esp. summary p. 164, concludes that "providential nationalism" was "New England writ large" before the War of 1812, and that the New England version became local (Federalist) during that war, while what he calls the providential consensus—the providential interpretation of American history—had become "the mainstream of American thought," although it would be "strained" by the North-South split. I would argue that the New England nationalist version, with its core value of historical whiteness, was reinvigorated precisely by that North-South split, coupled with the determination of New England political leadership to regain the power lost during the 1812–14 political struggles.

[53] Sheidley devotes an entire chapter of "Sectional Nationalism" to a careful analysis of Webster's speech as the articulation of New England nationalism, showing how he "was able to transfer the burden of disunionist sectionalism, which had been New England's for so many years, to the South. New England's own defensive sectionalism was . . . recast as an aggressive nationalism" (p. 380). Her argument emphasizes the importance of the speech as a bid for power on the part of elite Massachusetts conservatives (chap. 7, "Daniel Webster and the Promulgation of New England's Nationalism," esp. p. 379). I would emphasize that although Webster may have had this narrow objective in mind, his speech in fact articulated a much more broad-based and compelling expression of New England political culture with which northerners of every, and no, political stripe could and did identify. Unlike Sheidley, I argue for the importance and appeal of the implicit "whiteness" at the core of New England's historical interpretation, as laid out by Webster, in isolating the slave South and invigorating opposition to it.

and West made by Senator Robert Young Hayne of South Carolina. After an initial exchange and a second elaboration on the part of Hayne, Webster's Second Reply articulated a clear and compelling vision of an American nation made up of the union of northern and western states, bonded by an interpretation of the origin and meaning of the union and the U.S. Constitution and reflecting the core values of New England political culture and history. Coded implicitly among those essential values were claims to historical freedom and whiteness, against which Webster could effectively contrast a South isolated by its historical commitment to slavery. Such an interpretation, appealing as it did to the widespread desire among northern states outside New England to eradicate their black populations and achieve a "whiteness" like that of New England, could rally and solidify northern opposition to the Slave Power.

Webster's four main points together served to nationalize positions identified with New England interests and to marginalize opposing southern positions as narrowly sectional. First, he responded to Hayne's construction of a reference he had made, in his reply to Hayne's original speech on the public lands resolution, to the Ordinance of 1787 for the governance of the Northwest Territory, which prohibited slavery northwest of the Ohio River. Webster had praised the provision and its framer, Nathan Dane of Massachusetts. Hayne had objected, understanding this position as a frank attack on the domestic institution of slavery.[54] This gave Webster an opportunity to point out the threat posed by the Slave Power—"the peculiar effect which the magnitude of that population [of slaves] has had in the distribution of power under this federal government" and the "great advantage in that respect . . . enjoyed by the slave-holding States"—all the while disclaiming any desire to "overstep the limits of constitutional duty, or to encroach on the rights of others. The domestic slavery of the Southern States I leave where I find it,—in the hands of their own governments. It is their affair, not mine."[55] More important, defending Dane and the antislavery provisions of the Northwest Ordinance gave Webster the opportunity to invoke, by implication, the historical "whiteness" of the states later formed out of the Northwest Territory, to claim New England authorship of that "whiteness," and thus to establish a crucial kinship between those states and New England against the asserted political "advantage" of the South.[56]

[54] *The Great Debate between Robert Young Hayne of South Carolina and Daniel Webster of Massachusetts,* ed. Lindsay Swift (New York: Houghton Mifflin, 1898), p. 122.

[55] Ibid., p. 127.

[56] Sheidley "Sectional Nationalism," does not describe Webster's defense of both Dane and the exclusion of slavery in the Northwest Ordinance as a separate and significant element

Next, he defended New England congressmen against Hayne's accusation that they had been working to retard the growth of the West and to enhance their own region's commerce at the West's expense. Webster insisted that, on the contrary, New Englanders historically had supported internal improvements that enhanced the development of the West: "We [people of New England] look upon the States, not as separated, but as united. . . . We do not impose geographical limits to our patriotic feeling or regard. . . . I observed, when speaking on this subject before, that if we looked to any measure, whether for a road, a canal, or anything else intended for the improvement of the West, it would be found that, if the New England *ayes* were struck out of the list of votes, the Southern *noes* would always have rejected the measure."[57] He concluded this argument with a defense of the doctrine of federal responsibility for internal improvements, recasting a program especially beneficial to New England commercial interests in a national context.

Third, Webster offered an eloquent historical interpretation of the central role of New England as birthplace of the nation and steadfast, loyal defender of the union, challenging Hayne's charge of parochial party interest. He began by recalling the region's loyalty to Washington in the face of "abusive" and "scurrilous" attacks "from presses south of New England." He then moved to a vigorous and rather long-winded refutation of Hayne's allegations of New England disloyalty surrounding the Hartford Convention, denying "any such purpose as breaking up the Union" on the part of the convention delegates and implying that the "recently promulgated South Carolina opinions" (on nullification) might properly be queried in the same regard.[58] Here he evoked the Revolutionary origins of the republic in stirring images from New England history:

There is Boston, and Concord, and Lexington, and Bunker Hill; . . . where American liberty raised its first voice, and where its youth was nurtured and sustained, there it still lives in the strength of its manhood and full of its original spirit. If discord and disunion shall wound it; if party strife and blind ambition shall hawk at and tear it; if folly and madness . . . shall succeed in separating it from that Union by which alone its existence is made sure,—it will stand, in the end, by the side of that cradle in which its infancy was rocked; it will stretch forth its arm with whatever of vigor it

---

of his Second Reply, but this is the element that most effectively allows Webster to draw the Midwest into the New England sphere of influence under the rubric of historical freedom and "whiteness."

[57] *Great Debate*, pp. 141–42, 144.
[58] Ibid., pp. 170, 177–78.

may still retain over the friends who gather round it; and it will fall at last, if fall it must, amidst the proudest monuments of its own glory, and on the very spot of its origins.[59]

Fourth, Webster laid out his construction of the Constitution, opening this final section of his speech with an indictment of Hayne's "South Carolina doctrine" of the right of state legislatures to nullify acts of Congress. After examining the origins of the government and the source of its power, and locating them in the Constitution, Webster concluded, "At no time and under no circumstances has New England, or any State in New England, or any respectable body of persons in New England, or any public man of standing in New England, put forth such a doctrine as this Carolina doctrine.... New England has studied the Constitution in other schools and under other teachers."[60] In short, New England, birthplace of the republic, was also the most trustworthy guardian of its most sacred and supreme law: the Constitution that shaped, sustained, and gave it agency.

The four seemingly rather disconnected portions of the Second Reply were unified by certain insistent themes: an identification of New England interests with the good of the nation as a whole; a definition of "the nation" as those sections that subscribed to an interpretation of the Constitution as the supreme law and cherished a narrative of national history that located its birthplace within New England; the location of the source and strength of American nationalism within the ideals and policies of New England leaders, especially freedom from slavery as codified in the Northwest Ordinance. Nowhere in this speech did Webster refer to "Negroes" or to "whites," yet a compelling aspect of his speech was its implicit call to the rest of the northern "free" states to join a historically free and white republic of New England to achieve political dominance over a "Negroized" South.

Within four months Webster's speech had appeared in newspapers across the country and in pamphlet form in some twenty editions, just one of which was printed in forty thousand copies.[61] Harlow Sheidley describes in detail the outpouring of congratulation Webster received from all quarters in the ensuing months. The responses fell into two basic types: admiration for his defense of New England as a sectional victory over southern slaveholders, and appreciation for his constitutional nationalist argument as offering reassurance that the Union might indeed be preserved. Web-

---

[59] Ibid., p. 181.
[60] Ibid., pp. 182–83, 186–93.
[61] See Maurice G. Baxter, *One and Inseparable: Daniel Webster and the Union* (Cambridge: Harvard University Press, 1984), p. 188.

ster appeared at that moment to be, in Sheidley's words, a kind of "personification of the Union."[62] More significantly, perhaps, he had made an opening argument for New England as the personification of the Republic.

By 1845 that argument seemed a commonplace. In that year Jesse Hutchinson Jr. of the renowned Hutchinson Family Singers published a successful songster in Boston aimed at the growing audience of anti-(southern)-slavery sympathizers. "The Fugitive's Song" capitalized on both the fame of Frederick Douglass and the reputation of New England as a beacon of freedom. The cover illustration depicts a young Douglass, knapsack in hand, pointing toward a sign reading "New England"; behind him, mounted slave catchers and bloodhounds are stymied by a wide river he has somehow crossed (Figure 8). The lyrics—which begin "I'll be free! I'll be free!"—describe the determination of a slave to gain freedom in New England. The third verse reads:

> New England! New England! thrice blessed and free,
> The poor hunted slave finds a shelter in thee,
> Where no bloodthirsty hounds ever dare on his track;
> At thy stern voice, New England! the monsters fall back!
> Go back! then, ye blood-hounds, that howl on my path,
> In the Land of New England I'm free from your wrath,
> And the Sons of the Pilgrims my deep scars shall see,
> Till they cry with one voice "Let the Bondmen go free."

The fourth verse predicts the conversion of the entire North by the power of this New England commitment to freedom:

> That voice shall roll on, 'mong the hills of the North,
> In Murmurs more loud 'till its thunders break forth; . . .
> Like the tempests of Heaven, shaking mountain and sea,
> Shall the North tell the South, "Let the Bondmen go free!"[63]

By 1862, the first effort was afoot to replicate the converted North in the South. In that year, fifty-three northern teachers and missionaries known as "Gideon's Band" went south to teach and preach among some ten thousand slaves abandoned by their fleeing owners in the Union bombardment of the Sea Islands off the coast of South Carolina in the fall of 1861. This "rehearsal for Reconstruction," as Willie Lee Rose memorably called it, was

[62] Sheidley, "Sectional Nationalism," pp. 407–10.
[63] Jesse Hutchinson Jr., *The Fugitive's Song* (Boston: Henry Prentiss, 1845), p. 5.

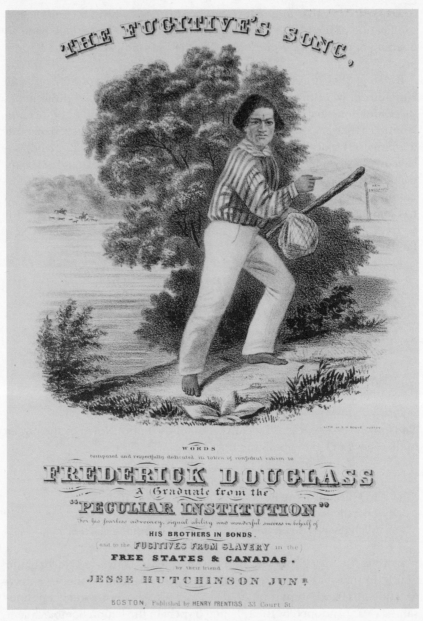

Figure 8. Cover of 1845 songster. Courtesy of the Library Company of Philadelphia

an unabashed test of the ability of ex-slaves to absorb northern values and free labor ideology. In Rose's words, the Gideonites went south with "the exalted aims of remodeling Southern society and spreading New England civilization."[64]

The Gideonites came from Boston, New York, and, later, Philadelphia. The Boston contingent consisted of prominent, well-educated abolitionists, most of whom were young Unitarians; some had been members of the Kansas Emigrant Aid Society. The New Yorkers were evangelicals affiliated with Lewis Tappan and the American Missionary Association. The Philadelphia group contained abolitionists of both religious perspectives. Although there was persistent friction among the groups, they clearly shared a single vision of an orderly, productive, chaste society that they would diligently strive to replicate among the freedmen. Rose is speaking specifically of the Bostonians when she notes the Gideonites' expectation that "the decadent South, with its antique civil arrangements, would be regenerated by the vigorous institutions of New England, the public school system, 'liberal Christianity,' and even the town meeting, if possible," but throughout the book she demonstrates that these ideas lay at the heart of a common northern vision of the well-ordered society. In an epilogue evaluating postwar developments, she observes that "the Sea Islanders had learned the lessons of freedom, and they became, in their own way, as self-governing as many a small New England town."[65]

A New England native living in South Carolina at the time of Webster's speech had written to commend Webster's "able and manly defence of *my Country*—the Country of Yankees."[66] By 1860 the historically free, white "Country of Yankees" had encompassed the entire Union outside the South. The semantic development of the term "Yankee" neatly parallels the expansion of "New Englandism" as an advancing trope of historical freedom and whiteness. According to *A Dictionary of American English on Historical Principles* (1944) this term seems to have emerged at the end of the seventeenth century, although none of the speculative theories of its origin in corruptions of Dutch or Native American proper names, or in Native American corruptions of English names, are convincing. More significant are the three major meanings of "Yankee" as traced by the dictionary.[67]

---

[64] Willie Lee Rose, *Rehearsal For Reconstruction: The Port Royal Experiment* (New York: Bobbs-Merrill, 1964), pp. 36–42.

[65] Ibid., pp. 38, 407.

[66] J. W. Scott to Daniel Webster, February 12, 1830, in *The Letters of Daniel Webster, from Documents Owned Principally by the New Hampshire Historical Society*, ed. Claude H. Van Tyne (New York, 1902), p. 146, quoted in Sheidley, " Sectional Nationalism," p. 408.

[67] *A Dictionary of American English on Historical Principles* (Chicago: University of Chicago Press, 1944), s.v. "Yankee," 4:2514–15.

The first of these is "a nickname applied originally to New Englanders," appearing by 1765. The dictionary quotes a British visitor's comment on American usage in 1784—"The New Englanders are disliked by the inhabitants of all the other provinces, by whom they are called *Yankeys*"—and gives other examples through 1903.

The second meaning, "a native or inhabitant of the United States; an American," appeared around the time of the American Revolution and was used by the British to identify residents of their former colonies; in 1800 a British visitor described a "Yankee" and noted, "We apply this designation . . . to the inhabitants of all parts of the United States." Examples are nearly all British until after the Civil War.[68] The first instance given of an American use of "Yankee" to mean "American" is from the *Congressional Record* in 1874, which quotes a congressman as saying, "When I say a Yankee, I mean an American." All examples thereafter are from American sources.

Under the third meaning, "Used, esp. by Southerners during the Civil War, of Federal soldiers," the major subcategory is "an inhabitant of the northern states." The example is from 1865: "[The] newspapers have persuaded the masses that the Yankees (a phrase which they no longer apply distinctively to New Englanders, but to every person born in the North) . . . are arrant cowards."

The extension of the scope of "Yankee" in American usage from "New England" to "the North" during the antebellum period and then, following the Union victory in the Civil War, to "America" charts the triumphant course of New England nationalism and embodies the stunning success of the cultural imperialism that was one of its salient features. The Pilgrims and the Puritans, the Boston Tea Party and Paul Revere, that very specific City on a Hill, had by the Civil War become part of the personal heritage of every individual who could claim a history of freedom—no slavery, no enslavement. With the success of this narrative, New England had *become* the nation and, in the process, the nation had become New England.

Cunningly concealed within that New England nationalist conception, of course, was a compelling historical interpretation of America—the *true* America, the free America outside the South—as a white republic. The consequence of that interpretation for northern free people of color, in

---

[68] Alexander Saxton notes an early appearance of "the Yankee" in the person of a character named Jonathan in Royall Tyler's 1787 play *The Contrast*, and argues for his "authentic personification of American identity." But Jonathan is a "regionally distinct vernacular character"—a New Englander—as Saxton also notes (*The Rise and Fall of the White Republic: Class Politics and Mass Culture in Nineteenth-Century America* [New York: Verso, 1990], p. 116). Saxton is concentrating on issues of class associated with vernacular speech and arguing that vernacular characters nationalized theater in this period; in so doing, he undervalues the play's quite strong identification of "the Yankee" with New England.

effacing their history of enslavement, was to render them an unaccountable population of innately and permanently degraded "aliens and outcasts in the midst of the people," as Connecticut colonizationist Leonard Bacon had observed. Bacon thought that this conception held sway "in the estimation of the [white] community and in their [free blacks'] own consciousness."[69] The first assumption was largely true; the second emphatically was not.

[69] Bacon, *A Plea for Africa*, p. 13.

7

"We Are the Alphabet": Free People
of Color and the Discourse of "Race"

If free people of color in New England had anticipated enacting their
freedom as an entitlement, under the same terms as whites enacted
theirs, they soon learned that whites' understanding of antislavery and
Revolutionary rhetoric was quite different from their own. As whites' eighteenth-century observation that servitude made slaves servile hardened
into their nineteenth-century conviction that all people of color were inherently servile—freed slaves perhaps, but free people, never—people of
color struggled to adapt their expectations of citizenship to the grim truth
of mounting hostility, ridicule, and escalating efforts to control and even
eliminate their presence.

From the late 1780s through the early 1800s, free people of color employed a range of strategies to better their economic circumstances, to advance their political and social situation, to evade or stymie the harsh
machinery of social control, and to resist the "racial" explanations of whites
for their condition. Black intellectuals debated the efficacy of competing
strategies, and the meaning of "race" itself, in sermons and speeches and,
after 1827, in newspapers and on the floor of national and regional conventions. These debates were considerably complicated by the persistence
of slavery in the southern states at a time when the recollection of local
slavery on the part of whites in New England was rapidly dimming. In the
1850s, against this backdrop, three explosive novels by writers of color interrogated the stability of meaning of these oppositions and the relation-

ships among them: black/white, free/slave, and North/South.

The post-Revolutionary "racialization" of difference provided the context in which free people of color struggled to become independent citizens as gradual emancipation slowly increased their numbers after 1780. It should not be assumed that their actions and ideas had no effect upon the gradual embodiment of "race" at the turn of the nineteenth century. Far from being external observers of this ideological process, at all levels of the economic scale they were its active participants as well as its ultimate casualties.

Although the poorer people of color rarely left records demonstrating that they acknowledged "racial" characterizations as meaningful, they both resisted and participated in "racialization" in subtle ways. Sometimes their approach was a kind of passive resistance. For example, in their encounters with town authorities concerning their legal settlement, most seem to have ignored the struggles of white clerks to identify them "racially." Although they gave detailed stories of their lives, children, and places of settlement, it is clear from the "racial" designations hazarded by the clerks, often with one or two alternatives offered ("Elizabeth Gardner an Indian or Molatto Woman"), that the individuals so designated made no effort to identify themselves racially or to clarify the clerks' uncertainty.[1]

Only occasionally did a poor person of color engage in the racial naming game, and then for some strategic purpose. A good example is the case of John Hammer, mentioned earlier, who complained to a Hopkinton, Rhode Island, Justice Court that the warrant identifying him as a "black man" was flawed because he was "an Indian man."[2] By claiming an "Indian" identity, Hammer sought to void the warrant; but by failing to identify himself specifically as Narragansett, he participated at the same time in the effacement of distinct tribal identities by the terms "Indian" and "Negro," imposed by Europeans.[3] Occasionally, too, persons of color seem to have used a "racial" characterization as part of their nickname, or at least answered to such a name, however it may have been assigned, as in the case of "Black Bets" of Sandwich, Massachusetts.[4] Such instances were relatively rare, however.

For the most part, poor people of color seem to have ignored "racial"

---

[1] Providence Town Papers, 6:150, July 23, 1782.

[2] Hopkinton Justice Court Records, October 8, 1793.

[3] Ruth Wallis Herndon and Ella Wilcox Sekatau, in "The Right to a Name: The Narragansett People and Rhode Island Officials in the Revolutionary Era," *Ethnohistory* 44 (Summer 1997): 445–46, discuss the redesignation of persons with Narragansett ancestry successively as "Indians," "Mustees," and finally "blacks" or "negroes."

[4] Providence Town Council Records, 4:215, July 24, 1782.

characterizations as part of the overall institutional framework of control that they sought to evade whenever possible. Such evasions constituted a form of resistance at the very moment, ironically, that this and other refusals to participate in the arbitrary mechanics of so-called good citizenship—failing to abide by the legal settlement system in choosing their places of residence, failing to adopt European marriage customs—were being interpreted as just the sort of disorderly behavior to be expected of exslaves: that is, as "racial" behavior.

"Racial," too, was the judgment rendered by whites on behavior they interpreted as dependent, although much of this behavior was viewed quite differently by people of color themselves. A particularly vivid example of this phenomenon centered on the frequent reliance of freed slaves upon the economic support of their former owners, as when Jeney sought help from her former owner, Moses Brown (Chapter 5). Whites considered such reliance evidence of the slavelike dependence that they had expected would persist in freed slaves, dependence that antislavery activists had warned must be discouraged by the postemancipation guidance of whites in the form of stern admonitions to work. To most whites, the willingness to accept assistance from former owners could be the refuge only of lazy, shiftless people, people constituted as "racially" dependent, who thereby forfeited any claim they might make to independent citizenship.

To many people of color, however, support from their former owners was an entitlement rooted in the tradition established by the earlier colonial laws that had required owners to remain accountable for slaves they emancipated individually. These laws had enlisted town governments to enforce the former owners' accountability. In the course of post-Revolutionary emancipation, such laws had been rescinded, placing impoverished freed people of color at the mercy of town charity under the jurisdiction of the Poor Laws. In effect, the new system transferred liability for the consequences of enslavement—former slaves' need for financial assistance—from the private to the public purse, while removing blame for these consequences from the perpetrator and embodying it in the victim. Former slaves resisted the transfer of both kinds of responsibility, continuing to hold slaveholders both financially and morally accountable for their dependent condition. Statements such as the often quoted "Masa eat the meat; he now pick the bone,"[5] usually reported to illustrate the astuteness of individual slaves who refused to accept freedom when it entailed the

---

[5] William D. Piersen, *Black Yankees: The Development of an Afro-American Subculture in Eighteenth-Century New England* (Amherst: University of Massachusetts Press, 1988), pp. 33–34, citing J. H. Temple, *The History of Framingham, Massachusetts* (Framingham, Mass., 1887), p. 237, and other examples.

near-certainty of extreme want in their old age, can be understood in their larger context as the assumption by former slaves of personal responsibility for the enforcement of an obligation once mandated by law. This behavior, too, can be understood as a form of resistance to "racialization," in that it represented a determination to maintain the accountability of an external and historical factors—prior enslavement—for the present circumstances of poverty, unemployment, and so on.

Working persons of color resisted being shoehorned into "racial" categories and characterizations in several ways. Simply achieving a level of comparative success by inserting themselves into an economy and, sometimes, a polity in which they were assumed to be unable to function constituted one potent form of resistance. Probates, ledgers of local businesses, and other records reveal a startling diversity of role and status which gives the lie to the condition of dependency and disorder that came to characterize whites' imaginative construction of "free people of color." By the 1790s, persons of color had begun to appear among the creditors listed in the estate inventories of whites, as owners of estates themselves, as holders of securities, and, rarely, as bondholders of laborers of color. For example, among the creditors of Rowse Helme, scion of a prominent Rhode Island slaveholding family who nonetheless died insolvent, was John Robinson, listed as "Mustee." Another claim was made by Sylvester Fuller for the "Publick Securities" of Scipio Brown, also a man of color. Maria Slade, a free woman of color of Swansey, Massachusetts, who was bound out by her mother, had her time purchased by "Samuel Cole, a Negro man of Attleborough [Massachusetts]."[6]

Some persons of color owned successful businesses. George T. Downing of Newport was not the only famous caterer in Rhode Island; Scipio Brenton of Providence, described as the "Prince of Caterers" in some accounts, owned the building on Snow Street in which he operated his catering business and maintained an expensive fire insurance policy on it.[7] In myriad account books, black men and women appear frequently as spinners, weavers, and skilled workers in other trades. For example, from 1792 to 1794, Jeremiah Negro was employed on a contract basis by Joel Foote, owner of a Colchester, Connecticut, dyeing and fulling mill, to spin and break wool and to press, dye, dart, and dress fabric.[8] Phillis, wife of Prince Alderedg [Aldridge], was a warp spinner, as were both Brister Rhodes and

[6] South Kingstown Town Council and Probate Records, 6:287–90, September 1793; Providence Town Council Records 7:145, January 29, 1791.

[7] Elisha Dyer, "Reminiscences of the South Side of Westminster Street," Manuscripts of the Rhode Island Veteran Citizens Historical Society; and Providence Mutual Insurance Co., Fire Records, 1:386, 1807, both in Rhode Island Historical Society.

[8] Account Book of Joel Foote, 1791–1810, Connecticut Historical Society.

his (unnamed) wife.[9] Prince Green and Ben Lippet of East Greenwich, Rhode Island, listed as "Negrow," were musicians who regularly purchased violin strings and household goods from William Arnold, Merchant, and periodically paid their bills with "1 evening fidlen."[10] There were hundreds of such people, often living on the margins of white communities but working in their midst. The visible participation of such hard-working people on a day-to-day basis in the ongoing economic life of their communities offered potent resistance to assumptions about the inherent dependency and disorderliness of free people of color. Nonetheless, because the rewards of such industry for the majority were low pay, uncertainty and irregularity of employment, and relegation to housing of poor quality, their living conditions often confirmed, rather than refuted, claims of the "degraded condition" of people of color.

Leaders and intellectuals of color engaged the issue of "condition" theoretically, in heated debates over its causes. The condition argument can best be understood as their attempt to account for the failure of republican ideology to deliver on its Revolutionary promises as they had understood them—that is, an attempt to account for the "racial" stratification of post-Revolutionary America which left most of them suffering systematic "prejudice," poverty, unemployment, and overall marginalization. Black intellectuals endlessly debated the problems of locating responsibility for this "degraded condition" (the phrase most commonly used by people of color themselves as well as by whites), of understanding its relation to the pervasive "prejudice" of whites, and of determining a course of action that could ameliorate both condition and prejudice, thereby enabling people of color to become full and equal inheritors of the republican promises of opportunity for self-making and of citizenship.

People of color identified three broadly conceived sources of blame and targets for change and discussed them in numerous permutations: slavery and ongoing oppression in various forms by whites; choices made by people of color themselves since their emancipation; and the "essential nature" of people of color as possibly distinct from that of whites. The discourse of condition was the discourse of "race" and identity; "condition" provided the context in which people of color interrogated the meaning and permanence of physical difference, the precise terminology that they should use to identify themselves as a group, and the source of the persistent "prejudice" of whites against them. These issues in turn informed an

[9] Account Book of Almy & Brown, Providence, vol. 67, 1785–90, Rhode Island Historical Society.

[10] Ledger of William Arnold, 1786–1807, esp. August 1792 to August 1804, Rhode Island Historical Society.

ongoing debate over what exactly it was, if anything, that defined them as a group separate and distinct from other Americans and that could constitute a common identity. Was it their shared descent from African peoples? a shared experience of oppression? a common range of skin color and other physical characteristics?

At the outset of gradual emancipation, free people of color clearly recognized in their condition the consequences of enslavement and the legacy of failed Revolutionary promises. In 1780 in Dartmouth, Massachusetts, for example, a small group petitioned the revolutionary legislature to relieve them of poll and estate taxes on the grounds that "we are not allowed the Privilege of freemen of the State having no vote or Influence in the Election of those that Tax us." They described their condition as "the poor Dispised miserable Black people" and noted that "by Reason of Long Bondag and hard Slavery we have been deprived of Injoying the Profits of our Labouer or the advantage of Inheriting Estates from our Parents as our Neighbouers the white peopel do.[11]

By the turn of the nineteenth century, nearly twenty years after gradual emancipation statutes had begun to swell the numbers of free people of color, their condition had not improved. Nonetheless, black leaders of the Revolutionary generation still expected that the republican promise would be fulfilled for them, and they still retained a vivid memory of the experience of slavery. Linking these two factors, they sought to explain their persistent suffering as the failure of republicanism to overcome slavery's legacy of despotism.

An exemplar of this kind of thinking was Lemuel Haynes, black minister and Revolutionary veteran. In an 1801 Fourth of July address, "The Nature and Importance of True Republicanism," Haynes set out several of the themes that would become elements of intense argument among free people of color in the ensuing years, against a backdrop of their recent experience of local enslavement. Asking a Vermont audience of whites to consider "the poor Africans, among us," he inquired, "What has reduced them to their present pitiful, abject state? Is it any distinction that the God of nature hath made in their formation? Nay—but being subjected to slavery, by the cruel hands of the oppressors, they have been taught to view themselves as a rank of beings far below others, which has suppressed, in a degree, every principle of manhood, and so they become despised, ignorant, and licentious. This shews the effects of despotism."[12] Haynes, re-

---

[11] "Negroes Protest against Taxation," in Herbert Aptheker, ed., *A Documentary History of the Negro People in the United States* (New York: Citadel Press, 1951), pp. 14–16.

[12] Richard Newman, ed., *Black Preacher to White America: The Collected Writings of Lemuel Haynes, 1774–1833* (Brooklyn, N.Y.: Carlson, 1990), p. 82.

jecting biological explanations of difference, forcefully indicted slavery as the original cause of the "pitiful, abject state" of free people of color; at the same time, he found the behavior of people of color themselves to be the proximate cause of their "abject" condition, invoking environmental theories of difference to argue that their behavior had been corrupted by the "effects of despotism." Drawing upon republican ideas of benevolence and affection as the ties that would bind together a republic, Haynes saw clearly that it was the responsibility of whites to undo the effects of despotism by extending benevolence to people of color, "to meliorate the troubles of life, and to cement mankind in the strictest bonds of friendship and society."[13] Haynes, black minister to a white parish, was convinced that whites both had the power to unite their interests with those of people of color and could be persuaded to do so by the compelling argument that the virtue and well-being of the republic depended upon this union. In a reciprocal exchange of benevolence with whites, free people of color could shake off their "ignorance and licentiousness"—the legacies of despotism—and regain their "principles of manhood": the pride, dignity, and strength of character common to all free human beings.

By the 1820s and 1830s, however, the context for discussing the plight of free people of color and the frame of reference of leaders of color themselves had both changed dramatically. New black leaders who confronted the "degraded" condition of free people of color in New England were a generation distant from the personal experience of enslavement—their own or that of family and friends. Fundamental attitudes in the white community toward the effects of enslavement on "character" had changed as well. Most northern whites had allowed the middle member in the progression "'negro' > slave > servile" to wither along with the institution of slavery itself, fixing permanent inferiority upon people of color as a group and undermining prospects for Haynes's hoped-for extension of benevolence. The new "racial" antipathy could be demonstrated by the fate of Haynes himself, who was dismissed from his parish after twenty years of service at least partly because, as an acquaintance said Haynes had told him wryly, "the congregation had just then discovered that he was a colored man."[14]

The growing enmity on the part of whites was clearly reflected in their

[13] Ibid., pp. 80–84. I owe my interpretation of Haynes's position on the relationship between American post-Revolutionary "racial" problems and republicanism to John Saillant's illuminating "Lemuel Haynes's Black Republicanism and the American Republican Tradition, 1775–1820," *Journal of the Early Republic* 14 (Fall, 1994): 293–324.

[14] Ebenezer Baldwin, *Observations on the Physical, Intellectual, and Moral Qualities of our Colored Population: with remarks on the subject of Emancipation and Colonization* (New Haven, Conn.: L. H. Young, 1834), p. 46.

public language; the use of the word "nigger" in particular seemed to operate as a kind of coagulate of the resentments that had been growing in white communities in tandem with the size and visibility of the population of free people of color. People of color themselves understood clearly how the term served to enact the embodiment of innate, permanent inferiority. Hosea Easton described the process in his 1837 *Treatise on the Intellectual Character, and Civil and Political Condition of the Colored People of the United States:*

> Negro or nigger, is an approbrious [*sic*] term, employed to impose contempt upon them as an inferior race, and also to express their deformity of person. Nigger lips, nigger shins, and nigger heels, are phrases universally common among the juvenile class of society, and full well understood by them. . . . Children in infancy receive oral instruction from the nurse. The first lessons given are, . . . go to sleep, if you don't the old *nigger* will care [*sic*] you off; don't you cry—Hark; the old *nigger's* coming— how ugly you are, you are worse than a little *nigger*. . . . to inspire their half grown misses and masters to improvement, they are told that if they do this or that, . . . they will be poor or ignorant as a nigger, or that they will be black as a nigger; or have no more credit than a nigger.[15]

In an explicit reference to the scurrilous, lampooning broadsides then circulating widely in the streets of Boston (see Chapter 5), Easton noted, "This kind of instruction is not altogether oral. Cuts and placards descriptive of the negroe's deformity, are every where displayed to the observation of the young, with corresponding broken lingo, the very character of which is marked with design. Many of the popular book stores, in commercial towns and cities, have their show-windows lined with them. The barrooms of the most popular public houses in the country, sometimes have their ceiling literally covered with them."[16]

This language and these practices were not universal among whites; some, among them many abolitionists, publicly espoused social and political equality for free people of color as a matter of political conviction. But most did not, and of those who did, many seemed unable or unwilling to enact their public stance in their personal relations; even well-intentioned

---

[15] Hosea Easton, *A Treatise on the Intellectual Character, and Civil and Political Condition of the Colored People of the U. States, and the Prejudice Exercised Towards Them. By Rev. H. Easton, A Colored Man* (Boston: Isaac Knapp, 1837), pp. 40–41.

[16] Easton, *Treatise*, pp. 41–42. Note Easton's awareness of the use in the broadsides of eye dialect or invented forms ("broken lingo . . . marked with design"), as discussed in Chapter 4.

abolitionists often demonstrated a virtual blindness to the implications of their words and actions. "Whatever they do for us savors of pity, and is done at arm's length, on a sort of *noli me tangere* principle," observed Samuel Ringgold Ward in disgust.[17]

People of color recognized that ridicule, discrimination, and rigid assumptions about their "racial" inferiority were a worsening problem, even though the actual "condition" of the vast majority remained largely unchanged. As Abraham Shadd put it in his address to the Third Annual Convention of the Negro People in 1833, "A deep and solemn gloom has settled on that once bright anticipation [of freedom], and that monster, prejudice, is stalking over the land, spreading in its course its pestilential breath."[18]

Although people of color clearly recognized "prejudice" as an important factor in their oppression, there was considerable disagreement about how it related to physical difference, and what in fact the meaning of physical difference was. They were as keenly interested as whites in explaining human variety. Some continued to insist upon environmental explanations of physical difference, attributing variety in skin color to diet, culture, and climate long after most authorities had succumbed to biological theories. James McCune Smith, a physician, even elaborated a theory linking human character traits with culturally distinct modes of intake of food and use of air.[19] Nonetheless, the increasing popularity of an essentialist vocabulary of nature and "blood" to explain human behavior frequently led people of color to confront essentialist constructions of their own difference in equally essentialist terms.

Although nearly all people of color vigorously rejected interpretations of their oppressed status as evidence of innate inferiority, they often adopted the language of "biology" and "innate character" to describe what they continued to regard as a mutable condition. Martin Delany, for example, quite self-consciously explored the connection between experience and biology, noting that "the degradation of the slave parent has been entailed upon the child, ... in regular succession handed down from father to son—a system of regular submission and servitude, menialism and dependence, until it has become almost a physiological function of our system, an actual condition of our nature. Let this no longer be so."[20] The adop-

[17] *Frederick Douglass' Paper,* April 13, 1855.

[18] "Minutes and Proceedings of the Third Annual Convention, for the Improvement of the Free People of Colour" (New York, 1833), p. 32, in Howard H. Bell, ed., *Minutes of the Proceedings of the National Negro Conventions, 1830–1864* (New York: Arno Press, 1969).

[19] *Anglo African Magazine,* January 1859, pp. 5–9. Earlier examples are *Freedom's Journal,* May 18, 1827; May 2, and September 19, 1828.

[20] Martin Robison Delany, *The Condition, Elevation, Emigration, and Destiny of the Colored People of the United States, Politically Considered* (Philadelphia: By the Author, 1852), pp. 47–48.

tion of such essentialist language by leaders of color as a goad to induce change in their own constituency was a common tactic and one that may have been intended at least partly to subvert the essentialist construction itself. In a discourse of black inferiority so pervasive, however, this strategy undoubtedly had an unintentionally reinforcing effect.

By the 1820s and 1830s the dominant discourse of variety or difference had become one of hierarchy, soon to be supported by an emerging "science" of "race" together with long-standing biblical arguments concerning the curse of Canaan, son of Ham.[21] Many black intellectuals challenged these views. *Freedom's Journal* insisted editorially that "there are no facts . . . which authorise the conclusion that any one of the several varieties of our [human] race is either intellectually or morally superior to the rest."[22] Hosea Easton thought it "a settled point with the wisest of the age, that no constitutional difference exists in the children of men, which can be said to be established by hereditary laws. . . . whatever differences exist, are casual or accidental."[23] Of course, a great and growing number of whites held otherwise, and by the late 1820s some intellectuals of color had begun countering widespread assumptions of "natural" black inferiority with claims of innate black superiority. There were many variants of these arguments, but they can be divided into two broad categories: those based on physical comparisons, and those rooted in historical claims.

As early as 1827 *Freedom's Journal* was quoting Herodotus on the physical superiority of Africans to whites.[24] By 1859 John Rock of Boston, a dentist who was also an attorney, was lecturing regularly on the greater physical beauty and strength of constitution of people of color, contrasting their "beautiful, rich color" with whites' "wan color," their "gracefully frizzled hair" with whites' "lank hair," and so forth.[25] More subtly, Henry Highland Garnet sometimes referred to whites as "our colorless brethren."[26] Insistence upon the special beauty of people of color and interpretations of their physical distinctiveness as a mark of God's favor served to support the notion of their providential role in the redemption of the world, as promised in a frequently cited biblical passage. "Princes shall come out of Egypt; Ethiopia shall soon stretch out her hands unto God."[27]

More than a defense against assumptions of inferiority, people of color

[21] See Chapter 4.

[22] *Freedom's Journal,* July 13, 1827.

[23] Easton, *Treatise,* p. 5.

[24] *Freedom's Journal,* March 20, 1827; see also February 14, 1829.

[25] *Liberator,* March 12, 1858.

[26] Henry Highland Garnet, *The Past and Present Condition, and the Destiny, of the Colored Race* (Troy, N.Y., 1848; facsimile rpt. Miami, Fla.: Mnemosyne, 1969), p. 11.

[27] Psalms 68:31. On the origins of "black messianism," see Wilson Moses, *Black Messiahs and Uncle Toms: Social and Literary Manipulations of a Religious Myth* (University Park: Pennsylvania State University Press, 1982), pp. 1–16.

longed for a unifying identity powerful enough to allow them to contest whites' exclusive claim to the all-powerful identity "American citizen," to which people of color felt entitled but were unable to claim successfully. They sought this identity in the languages of descent ("African") and physiognomy ("black" and "of color").

For the first two centuries, people of African descent in New England called themselves variously "Blacks," "Negroes," and "Africans." In *Slave Culture* (1987), Sterling Stuckey suggests that "African" or "Free African" were most common in the North over the course of the nineteenth century, but he may overestimate the ubiquity of these terms.[28] Early petitions use "black," "Negro," and "African" indiscriminately, sometimes in the same petition.[29] People of color did tend to use the term "African" for the independent institutions they began to form in the last two decades of the eighteenth century and the first decade of the nineteenth, following the lead of Absalom Jones and Richard Allen in their establishment of the Free African Society in 1787 in Philadelphia.[30] Although Stuckey finds "direct African cultural influence" to be the primary factor in the early institutional use of "African" by people of color in the North, a combination of factors may have been at work.[31] "Africans" was conventionally used by Europeans as a term for slaves in the seventeenth and the early eighteenth century. The use of "African" by people of color almost certainly reflected in part the desire among a largely enslaved people to define themselves by a point of origin at which they or their ancestors had been free. It is also true that even as late as the turn of the century, many people of color in New England had themselves been captured, or were children of those who had been captured, on the coast of Africa, reflecting the renewed influx of Africans in New England during the mid-1700s.[32] It is difficult, though, to distinguish attachment to African cultural values and spirituality from insistence upon an original identity as free persons—especially since, as Stuckey notes, people of African descent in America were forced

[28] The most comprehensive discussion of "the names controversy" among antebellum people of color is Sterling Stuckey, "Identity and Ideology: The Names Controversy," in his *Slave Culture: Nationalist Theory and the Foundations of Black America* (New York: Oxford University Press, 1987), pp. 193–244.

[29] See, e.g., the 1779 petition to the Connecticut General Assembly of Prime and Prince, who refer to themselves as "Negroes in the Towns of Stratford and Fairfield" and later as "poor Ignorant Africans"; and the 1777 petition of "A Great Number of Blackes" to the Massachusetts Bay House of Representatives, both in Aptheker, *Documentary History,* pp. 9–12.

[30] See Carol V. R. George, *Segregated Sabbaths: Richard Allen and the Emergence of Independent Black Churches, 1760–1840* (New York: Oxford University Press, 1973), on the establishment of African American denominations.

[31] Stuckey, *Slave Culture,* pp. 199–200.

[32] Piersen, *Black Yankees,* p. 7; Ira Berlin, "Time, Space, and the Evolution of Afro-American Society on British Mainland North America," *American Historical Review* 85 (February 1980): 51–53.

to homogenize their religious and ethnic specificity into the all-encompassing term "African."[33]

In any case, after 1820 free people of color increasingly substituted "colored" (or "coloured") and sometimes "black" for the term "African." Stuckey attributes the decreasing use of "African" to the perception that it had become dangerous for people of color to suggest an origin or allegiance outside the United States in the face of the American Colonization Society's determination to send them "back" to their "homeland."[34] That is a persuasive argument, but again, there may have been other factors at play. People of color were not isolated from the increasingly pervasive discourse of "race" that was becoming dominated by the language of physical difference and "essence" by 1800; the growing use of terms such as "black" and "colored" in preference to "African" may reflect this influence as well. Even so nationalist a speaker as David Walker, widely regarded as one of the earliest advocates of Pan-Africanism, addressed his 1829 *Appeal* to "the Coloured Citizens of the World." In a note to the third edition of the *Appeal*, "we, the Blacks or Coloured People" are distinguished from "the White Christians of America"; elsewhere in the text Walker spoke of "the blacks of Africa," "the mulattoes of Asia," and "the whites of Europe."[35] Clearly, Walker found power in an appeal to physical difference as a badge of nationhood.[36]

A few people, however, may have seen that the turn toward physical language had disempowering as well as unifying implications; some, at least, vehemently opposed its use, although it is difficult to pin down the precise meaning of their opposition. William Whipper, a lumberman from Pennsylvania, led the charge against language that supported what he called "complexional distinctions" of any kind. At the Fifth Annual Convention for the Improvement of the Free People of Colour in 1835, he offered a resolution asking black people to abandon the use of the word "colored" as well as the title "African."[37]

[33] Stuckey, *Slave Culture*, p. 119.

[34] In ibid., pp. 203–22, Stuckey describes the efforts of William Whipper and others to discard the words "colored" and "African" and to dissolve organizations based in "complexional distinctions" as part of an integrationist position that dominated the leadership of free people of color in the mid-1830s; he sees a countervailing nationalist position, represented by Garnet and others, becoming dominant after 1840.

[35] David Walker, *Appeal to the Colored Citizens of the World*, in *One Continual Cry*, ed. Herbert Aptheker (New York: Humanities Press, 1965), pp. 61, 62, 80.

[36] Walker's ideas and their context and sources are examined in Peter P. Hinks, *To Awaken My Afflicted Brethren: David Walker and the Problem of Antebellum Slave Resistance* (University Park: Pennsylvania State University Press, 1997), esp. pp. 173–236.

[37] "Minutes of the Fifth Annual Convention for the Improvement of the Free People of Colour" (Philadelphia, 1835), pp. 14–15, in Bell, *Proceedings*.

Whipper's denunciation of "color-phobia" on the part of people of color themselves, and his injunction to blacks to "throw off the distinctive features in the charters of our churches and other institutions," are read by Sterling Stuckey as shame at being of African ancestry. Stuckey calls Whipper "Mr. Cosmopolite, the archetypal 'integrationist' of antebelllum America."[38] Yet another reading is possible, especially in light of Whipper's apparent move toward a nationalist position after 1849, when he called for "a distinct civil and religious code" and a "new religion" as strategies for giving substance to a "national existence as a people."[39] This was a nationalist position rooted in notions of a common consciousness and social experience. Whipper's earlier denunciations of "complexional" terms and even institutions were not necessarily in conflict with such a position; rather, they seem to have reflected a rejection of physical difference as the basis of social organization and physical language as the expression of identity.[40]

Some people of color continued to use the term "African" in the early antebellum years in preference to "of color," without any apparent objection to the physicality of the latter term but with a different agenda. Maria Stewart, Hartford-born woman of color who became a Boston lecturer, writer, and celebrity (reputedly the first American-born woman to address an audience of mixed gender on a political subject), commonly referred to men and women of color as "daughters of Africa" and "sons of Africa" in contradistinction to "the Americans" (whites). For example, she noted in 1831, "The American ladies have the honor conferred on them, that by prudence and economy in their domestic concerns . . . they laid the foundation of their becoming what they now are. . . . Shall it any longer be said of the daughters of Africa, they have no ambition, they have no force?"[41] A profound admirer of David Walker, Stewart insisted, as he did, upon a distinct identity for people of color and a leadership role for them in ame-

[38] *Colored American*, January 12, 1841; Stuckey, *Slave Culture*, pp. 210–11.

[39] *North Star*, November 23, 1849. By 1853 Whipper was advocating separate schools to meet the special needs of children of color; see "Proceedings of the Colored National Convention" (Rochester, 1853), pp. 22–23, in Bell, *Proceedings*.

[40] The deteriorating position of free people of color is usually cited as the basis for the transformation in thinking, strategy, outlook, and language of Whipper and others who embraced nationalism in the late 1840s and especially after 1850. See, e.g., Jane H. Pease and William H. Pease, *They Who Would Be Free: Blacks' Search for Freedom, 1830–1861* (1974; Urbana: University of Illinois Press, 1990), pp. 251–76. I do not disagree, but I would argue that some seemingly antinationalist or integrationist thinking of the 1830s may reflect a more complex awareness of the political implications of the embodiment of "race" and its expression in language by people of color themselves.

[41] Maria Stewart, "Religion and the Pure Principles of Morality: The Sure Foundation On Which We Must Build," in *Maria Stewart, America's First Black Woman Political Writer: Essays and Speeches*, ed. Marilyn Richardson (Bloomington: Indiana University Press, 1987), p. 37.

liorating their condition in the North as well as in ending slavery. But by continuing to use the term "African," Stewart seemed to reach beyond its earlier connotations of free origin and cultural distinctiveness to root a claim to nationhood for people of color in their historical presence in a specific homeland, Africa. Perhaps she was borrowing the strategy of the national liberation movements of Greece and Poland of the 1820s, as reported in *Freedom's Journal* as well as in mainstream newspapers.[42]

In addressing African men and women as sojourners, marooned in a country in which by their labor they had earned a property right but had been unable to claim a citizenship right, she was apparently oblivious to the danger (of acute concern to others) that the term "African" might weaken their claims to an enfranchised American citizenship. As a woman often shaping her remarks to women, however, she may have found the issue of literal enfranchisement somewhat irrelevant, since women would be excluded even if the vote were extended to men of color. To Stewart, a more compelling issue undoubtedly was the practical citizenship of material opportunity and achievement, a topic she addressed frequently: "Unite and build a store of your own," she insisted.[43] If people of color, and especially women of color, were to be refused American citizenship rights, they could nonetheless act to realize some of the tangible fruits for themselves while remaining African "citizens." But Stewart was the exception in a swelling chorus of voices making "coloured citizens" and their welfare the subject of their struggle.

Establishing a collective name was not only, or even primarily, a strategic choice between an integrationist approach (employing no distinctive name at all) and a nationalist one (using "African" or "colored"). It also involved, quite importantly, another kind of strategic choice—a Hobson's choice, in fact. People of color could locate the source of a distinctive collective identity in the body, a dangerous course given the assumptions about innate mental and moral incapacity that had become fused with it in the course of gradual emancipation; or they could fashion a coherent, European-style national origin out of Africa, which might encourage efforts to expatriate them and heighten their identification with peoples thought to be sunk in darkness and depravity. Many leaders of color of the 1830s and after resolved this dilemma by adopting elements of both strategies and employing the strengths of one to counter the damning aspects of the other. They chose the language of physical difference as their pri-

---

[42] *Freedom's Journal,* May 4, 1827, p. 31, reported that people of color had given generously to the Fund for Greek Independence in Boston, which had raised $11,000 by May of 1827.

[43] Stewart, "Religion and the Pure Principles," p. 38.

mary form of identifying a present, living group in order to avoid weakening their claim to American citizenship; at the same time, they renewed their historical identification with the Africa of antiquity, whose achievements stood as a powerful rebuttal to the accusations of innate inferiority associated with that physical identity.

Throughout the antebellum period, leaders of color drew upon ancient African history as a source of collective legitimacy. *Freedom's Journal, Rights of All,* and the *Colored American* printed articles describing ancient African civilizations, especially those of Egypt and Ethiopia. The contrast between the glorious history of Africans in antiquity and their oppressed and degraded present was a common theme. For example, in *The Past and Present Condition, and the Destiny, of the Colored Race,* Henry Highland Garnet described "the ancient fame of our [Egyptian] ancestors," which "arose from every virtue, and talent, that render mortals pre-eminently great," from "the conquests of love and beauty, from the prowess of their arms, and their architecture, poetry, mathematics, generosity, and piety." He cited Cleopatra, Hannibal, Terence, Euclid, Cyprian, Origen, and Augustine as among the great Africans of past ages, noting that "when these representatives of our race were filling the world with amazement, the ancestors of the now proud and boasting Anglo Saxons were among the most degraded of the human family."[44] In this way Garnet and others claimed for people of color a future—a "destiny"—equal in greatness to Africa's ancient past, while avoiding any identification with the "dark, degraded, ignorant Africa" of the recent past and present, which could lend support to the American Colonization Society program and reinforce prejudice.[45] Identifying themselves in the present in physical language as "the colored race"[46] accomplished the second half of this delicate maneuver (at the expense, again, of reifying "race").

Of course, it was not a distant, glorious past in Africa but a devastating experience of slavery in America that had resulted in the condition of poverty of northern free people of color and the climate of persistent prejudice against them. But *which* slavery—the slavery of their own northern ancestors in the past, or the ongoing bondage of the majority of American

[44] See, e.g., *Freedom's Journal,* April 6, July 6 and 13, August 31, 1828, and February 7, 1829; Garnet, *Past and Present Condition,* pp. 11–12.

[45] Jonathan Mayhew Wainwright, *A Discourse, on the Occasion of Forming the African Mission School Society, Delivered in Christ Church, in Hartford, Connecticut on . . . August 10, 1828. . . .* (Hartford, Conn.: L. H. & F. J. Huntington, 1828), p. 20.

[46] Garnet saw the danger in this language, at least from a theological perspective: "In order to pursue my subject I must, for the sake of distinction, use some of the improper terms of our times. I shall, therefore, speak of *races,* when in fact there is but one race, as there was but one Adam" (*Past and Present Condition,* p. 6).

people of color in the South? And how exactly was either experience of slavery related to prejudice? These were linked questions, and they were not theoretical ones; upon them turned all the most important decisions facing free people of color as to what course of action would best achieve what all agreed were their paramount goals: to end their oppression in all its forms, and to become independent, fully enfranchised citizens. In the antebellum years northern people of color engaged in endless chicken-and-egg arguments over slavery, prejudice, and condition.

Charles B. Ray, editor of the *Colored American,* saw "prejudice" as the source of the oppression of northern people of color. He endorsed the argument of abolitionist Charles Goodell, who in turn concurred with "the South, which points to the colored people of the north, trodden under the iron hoof of this *prejudice, more* grievously than they are in the south, and asks us if we would have slavery abolished while this *prejudice remains?"*[47] Such statements had the effect of establishing a kind of moral and practical equivalency between prejudice and slavery; such an equivalency substituted prejudice itself for the experience of slavery and gradual emancipation of which it was a legacy, contributing to the effacement of the historical experience of slavery in the North.

Hosea Easton, also saw causal links between slavery and prejudice and between prejudice and condition, but even he, a Boston minister descended from New England slaves, left the historical dimension barely implicit with respect to the North in his careful exposition of these relationships. After defining "prejudice" as the malignant feelings held by one group against another that the first group has injured, Easton explained: "The colored population are the injured party. And the prejudice of the whites against them is in exact proportion to the injury the colored people have sustained. . . . The true cause of this prejudice is slavery. . . . The system of slavery in its effects, is imposed on the injured party in two forms, or by two methods. The first method is, by a code of laws, originating in public sentiment, as in slave states. The other is, prejudice originating in the same, as it exists in free states. . . . Slavery, in the form and character of prejudice, is as fatal, yea, more fatal than the pestilence."[48] Easton was apparently using the term "slavery" in two different ways. In one sense, "slavery" was an abstract and universal expression of the relationship of oppressed/oppressor, originating in the collective mind of the white public ("the public sentiment"). This "slavery" in turn engendered two parallel systems of oppressive practices as its "effects": one, also called "slavery,"

[47] *Colored American,* March 18, 1837.
[48] Easton, *Treatise,* pp. 35–36, 45.

that was encoded in law in the South; the other, called "prejudice," that was encoded (by implication) in custom in the North. Easton in effect substituted a metaphorical, universal "slavery" for the legally constituted northern system of enslavement that had ended only by statutory action and constitutional interpretation—a slavery experienced by real slaves, which *could* provide a material explanation for northern "prejudice." (The same Hosea Easton could interpret his own individual "condition" historically, however: "I wonder that I am a man; for though of the third generation from slave parents, yet in body and mind nature has never been permitted to half finish her work.")[49]

Theodore Wright, too, thought of slavery in universal terms. He considered "the giant sin of prejudice, this foul monster" to be "at once the parent and the offspring of slavery," implying that prejudice emerged autonomously and spontaneously as a precondition of slavery but then was continually reinforced by it.[50] But Wright, like most black abolitionists as well as white ones, tended to use the term "slavery" as if the institution were one great monolith or abstraction.

Disconnected from historically specific practices and relations of power, attributed to "public sentiment," "prejudice" could be interpreted as a sinful attitude that floated about and could be caught like the common cold, even by people of color themselves. Thus, in 1840, the *Colored American* debated whether, as some members of the community charged, "this spirit color-phobia, prejudice, exists among ourselves toward each other, and based on complexion."[51] Eight years later Henry Highland Garnet, speaking of "party feuds" and "dissensions" among people of color, noted disapprovingly that "some . . . would form factions upon the shallow basis of complexion."[52] Although some people of color undoubtedly were biased against dark skin, only in the absence of a clear, living history of slavery and emancipation *in situ* could the two "prejudices" be understood as the same phenomenon.

"Prejudice" could also be explained as the result, rather than the cause, of the "debased condition" of northern free people of color. "W" told readers of the *Colored American:* "The truth is, that the real ground of prejudice is not the *color of the skin,* but the *condition.* We have so long associated *color* with *condition,* that we have forgotten the fact, and have charged the offence to the wrong account."[53] Frederick Douglass observed wryly, "The

[49] Ibid., p. 26.
[50] "Minutes of the New York Antislavery Society," in August Meier and Elliott Rudwick, *From Plantation to Ghetto: An Interpretive History of American Negroes* (New York: Hill & Wang, 1966), p. 106.
[51] *Colored American,* September 26, 1840.
[52] Garnet, *Past and Present Condition,* pp. 18–19.
[53] *Colored American,* June 24, 1837.

inferiority is not by color . . . but by condition. With a hundred thousand dollars . . . I could make a very black man white."[54] But what, then, was the source of that condition?

The *Weekly Advocate* offered one of the few assessments that could be read as fixing the blame for the oppressed condition of northern people of color squarely on the shoulders of those who had enslaved them: the "prejudice which was always felt against [people of color] because they were slaves" had "descended like a curse upon their free children."[55]

Rarely, a voice called upon all free people of color to remember the past enslavement of their own families. A poem by Sarah Forten, "Our Sires Who Once in Freedom's Cause," reminded readers of the *Liberator:* "Oh, surely they [the sons of Revolutionary veterans] have quite forgot, / That bondage once had been their lot; / The sweets of freedom now they know, / They care not for the captive's woe."[56] In these lines Forten neatly appealed to both black and white readers whose ancestors fought in the Revolution, evoking the metaphorical enslavement of whites by Britain as well as the physical bondage of people of color to white slaveowners. This was a fairly circumspect appeal, however; few were willing to resurrect the memory of northern slavery as bluntly as had the *Weekly Advocate.* To do so was surely to risk alienating northern whites who, after all, represented potential allies.

Absent an explanation rooted in the historical experience of slavery, the debased condition of free people of color could be seen as sui generis, be understood as the logical consequence of their own innate inferiority, as many colonizationist sermons and burlesquing broadsides claimed. Although people of color rejected this interpretation, they did frequently blame their debased condition on their own lack of effort or misplaced goals. For example, in 1831 a convention address suggested "deliberate reflection on the dissolute, intemperate and ignorant condition of a large portion of the colored population"; two of the three descriptive terms implied strongly that their condition was the consequence of deliberate choices freely made by people of color themselves, rather than the result of oppressive actions taken against them by whites, whether past or present. The newspaper *Rights of All* saw lax and improper behavior as one of the foremost problems of free people of color and made its correction a key purpose, announcing in its first issue in 1829, "It will be the constant aim of the Editor, as far as in his power, to remove the many abuses which exist among his brethren, to promote habits of industry and economy, and

[54] *Frederick Douglass' Paper,* July 22, 1853.
[55] *Weekly Advocate,* February 11, 1837.
[56] *Liberator,* April 16, 1831.

to inculcate the importance of an improved education."[57] The *Coloured American* went so far as to accuse free people of color of being "greatly deficient and deeply criminal" in making "fine dress and luxurious living . . . the summit of our ambition" and admonished them to "spend little upon our outward man but husband EVERY DOLLAR for the purpose of . . . improving our condition."[58]

Even when free people of color specifically indicted their earlier enslavement for their present plight, they often focused on its residual effects on their own behavior, not on the behavior of the whites who continued to oppress them. The *Colored American* reminded readers in 1837 that "the first thing to be done by our people in the elevation of their moral and civil condition is, to change long-standing habits . . . [in which may be seen] the effects of slavery."[59] This reasoning tended to support the contention that the characteristics of servility had survived slavery and had become fixed elements of the behavior of free people of color.

The fading away of a legitimizing historical context for the oppressed condition of people of color lent a special urgency to the program of self-improvement or "uplift" that constituted the dominant strategy of a majority of northern leaders of color of the 1830s and 1840s.[60] These efforts included establishing independent institutions that could devise plans of action, serve as forums for debating these plans, and assist in implementing them. Such institutions included mutual benefit societies, churches, schools, businesses, conventions, and an independent press. The self-improvement agenda challenged charges that people of color were innately mentally incapable by demonstrating their potential for achievement; it countered claims that they were naturally immoral by demonstrating their capacity for moral transformation. *Freedom's Journal* editorialized in 1827, "It is for us to convince the world by uniform propriety of conduct, industry and economy, that we are worthy of esteem and patronage."[61] "Educa-

---

[57] *Rights of All*, February 28, 1829.

[58] *Colored American*, May 6, 1837.

[59] Ibid., May 13, 1837.

[60] James Oliver Horton and Lois E. Horton have explored the communities and culture of free people of color in *In Hope of Liberty: Culture, Community, and Protest among Northern Free Blacks, 1700–1860* (New York: Oxford University Press, 1997), chaps. 4–10. A clear, detailed analysis of the concerns, goals, and strategies of northern free people of color from 1830 to the eve of the Civil War is Pease and Pease, *They Who Would Be Free*. Leon F. Litwack, *North of Slavery: The Negro in the Free States, 1790–1860* (Chicago: University of Chicago Press, 1961), remains the classic exposition of the social and political context in which they struggled. A later work, Harry Reed, *Platform for Change: The Foundations of the Northern Free Black Community, 1775–1865* (East Lansing: Michigan State University Press, 1994), compares the development of infrastructure in the black communities of Boston, New York, and Philadelphia.

[61] *Freedom's Journal*, March 30, 1827.

tion, Temperance and Economy, are best calculated to promote the elevation of mankind to a proper rank and standing among men, as they enable him to discharge all those duties enjoined on him by his Creator," intoned the report of the Committee on the Condition of the Free People of Colour of the United States to the First Annual Convention of the People of Colour.[62] Powerless to demand accountability from whites for their condition, people of color had little choice but to accept the burden of proof of their inherent worthiness.

In this way, their oppressed and degraded condition confronted people of color with yet another of the many paradoxes they had faced in slavery and in freedom since their appearance in the Americas. In a climate of increasing political and economic hostility, any effort to hold whites accountable for the condition of their former slaves and their descendants could only alienate them still further and reinforce the perception that people of color themselves were incapable and dependent. Yet to hold themselves responsible for ameliorating their own condition was to demand personal achievement and social transformation from the group with the least political and economic power to effect either one. Modeled on moral suasion abolitionism, which attempted to induce self-criticism in the powerful—slaveholders—and awaken them to sin, the movement for self-improvement among people of color targeted the disempowered for self-criticism and transformation. But no demonstration of thrift, honesty, and industry could overcome the hostility of the whites who controlled most employment opportunities, most housing, most facilities for higher education, and all political institutions.

By the early 1840s, leaders of color had begun calling more explicitly for change in the surrounding society, although many still saw moral improvement among people of color as an essential tool with which they might effect that change. For example, Samuel H. Davis, chairman pro tem of the 1843 National Convention of Colored Citizens, held at Buffalo, insisted, "If we are not willing to rise up and assert our rightful claims and plead our own cause, we have no reason to look for success. . . . We must learn to act in harmony with the principles of God's moral government."[63] This was the same convention, of course, at which Henry Highland Garnet uttered his call to the slaves to rise on their own behalf: "TO SUCH DEGRADATION [American slavery] IT IS SINFUL IN THE EXTREME FOR YOU TO MAKE VOLUNTARY SUBMISSION. . . . IT IS YOUR SOLEMN AND IMPERATIVE DUTY TO USE EVERY MEANS, BOTH MORAL, INTELLECTUAL, AND PHYSICAL THAT

[62] "Minutes and Proceedings of the First Annual Convention of the People of Colour" (Philadelphia, 1831), p. 5, in Bell, *Proceedings*.

[63] "Minutes of the National Convention of Colored Citizens" (Buffalo, 1843), p. 7, in Bell, *Proceedings*.

PROMISES SUCCESS."[64] Both calls were framed as moral imperatives; both also reflect the determination that people of color should take responsibility for transforming their own condition and the belief that they could in fact prevail. (Not all convention delegates agreed; Douglass, for one, thought that Garnet's address would provoke insurrection, which could only end in "catastrophy."[65])

Strategies for advancement focused more intently on practical self-help and economic achievement than on moral uplift after 1840. Although the positive moral effects of material progress were always carefully stressed, development of the mechanical arts, commercial enterprise, and entrepreneurship plus the purchase of farmland and the development of agricultural skills dominated the agenda. At the 1847 national convention the Committee on Commerce recommended, "To Commerce, America owes her present importance, and we, too, if we would acquire any very great influence for good, must join in the march of Commerce"; the same convention passed a resolution to explore the establishment of a separate bank. At the same time, the Committee on Agriculture had a different theory: "[Agriculture] was the primitive pursuit of life, the calling of earth's first born ones, the mode of subsistence and happiness prescribed by God himself, therefore the true mode by which to live, the best mode. . . . [It] tends to equality in life."[66] Many black leaders, however, were also turning their attention to political means and ends to improve their condition, focusing on gaining or regaining an unrestricted franchise as an important vehicle for advancement.[67]

As complex and dynamic and responsive to developments in its immediate context as it was, the entire northern black agenda of self-improvement strategies, from relatively passive moral uplift to aggressive economic and political advancement, suffered from a kind of double consciousness imposed upon it by the problem of southern slavery. Every strategy for the advancement of free people of color was also endlessly debated and judged by ardent supporters of abolition for its potency as an antislavery strategy. The condition of more than three million people of color still enslaved in 1800, mostly in the southern states—a number that would grow to four

[64] Garnet's "Address," in Aptheker, *Documentary History*, p. 229.
[65] "Minutes of the National Convention of Colored Citizens" (Buffalo, 1843), p. 13, in Bell, *Proceedings*.
[66] "Proceedings of the National Convention of Colored People, and Their Friends" (Troy, N.Y., 1847), pp. 23, 15, in Bell, *Proceedings*; see also pp. 25, 28, and 29 for calls for specific commercial and agricultural initiatives.
[67] Only in Massachusetts, Vermont, New Hampshire, and Maine did free people of color enjoy an unrestricted access to the ballot, and even in those states, custom discouraged widespread voting; see Litwack, *North of Slavery*, pp. 74–93, esp. 91–92.

million by 1860—morally overwhelmed the problems of a free population just a tenth that size. But the role of abolition in the northern black agenda did not depend simply on the moral obligation of one to the welfare of the other. More important, and much more contentious, was the complex way in which the political, social, and economic condition of each group defined and limited the condition of the other.[68]

Throughout the antebellum period free people of color consistently framed their relationship to slaves by the term "brethren." "We will never separate ourselves voluntarily from the slave population in this country," resolved an 1817 conference. "They are our brethren by the ties of consanguinity, of suffering, and of wrong, and we feel that there is more virtue in suffering privations with them, than fancied advantages for a season."[69] In 1827, when *Freedom's Journal* referred to free people of color as "pioneers of their less favoured brethren who yet remain in a moral and physical bondage," enslavement and freedom were posited as locations on a continuum of time, space, and experience along which people of color traveled as one single people; in these terms, "slave" and "freeman" were stops on a journey that united them rather than distinct statuses or identities that separated them.

Nonetheless, their leaders recognized that the problems free people of color faced differed in kind as well as degree from those suffered by slaves. Samuel Cornish, in his presidential address to the 1834 national convention, reflected that "the present form of society divides the interest of the community into several parts. Of these, there is that of the white man, that of the slave, and that of the free coloured man. . . . Under present circumstances it is highly necessary [that] the free people of colour should combine, and closely attend to their own particular interest."[70] Cornish was not disavowing the cause of antislavery but rather identifying and validating the separate interests of free people of color. Five years later the

---

[68] Some historians have argued that abolition was a generally low priority among northern blacks absorbed in their self-help agenda; see Frederick Cooper "Elevating the Race: The Social Thought of Black Leaders, 1827–50," *American Quarterly* 24 (December 1972): 604–25. James Oliver Horton refutes this claim, arguing that Cooper "drew too sharp a distinction between self-help and antislavery, assuming that commitment to one lessened involvement in the other" and "failed to appreciate the bond between slaves and free blacks" (*Free People of Color: Inside the African American Community* [Washington: Smithsonian Institution Press, 1993], pp. 54–55). For another vigorous refutation of Cooper, see Hinks, *To Awaken My Afflicted Brethren*, p. 110. None of these scholars fully addresses the complex relation of the condition of each group to that of the other, in fact and in perception.

[69] Resolution passed at a meeting of free people of color in Philadelphia, 1817, in Aptheker, *Documentary History*, p. 71.

[70] "Minutes of the Fourth Annual Convention for the Improvement of the Free People of Colour in the United States" (June 1834), pp. 3–4, in Bell, *Proceedings*.

Colored American hinted that the interests of slaves and free people of color might be competing interests in some sense, complaining that "at this moment more is known among abolitionists of slavery in the Carolinas, than of the deep and damning thralldom which grinds to the dust the colored inhabitants of New York."[71]

Free black leaders creatively combined and contrasted these interests rhetorically, and sometimes played them off against each other, in order to inspire their constituency to aggressive action in one or the other or both causes. For practical reasons, the uplift agenda of the 1820s and 1830s focused on the particular economic, educational, and political needs of free blacks themselves. No matter how deep their devotion to the common cause of all "brethren," no matter how powerful their hatred for the institution of slavery, most free people of color—mired as they were in the "deep and damning thralldom" of economic uncertainty and political powerlessness—had few resources and little energy left unspent in their own struggle. Samuel Cornish had acknowledged this dilemma in 1829 when he advocated that they leave antislavery agitation to the whites and concentrate on uplift.[72] Nearly a decade later Cornish still held this position, arguing that "the low condition of the free colored people at the North soothes the conscience of the Southern slaveholder."[73]

But the uplift agenda struck other leaders as an abandonment of their "brethren" to the terrors of bondage. In 1838 the *Colored American* railed at free people of color to "witness our criminal apathy and idiot coldness in the antislavery cause!"[74] To stimulate support for abolition, many leaders attempted to reinvigorate the notion of a common and inseparable bond between slave and free by shaking the latter's complacency. Along with "W," they insisted, "Slavery must be *abolished* before the colored man can *rise*."[75] Frederick Douglass boldly charged free people of color with outright complicity in the persistence of slavery. In his address to the 1848 national convention he insisted, "In the Northern states, we are . . . far enough removed from the actual condition of the slave to make us largely responsible for their continued enslavement. . . . Every one of us should be ashamed to consider himself free, while his brother is a slave." But if Douglass was willing to hold free people of color responsible for the condition of slaves in order to motivate them to antislavery action, he could

[71] *Colored American*, May 18, 1839.
[72] *Rights of All*, September 18, 1829.
[73] "Proceedings of the Colored National Convention" (Rochester, 1853), p. 38, in Bell, *Proceedings*.
[74] *Colored American*, May 3, 1838.
[75] Ibid., June 24, 1837.

also reverse the argument, holding slavery responsible for the condition of free people of color; later in the same talk he said, "We ask you to devote yourselves to this cause as one of the first and most successful means of self-improvement."[76] The argument that southern slavery was the real source of northern "prejudice," and that abolition offered the only hope of advancement for free people of color in the North, shifted the focus of their agenda back to the slavery issue without requiring them to abandon their own interests—indeed, promised that it would advance those interests.

This was just one factor however, in the surge of renewed commitment to the antislavery struggle in the 1840s and especially the 1850s in the North. Another was a shift in leadership of northern free people of color. The Revolutionary generation of spokespersons such as Lemuel Haynes had all been native-born northerners, intimately familiar with northern slavery. By 1830, not only did the new generation of northern-born leaders have no personal memory of slavery, but a growing number of lecturers and leaders in the northern states were former southern slaves—David Walker, Samuel Ringgold Ward, and Frederick Douglass—whose personal frame of reference for northern "race" hatred was the persistent enslavement of people of color in the South. The shift in leadership itself mirrored the changing demographics of northern cities. By 1855, for example, as James Oliver Horton points out, 55 percent of black Bostonians had been born outside Massachusetts, one-third of them in the South.[77] It is not surprising that by the 1840s the historical dimension of northern blacks' condition was dropping out of national discussion in favor of the problem of concurrent southern enslavement.

Still another factor that had an enormous impact on the northern black agenda was the passage of the 1850 Fugitive Slave Law. By making reenslavement subject to a master's affidavit and freedom contingent upon positive proof, and by requiring all citizens to assist in the return of claimed fugitives, the law essentially identified every person of color as a potential slave and threatened them all with reenslavement. In the words of Samuel Ringgold Ward, "The business of catching slaves, or kidnapping freemen, is an open warfare upon the rights and liberties of the black men of the North."[78]

The Fugitive Slave Law effectively reunited the interests of the free and the enslaved, making them one "whole people" again, catapulting abolition (along with "public safety," or strategies to combat kidnapping) to the

[76] "Report of the Proceedings of the Colored National Convention" (Cleveland, 1848), p. 18, in Bell, *Proceedings*.

[77] Horton, *Free People of Color*, pp. 26–27.

[78] *Impartial Citizen*, quoted in *Liberator*, October 11, 1850.

top of their national agenda.[79] By transforming all northern people of color into victims of southern slavery, the law further effaced the memory of northern slavery and its historical accountability for "prejudice." Achieving economic and social advancement and overcoming this "prejudice" remained high priorities for northern free people of color, but after 1850 the politics of these imperatives increasingly overshadowed their moral dimension and looked steadfastly southward. Even those who felt that southern slavery had historically received a disproportionate share of attention framed their call for new efforts toward advancement of the free within the rubric of antislavery, as this carefully worded lament at the Colored National Convention in 1855 attests:

> Years of well-intended effort have been expended for the especial freedom of the slave, while the elevation of the free colored man as an *inseperable* [sic] *priority* to the same, has been entirely overlooked. . . . the whole process of Operation against the huge and diabolical system of oppression and wrong, has been shorn of more than half its strength and efficacy, because of this neglect of the interests of the Free People of Color. . . . the elevation of the free man is inseperable from, and lies at the very threshold of the great work of the slave's restoration to freedom, and equally essential to the highest well-being of our own common country.[80]

The Fugitive Slave Law also served to reinforce the common "racial" identification of all people of color. By potentially reenslaving northern free people of color and thus reunifying them with southern slaves, it underscored their common African descent and reanchored their identity in one "blood" with distinct "national" interests. It also seemed to some to reinforce their estrangement from whites and to clarify the extent to which their survival and advancement as a free people depended upon their efforts alone.

The upsurge in black nationalist thinking, fueled by the Fugitive Slave Law and the fear of reenslavement, was reflected in two kinds of activities. First, some leaders proposed new schemes for independent institution-building within the United States, schemes far more ambitious and broader in scope than earlier proposals for annual conventions or a single

---

[79] Pease and Pease provide a good summary of resistance to the Fugitive Slave Law, including the formation of Vigilance Committees in major cities (*They Who Would Be Free*, pp. 218–32).

[80] "Proceedings of the Colored National Convention" (Philadelphia, 1855), p. 4, in Bell, *Proceedings*.

industrial college. For example, the National Council of the Colored People, conceived at an organizational meeting in 1853 by elected delegates representing ten states, was designed to implement and oversee a complex institutional network of programs for education (with library and museum components), collective purchasing, and job placement. The council itself was to be a body of representatives chosen by state councils, themselves selected by general election among black residents. The council would govern the institutional components through four executive committees. The plan even provided for an arbitration system that would enable people of color to bypass the American courts.[81]

The National Council met periodically for about two years, but the components providing actual services—school, library, and so on—were never implemented. Still, the decision to proceed separately to organize a central institutional framework for the national community of people of color—a kind of state-within-a-state that would coordinate elements attacking a range of problems: employment, education, economic development—suggests the level of frustration that free people of color had reached with conventional avenues of advancement in American society at large. It also reveals a new determination to look inward for economic and political strength instead of promoting commercial relations between people of color and the white-controlled mainstream economy. Proposals such as the National Council plan reflected a nationalist determination to withdraw from what seemed increasingly to be one single, national, enslaving white body politic into a parallel one that would be separate, safe, and black, but stateless.

Although the "nation" of people of color reflected in the conception of the National Council was dispersed throughout the country, some in New England adopted a degree of regional identity that might be considered a kind of counterpart to whites' specifically New England nationalist impulse, (discussed in Chapter 6). This identity, manifested in the call to gather at a New England Colored Citizens Convention held in Boston in 1859, coalesced in response to the Fugitive Slave Law and the Dred Scott decision of 1857. William Wells Brown opened the convention by calling upon the free people of color of New England to "bid defiance to the Fugitive Slave Law, Dred Scott Decision, and every thing that shall attempt to fasten fetters upon us."[82] Although free people of color held state conven-

[81] "Proceedings of the Colored National Convention" (Rochester, 1853), pp. 18–19, 30, in Bell, *Proceedings*.

[82] "Minutes of the New England Colored Citizens Convention, August 1, 1859," in *Proceedings of the Black State Conventions, 1840–1865*, ed. Philip S. Foner and George E. Walker (Philadelphia: Temple University Press, 1980), p. 208.

tions in several western, mid-Atlantic, New England, and even southern states during the antebellum period, this was the only convention that asserted a regional identity.

A New England identity remained somewhat appealing because for over half a century the idea of New England as a refuge of freedom had retained a stubborn hold on the imagination of people of color, despite bitter experience to the contrary. Even though, as gradual emancipation followed slavery into an ever receding past, "racial" thinking and practices in New England became increasingly oppressive, New England *was* free in the technical sense that the legal machinery of slavery had generally ceased to function there. It was for this reason that as late as 1845 William C. Nell and other people of color could form the New England Freedom Association to assist fugitive slaves who "by the welcome light of the North Star, reach a haven where they can be protected from the grasp of the manstealer."[83] This "freedom," of course, coincided with the kind of unfreedom characterized by widespread, systematic associations of "nigger" with degrading functions and offensive phenomena (as reported by Hosea Easton in 1837) and structured by the ideology reflected in the scurrilous broadsides described earlier. Nonetheless, conditions could be said to have improved in some formal ways in the 1840s; for example, in Rhode Island a peculiar alignment of political rivals in 1842 enabled free people of color to regain the franchise they had lost in 1822.[84] As late as 1848, Frederick Douglass could assert that "great changes for the better have taken place and are still taking place. The last ten years have witnessed a mighty change in the estimate in which we as a people are regarded in this and other lands. . . . Mountains of prejudice have been removed, and truth and light are dispelling the error and darkness of ages."[85]

But the Fugitive Slave Law of 1850 stripped away even the legal convention of "freedom" and overshadowed the few formal advances, laying bare the reality of northern "racial" thinking and practices. Martin Delany spoke for a growing number of distinctly disenchanted northern people of color in 1852 when he stated baldly that the "free" states were nothing of the kind:

[83] *Liberator,* December 12, 1845.

[84] On the alliance of free people of color with conservative whites in opposition to Thomas Dorr's rebellion against restricted suffrage under the Rhode Island constitution, see Irving Bartlett, *From Slave to Citizen: The Story of the Negro in Rhode Island* (Providence: Urban League of Greater Providence, 1954), pp. 39–43; and J. Stanley Lemons and Michael A. McKenna, "Re-enfranchisement of Rhode Island Negroes," *Rhode Island History* 20 (Winter 1971): 3–13.

[85] "Report of the Proceedings of the Colored National Convention" (Cleveland, 1848), pp. 17–18, in Bell, *Proceedings.*

Are we willing to raise ourselves superior to the condition of slaves, or continue the meanest underlings, subject to the beck and call of every creature bearing a pale complexion? If we are, we had as well remained in the South, as to have come to the North in search of more freedom. What was the object of our parents in leaving the South, if it were not for the purpose of attaining equality in common with others of their fellow citizens? . . . They heard of liberty and equality here, and they hastened on to enjoy it, and no people are more astonished and disappointed than they, who for the first time, on beholding the position we occupy here in the free north—what is called, and what they expect to find, the free States. They at once tell us, that they have as much liberty in the south as we have in the north.[86]

Douglass, too, had abandoned all suggestions of northern "racial" progress by 1853 and asked scathingly, "What stone has been left unturned to degrade us? What hand has refused to inflame the popular prejudice against us? . . . What wit has not laughed at us in our wretchedness? . . . Few, few, very few."[87]

In blacks' evolving view of the white North we can see the emergence of a conception of a "white" New England, quite parallel to whites' own conception of it, as a place where whites belonged and people of color did not, where people of color and whites were fundamentally estranged. In the black conception, however, it was the whites who had become strangers by willfully withdrawing from the people of color. In Douglass's words, "Our white fellow-countrymen do not know us. They are strangers to our character, ignorant of our capacity, oblivious of our history and progress."[88]

But people of color clung to the founding ideal of America as fundamentally republican and inclusive, even if that ideal had been distorted by centuries of slavery, and they continued to identify New England as the site of the original experiment in liberty. At the New England Convention of 1859, whose program was otherwise undistinguished from those of the state and national conventions—advocating education, temperance, the franchise, and opposition to the American Colonization Society (as well as the African Civilization Society)—the convention president, George T. Downing of Rhode Island, made an explicit claim on behalf of New England people of color to a central role in the providential and perfectionist mission of America as it had been initiated at Massachusetts Bay. He

[86] Delany, *Condition*, p. 46.
[87] "Proceedings of the Colored National Convention" (Rochester, 1853), pp. 16–17, in Bell, *Proceedings*.
[88] Ibid.

declared: "We are the life of the nation's existence. . . . All of the great principles of the land are brought out and discussed in connection with the Negro. . . . We are the alphabet; upon us, all are constructed. We, the descendants, to a great extent, of those most unjustly held in bondage, . . . these were the most fit subjects to be selected to work out in perfection the realization of a great principle, *the fraternal unity of man.* This is AMERICA'S MISSION."[89]

This was an assertion of indivisible substance with American nationhood, a claim that people of color collectively embodied the very principle of inclusive citizenship identical with the American mission itself. Downing's embrace of "America's mission" at a New England convention, so clearly invoking the conception of John Winthrop's "City upon a Hill," endorsed a version of New England nationhood that was consonant with the cultural imperialist claims of whites, made with reference to a (Jacobin, slaveholding) South. The difference was that Downing's version insisted upon the centrality of people of color to the realization of those claims and attempted to structure a key role for them as New England's core citizenry.

Besides these varieties of stateless nationalism, the Fugitive Slave Law reinvigorated another nationalist movement whose antecedents stretched back to the 1780s: the emigration movement, which proposed the literal, physical withdrawal of people of color from the United States. Martin Delany, James Theodore Holly, Henry Highland Garnet, and others, most of whom had been proponents of uplift ideology and active participants in the abolition movement before 1850, now turned to the creation of a separate nation of color outside U.S. boundaries as the only reasonable solution to the prospect of effective reenslavement and permanent oppression posed by the Fugitive Slave Law.[90]

The new wave of emigration sentiment appeared to represent a sharp about-face from the earlier, near-universal condemnation of emigration in the guise of the American Colonization Society's project to colonize Liberia with free people of color. Although a small number of distinguished black leaders had willingly participated in the ACS project between 1820 and 1850, the great majority had seen it as David Walker had in 1829: "a plan got up, by a gang of slaveholders to select the free people of colour from among the slaves, that our more miserable brethren may

[89] "Minutes of the New England Colored Citizens Convention," in Foner and Walker, *Proceedings,* p. 211.

[90] The most comprehensive description of the antecedents and antebellum flowering of the emigration movement among free people of color remains Floyd J. Miller, *The Search for a Black Nationality: Black Emigration and Colonization, 1787–1863* (Urbana: University of Illinois Press, 1975).

be the better secured in ignorance and wretchedness, to work their farms and dig their mines, and thus go on enriching the Christians with their blood and groans."[91] Throughout the 1830s and 1840s, free people of color had excoriated colonization as white-controlled, involuntary removal of people from a country in which they were entitled to full citizenship rights because they had earned them with their sweat and blood. If colonization had seemed to many whites the last hope for the fulfillment of the antislavery promise—the disappearance of slaves/blacks—most people of color themselves, understanding the same promise quite differently as consisting of incorporation and enfranchisement, had seen abolition and advancement as the only strategies that might fulfill it.

But the Fugitive Slave Law, by reversing the tide of antislavery progress, nullified the antislavery promise to people of color. Whereas before 1850 the emigration of northern free people of color could be condemned as abandonment of their enslaved southern brethren, the Fugitive Slave Law effectively erased the difference between the free and the enslaved. In the words of Martin Delany, "By the provisions of this bill, the [free] colored people of the United States are positively degraded beneath the level of the whites. . . . We are slaves in the midst of freedom, waiting patiently, and unconcernedly—indifferently, and stupidly, for masters to come and lay claim to us. . . . The slave is more secure than we; he knows who holds the heel upon his bosom—we know not the wretch who may grasp us by the throat."[92] Thus the emigration of free people of color could now be viewed as the escape of one group of slaves who, having transformed themselves by this act into "freemen," might work successfully to achieve the emancipation of the others. It was in this new sense of "free" that Delany, proposing emigration to Central or South America or to the British West Indies, went on to insist: "Therefore, to elevate the free colored people of America anywhere upon this continent; forebodes the speedy redemption of the slaves."[93] There were many competing emigration proposals: Delany himself later refocused on the Yoruba Valley in Africa, as did Henry Highland Garnet in conjunction with the African Civilization Society; James Theodore Holly suggested emigration to Haiti.[94]

Although these proposals seemed to be variations on the American Colonization Society's Liberian emigration plan—differing principally in their black rather than white authorship[95]—what they closely resembled

---

[91] *Walker's Appeal*, in Aptheker, *One Continual Cry*, p. 121.

[92] Delany, *Condition*, p. 155.

[93] Ibid., p. 205.

[94] See Miller, *The Search for a Black Nationality*, pp. 105–249, for details of these proposals.

[95] These projects, especially that of the African Civilization Society, received the support

in some respects was the ideal of a homogeneous, racialized nation-state conceived by whites as the ultimate result of gradual emancipation in New England: the white New England nation-state that would be realized once slaves/people of color had been eliminated and their history forgotten. Antebellum black nationalism and antebellum New England nationalism thus shared a common racialized ethos. In addition, emigration plans suggested for free people of color a role as the "saving remnant," quite similar to the one the New England Puritans had envisioned for themselves with respect to England. That is, by removing themselves from American society and establishing a new society based on republican principles, free people of color hoped to influence America to abolish slavery and to enact equality. At the same time, the agriculture and trade they would establish (especially the cultivation and sale of cotton) could commercially undermine the South and thus contribute to the collapse of slavery. In this sense, antebellum black nationalists shared a common Puritan vision with the first English settlers of Massachusetts Bay; they advocated instituting a model black "City upon a Hill" elsewhere as an inspiration to both the corrupted original and the slaveholding South to remake themselves in its image.[96]

Both kinds of nationalist response to the Fugitive Slave Law—alternative, stateless nation formation within the United States, and external state formation by emigration—demonstrate how the law operated as an engine of racialization by reunifying people of color around their shared physical difference in disregard for their social identity and status, free or enslaved. In New England the Fugitive Slave Law in a sense turned back the clock, returning every person of color in 1850 to the status of presumptive slave which had characterized the state of being "negro" a century before, when slavery was widespread and sanctioned by law and social custom. In that earlier New England society, when all people of color were likely to be slaves, few claimed free status, and their claims were relatively easy to establish according to the many conventions of securing, transferring, and relinquishing property in slaves. But the New England of 1850 was no longer such a society; the Fugitive Slave Law made a group of people subject to seizure by their presumptive status in a society in which the formal conventions and legal machinery offering legal proof of exclusion from it no longer existed. How, in the absence of bills of sale, passes, manumission

---

of influential whites in the United States, Canada, and England at one point or another but were led by persons of color and sustained by the wave of emigration interest that swept North American communities of color in the 1850s.

[96] See, e.g., an 1859 speech by Henry Highland Garnet on behalf of the African Civilization Society, in *Weekly Anglo-African*, September 10, 1859.

papers, authorizations of emancipation by town officials—legal evidence of status—could freedom be proved?

In fact, by 1850, when virtually everyone in New England could be assumed to be "free" yet all people of color were conventionally seen as permanently and innately "servile," the question had become not "Which Negroes are slaves?" but "Which persons are Negroes?" Hence the Fugitive Slave Law not only reunified southern slaves and northern free people of color around shared physical difference but also revivified the association of unfree status before the law with physical characteristics. In a sense, then, it theoretically required people to be able to prove not that they were free but that they were white.

In 1837 Hosea Easton had foreshadowed the transformation of the problem of proving status (enslaved or free) into a problem of determining "race" when he wrote, concerning the return of fugitive slaves at that time (still under the provisions of the Federal Fugitive Slave Law of 1793), "Only think, if one is claimed who is black, or who is a descendant of a black, (though he be whiter than a white man,) he must be given up to hopeless bondage . . . whereas, if a white person be claimed, if he is half negro, if he can prove himself legally white, or of white parentage, he is acquitted."[97] Easton obviously considered the formulations "white black" and "negro white"—two seemingly equivalent terms operating in different semantic fields, one purely descriptive and the other essential—quite conventional by 1837. In the ensuing years, both "racial" identity and legal status had become increasingly difficult to pin down as more and more people of color, many of them light-skinned, left the South and their legal status behind and came North seeking freedom or, if free, increased economic opportunity. They joined a northern population that was itself of increasingly mixed descent and presumptive but unprovable "free" status. Thus when the 1850 Fugitive Slave Law made freedom contingent upon the certainty of "racial" identity, it posed a threat to every northern person, black and white.

On its face, the law made "slaves" of whites along with free people of color because it demanded that they become complicit in southern slaveholding and threatened them with imprisonment if they refused—a clear abrogation of both their own rights as free citizens and the general right to freedom conferred upon unfree persons by their entry into a free state. In the latter sense it was a northern states' rights issue, and abolitionists black and white seized upon this argument as a strategy for enlisting widespread support among northern whites, not only against the law per se but also for antislavery itself.

[97] Easton, *Treatise*, p. 33.

But some abolitionists were obviously aware of the other, subtler racializing effect of the law—its conflation of physical characteristics with legal status—and exploited it to arouse the fears of whites against the law itself and against the Slave Power. For example, when William Lloyd Garrison was invited to speak at the 1859 New England Colored Citizens' Convention, after insisting upon his pleasure at "the reputation he had gained of being a black man" among those who had never seen him in the flesh, he proclaimed, "'To this complexion had it come at last,' that color was no protection against the encroachments of the Slave Power; whites as well as blacks were alike slaves upon the plantation. It was absurd for any to suppose that color would protect them from being made slaves."[98] Horace Mann of Massachusetts took the same tack, elucidating the logic by which the law collapsed "race" and status into one arbitrary category. Speaking before the House of Representatives in February 1851, Mann explained that if it was "universal and indisputable" that "the right to freedom in a free state, and the right to be held and treated by the courts as a freeman, has no relation to complexion," then, under the Fugitive Slave Law, "*all* white men may be arbitrarily presumed to be slaves, and be deprived of the form of trial, secured to them by the constitution, just as well as any colored man can."[99] This was metaphor flirting with materiality: anyone provably white was safe from literal enslavement; anyone not provably white could theoretically be in jeopardy.

But who was "white"? "White" as an essential identity, fused within the body, and "white" as a physical marker, manifest on its surface, did not necessarily coincide. As Hosea Easton had observed as a commonplace in 1837, "white blacks" and "negro whites" were everywhere. While it was miscegenation in the context of slavery that had actually destabilized the comfortable essentialism of "white" by em-bodying potential slave status in persons with the appearance of whites, it was the Fugitive Slave Law that made the potential consequences of this phenomenon for "free," "white" people manifest and threatening. In this sense, the law offered an ironic challenge to the ironclad associations of whiteness with citizenship and blackness with servility which white authors had worked through with such anxiety and ultimate triumph in the post-Revolutionary role reversal literatures. During the Civil War, Abolitionists played upon the anxiety aroused

---

[98] "Minutes of the New England Colored Citizens' Convention, August 1, 1859," in Foner and Walker, *Proceedings,* pp. 217–18.

[99] Horace Mann, "Speech delivered in the House of Representatives of the United States, in Committee of the Whole on the State of the Union, February 28, 1851, on the Fugitive Slave Law," in *Slavery Letters and Speeches by Horace Mann,* Research and Source Works Series 350, Sources of Negro History and Culture 2 (Boston: Burt Franklin, 1851), p. 417.

EMANCIPATED SLAVES.

Brought from Louisiana by Col. Geo. H. Hanks.   The Children are from the Schools established by order of Maj. Gen. Banks.

WILSON CHINN.   MARY JOHNSON.   ROBERT WHITEHEAD.
        CHAS. TAYLOR.   AUGUSTA BROUJEY.   ISAAC WHITE.   REBECCA HUGER.   ROSINA DOWNS.

Entered according to Act of Congress, in the year 1863, by PHILIP BACON, in the Clerk's Office of the United States for the Southern District of New-York.

Photographed by M. H. Kimball, 477 Broadway, N.Y.

Figure 9. Courtesy of the Library Company of Philadelphia

by these implications to stiffen northern resolve, exhibiting groups of freed slaves that included apparently "white" individuals (see figure 9).

People of color were far from blind to this irony. African American authors responded with a new generation of role reversal literature that questioned the implications of "white black" and "black white" identities for assumptions about "racial" suitability for citizenship and enslavement. The first two full-length works of fiction by African Americans, both written af-

ter 1850, offered complex plots driven by a variety of circumstances of role
reversal, "passing," and mistaken "racial" identity. The first, situated almost
entirely in the South, considered the interplay of apparent and essential
"racial" identities in the context of a southern society organized by the laws
of slavery; the second investigated the interplay of such identities in a
northern environment where social behavior was organized by "race" itself.

Clotel; or, The President's Daughter, published by William Wells Brown in
1853, frankly examines the meaning of "white" in the context of slavery
and weighs the relative heritability of physical markers and status. It explores the paradox of inescapable slave status that poisons the lives of ever
"whiter," and ever more exemplary, descendants of the union of a slave and
a white republican hero in the antebellum South by chronicling the struggles of three generations of women of color: Currer, a light-skinned mulatto housekeeper who is identified as Thomas Jefferson's paramour;
Clotel and Althesa, their white-appearing daughters; Mary, Clotel's child
by a faithless white man who "marries" and abandons her; and Ellen and
Jane, daughters of Althesa by an honorable white man who marries and remains with her until their deaths in an epidemic. The loosely constructed
plot traces the arbitrary paths of these women from enslavement through
periodic episodes of false freedom to reenslavement or death for all but
Mary.

One of Clotel's digressive subplots, based on an actual incident in
Louisiana, deals with Salome Müller, a white European who had been enslaved since shortly after her emigration from Germany and subsequent
separation from her parents, because no one could attest to her free birth.
In the fictional version it is Althesa, a white-appearing quadroon, who hires
Salome from her owner, then discovers the truth and arranges Salome's
freedom. A neat reversal of the mistaken identity trope serves to illuminate
the troubling implications of an essential yet unmarked "racial" identity:
Salome's children, born of her forced relationship with a black slave and
long separated from her, remain enslaved. Although visibly black, they
should by law have been free, following their mother's condition; but they
have no more access to proof of their invisible free identity than do northern free blacks—or putative whites.[100] Even though the incident on which
this anecdote was based actually took place in 1844, Brown was clearly
aware of its post-1850 implications when he chose to include it in Clotel.

Brown alluded to other mistaken identity cases as well. Without fictional embellishment, he reported two incidents in northern states in which

[100] William Wells Brown, Clotel; or, The President's Daughter (1853; New York: Carol, 1989),
pp. 145–48.

white members of Congress were mistaken for people of color and denied accommodations. One of these was especially ironic, since it involved Daniel Webster, New Hampshire senator and secretary of state under President Millard Fillmore, who strenuously supported the Fugitive Slave Law.

Frank J. Webb's *The Garies and Their Friends,* published in 1857 in London, also explores the implications of essential, unmarked "racial" identity, this time in northern contexts. The story takes place largely in Philadelphia, New York, and Sudbury, Massachusetts, and follows the vicissitudes of two families, the Garies and the Ellises. Clarence Garie, a white plantation owner, and Emily, the near-white slave who lives with him as his wife, have two completely white-appearing children who are also Garie's slaves by law. Ellen and Charles Ellis are dark-skinned free people of color who have three children. Other characters include George Winston, a white-appearing ex-slave who is Emily's cousin and a friend of the Ellises, and who passes for white; and a Mr. Walters, also a friend of the Ellises, a free, wealthy, and successful dark-skinned Philadelphia businessman whose money earns him a surface respect from whites who, he knows, despise his color.

Near the beginning of the novel, Garie places his Georgia estate in the hands of an overseer and moves his family to Philadelphia, where he may legally marry Emily and free his children, and where the third child they are expecting may be born free. Once there, Emily Garie renews her childhood acquaintance with Ellen Ellis. The Garies purchase a home and enroll their children in an excellent private school. When it becomes known that young Clarence and Emily Garie are "black," however, they are forced to leave the school. Shortly thereafter, Mr. and Mrs. Garie are killed during a "race" riot, Clarence by a pistol shot and Emily while she is hiding in the woodshed giving premature birth to an infant who also dies. Mr. Ellis is permanently disabled in the same riot, and his family is taken in by Mr. Walters, the wealthy black entrepreneur; ultimately, the eldest Ellis daughter, Esther, marries him. Young Clarence Garie is sent away to a private school in Sudbury, Massachusetts, where he passes for white. His engagement to a wealthy young white woman is destroyed when her father learns that Clarence is black; Clarence becomes consumptive, falls into a decline, and dies. Young Emily Garie remains among people of color and eventually marries the Ellis's son Charles, who has overcome intense discrimination to become a successful engraver.

In the northern cities depicted in *The Garies,* "being white," like "being negro or black," is both a way of life and an essential identity only arbitrarily related to physical appearance. Webb treats passing for white as the literal equivalent of being a runaway slave. Although he was undoubtedly well aware of the implications of the Fugitive Slave Law for white as well as black freedom (he cleverly includes a white character beaten nearly to death by white racists who mistake him for a man of color),[101] Webb's argument concerned "race," not slavery; his point was that by 1850 in the North "race" had come to perform the same function in social relations that the law performed in legal ones. Hence he placed at the center of his narrative a white southerner who relocates his white-appearing "wife" and children to the North in order to free them, only to find that the implacable hatred generated by their essential although invisible "blackness" is more immobilizing than their former bondage, ultimately killing both adults and their baby.

Like the earlier role reversal narratives written by whites, these stories also interrogated the equation of "race" and citizenship, but from an opposing perspective. The earlier narratives had tested the reliability of "blackness" and "whiteness" as clues to eligibility or ineligibility for republican citizenship in potentially transformative situations—emancipation in the northern states, enslavement on the coast of Africa. In contrast, *Clotel* and *The Garies* slyly tested the reliability of principled behavior and good citizenship as clues to "racial" identity in situations in which white-appearing characters have been transplanted—by sale, escape, distant marriage, or other relocation—to communities in which their antecedents are unknown, or in which their circumstances undergo a radical transformation. In these works, whites insist upon the reenslavement or social exclusion of white-appearing people of color once they are discovered to "be" black, because the whites equate that "inner blackness" with "natural" servility; yet at the same time, white-appearing people can "pass" successfully as exemplary citizens (until their "racial" identity is disclosed in some unfortunate fashion) precisely because they have a "natural" aptitude for republican behavior.

In *Clotel* a "republican nature" is represented as incipient in humans in general, irrespective of "race," but most responsive to the kind of education and social nurturing commonly afforded whites; white-appearing characters who "are" black by descent behave virtuously when they have received the benefits of principled education and training. In other words, Brown saw the relationship between culture and virtuous republican behavior as systematic, the relationship between color and such behavior as arbitrary and unpredictable. Slavery, however, was the worm in the culture apple for Brown. In *Clotel,* many white characters presumably raised ac-

---

[101] Frank J. Webb, *The Garies and Their Friends* (London, 1857); (New York: Arno Press and the New York Times, 1969), pp. 188–91.

cording to the principles of republican citizenship do not in fact behave as principled citizens because slavery has undermined these principles, whereas characters of color raised and educated in like manner uniformly exhibit principled and virtuous behavior.[102] In this sense, Brown confirmed the possibility that people of color are "natural" republicans and innately good citizens, inverting the "racial" equation made by most whites.

The white-appearing women of color in *Clotel* are prized, and enslaved, for their whiteness, and Brown represented the irony of their situation and the depth of their tragedy as their inability to realize their "whiteness" by living "white" lives. Explicitly rejecting the equation of lighter skin with intellectual or social superiority, he represented a conversation among slaves favoring "light-coloured" mulattoes over "common darkies" as "unmistakeable evidence that caste is owing to ignorance";[103] nonetheless, he did endorse "white" lives as the entitlement of all Americans. Brown attempted to point out to slaveowners and legislators that the logic of the laws supporting slavery placed them in the position of enslaving persons who could not be distinguished from themselves, and that by extension the same logic might one day result in their own loss of "white" lives—that is, in enslavement. He suggested that "blackness" and "whiteness" have essential meaning beyond the accident of appearance only as cultural effects of slavery.

Webb, on the other hand, emphatically endorsed the existence of an essential "blackness" that transcends both appearance and culture and is equal if not superior to "whiteness," even as he decried whites' construction of it as innate inferiority. Virtually all his characters of color suffer for their essential "black" identity at the hands of whites, but those who remain loyal to it are ultimately redeemed by their allegiance. Mr. Walters, the darkest character, retains his wealth and influence in the face of persistent prejudice and the attack of the mob. The Ellis family, proudly black, survives the incapacitation of the father by the mob and achieves financial stability. Esther's marriage to Mr. Walters and the marriage of Caddy, a second daughter, to another (minor) dark-skinned character are happy and produce children who are explicitly described as unusually high achievers. Charles, the son, wins economic success as an engraver. He marries young Emily Garie, a white-appearing character who chooses to remain "black"

---

[102] Thomas Jefferson himself, as progenitor in the novel of the beautiful near-white women, is the quintessential example of the faithless republican character (p. 64); Clotel, his quadroon granddaughter, exemplifies "pure mind" (p. 111), as do George, white-appearing son of "another American statesman" (p. 224), and Jefferson's other quadroon and octaroon descendants.

[103] Brown, *Clotel*, pp. 132–33.

and thus earns a tranquil future that redeems her from her family's tragic past.

Passing for white destroys Emily's equally white-appearing brother, however. It is not the act of passing per se that condemns young Clarence Garie but the corrosive effect of the overwhelming fear of discovery that distances him from family and friends. Mr. Walters foreshadows the result of the deception when, with great reluctance, he acquiesces in the plan of Mr. Balch, a white friend, to send young Garie away on the grounds that passing for white will be the boy's best opportunity for advancement after the death of his parents. "There's no doubt, my dear sir," Walters tells Balch, "but what I fully appreciate the advantage of being white. Yet, with all I have endured, and yet endure from day to day, I esteem myself happy in comparison with that man, who, mingling in the society of whites, is at the same time aware that he has African blood in his veins, and is liable at any moment to be ignominiously hurled from his position by the discovery of his origin."[104] Later, fully committed to the deception and newly engaged to a white woman who believes he is white, Clarence himself describes the disengagement from the community of people of color that his situation demands:

> I can't be white and coloured at the same time. . . . my education, habits, and ideas, all unfit me for associating with the latter; and I live in constant dread that something may occur to bring me out with the former. I don't avoid coloured people because I esteem them my inferiors in refinement, education, or intelligence; but because they are subjected to degradations that I shall be compelled to share by too freely associating with them. . . . It is a pity . . . that I was not suffered to grow up with them, then I should have learnt to bear their burthens. . . . Now it would crush me, I know. It was a great mistake to place me in my present false position, . . . it has cursed me.[105]

Webb considered social solidarity the key to survival for people of color in the North, and the acknowledgment of one's essential identity as "black," regardless of appearance, as its cornerstone. For him, such identity was not rooted in African descent; like Brown, Webb was a civilizationist and clearly saw the culture that Europeans had developed in America as the desirable entitlement of the descendants of the Africans enslaved there. Rather, he understood essential "black" identity as rooted in a spe-

---

[104] Webb, *The Garies*, p. 276.
[105] Ibid., p. 323.

cial capacity to confront and overcome oppression, to be virtuous and honest in the face of hypocrisy and dishonesty. Webb saw these as qualities uniquely inherent in "black" people, qualities that should be preserved, strengthened, and expressed in community. He regarded people of color not only as naturally republican but as uniquely so.

Although both narratives suggested that "blackness" and "whiteness" had some meaning as essential identities, Brown, himself a runaway slave, saw their substance as a kind of intermediate product of the law of slavery, sustained by whites, which would evaporate when slavery itself ended; to him, then, such categories provided no more clues to capacity for citizenship than did the physical characteristics of "race." For Webb, however, a northern free man of color, "black" and "white" were not vestigial legal categories sustained by the persistence of slavery; rather, they were independent social identities—only arbitrarily related to physical characteristics—which had become institutionalized as successors to the legal categories of "slave class" and "slaveowning class" and performed the same function: to organize labor and social relations. He considered these identities essential, innate, and permanent—that is, "racial." For Webb, an essential "black" identity represented a special aptitude for republican citizenship which must be enacted corporately; presumably it could be realized in civic empowerment wherever communities of color formed to act in concert.

By the mid-1850s, conceptions such as Webb's of an essential black identity, along with various black nationalist proposals and positions that implicitly acknowledged an essentialist notion of black identity at their core, had become prominent in the thinking of many leaders and intellectuals of color.

Many, but not all, of these conceptions reflected a deeply gendered notion of blackness. The empowerment of free people of color was commonly identified in the discourse of men, and often women as well, with the restoration of black "manhood," a term that was near-ubiquitous in convention addresses, antislavery lectures, and editorial arguments made by people of color in the early nineteenth century.[106] For example, Martin Delany insisted in 1852 that "the force that elevates us to the position of manhood's considerations and honors, will cleft the manacle of every slave in the land"; the call to the 1855 Colored National Convention in Philadelphia stressed the "Political and Social Rights that lie at the very

[106] On the ideal of black manhood in the early nineteenth century, see James Oliver Horton and Lois Horton, "Violence, Protest, and Identity: Black Manhood in Antebellum America," in Horton, *Free People of Color*, pp. 80–96.

foundation of our manhood"; at the New England Convention, George T. Downing called upon his 1859 listeners to stay in New England, "in a climate and a home congenial to us, and to the development of mind and manhood."[107]

The use of the term "manhood" to describe that aspect of the humanity of people of color most profoundly compromised by slavery and "racialization" can be attributed to several historical factors: the inability of slaves to assert roles that were traditionally male in African and European societies; the importance of the loss of the franchise, an explicitly male prerogative, as an obstacle to the exercise of citizenship by free people of color; and the general universalizing of male experience reflected in English language usage.[108] Although black newspapers frequently dispensed advice on how women might best be good wives and mothers, there was little implication in any of these articles that such behavior would exemplify "blackness," as appropriate male behavior might do. Women's education was understood to be important because of their pivotal role in "domestic and social relations," and women such as Maria Stewart sometimes suggested to "daughters of Africa" that efforts at self-improvement might "show forth to the world that ye are endowed with noble and exalted faculties" and thus assist in uplifting the race. But uplift itself was most frequently characterized in masculinist terms and as a task within the province of masculine responsibility.[109]

In the 1850s, however, discussions of the role of women in uplifting the "race" underwent a subtle transformation. At the 1853 Colored National Convention in Rochester, the Committee on Social Relations and Polity suggested that the key to the continuing degraded condition of free people of color lay in differences between "our homes and the homes of our white neighbors" and explicitly charged that "the burthen of our disabilities, moral, social and political, finds its issue in these differences. . . . The white American's hearth-stone finds around it a cluster of vigorous youth, preparing successfully for the more vigorous battle of life; the colored American's, a few ill-trained and often worse-governed youth groping in the gloom and mist of uncertainty." The committee's report urged that the

---

[107] Delany, *Condition*, p. 206; "Proceedings of the Colored National Convention" (Philadelphia, . . . 1855), p. 5, in Bell, *Proceedings;* "New England Colored Citizens' Convention," in Foner and Walker, *Proceedings*, p. 211.

[108] For a thorough discussion of the origins and operation of gender ideals in antebellum black society, see James Oliver Horton, "Freedom's Yoke: Gender Conventions among Antebellum Free Blacks," *Feminist Studies* 12 (Spring 1986): 51–76. A somewhat revised version of this article appears as chap. 5 in Horton, *Free People of Color*, pp. 98–120.

[109] See, e.g., *Colored American*, March 18 and June 17, 1837; Maria Stewart, "Religion and the Pure Principles," p. 30.

social elevation of people of color be accomplished through two branches of education, "that of the School-Room and that of the Fire-Side," and went on to focus on the importance of the latter: "It is but too apparent that we have made too little progress in the fire-side culture of our youth," and "this neglect enters too largely into all the ramifications of our social state, affecting its present and prospective advancement. . . . comfortable homes and hearths, and correct culture and habits, tend to the increase of a people; the reverse to their diminution."[110]

Emphasis on "fire-side culture" elevated the importance of the domestic sphere and suggested that the advancement of the whole people of color lay substantially within the responsibility of women. In one sense such an argument elevated the significance of women in uplifting the "race," yet it also seemed to blame the domestic sphere, and thus women, for the oppressed condition of free people of color. But white and black households were seldom comparable. A much larger proportion of women of color than of white women worked long hours outside their homes; many more households of color included transient members only sporadically present, or were themselves transient; many were substantially poorer than most white households.[111] The committee's critique seemed to suggest that these conditions were consequences of a failed fireside culture rather than material circumstances that made it extremely difficult to organize a comparable fireside culture. Insofar as the advancement of the "race" was understood generally by the 1850s to be closely linked to the full realization of an essential "black" identity, women of color were thus held especially accountable for failing to provide the "homes and hearths" under which this identity might effectively be nourished and reproduced.

By the eve of the Civil War, then, most northern free people of color were willing to see their greatest possibilities for advancement in strengthening their own fireside culture, in working together in loyal community, and in overcoming white prejudice by example and especially by ending slavery. Although the myth of the "free" North had been severely eroded by intensifying antiblack discrimination and violence, and especially by the enactment of the Fugitive Slave Law, most people of color were still willing to

[110] "Proceedings of the Colored National Convention" (Rochester, 1853), pp. 20, 22–24, in Bell, *Proceedings*. The committee consisted of three men: Charles B. Ray, former editor of the *Colored American*, by this time defunct; William Whipper, former Garrisonian and foe of institutions formed on the basis of "complexional distinctions" who now, with the rest of the committee, advocated separate schools sympathetic to the particular needs of people of color; and William J. Wilson, Brooklyn correspondent for *Frederick Douglass' Paper*.

[111] See the discussions of economic levels, occupational profiles, and transiency in black communities in Chapters 3 and 4.

lay the largest measure of blame for northern "prejudice" on the persistence of southern slavery and to claim Yankee culture as a positive model.

In 1859 an obscure woman of mixed "race" published a novel in Boston that offered a devastating critique of all these contentions. *Our Nig; or, Sketches from the Life of a Free Black,* by Harriet E. Wilson, is an apparently autobiographical novel that depicts the life of a mulatto indentured servant in New Hampshire and Massachusetts in the early decades of the nineteenth century.[112] Like *The Garies,* it is a novel about "race" in the "free" states; unlike *The Garies,* it follows one character closely, in the manner of a slave narrative, except that it is written almost entirely in the third person. Although Wilson notes in her preface that she wrote the novel in the hope of raising money to support herself and reclaim her son from foster care, it probably failed to achieve those ends. As Henry Louis Gates points out in his introduction to the second edition, its publication generated no notices or reviews (unlike other early black fiction such as Brown's *Clotel* and Delany's *Blake, or The Huts of America,* which did elicit notices in British periodicals and American antislavery organs), and no editions were published between the first in 1859 and the second in 1983.[113] This is really not surprising, for on one score or another *Our Nig* critiques the assumptions and positions of virtually every constituency that might have been expected to support its publication and to buy it. Moreover, Wilson offers an interpretation of the "condition" question quite different from those debated by both black and white men during the preceding half-century, and interrogates constructions of both essential blackness and essential whiteness.

First, she explodes the notion of the model of white fireside culture, in which a tightly knit family group is overseen by a virtuous and pious female nurturer. The novel opens with the words "Lonely Mag Smith!" describing a white woman "deprived of parental guardianship, far removed from rel-

---

[112] Harriet E. Wilson, *Our Nig; or, Sketches from the Life of a Free Black* (1859; New York: Random House, 1983).

[113] Henry Louis Gates, introduction to *Our Nig;* Martin Robison Delany, *Blake; or, The Huts of America,* serialized in *Anglo-African,* January–July 1859, and in *Weekly Anglo-African,* November 26, 1861–May 24, 1862. Although Gates implies that *Our Nig* is singular in receiving no reviews, in fact *The Garies* is also absent from his list of early black literature that did get public notice—and with good reason, for it too critiques the underlying "racial" structure of society in the so-called "free" states, and both books represent "interracial" marriage in a positive light. Gates says, "Never . . . was miscegenation depicted with any degree of normality before *Our Nig,*" (p. xxvii), but here again he overlooks *The Garies,* which represents such a marriage much more positively: Wilson's white bride did care for her ailing black husband but "only as a means to subserve her own comfort" (*Our Nig,* p. 15), whereas Webb's white husband moves out of the South in order to marry his mulatto wife and free their children, and he is killed defending his family in a race riot (*The Garies,* pp. 223–24).

atives." Next, a second fractured white family coalesces around Mag and quickly evaporates, as she is seduced and abandoned by a white lover and produces an illegitimate infant who dies. Ultimately, she is driven by want to descend "another step down the ladder of infamy": she marries a black man and produces two children; one of these is Frado, half black and half white, the subject of the remaining narrative.[114]

The third white household encountered in the narrative is the home of the Bellmonts, where Frado's mother abandons her at six years of age after the father has died, leaving Mag and a new liaison destitute. This family is a demonic inversion of the fireside culture model. The matriarch is a tyrant who virtually enslaves Frado and administers unending physical and mental abuse; her oldest daughter is her carbon copy. The father is kind but weak, the antithesis of the benevolent patriarch of conventional Victorian culture; when it is suggested that he should rule his own household and restrain his termagant wife, he responds, "And live in hell meantime." Other female family members are elderly or disabled or otherwise powerless; other male family members are well-meaning and sometimes intervene usefully on Frado's behalf but disappear at key moments and are generally inconsistent in their support. Near the end of the novel a physically broken Frado, having reached the end of her indenture (which probably would have been obtained from town officials sometime after her abandonment; this is never explained), lives and works in several other white households. She receives clearly compassionate treatment in only one of these, and it is not a model family but a wife and four children abandoned by a father who has "gone West."[115]

Frado finally establishes her own family with a black man who claims to be a fugitive slave, and they produce a son. But this black family is not a stable or nurturing unit either; the man proves to be a fraud as well as an unreliable husband and source of support. Eventually he disappears and then dies.[116] Here Wilson seems to be deriding the equation of essential blackness with natural republican virtue, made by Webb and others, and suggesting that domestic models based on loyalty to this essential identity are as flawed as models of white fireside culture.

There is one functional family in the book, but its constitution is deeply ironic. The only first-person pronouns used in connection with Frado appear in the first three chapter headings: "my mother," "my father," and "me."[117] Taken together, these elements construct the only stable, nurtur-

[114] Wilson, *Our Nig*, pp. 5, 6, 13.
[115] Ibid., pp. 15–24, 44, 117–25.
[116] Ibid., pp. 126–28.
[117] The chapters are headed "Mag Smith, My Mother"; "My Father's Death"; and "A New

ing family unit in the novel. But this is a black-white household with black-white children—the very model of race mixing and disorder, the very antithesis of the patriarchal good citizenship represented by whites as the bedrock of the republic and held up by the 1853 Committee on Social Relations and Polity as a model for families of color to emulate. Here, Wilson seems not so much to be advocating "race" mixing per se as demonstrating the liberating possibilities that lie outside the narrow range of acceptable models of family life defined in "racial" terms.

If part of Wilson's project was to expose conventional "racial" models of domestic life as delusory, and especially to unmask the domestic moralism of the "good white New England household" proposed so effectively by writers such as Stowe, an equally important goal was to link the "racial" organization of households with the social "condition" of people of color in the northern states. Frank Webb had already exposed the terroristic racism that organized the material relations of whites with people of color in the public sphere in the North and thus produced their "condition"; Harriet Wilson brought the condition argument into the domestic sphere and demonstrated how it was reproduced in household relations and in the relations of the household with the larger community. In this way she showed how the oppression of people of color by whites was naturalized as an indivisible element of northern nationalism itself, yet self-consciously suppressed within the conventional opposition between "slave South" and "free North."

Wilson describes, among Frado's "adventures" after the death of her husband, being "watched by kidnappers" and "maltreated by professed abolitionists, who didn't want slaves at the South, nor niggers in their own houses, North." Although Wilson never characterized her region more narrowly than "the North," it is clear from her text that she spent her life in New England. She lived in a state bordering Massachusetts (New Hampshire, according to an appended letter by one "Allida") before her husband's death and in Massachusetts while writing the narrative, which was published in Boston. Gates's research suggests that she was listed in the fed-

---

Home For Me" (ibid., pp. 1, 14, 24). Gates (p. xxxvi) refers to these as "first-person lapses" and regards them as evidence of tensions between autobiography and fiction in Wilson's writing. But I would read them as demarcating that time during which Frado "owned herself." The first three chapters chronicle Frado's life from the circumstances of her conception through the first three years of her enforced service in a white household, when she is allowed to go to school. During this period some part of her experience is "free," and she is able to engage on her own terms with others as an individual "I" or "me." At the outset of chap. 4, however, as Wilson says, "Her education completed, as *she* said, Mrs. Bellmont felt that her time and person belonged solely to her" (p. 41). I would argue that first-person pronouns cease when Frado's objectification by Mrs. Bellmont as a virtual slave becomes complete.

eral census of 1850 for New Hampshire and may have been born there.[118] Her text would have been perceived as a New England narrative by most readers, and it is as a New England narrative—a New England slave narrative—that the text is most subversive.

The very wording and organization of the six lines on the title page reflect the irony of this situation. In the first three lines, "Our Nig; / or, / Sketches from the Life of a free Black," the "or," commonly used to elaborate an initial element in antebellum titles, here introduces the suggestion of alternative or oppositional meaning: the title character is defined by a pronoun of ownership and an epithet of derogation, but she is "free." The opposition is repeated in the fourth and fifth lines, in which the "free" status suggested by placement of the tale in a "Two-Story White House, North" is undermined by the subsequent assertion that "Slavery's Shadows Fall Even There." The sixth line reads "By 'Our Nig'; of the alternative free and unfree identities posed in the title, Wilson chooses to claim authorship as the latter, not as a "free Black."[119] Here again she is deeply ironic; although she suggests that her situation has finally reduced her to this truncated, objectified status—an identity that allows her, however, to claim authority as an expert on the conditions under which such transformations take place—she refutes that identity by the polished writing that follows, her wide reading evidenced in carefully chosen epigraphs.

The situation Wilson suggested on the title page and detailed in the text is one of slavery in all but the most legalistic sense, and her prefatory apologia's disclaimer of intention to "provoke shame in our good anti-slavery friends at home" must be read as ironically as her title—especially in light of her final frank indictment of "professed abolitionists" who don't want "niggers in their own houses, North." Her demure insistence that she did not intend to "palliate slavery at the South, by disclosures of its appurtenances North" served in fact to equate the two conditions, and in immediately casting Mrs. Bellmont's behavior as uncharacteristic of New England—"My mistress was wholly imbued with *southern* principles"—she in fact located such principles squarely in New England and further eroded the distinction between the "free" and slave states on which New England nationalist assumptions were fondly based.[120]

At the same time, Wilson also critiqued the kind of black nationalist strategy whereby Webb proposed to render white racism irrelevant. Wilson used Frado's situation of extreme isolation, into which briefly comes a lone itinerant man of color whose antecedents are unknown and who proves to

[118] Ibid., pp. 129, 134, xiv.
[119] Ibid., title page. The author's own name appears only on the verso: "Entered according to Act of Congress in the year 1859, by Mrs. H. E. Wilson."
[120] Ibid., Preface, p. 129.

be a fraud, to demonstrate that Webb's model of social solidarity for free people of color—consisting of closely knit, supportive networks of black families and friends which constitute self-sufficient and self-empowering communities—was simply an unrealistic fantasy for many people of color, especially women, in New England. There, single families of color, let alone unrelated individuals "living out" in white families like Frado or else "working out" and living as boarders or tenants of (often exceedingly marginalized) whites, could not easily find power in a nationalist group strategy of solidarity around "essential blackness."

What Harriet Wilson published in 1859 was a remarkably clear-eyed assessment of the racialized structure of New England life which had developed in the more than half a century following the first steps toward emancipation of New England slaves. Her blunt portrayal of the mechanics of "racial" essentialism and its reproduction in white New England households dismantled the mythology of the New England "free" states and indicted the model of "fire-side culture" that was the engine of its reproduction. Although she exposed New England nationalism as a fundamentally white "racial" construction, she also rejected black essentialism and black nationalist domestic models as potential cornerstones of resistance and empowerment.

Wilson proposed no solutions to the racialized structure of New England life. Even though she presented a relatively successful "racially" mixed family as a critique of the dysfunctional essentialist models, black as well as white, she did not suggest that such pattern could either transcend or transform the racial essentialism that surrounded and marginalized it. Rather, her project seems to have been a straightforward exposé, laying bare the false assumptions and hypocrisy of both white and black New England nationalisms in a cathartic expression of disgust.

Wilson's book was ignored by both the black and the white press of its time, passing, like the enslavement and emancipation of which its author's experience was the logical sequel, into historical oblivion. No other author attempted anything like her textured and profoundly insightful critique of the "racial" dynamics of antebellum New England life. The assumptions and pretensions she sought to expose remained relatively undisturbed. The engagement of New England in the Civil War can be read, as Lewis Simpson suggests, as a nationalist and culturally imperialist enterprise fueled at least in substantial part by the "racial" essentialism on the one hand and the mythology of "freedom" on the other which Wilson so shrewdly dissected.[121]

[121] Lewis P. Simpson, *Mind and the American Civil War: A Meditation on Lost Causes* (Baton Rouge: Louisiana State University Press, 1989).

Ultimately, of course, the Civil War ended American slavery finally and completely, but northern people of color were not thereby released from racial thinking and practices whose origins were lost in a largely suppressed history of northern slavery and gradual emancipation. Indeed, the ante-bellum struggles of free people of color to define and assert an identity that would empower them, and their efforts to explain and transform their condition, had *shaped* as well as been shaped by the post-Revolutionary dis-course of "race" that emerged in the context of that first emancipation.

Long after the war had ended, the presence of people of color in New England continued to be regarded by many whites as unaccountable, a puzzling and irritating refusal of "the Negro" to follow the dodo into extinction as Emerson—echoing the implicit promises of antislavery activists in the Revolutionary period—had so confidently predicted.[122]

[122] *The Journals and Miscellaneous Notebooks of Ralph Waldo Emerson*, ed. William H. Gilman et al. (Cambridge: Harvard University Press, Belknap Press, 1960–82), 13:286, quoted in Simpson *Mind and the American Civil War*, p. 54.

Index